W9-AZM-260

TRANSMATH™

Developing Number Sense

John Woodward
Mary Stroh

Cambium
LEARNING®

BOSTON, MA | LONGMONT, CO

Copyright 2010 Cambium Learning Sopris West®.
All rights reserved.

6 7 8 9 10   RRDGMWI   14 13 12 11 10

No part of this work may be reproduced or transmitted in any form or by any means,
electronic or mechanical, including photocopying or recording, or by any information
retrieval system, without the express written permission of the publisher.

ISBN 13: 978-1-60697-040-9
ISBN: 1-60697-040-2

181956/10-10

Printed in the United States of America
Published and distributed by

Cambium
LEARNING®
Sopris West®

4093 Specialty Place • Longmont, CO 80504 • (303) 651-2829
www.sopriswest.com

Table of Contents

UNIT 1

UNIT 2

UNIT 2 (*continued*)

UNIT 3

UNIT 4

UNIT 5

UNIT 5 (continued)

UNIT 6

A wise man once said...

"If you think dogs can't count, try putting three dog biscuits in your pocket and then giving Fido only two of them."

= arf arf arf

Amazing Math Dogs
True Stories

Dave the Math Dog shows off his math skills on national TV and to math students in Illinois. This Golden Retriever can count, add, subtract, and do other math problems by patting the answers in his owner's paw, er, hand.

Maggie the Wonder Dog, a zippy Jack Russell Terrier, taps out her mathematical solutions with her tiny white paw.

In China, a small white dog named "Wawa" barks the answers for math equations that use numbers up to 10.

OBJECTIVES

Building Number Concepts

- Determine the place value of digits in a whole number
- Find sums of whole numbers with and without regrouping
- Round and estimate with whole numbers

Problem Solving

- Read and interpret word problems
- Create, read, and interpret bar graphs
- Create pictographs

▶**Place Value in Whole Numbers**

Vocabulary

digits
place value
place-value chart

How does a digit get its value?

We can write any number using the **digits** 0 through 9. The digits of a number have different values based on their position in the number. This is called the **place value** of the digit.

We can use a **place-value chart** to help determine the value of each digit in a number.

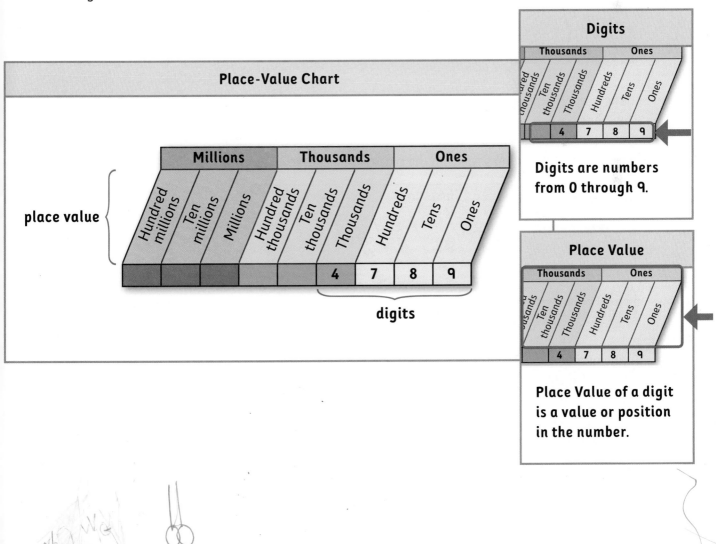

Digits

Digits are numbers from 0 through 9.

Place Value

Place Value of a digit is a value or position in the number.

How does the position of the digit affect its value?

The value of a digit and its position in the place-value chart are related. Look at the example below.

Example 1

Find the value of the digits.

Look carefully at the number 285 in the place-value chart:

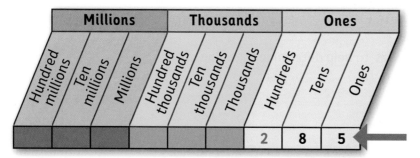

In the number 285, the digit 2 is in the hundreds place.
The 2 has a value of **2 hundreds**, or **200**.

Now look at the number 25,981 in the place-value chart:

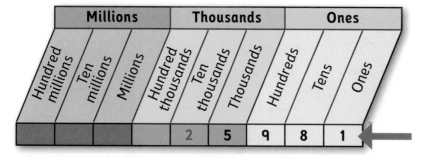

In the number 25,981, the digit 2 is in the ten thousands place.
The 2 has a value of **2 ten thousands**, or **20,000**.

The digit 2 is farther to the left in **25,981** than in **285**.
The place value of the digit 2 is greater in 25,981 than in 285.

How do we read and write numbers?

When we read and write numbers, we separate them into groups of three digits.

To read a number, we say the one-, two-, or three-digit number for each group, and then we say the name of the group.

Example 1

Read the number in the place-value chart.

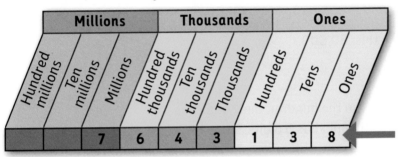

We read the number in the place-value chart as
7 million, 643 thousand, 138. We do not need to say 138 ones.

To write a number, separate each group with a comma. Start with the ones digit, and place a comma after every three digits.

The number in the place-value chart above is written 7,643,138.

Improve Your Skills

How would we write five thousand forty-one?

Common mistakes:

541	five hundred forty-one
500,041	five hundred thousand forty-one
5,000,401	five million four hundred one

We can avoid these mistakes if we use place value.

The correct way to write the number is 5,041.

How does the greatest place value of a number relate to the number of digits in that number?

Thinking about the greatest place value in a number helps us write the correct number of digits for that number.

Improve Your Skills

Marvin's teacher asked him to write the number

six hundred thousand five hundred nine.

Marvin wrote the number like this: 60,509.

ERROR

The table shows that any number in the hundred thousands has 6 digits. The number Marvin wrote only has 5 digits, so we know he is incorrect.

Greatest Place Value	Number of Digits	Example
Ones	1 digit	5
Tens	2 digits	35
Hundreds	3 digits	135
Thousands	4 digits	4,135
Ten thousands	5 digits	54,135
Hundred thousands	6 digits	654,135
Millions	7 digits	2,654,135
Ten millions	8 digits	82,654,135
Hundred millions	9 digits	782,654,135

We correctly write the number as 600,509.

 **Apply Skills**
Turn to *Interactive Text*, page 2.

mBook Reinforce Understanding
Use the *mBook Study Guide* to review lesson concepts.

▶**Problem Solving: Reading Word Problems Carefully**

What are the first steps in solving word problems?

Solving word problems can be difficult. There can be a lot of information to read. Before solving any problem, we must read it carefully.

To begin solving a word problem, we should:

- Figure out what the problem is asking.
- Rewrite what the question is or what the problem is asking.

Example 1

Solve the word problem.

Problem:

There are 64 teams in the first round of a college basketball tournament. There are 4 divisions with an equal number of teams in each division. Each team plays until they lose a game. There are 2 teams in the finals. How many teams are in each division in the first round of the basketball tournament?

- **Figure out what the problem is asking.**
  The last sentence tells us what the problem is asking.

- **Rewrite the question or what the problem asks.**
  How many teams are in each division in the first round of the basketball tournament?

> Remember to read the problem carefully before beginning to solve it.

Problem-Solving Activity
Turn to *Interactive Text*,
page 4.

mBook Reinforce Understanding
Use the *mBook Study Guide*
to review lesson concepts.

Homework

Activity 1

Write the value of the digit.

Model   In the number 4,237,001, what is the value of the 7?   Answer: 7,000

1. In the number 12,005,999, what is the value of the 2?

2. In the number 3,567, what is the value of the 7?

3. In the number 16,295,001, what is the value of the 9?

4. In the number 27,095, what is the value of the 0?

5. In the number 632,981,075, what is the value of the 1?

Activity 2

Write the value of the digit that is underlined.

Model   45,079   Answer: 5,000

1. 10,119	2. 5,092	3. 29,010
4. 5,376	5. 129,020	6. 3,506,999
7. 62,125	8. 25,000,210	9. 529,023,311

Activity 3

The number is written in words.
Write how many digits the number has.
Then write the number.

		Digits?	Number
Model	seven thousand twelve	4 digits	7,012
1.	sixty five thousand twenty-nine		
2.	seventy four thousand one hundred sixty		
3.	eight hundred thirteen		
4.	four million twenty-five		

Activity 4 • Distributed Practice

Add. Try to find the sum mentally.

1. 8 + 3	2. 5 + 2	3. 9 + 4	4. 7 + 8
5. 8 + 0	6. 1 + 5	7. 6 + 4	8. 7 + 7

Lesson **2** | Thinking About Numbers by Place Value

Problem Solving:
Reading Important Information

▶Thinking About Numbers by Place Value

Vocabulary

basic addition facts
extended addition
  facts
power of 10
standard form
expanded form

What are basic and extended addition facts?

Basic addition facts are one-digit math facts that we either memorize or compute quickly in our heads. Here are some examples.

| $4 + 9 = 13$ | $6 + 5 = 11$ | $4 + 8 = 12$ | $9 + 8 = 17$ |

Extended addition facts are basic facts multiplied by a **power of 10**. An extended fact looks like a basic fact, except each number has one or more zeros after it. It has been multiplied by 10, 100, 1,000, or another power of 10.

Powers of 10

$10 = 10$
$100 = 10 \times 10$
$1,000 = 10 \times 10 \times 10$

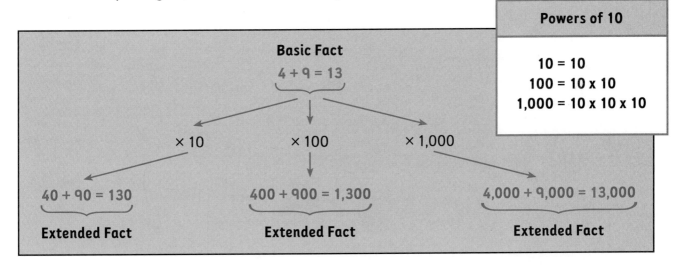

Basic Fact
$4 + 9 = 13$

$\times 10$ $\times 100$ $\times 1,000$

$40 + 90 = 130$ $400 + 900 = 1,300$ $4,000 + 9,000 = 13,000$

Extended Fact   **Extended Fact**   **Extended Fact**

Extended addition facts are created by multiplying each digit in the basic addition fact by a power of 10.

Example 1

Write extended facts for the basic fact 8 + 3 = 11 by multiplying the fact by powers of 10.

Basic fact: **8 + 3 = 11**   Extended facts: **80 + 30 = 110**
                                                   800 + 300 = 1,100
                                                   8,000 + 3,000 = 11,000

Seeing the relationship between basic facts and extended facts helps us add large numbers in our heads.

What is expanded form?

The way we usually write numbers is called **standard form** . The number 328 is written in standard form.

Sometimes it is helpful to write a number in a way that shows the place value of each digit. This is called **expanded form** . It shows the number as a sum of the values of its digits. Let's look at some examples of standard and expanded form.

Example 1

Write 328 in expanded form.

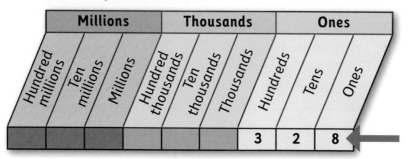

The place-value chart shows that **328** is
3 hundreds, 2 tens, and 8 ones.

| 328 | **3** hundreds | + | **2** tens | + | **8** ones |
| 328 | **300** | + | **20** | + | **8** |

The expanded form of the number 328 is 300 + 20 + 8.

How we read numbers is very different from how we write them in expanded form.

Example 2

Write 906,081 in expanded form.

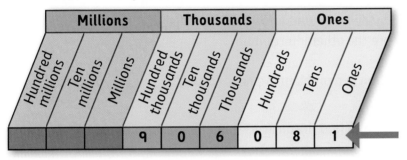

The number 906,081 is read *nine hundred six thousand eighty-one*. We do not say the ten thousands and hundreds place values because their value is 0. In expanded form, we write a zero for these place values.

The expanded form of the number 906,081 is
900,000 + 0 + 6,000 + 0 + 80 + 1.

We can use the greatest place value of the expanded form to tell how many digits the number has when written in standard form.

Example 3

Write 90,000 + 0 + 500 + 80 + 2 in standard form.
When the greatest place value in a number is ten thousands, the number has 5 digits. The number in this problem should have five digits.

The standard form of 90,000 + 0 + 500 + 80 + 2 is 90,582.

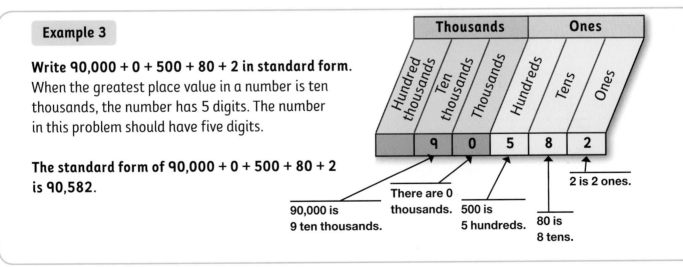

90,000 is
9 ten thousands.

There are 0 thousands.

500 is
5 hundreds.

80 is
8 tens.

2 is 2 ones.

Apply Skills
Turn to *Interactive Text*, page 6.

mBook Reinforce Understanding
Use the *mBook Study Guide* to review lesson concepts.

How do we find important information?

One of the first steps of problem solving is identifying what the problem is asking. Let's look at another step in problem solving—finding the important information in a problem.

We are often given more information than we need to solve a problem. This means we have to identify the important information needed to solve a problem and then ignore the other information.

To find the important information in a problem, we need to answer the following:

- What information do I need to find the answer?
- Is there any information I do not need?
- Could I explain to a classmate what I am supposed to find?

Steps for Solving a Word Problem:

STEP 1
Figure out what the problem is asking and rewrite what you find.

STEP 2
Decide what information you need to find the answer.

STEP 3
Find the important information in the problem.

POWER CONCEPT

Identifying what a problem asks for and finding the important information needed to solve it are the first steps of problem solving.

We already figured out what the following word problem is asking. Now, we should identify the important information in the problem.

Example 1

Find the important information in this problem.

Problem:

There are 64 teams in the first round of a college basketball tournament. There are 4 divisions with an equal number of teams in each division. Each team plays until it loses a game. There are 2 teams in the finals. How many teams are in each division in the first round of the basketball tournament?

> Always try to separate the information you need from the information you don't need.

STEP 1
Figure out what the problem is asking, and rewrite what you find.
How many teams are in each division in the first round of the basketball tournament?

STEP 2
Decide what information you need to find the answer.
We need to know the number of teams in the first round and the number of divisions.

STEP 3
Find the important information in the problem.
The first two sentences include the important information.

It is important to identify what the problem is asking when you explain how you solve problems.

 Problem-Solving Activity
Turn to *Interactive Text*, page 8.

 mBook **Reinforce Understanding**
Use the *mBook Study Guide* to review lesson concepts.

Homework

Activity 1

Write the number in expanded form.

Model 293 Answer: 200 + 90 + 3

1. 75	2. 478	3. 290
4. 907	5. 555	6. 1,693

Activity 2

Write the number in standard form.

Model 500 + 20 + 7 Answer: 527

1. 80 + 9	2. 400 + 0 + 6	3. 500 + 80 + 0
4. 600 + 60 + 2	5. 900 + 90 + 9	6. 1,000 + 0 + 0 + 9

Activity 3

Use the place-value chart to answer the following questions.

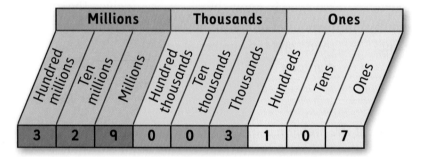

1. What is the value of the digit 9?

2. In which places are the zeros?

3. What is the digit in the ten millions place?

Activity 4 • Distributed Practice

Add. Try to find the sum mentally.

1. 9 + 1	2. 90 + 10	3. 7 + 7
4. 70 + 70	5. 6 + 2	6. 60 + 20

Lesson 3 ▶Addition Problems in Expanded Form

Problem Solving:
Finding What the Problem Is Asking For

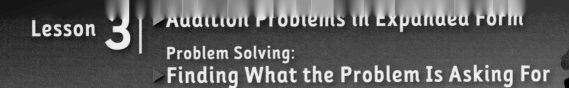

▶**Addition Problems in Expanded Form**

Vocabulary
place-value coins

How do we use expanded form in addition?

We know that coins have different values. A penny is worth 1 cent, and a dime is worth 10 cents. We can use **place-value coins** to help show place value. Place-value coins are worth 1, 10, or 100.

We can show the number 32 as 3 tens coins and 2 ones coins.

Tens	Ones	
10 10 10	1 1	} 32

When we add 3 to 32, we add 3 ones coins.

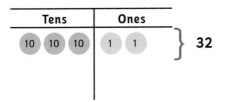

Tens	Ones	
10 10 10	1 1	} 32
	1 1 1	} + 3

The coins help us see the answer to 32 + 3 because they show place value. We use the same thinking when we do addition in expanded form.

In Lesson 2, we wrote numbers as a sum of the value of their digits. This is called expanded form. Now, we will learn to write addition problems in expanded form.

Sometimes it is easier to see what is happening in addition when we write a problem in expanded form. Writing an addition problem in expanded form helps us clearly see that we add ones to ones and tens to tens.

POWER CONCEPT

Writing an addition problem in expanded form helps us keep track of place value when we add.

Example 1

Write the addition problem $\begin{array}{r} 42 \\ + 35 \\ \hline \end{array}$ in expanded form.

The expanded form of 42 is 40 + 2.
The expanded form of 35 is 30 + 5.

The expanded form of $\begin{array}{r} 42 \\ + 35 \\ \hline \end{array}$ is $\begin{array}{r|r} 40 & 2 \\ + 30 & 5 \\ \hline \end{array}$.

 Apply Skills
Turn to *Interactive Text*,
page 10.

 mBook Reinforce Understanding
Use the *mBook Study Guide*
to review lesson concepts.

▶**Problem Solving: Finding What the Problem Is Asking For**

How do we know if we answered the question being asked?

When we solve a word problem, we must decide what the problem is asking. One common error when solving word problems is answering a question that is not asked.

Let's show how a student did the calculation correctly, but found the answer to a question that was not asked. Following the problem-solving steps is a good way to avoid making this common mistake.

Example 1

Solve the word problem.

Problem:

Michael has two brothers. One brother is 3 years older than Michael, and the other is 3 years younger. If the youngest brother is 12 years old, how old is the oldest brother?

Samantha solved the problem and wrote her solution on the board:

$12 + 3 = 15$

Michael is 15 years old.

Is Samantha's answer correct?

No, because the problem did not ask for Michael's age. The problem asked, "How old is the oldest brother?"

The correct solution is:

Youngest brother's age: 12

Michael's age: $12 + 3 = 15$

Oldest brother's age: $15 + 3 = 18$

The oldest brother is 18 years old.

Steps for Solving a Word Problem:

STEP 1
Figure out what the problem is asking, and rewrite what you find.

STEP 2
Decide what information you need to find the answer.

STEP 3
Find the important information in the problem.

 Problem-Solving Activity
Turn to *Interactive Text*, page 11.

 mBook Reinforce Understanding
Use the *mBook Study Guide* to review lesson concepts.

Activity 1

Write the number in expanded form.

| **Model** | 293 | Answer: 200 + 90 + 3 |

1. 85　　　　　　　　2. 387　　　　　　　　3. 175

Activity 2

Rewrite the problem in expanded form. Do not find the sum.

Model	Answer:
37	30 | 7
+ 49 →	+ 40 | 9

1.　　35　　2.　　47　　3.　　47　　4.　　95
　　+ 28　　　　+ 80　　　　+ 65　　　　+ 62

5.　　38　　6.　　90　　7.　　60　　8.　　82
　　+ 51　　　　+ 20　　　　+ 72　　　　+ 12

Activity 3

Write what the problem is asking for. Do not solve.

Model　A CD store sells about 200 CDs each day. The store manager wants to know about how many CDs the store sells in a week. The 20 best-selling CDs are in the rock/pop category. The store also sells a lot of movie soundtracks.

Q: What is the problem asking for?

A: About how many CDs does the store sell in a week?

1. The human heart beats about 72 times per minute. It pumps blood at a rate of about 5 liters per minute. How many times does the heart beat in an hour?

2. The world population increases by 240,000 people daily. Population experts want to know how much the world's population grows in a week. Half the world's population lives in just 6 countries. Many of these countries are very poor. How much does the world's population grow in a week?

Activity 4 • Distributed Practice

Add.

1. 7 + 9　　　　2. 90 + 10　　　　3. 900 + 700　　　　4. 300 + 400

▶Expanded Addition

Problem Solving:
▶Using Bar Graphs to Display Data

▶**Expanded Addition**

How do we add using expanded form?

Remember that we model addition with place-value coins.
Look at how the numbers 43 and 26 are shown with the coins.

We can use the coins to help us find the sum of the numbers
43 and 26. We add the ones coins from both numbers, then
we add the tens from both numbers.

When we add numbers in expanded form, we use
expanded addition . There are steps to solving problems in
expanded addition.

Vocabulary
expanded addition

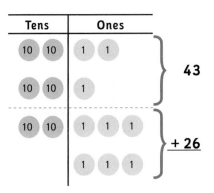

Example 1

Add using expanded addition.

STEP 1
Write the addition problem
in expanded form.
Now, we can add by place value
like we did with the coins.

$$\begin{array}{r} 43 \\ + \ 26 \end{array} \rightarrow \begin{array}{r|r} 40 & 3 \\ + \ 20 & 6 \end{array}$$

STEP 2
Add the ones column.
Then add the tens column.

$$\begin{array}{r|r} 40 & 3 \\ + \ 20 & 6 \\ \hline & 9 \end{array} \qquad \begin{array}{r|l} 40 & 3 \\ + \ 20 & 6 \\ \hline 60 & 9 = 60 + 9 \end{array}$$

STEP 3
Write the sum in standard form.   60 + 9 = 69   **The sum is 69.**

 Apply Skills
Turn to *Interactive Text*,
page 13.

 Reinforce Understanding
Use the *mBook Study Guide*
to review lesson concepts.

▶**Problem Solving: Using Bar Graphs to Display Data**

Vocabulary

bar graph
title
horizontal axis
vertical axis
scale
interval

What are bar graphs, and how are they used?

Data can be displayed in many different ways. One common way to present data is with a **bar graph** . In this lesson, we begin following the CD sales of a band called The Scatter Plots by looking at the bar graph below.

The **title** of the bar graph tells us that the graph shows the CD sales for the Scatter Plots from January through April.

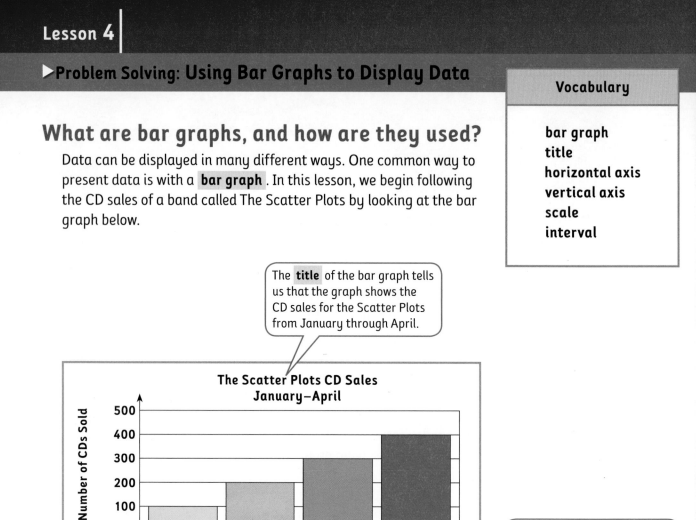

The line across the bottom of the graph labeled *Month* is the **horizontal axis** .

The line along the left side of the graph labeled *Number of CDs Sold* is the **vertical axis** . Notice the numbers along this axis: 0, 100, 200, 300, 400, and 500. This is the **scale** of the graph. The numbers in the scale are changing by 100, so the **interval** of the scale is 100.

The bar graph shows how many CDs the Scatter Plots sold over a period of four months:

Month	CDs Sold
January	100
February	200
March	300
April	400

Understanding Scale and Interval

It is important to understand the scale of the graph. Notice the scale of the bar graph ranges from 0 to 500, and the interval is 100. We can think of this as counting by 100 from 0 to 500.

This scale and interval were selected because they do a good job of representing the data shown in the graph.

> Pay close attention to the scale and the interval.

 Problem-Solving Activity
Turn to *Interactive Text*, page 14.

 Reinforce Understanding
Use the *mBook Study Guide* to review lesson concepts.

Homework

Activity 1

Write the number in expanded form.

Model 49   40 + 9

1.	35	**2.**	529	**3.**	812	**4.**	375
5.	16,020	**6.**	45,999	**7.**	6,015	**8.**	4,007

Activity 2

Add using expanded addition. Then write the sum in standard form.

Model

```
  28        20 | 8
+ 61  →   + 60 | 1
          80 | 9
```

80 + 9 Answer = 89

1.	17	**2.**	45	**3.**	54
	+ 82		+ 33		+ 22
4.	61	**5.**	32	**6.**	40
	+ 16		+ 25		+ 49

Activity 3

Copy and complete the chart of basic and extended facts.

Basic Fact	Extended Fact (Basic Fact × 10)	Extended Fact (Basic Fact × 100)
2 + 4	20 + 40	200 + 400
	20 + 80	
9 + 1		900 + 100
2 + 7		200 + 700
	30 + 30	
9 + 8		
		600 + 500

Activity 4 • Distributed Practice

Add.

1.	2 + 3	**2.**	20 + 30	**3.**	200 + 300
4.	2,000 + 3,000	**5.**	7 + 4	**6.**	700 + 400

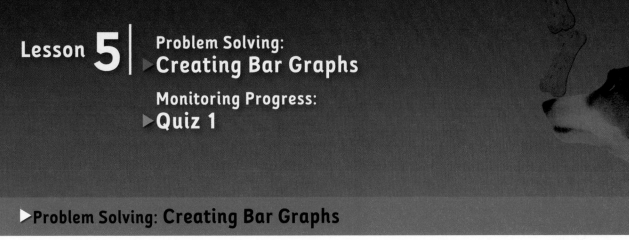

►**Problem Solving: Creating Bar Graphs**

How do we create a bar graph?

In Lesson 4, we learned the parts of a bar graph. It is important to understand these parts when reading and creating a bar graph.

Use this graph as a model for creating a bar graph. To be clear, a bar graph must be labeled. Also, its scale and interval must fit the data.

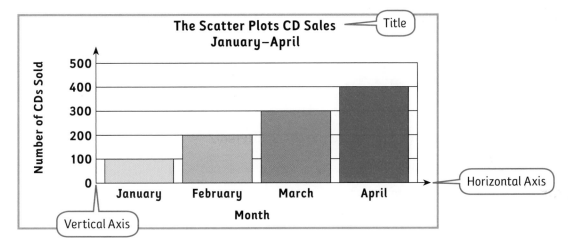

Labels

When creating a graph, we need to select a title that clearly tells the reader what is shown. As with the title, select labels that clearly describe the data that are shown on each axis.

Scale and Interval

When creating a bar graph, we need to select the scale and interval. Look at the lowest and highest value in the set of data to help decide this. In the graph above, the lowest value is 100, and the highest is 400. These data fit nicely in the scale 0–500.

 Problem-Solving Activity
Turn to *Interactive Text*, page 16.

 Monitoring Progress
Quiz 1

 mBook Reinforce Understanding
Use the *mBook Study Guide* to review lesson concepts.

Activity 1

Rewrite the problem in expanded form. Do not find the sum.

Model	Answer:
75	70 | 5
+ 22 →	+ 20 | 2

1. 36
  + 41

2. 13
  + 35

3. 70
  + 19

4. 62
  + 26

5. 25
  + 31

6. 22
  + 44

Activity 2

Use the graphs to answer the questions.

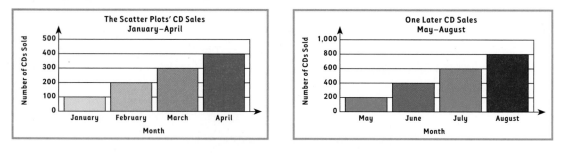

1. Notice the title of the graphs. How are the titles different?

2. What does the first graph show?

3. What does the second graph show?

4. What is the scale of the first graph? What is the interval?

5. What is the scale of the second graph? What is the interval?

Activity 3

Add.

1. 2 + 3

2. 700 + 300

3. 200 + 500

4. 200 + 300

5. 900 + 400

6. 90 + 90

7. 2,000 + 3,000

8. 80 + 20

9. 100 + 800

Lesson 6 ►More Expanded Addition
Problem Solving:
►Analyzing Data in a Bar Graph

►More Expanded Addition

How do we add three-digit numbers in expanded form?

We already know how to use ones and tens place-value coins. They are like pennies and dimes. Now we will add using the hundreds coin. It is like a dollar. Look at the number 245 shown with place-value coins.

Let's see what happens when we add 112 to 245.

Together, there are seven ones coins, five tens coins, and three hundreds coins.

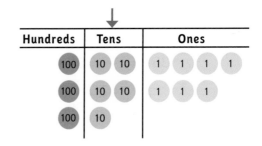

Hundreds	Tens	Ones	
100	10 10	1 1 1 1	} 245
100	10 10	1	
100	10	1 1	} + 112
300 +	50 +	7	357

We use the same thinking to add using expanded addition.

Starting in the ones place, we add 5 and 2. Because 5 + 2 = 7, we write 7 in the ones place.

```
  200 | 40 | 5
+ 100 | 10 | 2
      |    | 7
```

We can check this addition against the coin model. Seven ones coins are the same as the number 7 in the ones place in addition.

We can do the same thing for the tens place. Because 40 + 10 = 50, we write 50 in the tens place. We check by counting the coins. Five tens coins equals 50.

```
  200 | 40 | 5
+ 100 | 10 | 2
      | 50 | 7
```

Finally, we solve the hundreds place. Because 200 + 100 = 300, we write 300 in the hundreds place. In the coin model, we see that three hundreds coins equals 300.

```
  200 | 40 | 5
+ 100 | 10 | 2
  300 | 50 | 7
```

The sum is 357.

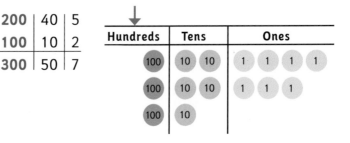

We know how to add two-digit numbers using expanded addition. The same method can be used for three-digit numbers.

Example 1

Find the sum of 321 and 473 using expanded addition.

```
  321          300 | 20 | 1
+ 473  →     + 400 | 70 | 3
             700 | 90 | 4      700 + 90 + 4 = 794   The sum is 794.
```

Let's look at an example of expanded addition that adds a three-digit number and a two-digit number. Notice how the ones and tens line up in this problem.

Example 2

Find the sum of 105 and 93 using expanded addition.

```
  105          100 | 00 | 5
+  93  →     +      | 90 | 3
             100 | 90 | 8      100 + 90 + 8 = 198   The sum is 198.
```

Let's add the same two numbers in two different orders.

Example 3

Show that the sum of 351 and 138 is equal to the sum of 138 and 351.

```
  351          300 | 50 | 1              138          100 | 30 | 8
+ 138  →     + 100 | 30 | 8            + 351  →     + 300 | 50 | 1
             400 | 80 | 9 = 489                     400 | 80 | 9 = 489
```

The sum of 351 and 138 is 489.   **The sum of 138 and 351 is 489.**

The order of the numbers does not matter in addition. The sum of both problems is the same.

 Apply Skills
Turn to *Interactive Text*,
page 18.

 mBook Reinforce Understanding
Use the *mBook Study Guide*
to review lesson concepts.

▶**Problem Solving: Analyzing Data in a Bar Graph**

Vocabulary
trend

What do we look for in a bar graph?

One advantage of using a bar graph is that we can make observations about the data, such as spotting a **trend** . A trend is a pattern in data over time.

In the graph below, the CD sales for the Scatter Plots go up each month. We say that this trend is *increasing sales*. This means that the sales are getting better over time.

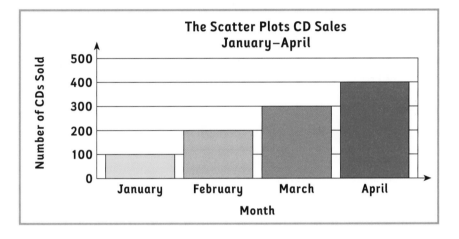

POWER CONCEPT

We use a bar graph to understand data and find trends.

With a bar graph, we can quickly make comparisons. For instance, the bar for April is taller than the bar for January, so the sales were greater in April than in January.

We can also use the bar graph to make calculations.

Example 1

Find the total CD sales during February and March.

February sales: 200 CDs

March sales: 300 CDs

200 + 300 = 500 CDs

The total CD sales during February and March were 500 CDs.

Problem-Solving Activity
Turn to *Interactive Text*,
page 19.

mBook Reinforce Understanding
Use the *mBook Study Guide*
to review lesson concepts.

Homework

Add.

1. $2 + 3$
2. $700 + 300$
3. $200 + 500$
4. $20 + 30$
5. $900 + 400$
6. $90 + 90$

Add using expanded addition. Then write the sum in standard form.

Model

$$\begin{array}{r} 432 \\ + 161 \\ \hline \end{array}$$

400	30	2
+ 100	60	1
500	90	3

$500 + 90 + 3$

Answer: 593

1. $\begin{array}{r} 228 \\ + 11 \\ \hline \end{array}$
2. $\begin{array}{r} 532 \\ + 23 \\ \hline \end{array}$
3. $\begin{array}{r} 954 \\ + 35 \\ \hline \end{array}$

4. $\begin{array}{r} 216 \\ + 122 \\ \hline \end{array}$
5. $\begin{array}{r} 432 \\ + 325 \\ \hline \end{array}$
6. $\begin{array}{r} 802 \\ + 103 \\ \hline \end{array}$

7. $\begin{array}{r} 102 \\ + 190 \\ \hline \end{array}$
8. $\begin{array}{r} 410 \\ + 410 \\ \hline \end{array}$
9. $\begin{array}{r} 102 \\ + 603 \\ \hline \end{array}$

Add.

1. $4 + 9$
2. $7 + 8$
3. $60 + 30$
4. $50 + 50$
5. $700 + 800$
6. $400 + 900$
7. $50 + 60$
8. $900 + 200$
9. $500 + 300$

Lesson 7 ▸Regrouping in Expanded Addition

Problem Solving:
Finding Information in Tables

▸**Regrouping in Expanded Addition**

Vocabulary
regroup

When do we have to regroup to add?

We know that we can model numbers with place-value coins. The number 57 is 5 tens coins and 7 ones coins as shown in the coin model below.

If we want to add 5 to 57, we add 5 ones coins to the ones column.

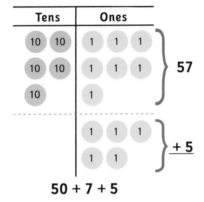

50 + 7 + 5

When we find the sum, we see that 5 ones coins and 7 ones coins combine to make 12 ones coins.

When we have ten ones coins, we can **regroup** them into 1 tens coin.

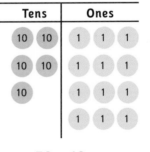

50 + 12

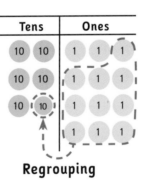

Regrouping

We use this model to learn how to regroup ones into tens when we have more than 9 coins in an addition problem.

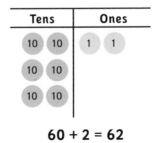

60 + 2 = 62

We have been adding numbers using expanded addition. Now, we will try some problems that need regrouping. We have to regroup ones to tens when the sum of the ones is greater than 9.

Example 1

Find the sum of 57 and 28 using expanded addition.

$$\begin{array}{r} 57 \\ + \ 28 \\ \hline \end{array}$$

STEP 1

Add the ones.

$$\begin{array}{r|l} 50 & 7 \\ + \ 20 & 8 \\ \hline & 1\,5 \end{array}$$

STEP 2

Write the sum in expanded form.
Because 15 is greater than 9, we have to regroup. Rewrite 15 as 1 ten and 5 ones.

$$\begin{array}{r|r} 50 & 7 \\ + \ 20 & 8 \\ \hline & 10 + 5 \end{array}$$

STEP 3

Regroup.
Regroup 1 ten from the ones column to the tens column.

$$\begin{array}{r|r} & 10 \leftarrow \\ 50 & 7 \\ + \ 20 & 8 \\ \hline & \cancel{10} + 5 \end{array}$$

STEP 4

Add the tens.

$$\begin{array}{r|l} 10 & \\ 50 & 7 \\ + \ 20 & 8 \\ \hline 80 & 5 \end{array}$$

STEP 5

Write the sum in standard form.

$$\begin{array}{r|l} 10 & \\ 50 & 7 \\ + \ 20 & 8 \\ \hline 80 & 5 \to 85 \end{array}$$

The sum is 85.

Example 2

Find the sum of 315 and 238 using expanded addition.

$$315$$
$$+\ 238$$

STEP 1
Add the ones.

300	10	5
+ 200	30	8
		1 3

STEP 2
Write the sum in expanded form.

Because 13 is greater than 9, we have to regroup. Rewrite 13 as 1 ten and 3 ones.

300	10	5
+ 200	30	8
		10 + 3

STEP 3
Regroup.

Regroup 1 ten from the ones column to the tens column.

	10 ←	
300	10	5
+ 200	30	8
		~~10~~ + 3

STEP 4
Add the tens.

	10	
300	**10**	5
+200	**30**	8
	50	3

STEP 5
Add the hundreds.

	10	
300	10	5
+200	30	8
500	50	3

STEP 6
Write the sum in standard form.

	10	
300	10	5
+200	30	8
500	50	3 → **553**

The sum is 553.

% ÷ **Apply Skills**
< × Turn to *Interactive Text*, page 21.

 mBook **Reinforce Understanding**
Use the *mBook Study Guide* to review lesson concepts.

▶**Problem Solving: Finding Information in Tables**

Vocabulary
table

How do we find information in a table?

Sometimes the information we need to solve a word problem is in a **table** . A table is another way to show information.

This table shows CD sales for five bands on Hipster Records.

Hipster Records CD Sales January–April	
Band	**CD Sales**
The Hammerheads	$30,000
One Later	$24,000
4 Floors Up	$19,000
The Scatter Plots	$12,000
Three Ears	$6,000

The column on the left shows the names of each different band. The column on the right shows how much money each band made selling CDs during the four-month period from January through April.

To read the table, we find the name of the band on the left, and read across to the right to find out how much money it made selling CDs from January through April.

Problem-Solving Activity
Turn to *Interactive Text*,
page 22.

mBook Reinforce Understanding
Use the *mBook Study Guide*
to review lesson concepts.

Lesson 7

Homework

Activity 1

Complete the following basic and extended facts.

1. 7 + _____ = 16
2. 90 + 70 = _____
3. 700 + 900 = _____
4. 7 + 8 = _____
5. 80 + _____ = 150
6. _____ + 800 = 1,500
7. 60 + 70 = _____
8. _____ + 600 = 1,300
9. 6 + _____ = 13

Activity 2

Rewrite the problem in expanded form. Do not find the sum.

Model
432
+ 161
400 | 30 | 2
+ 100 | 60 | 1

1.   327
      + 21

2.   220
      + 100

3.   500
      + 102

Activity 3

Add using expanded addition. Regroup when necessary.
Then write the answer in standard form.

Model
37
+ 46
30 | 7
+ 40 | 6
70 | 13
¹⁰
30 | 7
+ 40 | 6
80 | 3
80 + 3
Answer: 83

1.   327
      + 21

2.   220
      + 100

3.   54
      + 29

4.   78
      + 13

Activity 4

Use the bar graph to answer the following questions.

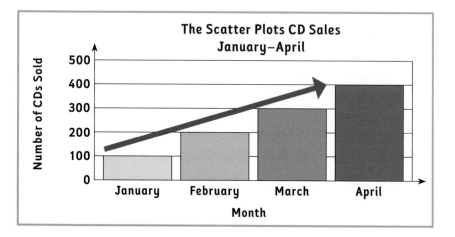

1. Suppose the Scatter Plots CD sales continue the same trend over the next three months. How many CDs will they sell in July?

2. If you were going to make a graph to show the CD sales from January to July, what scale and interval would you choose? What does the first graph show?

3. How would you change the scale and interval if the Scatter Plots CD sales had only increased by 50 each month over the next three months?

Activity 5 • Distributed Practice

Add.

1. $7 + 9$

2. $40 + 40$

3. $600 + 600$

4. $70 + 60$

5. $80 + 20$

6. $400 + 500$

Lesson 8 ▶ Comparing Methods of Regrouping

Problem Solving:
▶ Creating a Graph From a Table of Data

▶Comparing Methods of Regrouping

Vocabulary

traditional addition
algorithm

How is regrouping in expanded addition different from regrouping in traditional addition?

We have been using expanded addition to solve problems. Let's use another way to add. We will solve the following problem using **traditional addition** .

```
   37
 + 59
```

Steps for Using Traditional Addition:

STEP 1

Add the ones.

Since 7 + 9 = 16, we write 6 in the ones place of the answer.

```
   37
 + 59
    6
```

STEP 2

Regroup.

Write a small 1 above the tens column.

```
  1
   37
 + 59
    6
```

STEP 3

Add the tens.

Write 9 in the tens place of the answer.

```
  1
   37
 + 59
   96
```

The sum is 96.

A set of steps for solving a problem is called an **algorithm** . The three steps above show the algorithm for solving 37 + 59. The algorithm for traditional addition is different from the algorithm for expanded addition.

We have been adding numbers in expanded form, which clearly shows regrouping. Let's compare the way we add and regroup using expanded addition to the way we add and regroup using traditional addition.

Example 1

Use both expanded addition and traditional addition to find the sum of 47 and 28.

Expanded Addition	Traditional Addition
$\begin{array}{r} 47 \\ + 28 \end{array}$ → $\begin{array}{r|r} 40 & 7 \\ + 20 & 8 \end{array}$	$\begin{array}{r} 47 \\ + 28 \end{array}$
$\begin{array}{r|r} 40 & 7 \\ + 20 & 8 \\ \hline & 15 \end{array}$	$\begin{array}{r} 47 \\ + 28 \\ \hline 5 \end{array}$
$\begin{array}{r|r} 40 & 7 \\ + 20 & 8 \\ \hline & 10 + 5 \end{array}$	
$\overset{10}{\begin{array}{r|r} 40 & 7 \\ + 20 & 8 \\ \hline \cancel{10} + 5 \end{array}}$	$\overset{1}{\begin{array}{r} 47 \\ + 28 \\ \hline 5 \end{array}}$
$\overset{10}{\begin{array}{r|r} 40 & 7 \\ + 20 & 8 \\ \hline 70 & + 5 \end{array}}$ → 75	$\overset{1}{\begin{array}{r} 47 \\ + 28 \\ \hline 75 \end{array}}$

The sum is 75.

> **POWER CONCEPT**
>
> We use the traditional algorithm because it is faster and more efficient than expanded addition.

Traditional addition handles regrouping in a shorthand way.
This is sometimes called "carrying the one."

 Apply Skills
Turn to *Interactive Text*, page 24.

 mBook Reinforce Understanding
Use the *mBook Study Guide* to review lesson concepts.

▶**Problem Solving: Creating a Graph From a Table of Data**

How do we make a graph from a table of data?

Sometimes, the information found in a table is more clearly displayed in a bar graph.

The information shown in the table below is also displayed in the bar graph.

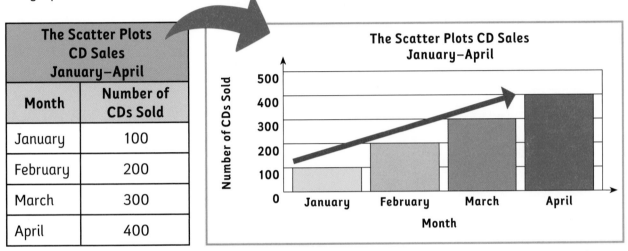

The Scatter Plots CD Sales January–April	
Month	**Number of CDs Sold**
January	100
February	200
March	300
April	400

Notice how the bar graph gives us information about the data at a glance. It helps us easily make comparisons and conclusions about the data. For example, it is easy to see that the most CDs were sold in April because the bar for April is the tallest one.

> Bar graphs help us see the data clearly.

 Problem-Solving Activity
Turn to *Interactive Text*, page 25.

 mBook Reinforce Understanding
Use the *mBook Study Guide* to review lesson concepts.

Homework

Activity 1

Add using expanded addition. Then write the answer in standard form.

Model

```
     28
   + 64
```

```
  20 |  8
 + 60 |  4
  80 | 10 + 2
```

```
       10
    20 | 8
   + 60 | 4
    90 | 2
```

90 + 2 = 92

Answer: 92

1.
```
    38
  + 15
```

2.
```
    16
  + 36
```

3.
```
    29
  + 58
```

4.
```
    64
  + 17
```

Activity 2

Add using traditional addition.

Model

```
    32
  + 18
```

```
     1
    32
  + 18
    50
```

32 + 18 = 50

Answer: 50

1.
```
    37
  + 24
```

2.
```
    20
  + 80
```

3.
```
    79
  + 13
```

4.
```
    31
  + 89
```

5.
```
    95
  + 27
```

6.
```
    87
  + 25
```

Activity 3 • Distributed Practice

Add.

1. 7 + 7

2. 60 + 20

3. 500 + 800

4. 70 + 60

5. 1,000 + 4,000

6. 600 + 200

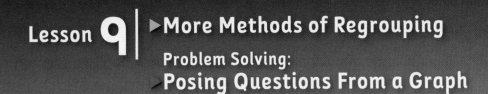

Lesson 9 | ▶More Methods of Regrouping

Problem Solving:
▶Posing Questions From a Graph

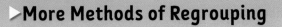

▶More Methods of Regrouping

How do we regroup to the hundreds place?

We have been adding two-digit numbers that need regrouping. Now we will work on problems that include three-digit numbers and need regrouping.

The number 168 can be shown as 1 hundreds coin, 6 tens coins, and 8 ones coins.

Hundreds	Tens	Ones	
100	10 10 10 10	1 1 1 1	} 168
	10 10	1 1 1 1	

To add 54 more, we add 5 tens coins and 4 ones coins.

	10 10 10 10	1 1 1 1	} + 54
	10		

There are more than 9 ones coins, so we must regroup.

Hundreds	Tens	Ones
100	10 10 10 10	1 1 1 1
	10 10 10 10	1 1 1 1
	10 10 10 10	1 1 1 1

There are more than 9 tens coins, so we must regroup again.

Hundreds	Tens	Ones
100	10 10 10 10	1 1
	10 10 10 10	
100	10 10 10 10	

The sum is 222.

Hundreds	Tens	Ones
100 100	10 10	1 1

200 + **20** + **2** **= 222**

In this problem, we regrouped coins from the tens place to the hundreds place the same way we regrouped from the ones place to the tens place.

Let's use this thinking with a problem in expanded addition.

Example 1

Find the sum of 197 and 35 using expanded addition.

STEP 1
Add the ones.

$$
\begin{array}{r|r|r}
100 & 90 & 7 \\
+ & 30 & 5 \\
\hline
 & & 1\,2
\end{array}
$$

STEP 2
Write the sum in expanded form.

$$
\begin{array}{r|r|r}
100 & 90 & 7 \\
+ & 30 & 5 \\
\hline
 & & 10+2
\end{array}
$$

STEP 3
Regroup.
Regroup 1 ten from the ones column to the tens column.

$$
\begin{array}{r|r|r}
 & 10 \leftarrow & \\
100 & 90 & 7 \\
+ & 30 & 5 \\
\hline
 & & \cancel{10}+2
\end{array}
$$

STEP 4
Add the tens.

$$
\begin{array}{r|r|r}
 & 10 & \\
100 & 90 & 7 \\
+ & 30 & 5 \\
\hline
 & 1\,30 & 2
\end{array}
$$

STEP 5
Regroup.
Regroup 1 hundred from the tens column to the hundreds column.

$$
\begin{array}{r|r|r}
 & 100 \leftarrow & 10 \\
100 & & 90 \quad 7 \\
+ & & 30 \quad 5 \\
\hline
 & \cancel{100}+30 & 2
\end{array}
$$

STEP 6
Add the hundreds.

$$
\begin{array}{r|r|r}
 & 100 & 10 \\
100 & 90 & 7 \\
+ & 30 & 5 \\
\hline
200 & 30 & 2
\end{array}
$$

STEP 7
Write the sum in standard form.

$$
\begin{array}{r|r|r}
 & 100 & 10 \\
100 & 90 & 7 \\
+ & 30 & 5 \\
\hline
200 & 30 & 2 \rightarrow 232
\end{array}
$$

The sum is 232.

Here is the same problem using traditional addition.

Example 2

Find the sum of 197 and 35 using traditional addition.

STEP 1
Add the ones.

$$197$$
$$+\ \ 35$$
$$\overline{\qquad 2}$$

POWER CONCEPT

Each addition algorithm has advantages. *Expanded addition* more clearly shows how to regroup. *Traditional addition* is faster, but we are more likely to make a regrouping mistake.

STEP 2
Regroup.

$$\overset{1}{1}97$$
$$+\ \ 35$$
$$\overline{\qquad 2}$$

STEP 3
Add the tens.
Think: 1 ten + 9 tens + 3 tens = 13 tens.

$$\overset{1}{1}97$$
$$+\ \ 35$$
$$\overline{\qquad 32}$$

STEP 4
Regroup.

$$\overset{1\ 1}{1}97$$
$$+\ \ 35$$
$$\overline{\qquad 32}$$

STEP 5
Add the hundreds.
Think: 1 hundred + 1 hundred = 2 hundreds.

$$\overset{1\ 1}{1}97$$
$$+\ \ 35$$
$$\overline{\quad 232}$$

The sum is 232.

Apply Skills
Turn to *Interactive Text*, page 27.

mBook Reinforce Understanding
Use the *mBook Study Guide* to review lesson concepts.

▶**Problem Solving: Posing Questions From a Graph**

How can we pose a question from a graph?

Most people use graphs to answer a particular question they are interested in. It is important that we become good at answering questions, based on the data in a graph. One way to practice this skill is to pose our own question about the data and then answer it.

Look at the bar graph.

Example 1 shows questions that can be answered by the graph.

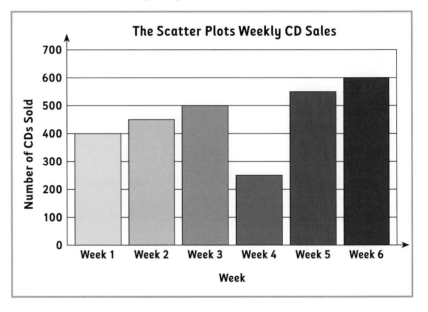

The Scatter Plots Weekly CD Sales

Example 1

The Scatter Plots manager, Ana, noticed that sometimes their CD sales drop from one week to the next. Pose a question about this situation and answer it.

Some possible questions are:
- When was the largest drop in sales?
- How many CDs were sold the week before the big drop?
- How many CDs were sold the week after the big drop?

We would answer these questions by looking at the bar graph for the biggest difference between two of the bars.
- The largest drop in sales occurred from Week 3 to Week 4.
- The week before the big drop, 450 CDs were sold.
- The week after the big drop, 550 CDs were sold.

 Problem-Solving Activity
Turn to *Interactive Text*, page 28.

 mBook Reinforce Understanding
Use the *mBook Study Guide* to review lesson concepts.

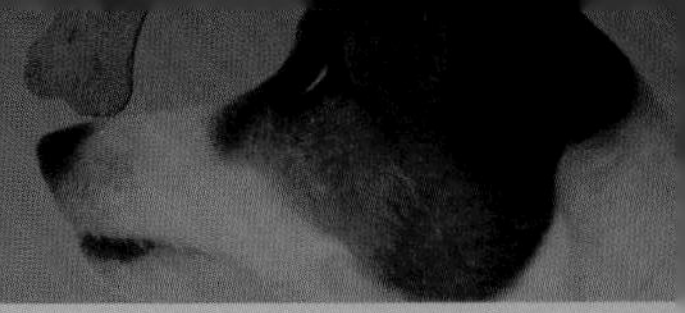

Homework

Activity 1	

Add using expanded addition. Write the answer in standard form.

Model

$$585 + 127 \rightarrow$$

500	80	5
+ 100	20	7
		12

	10 ← ⌐	
500	80	⦙ 5
+ 100	20	⦙ 7
		̶1̶0̶ + 2

100	10	
500	80	2
+ 100	20	7
	10	2

100	10	
500	80	2
+ 100	20	7
700	10	2

Answer: 712

1.
$$142 + 684$$

2.
$$493 + 278$$

3.
$$286 + 423$$

4.
$$216 + 596$$

Activity 2

Add using traditional addition.

Model

$$
\begin{array}{r}
566 \\
+259 \\
\hline
\end{array}
$$

$$
\begin{array}{r}
{}^{1} \\
566 \\
+259 \\
\hline
5
\end{array}
$$

$$
\begin{array}{r}
{}^{1}\;{}^{1} \\
566 \\
+259 \\
\hline
25
\end{array}
$$

$$
\begin{array}{r}
{}^{1}\;{}^{1} \\
566 \\
+259 \\
\hline
825
\end{array}
$$

Answer: 825

1.
$$
\begin{array}{r}
782 \\
+135 \\
\hline
\end{array}
$$

2.
$$
\begin{array}{r}
237 \\
+23 \\
\hline
\end{array}
$$

3.
$$
\begin{array}{r}
495 \\
+156 \\
\hline
\end{array}
$$

4.
$$
\begin{array}{r}
395 \\
+176 \\
\hline
\end{array}
$$

5.
$$
\begin{array}{r}
148 \\
+26 \\
\hline
\end{array}
$$

6.
$$
\begin{array}{r}
273 \\
+508 \\
\hline
\end{array}
$$

Activity 3 • Distributed Practice

Add.

1. $8 + 9$

2. $40 + 60$

3. $200 + 700$

4. $80 + 20$

5. $600 + 300$

6. $900 + 900$

Lesson **10** | ▶Numbers on a Number Line

Monitoring Progress:
▶**Quiz 2**

▶**Numbers on a Number Line**

How do we find numbers on a number line?

We use measuring tools in everyday life. Rulers measure distance. Fuel gauges measure how much gas is in a gas tank. These instruments help us understand a numerical value in a visual way.

Vocabulary
number line estimate round

A **number line** is a tool we can use to visualize numbers. Number lines help us see where numbers are in relation to each other.

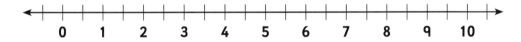

```
0  1  2  3  4  5  6  7  8  9  10
```

Number lines work as long as we have at least two numbers marked on them. Look at the number line to the right. We would have a hard time finding the number 50 on this line because there are no numbers.

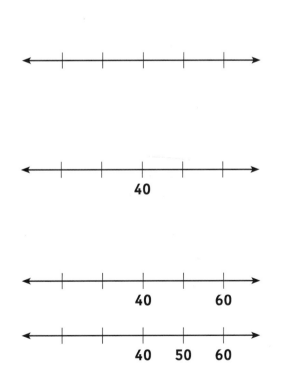

With this number line, we have a pretty good idea where 50 should be. It should be to the right of 40. But we don't know exactly where 50 should be yet.

40

After adding another number, we know where 50 should go. It goes between 40 and 60 on the number line.

40   60

40 50 60

As long as we have two numbers on a number line, we can find where any other number should go on the line.

When numbers are labeled on the number line, we can find their exact location.

Example 1

Find 50 on the number line.

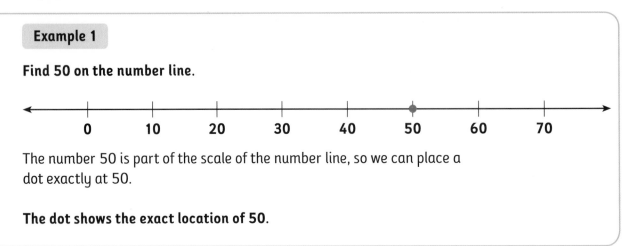

The number 50 is part of the scale of the number line, so we can place a dot exactly at 50.

The dot shows the exact location of 50.

It is a little more difficult to find the location of a number on a number line if the number is not labeled. In this case, we have to **estimate** the location of the number. This means we need to guess the number's location.

Example 2

Find 55 on the number line.

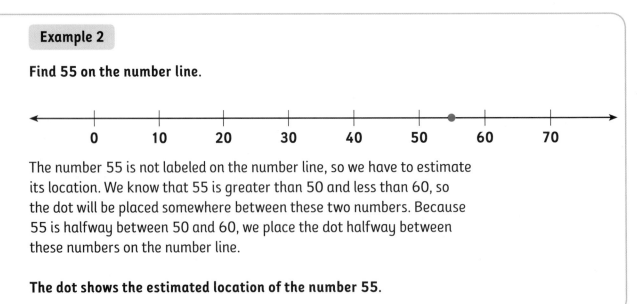

The number 55 is not labeled on the number line, so we have to estimate its location. We know that 55 is greater than 50 and less than 60, so the dot will be placed somewhere between these two numbers. Because 55 is halfway between 50 and 60, we place the dot halfway between these numbers on the number line.

The dot shows the estimated location of the number 55.

When we see a dot on a number line, sometimes we need to estimate the number represented by the dot. Example 3 shows estimations for several different dots on a number line.

Example 3

Estimate the number represented by each dot on the number line.

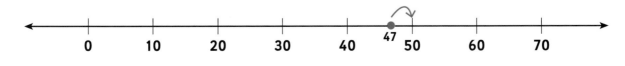

The number represented by **A** is about 5. The dot is halfway between 0 and 10.

The number represented by **B** is about 43. The dot is not quite halfway between 40 and 50. It is closer to 40.

The number represented by **C** is about 58. The dot is not quite halfway between 50 and 60. It is closer to 60.

How do we use number lines to round?

It is often easier to work with numbers using an estimation. For example, if we are asked to guess the number of people who attended a soccer game, we might say about 500, when the exact attendance was 487 people.

> When we estimate, more than one number can be considered a correct estimation.

When we use an estimation of a number, we **round** the number to the closest number on a number line.

Example 1

Use the number line to round to the nearest ten.
This number line is marked by tens. The number 47 is between 40 and 50. The number 47 rounds to 50 because it is closer to 50 than 40.

Example 2

Use the number line to round to the nearest hundred.

This number line is marked by hundreds. The number 320 is between 300 and 400. The number 320 *rounds down* to 300 because it is closer to 300 than 400.

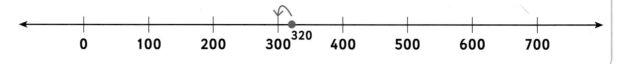

The most confusing case is when the number we are trying to round lies right in the middle of two numbers. In this case, we always round up to the greater number.

Example 3

Use the number line to round to the nearest ten.

This number line is marked by tens. The number 165 is halfway between 160 and 170. When a number lies exactly halfway between two numbers, we round up. So 165 rounds up to 170.

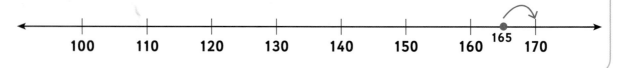

What are the rules for rounding?

We have learned that we can think about numbers on a number line to help us round. We can also use rules to help us round.

Rules for Rounding

To round to the nearest ten, look at the ones.

- If the ones are greater than or equal to 5, round up.   46 → 50
- If the ones are less than 5, round down.   32 → 30

To round to the nearest hundred, look at the tens.

- If the tens are greater than or equal to 5, round up.   180 → 200
- If the tens are less than 5, round down.   230 → 200

Improve Your Skills

How would we round 152 to the nearest hundred?

Common mistakes:

150   This number is 152 rounded down to the nearest ten, not the nearest hundred.

100   This number is 152 rounded down to the nearest hundred. Because there is a 5 in the tens place, we round up.

> Being able to estimate is an important skill.

The correct way to round 152 to the nearest hundred is to round up to 200.

 Apply Skills
Turn to *Interactive Text*, page 30.

 Monitoring Progress
Quiz 2

 mBook Reinforce Understanding
Use the *mBook Study Guide* to review lesson concepts.

Unit 1 • Lesson 10   49

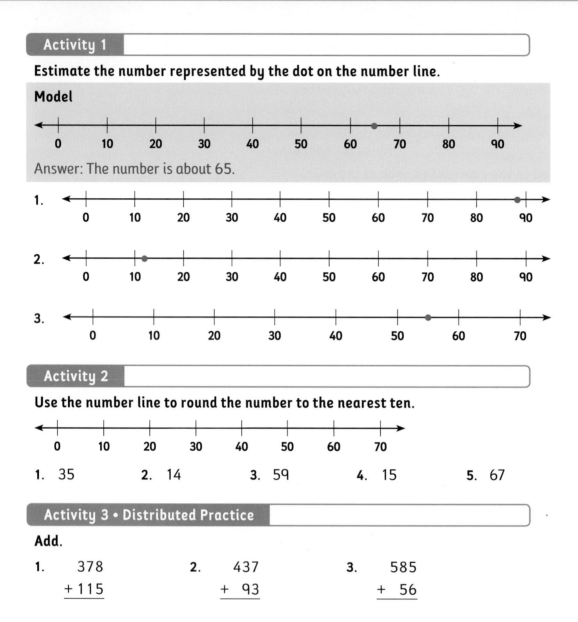

Activity 1

Estimate the number represented by the dot on the number line.

Model

Answer: The number is about 65.

1.

2.

3.

Activity 2

Use the number line to round the number to the nearest ten.

1. 35   2. 14   3. 59   4. 15   5. 67

Activity 3 • Distributed Practice

Add.

1.   378   2.   437   3.   585
     + 115   + 93   + 56

▸**Estimating Sums by Rounding**

How do we use rounding to estimate sums?

In Lesson 10, we used estimation to find numbers on a number line.
Now we will learn to estimate a sum using numbers on a number line.

Let's use estimation to find **77 + 32**.

We need to round the two numbers to estimate.

Look at the number line below.

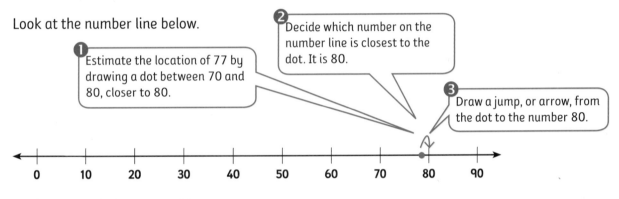

❷ Decide which number on the number line is closest to the dot. It is 80.

❶ Estimate the location of 77 by drawing a dot between 70 and 80, closer to 80.

❸ Draw a jump, or arrow, from the dot to the number 80.

We have rounded 77 up to 80.

Now let's round the number 32.

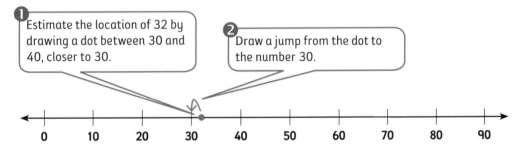

❶ Estimate the location of 32 by drawing a dot between 30 and 40, closer to 30.

❷ Draw a jump from the dot to the number 30.

We have rounded 32 down to 30.

We can rewrite the problem using the rounded numbers 80 and 30. This would give us an estimated sum. The rounded addition problem is an extended fact: **80 + 30 = 110**.

The estimated sum is 110.

Rounding helps us get a good idea about the sum of two numbers. It can turn a more difficult problem into an extended fact.

Example 1

Estimate the sum of 47 and 21.
Round each number to the nearest ten because the greatest place value in the numbers is the tens.

We round 47 up to 50 because 47 is closer to 50 than 40.

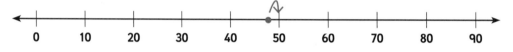

We round 21 down to 20 because 21 is closer to 20 than 30.

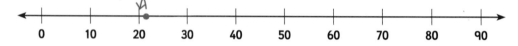

Use the rounded numbers to make the extended fact: 50 + 20 = 70.
The sum of the rounded numbers is 70.
The sum is about 70.

Now let's estimate a sum without using number lines.

Example 2

Estimate the sum of 586 and 801.
Round each number to the nearest hundred because the greatest place value in the numbers is the hundreds.

We round 586 up to 600 because 586 is closer to 600 than 500.
We round 801 down to 800 because 801 is closer to 800 than 900.

Use the rounded numbers to make the extended fact:
600 + 800 = 1,400.
The sum of the rounded numbers is 1,400.
The sum is about 1,400.

POWER CONCEPT

Even though estimating only gives us an answer that is close to the exact answer, it allows us to find a ballpark figure quickly in our heads.

How do we use rounding in the real world?

We round every day when we estimate a sum. For example, we estimate the total price of several items to be sure we have enough money to pay for them. Even though we do not know the exact sum, we can see whether we can afford the items.

Example 1

Which problem is easier to solve?

Problem 1

Jack buys a fish tank for $72 and a fish for $17. What is the total cost of the items?

> In Problem 1, we need to find the exact sum of 72 and 17.

Problem 2

Jack wants to buy a fish tank for $72 and a fish for $17. He has $200 to spend. Does Jack have enough money?

> In Problem 2, we need to estimate the sum of 72 and 17.

Problem 1 might look easier because there are only two numbers. But in Problem 1, we need to calculate the exact sum.

Problem 2 is easier because we can estimate the answer. $72 is less than $100, and $17 is less than $100.

Jack's total purchase will be less than $200.

We can also use estimation to check how reasonable an answer is.

Example 2

Is Martha's answer reasonable?

Martha added 586 and 801 on her calculator. She found the sum 667. Martha's answer seems too low. We can estimate to check if it is reasonable.

> You can make a mistake on a calculator or with a paper and pencil. Check your work!

The sum of 586 and 801 should be greater than 1,000 because the sum of 600 and 800 is 1,400.

Martha should try to find an answer closer to the estimate.

 Apply Skills
Turn to *Interactive Text*, page 32.

 mBook Reinforce Understanding
Use the *mBook Study Guide* to review lesson concepts.

▶**Problem Solving: Using Rounded Numbers in Bar Graphs**

How do we round numbers in a graph?

We have looked at graphs of CD sales in previous lessons. The graph below is a little different from the ones we have seen. Notice that the tops of some of the bars do not touch the lines of the scale.

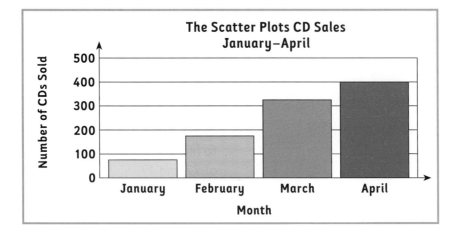

We need to round the numbers in the graph to the nearest hundred to make them easier to work with. To do this, we can use the height of the bars in the graph to estimate the sales for each month.

POWER CONCEPT

Rounding the data in a bar graph is a quick way to understand the information in the graph.

Example 1

Estimate the total CD sales for January and February.
To estimate the total CD sales for January and February, we need to round each month's sales.

Look at the bar for January in the graph above. It is between 0 and 100 on the scale. It is closer to 100, so we round the number for January to 100.

Now look at the bar for February. It is between 100 and 200 on the scale. It is closer to 200, so we round the number for February to 200.

Now we can create an extended fact: 100 + 200 = 300.
The total CD sales for January and February were about 300 CDs.

 Problem-Solving Activity
Turn to *Interactive Text*,
page 34.

 mBook Reinforce Understanding
Use the *mBook Study Guide*
to review lesson concepts.

Activity 1

Add using traditional addition.

1. $\begin{array}{r} 437 \\ + 192 \end{array}$ 2. $\begin{array}{r} 685 \\ + 97 \end{array}$ 3. $\begin{array}{r} 709 \\ + 206 \end{array}$

Activity 2

Round the numbers. Then estimate their sum.

Model	Answer:
47	50
+ 62	+ 60
	110

1. $69 + 81$ 2. $54 + 84$ 3. $94 + 59$

4. $499 + 799$ 5. $589 + 927$ 6. $369 + 481$

Activity 3

Round the numbers to the nearest hundred. Then estimate the sum.

1. Trandon and Latisha are collecting video arcade tickets. They plan to combine their tickets and trade them in for a big prize. Trandon has 787 tickets, and Latisha has 445 tickets. About how many tickets do they have altogether?

2. The Ruiz family traveled 227 miles on the first day of their trip, 329 miles on the second day, and 179 on the third day. About how far did they travel in all?

Activity 4 • Distributed Practice

Add. Try to find the sum mentally.

1. $8 + 9$ 2. $500 + 900$ 3. $4,000 + 9,000$

4. $70 + 60$ 5. $100 + 300$ 6. $80 + 40$

Lesson 12 | ▶Horizontal Expanded Addition
Problem Solving: ▶Horizontal Bar Graphs

▶Horizontal Expanded Addition

Vocabulary

horizontal expanded addition
commutative property

What is horizontal expanded addition, and why do we learn about it?

In previous lessons, we solved addition problems vertically using the traditional and expanded algorithms.

Traditional	Expanded
65	60 | 5
+ 31	+ 30 | 1

Another way to add is to use **horizontal expanded addition** . In horizontal expanded addition, we write the problems across the page on one line. Then we write a new line each time we do a step.

Steps for Using Horizontal Expanded Addition:

STEP 1

Rewrite the problem by putting addition signs in place of the vertical bars.

$$60 | 5 \qquad 60 + 5$$
$$+ 30 | 1 \qquad + 30 + 1$$

STEP 2

Move everything to one line.

$$60 + 5 + 30 + 1$$

Group the numbers together by place value. When the four numbers are written horizontally, the easiest way to add is to first add the tens, then add the ones.

$$60 + 5 \ + \ 30 + 1$$
$$\text{Tens} \qquad \text{Ones}$$
$$60 + 30 \ + \ 5 + 1$$

STEP 3

Combine the place values to find the sum.

$$90 + 6 = 96$$

The sum is 96.

Special rules, called properties, help us through each step of addition. The property that allows us to change the order of the numbers without changing the sum is called the **commutative property** .

$$3 + 7 \quad = \quad 7 + 3$$
$$10 \quad = \quad 10$$

We can write the problem as 3 + 7 or 7 + 3. The sum does not change.

Example 1

Find the sum of 57 and 11 using horizontal expanded addition.

STEP 1
Write the numbers in expanded form using an addition sign.

$$57 + 11 = \mathbf{50 + 7 + 10 + 1}$$

STEP 2
Group the numbers together by place value.

$$57 + 11 = \mathbf{50 + 7 + 10 + 1}$$
Tens   Ones
$$\mathbf{50 + 10 + 7 + 1}$$

We use the commutative property to change the order of the numbers being added.

STEP 3
Combine the place values to find the answer.

$$57 + 11 = \mathbf{50 + 7 + 10 + 1}$$
$$= \mathbf{50 + 10 + 7 + 1}$$
$$= \mathbf{60 + 8}$$
$$= \mathbf{68}$$

The sum is 68.

Horizontal expanded addition helps us understand place value in a different way and prepares us for algebra.

POWER CONCEPT

When we add numbers, the commutative property allows us to add the numbers in any order we want.

Apply Skills
Turn to *Interactive Text*, page 37.

 mBook **Reinforce Understanding**
Use the *mBook Study Guide* to review lesson concepts.

▶**Problem Solving: Horizontal Bar Graphs**

What are horizontal bar graphs?

We have been studying vertical bar graphs. On these graphs, the bars are drawn from bottom to top. Horizontal bar graphs are very much like vertical bar graphs. The difference is that bars are drawn from left to right. The scale is numbered on the horizontal axis, and the data labels are placed on the vertical axis.

Look at the horizontal bar graph below. It shows the CD sales for four different record companies.

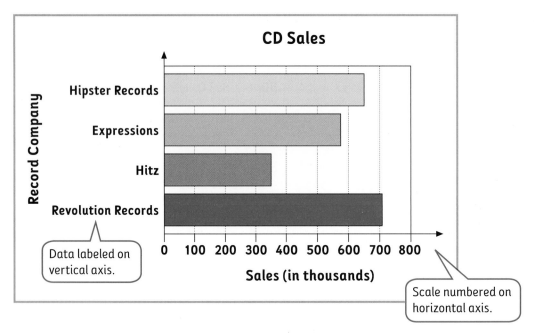

We can read a horizontal bar graph and use estimation to make conclusions about the data. For example:

- Revolution Records sold more than 700,000 CDs.

- Hitz sold the least number of CDs.

- Expressions sold more than 550,000 CDs but less than 600,000 CDs.

 Problem-Solving Activity
Turn to *Interactive Text*,
page 38.

 mBook Reinforce Understanding
Use the *mBook Study Guide*
to review lesson concepts.

Homework

Activity 1

Add using horizontal expanded addition. Write the answer in standard form.

Model

$70 + 21 = 70 + 0 + 20 + 1$

$70 + 20 + 0 + 1$

$90 + 1 = 91$

Answer: 91

1. $22 + 35$
2. $43 + 36$
3. $12 + 56$
4. $71 + 13$
5. $25 + 40$
6. $30 + 59$

Activity 2

Add using vertical expanded addition. Write the answer in standard form.

1.
$$\begin{array}{r} 364 \\ + \ 326 \\ \hline \end{array}$$

2.
$$\begin{array}{r} 607 \\ + \ 205 \\ \hline \end{array}$$

3.
$$\begin{array}{r} 293 \\ + \ 222 \\ \hline \end{array}$$

Activity 3

Add using traditional addition.

1.
$$\begin{array}{r} 129 \\ + \ \ 96 \\ \hline \end{array}$$

2.
$$\begin{array}{r} 399 \\ + \ 187 \\ \hline \end{array}$$

3.
$$\begin{array}{r} 904 \\ + \ \ 47 \\ \hline \end{array}$$

Activity 4 • Distributed Practice

Add. Try to find the sum mentally.

1. $70 + 60$
2. $100 + 800$
3. $8,000 + 6,000$
4. $90 + 30$
5. $700 + 700$
6. $10,000 + 20,000$

▶Horizontal Addition With Hundreds

How do we add hundreds using horizontal expanded addition?

Let's look at how we can add three-digit numbers using horizontal expanded addition. We group hundreds with hundreds, tens with tens, and ones with ones.

Example 1

Find the sum of 612 and 135 using horizontal expanded addition.

612 + 135 = 600 + 10 + 2 + 100 + 30 + 5

Hundreds		Tens		Ones	
600 + 100	+	10 + 30	+	2 + 5	
700	+	40	+	7	The sum is 747.

We can also add three-digit numbers with two-digit numbers this way. In this type of problem, there is only one hundreds number, so it is not grouped with another number. We continue by grouping tens with tens and ones with ones.

Example 2

Find the sum of 434 and 62 using horizontal expanded addition.

434 + 62 = 400 + 30 + 4 + 60 + 2

Hundreds		Tens		Ones	
400	+	30 + 60	+	4 + 2	
400	+	90	+	6	The sum is 496.

 Apply Skills
Turn to *Interactive Text*,
page 40.

 mBook **Reinforce Understanding**
Use the *mBook Study Guide*
to review lesson concepts.

▶Problem Solving: Collecting Data and Constructing Graphs

How do we construct graphs based on data?

Vocabulary
survey

In previous lessons, we created graphs from given tables of data. Before data are put into a table or graph, they must be collected.

There are many ways to collect data, such as using a survey . A survey is a study of people's opinions. It is conducted by asking a group of people about something. We can record the survey responses in a table of data like the one below and then use the table to create a bar graph.

The table below organizes the responses for the survey question: Which band do you like the best?

Which Band Do You Like the Best?		
Band	**Tally**	**Votes**
The Scatter Plots	ⅢⅠ Ⅰ	6
One Later	ⅠⅠ Ⅰ	3
The Hammerheads	ⅢⅠ ⅠⅠⅠⅠ	9
Three Ears	ⅢⅠ	5

> Bar graphs are a great way to take data from a survey and make it easier to understand.

We can use the data from this table to make a bar graph.

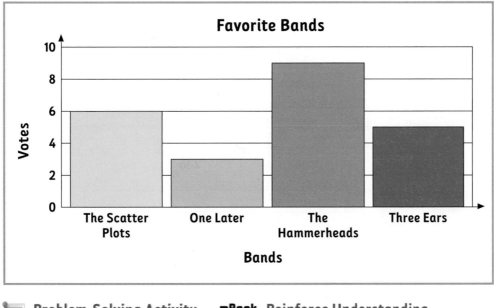

We can use the data from this table to make a bar graph.

Favorite Bands

 Problem-Solving Activity
Turn to *Interactive Text*, page 41.

mBook Reinforce Understanding
Use the *mBook Study Guide* to review lesson concepts.

Activity 1

Add. Try to find the sum mentally.

1. $7 + 8$	**2.** $80 + 70$	**3.** $700 + 800$
4. $9 + 6$	**5.** $60 + 90$	**6.** $900 + 600$
7. $8 + 5$	**8.** $80 + 50$	**9.** $500 + 800$

Activity 2

Add using horizontal expanded addition. Write the answer in standard form.

Model
$$432 + 161 = 400 + 30 + 2 \; + \; 100 + 60 + 1$$
$$400 + 100 \qquad + \; 30 + 60 \qquad + \; 2 + 1$$
$$500 \qquad\qquad + \quad 90 \qquad\qquad + \quad 3 \quad = 593$$

1. $228 + 41$	**2.** $534 + 34$	**3.** $216 + 127$	**4.** $407 + 92$

Activity 3

Estimate the number represented by the dot on the number line.

Model

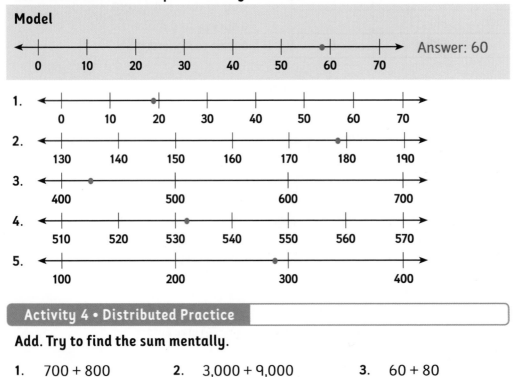

Answer: 60

Activity 4 • Distributed Practice

Add. Try to find the sum mentally.

1. $700 + 800$	**2.** $3,000 + 9,000$	**3.** $60 + 80$
4. $90 + 30$	**5.** $700 + 700$	**6.** $900 + 900$

Lesson 14 | Problem Solving: ▶ Creating a Pictograph

▶ **Problem Solving: Creating a Pictograph**

How do we create a pictograph?

We looked at how bar graphs can help us work with data. Another way to show data is to use a **pictograph**. A pictograph uses pictures, called **icons**, to show data. The icon stands for a certain amount. This amount is shown in a **key**.

Pictographs catch our eye because of icons. The icons usually have something to do with the type of data being displayed.

Look at the table below. It shows the number of tickets sold by the Hammerheads for several cities of its concert tour.

The Hammerheads Concert Tour	
City	**Number of Tickets Sold**
San Diego	600
Nashville	700
Boston	400
Dallas	350

Now look at a pictograph of the data.

The Hammerheads Concert Tour	
City	**Number of Tickets Sold**
San Diego	🎟🎟🎟🎟🎟🎟
Nashville	🎟🎟🎟🎟🎟🎟🎟
Boston	🎟🎟🎟🎟
Dallas	🎟🎟🎟🎟

key
🎟 = 100 tickets

The key tells us that each ticket icon represents 100 tickets. To show 600 tickets, we use six icons.

We can use half an icon to represent half of 100, or 50 tickets. Notice how the tickets for Dallas are represented with 3 and one-half icons: 100 + 100 + 100 + 50 = 350. We know there were 350 tickets sold for the Dallas concert.

Vocabulary

pictograph
icons
key

Pictographs are general displays of data that are fun. They are not good at accurately displaying data. It is hard to know how much the icon represents because we can only use full and half icons.

Example 1

Show the data using the given symbol. Round the data if necessary.

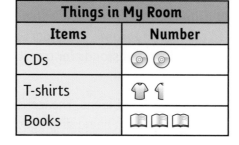

Things in My Room	
Items	Number
CDs	20
T-shirts	14
Books	32

Things in My Room	
Items	Number
CDs	◎ ◎
T-shirts	👕 ◖
Books	📖 📖 📖

key	
◎ = 10 CDs	
👕 = 10 T-shirts	
📖 = 10 books	

◎ For the CD data, the key tells us that each CD icon represents 10 CDs, so 2 CD icons represent 20 CDs.

👕 We represented T-shirts with one and one-half shirts. This is the most accurate way to represent the data. Each T-shirt icon represents 10 T-shirts, so one and one-half icons represent 15 T-shirts. This is very close to 14 T-shirts, but it is not exact. We had to round 14 to 15.

📖 We represented 32 books with 3 book icons. Each book icon represents 10 books, so 3 book icons represent 30 books. We rounded 32 down to 30 to place it in a pictograph.

Improve Your Skills

It is important to think about how we will use the data before we display it in a pictograph. If you have data where you need to know the exact amount, a pictograph is not the best option. A pictograph is good for getting a general idea about a subject.

 Problem-Solving Activity
Turn to *Interactive Text*, page 43.

 mBook Reinforce Understanding
Use the *mBook Study Guide* to review lesson concepts.

Activity 1

Complete the basic or extended fact.

1. 6 + _____ = 8
2. 60 + 20 = _____
3. 600 + _____ = 800
4. 4 + 3 = _____
5. 40 + _____ = 70
6. _____ + 400 = 700

Activity 2

Find the sum using traditional addition.

1.
$$\begin{array}{r} 919 \\ + 123 \\ \hline \end{array}$$

2.
$$\begin{array}{r} 727 \\ + 273 \\ \hline \end{array}$$

3.
$$\begin{array}{r} 641 \\ + 720 \\ \hline \end{array}$$

Activity 3

Add using horizontal expanded addition. Write the answer in standard form.

Model	182 + 16 =					
	100 + 80 + 2		+		10 + 6	
	100	+	80 + 10	+	2 + 6	
	100	+	90	+	8	= 198

1. 12 + 56
2. 150 + 29
3. 207 + 591
4. 45 + 34
5. 214 + 83
6. 512 + 487

Activity 4

Round the numbers to the nearest hundred. Then estimate the sum.

1. How many CDs were sold in January?
2. How many CDs were sold in April?
3. How many more CDs were sold in April than in January?
4. What is the trend?
5. If you were to try to predict the sales for May, what would your guess be?

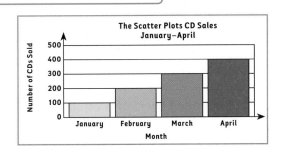

Activity 5 • Distributed Practice

Add. Try to find the sum mentally.

1. 70 + 20
2. 600 + 800
3. 1,000 + 4,000
4. 800 + 900
5. 30 + 60
6. 5,000 + 7,000

Problem Solving:
▶**Working With Data**

▶Addition

What are the different ways to think about addition?

In this unit, we learned different ways to think about addition. We also learned the importance of place value in addition.

Here are some examples of how place value is important.

Review 1

What forms of addition help us better understand place value?

Basic and Extended Addition Facts

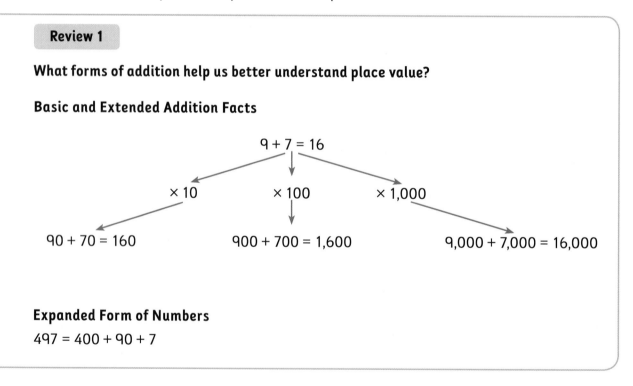

$9 + 7 = 16$

$\times\ 10$ $\times\ 100$ $\times\ 1{,}000$

$90 + 70 = 160$ $900 + 700 = 1{,}600$ $9{,}000 + 7{,}000 = 16{,}000$

Expanded Form of Numbers

$497 = 400 + 90 + 7$

Review 2

What are expanded and horizontal expanded forms of addition?

Expanded Addition	Horizontal Expanded Addition

$$\begin{array}{c}541 \\ +\,173\end{array} \rightarrow \begin{array}{c|c|c} 500 & 40 & 1 \\ +\,100 & 70 & 3 \\ \hline & & 4 \end{array}$$

$$\begin{array}{c|c|c} 500 & 40 & 1 \\ +\,100 & 70 & 3 \\ \hline & 110 & 4 \end{array}$$

100 ←

$$\begin{array}{c|c|c} 500 & 40 & 1 \\ +\,100 & 70 & 3 \\ \hline 700 & 100 + 10 & 4 \end{array}$$

$$700 + 10 + 4 = 714$$

$$54 + 32 \quad = \quad 50 + 4 \quad + \quad 30 + 2$$
$$50 + 30 \quad + \quad 4 + 2$$
$$80 \quad + \quad 6 \quad = 86$$

Expanded addition helps us think about numbers and the addition process.

Number lines can be used to round and estimate sums.

Review 3

How do number lines help us estimate?

Estimate the sum of 13 and 38.

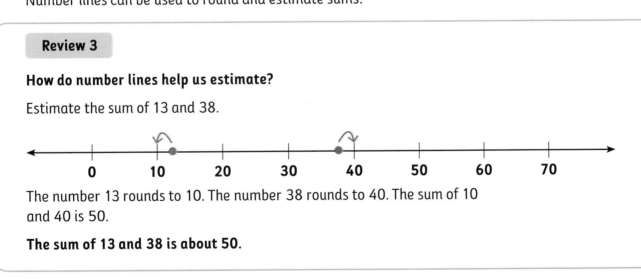

The number 13 rounds to 10. The number 38 rounds to 40. The sum of 10 and 40 is 50.

The sum of 13 and 38 is about 50.

We can use this understanding if we want to get an estimate, or a ballpark idea, of what an answer should be.

When we compare traditional addition with expanded addition, we see how we are regrouping tens into hundreds.

How do traditional addition and expanded addition compare?

Compare the traditional method of addition with the expanded form of addition.

Traditional Addition	Expanded Addition

Traditional Addition

541   →   541
+ 173   + 173

541
+ 173
  14

　1
541
+ 173
  14

　1
541
+ 173
714

Expanded Addition

500 | 40 | 1
+ 100 | 70 | 3

500 | 40 | **1**
+ 100 | 70 | **3**
          | **4**

500 | **40** | 1
+ 100 | **70** | 3
      | **110** | 4

100 ←
500 | | 40 | 1
+ 100 | | 70 | 3
700 | ~~100~~ + 10 | 4

100
500 | 40 | 1
+ **100** | 70 | 3
700 | 10 | 4

Traditional addition is more efficient than expanded addition. Expanded addition makes it easier to see place value.

In both cases, the sum is 714.

 Apply Skills
Turn to *Interactive Text*, page 45.

mBook Reinforce Understanding
Use the *mBook Study Guide* to review lesson concepts.

▶**Problem Solving: Working With Data**

What do we have to think about when we solve a problem with data?

Good problem solving always requires us to ask ourselves, "What is the problem asking for?" Then we can find the important information needed to solve the problem. It is helpful to underline this information. After solving a word problem, we should always check our answer to make sure that we answered the question being asked. It is easy to do the computations correctly, but we might find an answer that the problem did not ask for.

Tables and Bar Graphs

Sometimes, it is easier to see what information is important when it is presented in a graph. For example, here are two ways to show the number of meals sold on Friday.

Review 1

How are data tables and bar graphs related?

Compare data tables and bar graphs.

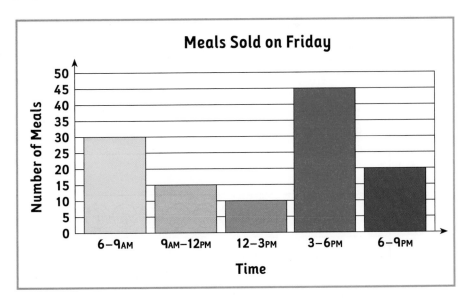

Meals Sold on Friday	
Time	Number of Meals
6 AM–9 AM	30
9 AM–12 PM	15
12 PM–3 PM	10
3 PM–6 PM	45
6 PM–9 PM	20

The bar graph makes it easier to see that most meals were sold between 3 pm and 6 pm. It is a little harder to see that in a table.

Pictographs

We have also learned that we can present information in tables with different kinds of graphs. We can take this same information and present it as a horizontal bar graph or as a pictograph.

Review 2

How do bar graphs and pictographs compare?

Compare the bar graph and pictograph.

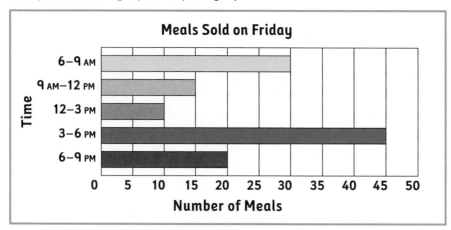

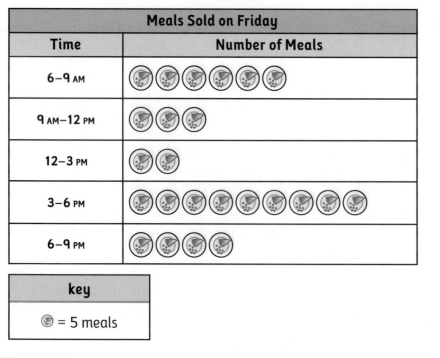

key
= 5 meals

 Problem-Solving Activity
Turn to *Interactive Text*, page 47.

mBook Reinforce Understanding
Use the *mBook Study Guide* to review lesson concepts.

CALVIN AND HOBBES (c) 1992 Watterson. Dist. By UNIVERSAL PRESS SYNDICATE.
Reprinted with permission. All rights reserved.

WHERE **DOES** THE 3 GO WHEN YOU SUBTRACT IT FROM 7?

7−3=4

OBJECTIVES

Building Number Concepts

- Understand the relationship between basic and extended subtraction facts
- Solve whole-number subtraction problems using a variety of strategies
- Estimate the solution to problems by rounding

Problem Solving

- Identify the question being asked in a word problem
- Read and analyze data in bar graphs and tables
- Solve word problems using whole-number subtraction

Lesson 1 ▸Addition and Subtraction Fact Families
Problem Solving:
▸ **Answering the Right Question**

▸Addition and Subtraction Fact Families

Vocabulary
fact family

How are addition and subtraction related?

There is a special relationship between addition and subtraction facts. This relationship can be seen in fact families. A **fact family** is a set of facts with the same three numbers.

In the following fact family, all four facts have the numbers 2, 8, and 10.

Fact Family for 2, 8, and 10	
8 + 2 = 10 2 + 8 = 10	10 − 2 = 8 10 − 8 = 2

Subtraction facts and addition facts are opposites. The answer at the end of an addition fact is at the beginning of a subtraction fact in its fact family. Look at the facts to see how the numbers move around.

Example 1

Write the fact family for 7, 8, and 15.

Fact Family	
Addition Facts: 7 + 8 = 15 8 + 7 = 15	Subtraction Facts: 15 − 8 = 7 15 − 7 = 8

Notice that the same three numbers are used, but in a different order. It is important to remember this difference when solving subtraction problems.

Example 2

Complete the subtraction fact using a related addition fact.

15 − 6 = _____

Think: 15 − 6 = _____ and 6 + _____ = 15 are in the same fact family.

Because we know 6 + 9 = 15, we also know 15 − 6 = 9.

The complete subtraction fact is 15 − 6 = 9.

> We can figure out the missing numbers in a subtraction fact by thinking about an addition fact in the same fact family.

What is the relationship between basic and extended subtraction facts?

We learned that once we know a basic addition fact, we can create extended addition facts. The same is true for subtraction.

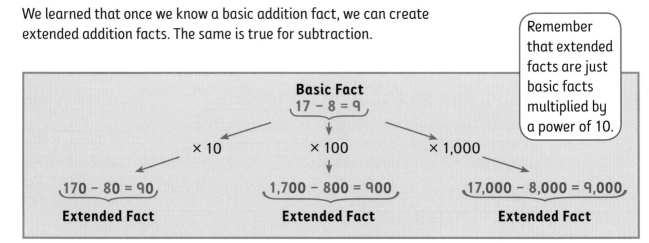

Remember that extended facts are just basic facts multiplied by a power of 10.

Basic Fact
17 − 8 = 9

× 10   × 100   × 1,000

170 − 80 = 90   1,700 − 800 = 900   17,000 − 8,000 = 9,000

Extended Fact   **Extended Fact**   **Extended Fact**

We also write fact families for extended facts. Look at the number of zeros in each of the extended facts. In the fact 170 − 80 = 90, each of the numbers has one zero. Notice the pattern in the other extended facts.

Example 1

Write the fact family for 70, 80, and 150.

70 + 80 = 150   150 − 80 = 70
80 + 70 = 150   150 − 70 = 80

 **Apply Skills**
Turn to *Interactive Text*,
page 51.

 mBook **Reinforce Understanding**
Use the *mBook Study Guide*
to review lesson concepts.

▶**Problem Solving: Answering the Right Question**

How do we answer the right question?

We learned how to be good problem solvers by identifying what a problem asks and finding the important information needed to solve it. Now we will learn that a good problem solver always checks the answer by asking, "Did I answer the question asked in the problem?"

Let's look at an example that shows how a student made the correct calculations but did not answer the question that was being asked.

Example 1

Problem:

Taylor has a gift card to the music store. She heard the Scatter Plots on the radio and wants to buy one of its CDs. If the difference between the costs of the group's newest CD and its first CD is less than $5, then Taylor will buy the newest CD. She also wants to buy a button and a poster. Which CD will she buy?

The Scatter Plots' Merchandise	Cost
Newest CD	$9
First CD	$7
Poster	$4
Button	$2

Your friend solved the problem:

$2 + $4 = $6

Taylor can buy a button and a poster because it would only cost $6.

Is her answer correct?

Your friend didn't answer the question the problem was asking. The problem wants to know, "Which CD will she buy?" Your friend's calculations are correct, but she did not answer the right question.

The right question is, "Which CD will Taylor buy?" We need to know the difference in price between the two CDs. Because $7 is $2 less than $9, Taylor will buy the newest CD.

The correct answer is Taylor will buy the newest CD.

> After solving a word problem, check to make sure you answered the question that was asked.

 Problem-Solving Activity
Turn to *Interactive Text*, page 52.

 **Reinforce Understanding**
Use the *mBook Study Guide* to review lesson concepts.

Homework

Activity 1

Write the fact family for the group of numbers.

Model 7, 8, and 15

$7 + 8 = 15$ $15 - 8 = 7$
$8 + 7 = 15$ $15 - 7 = 8$

1. 3, 9, and 12
2. 6, 7, and 13
3. 8, 6, and 14
4. 9, 8, and 17

Activity 2

Use a related addition fact to solve the subtraction fact.

Model $13 - 4 = $ _____
$4 + 9 = 13$
So $13 - 4 = 9$.

1. $15 - 7$
2. $11 - 6$
3. $120 - 40$
4. $140 - 90$

Activity 3

Write the extended fact family for the group of numbers.

Model 20, 60, and 80

$20 + 60 = 80$ $80 - 60 = 20$
$60 + 20 = 80$ $80 - 20 = 60$

1. 40, 50, and 90
2. 60, 80, and 140
3. 70, 90, and 160
4. 30, 90, and 120

Activity 4

Complete the table of basic and extended subtraction facts.

Basic Fact	Extended Fact (× 10)	Extended Fact (× 100)
$17 - 8 = 9$	$170 - 80 = 90$	$1,700 - 800 = 900$
	$120 - 60 = 60$	
$13 - 5 = 8$		
		$1,100 - 400 = 700$
		$1,500 - 900 = 600$
$14 - 6 = 8$		
	$160 - 90 = 70$	

Activity 5 • Distributed Practice

Add.

1. $\begin{array}{r} 77 \\ + 91 \\ \hline \end{array}$

2. $\begin{array}{r} 26 \\ + 66 \\ \hline \end{array}$

3. $\begin{array}{r} 378 \\ + \ 16 \\ \hline \end{array}$

4. $\begin{array}{r} 426 \\ + \ 14 \\ \hline \end{array}$

Lesson 2 ▸ Expanded Subtraction

Problem Solving:
▸ Analyzing Data Using Subtraction

▸ Expanded Subtraction

Vocabulary

expanded subtraction
difference

How do we write and solve subtraction problems in expanded form?

We learned how to use expanded addition to solve problems in Unit 1, Lesson 3. The expanded form is also used to solve subtraction problems. This is called **expanded subtraction**.

Look at how we model the subtraction problem 98 − 65.

Steps for Using Expanded Subtraction:

STEP 1
Write the numbers in expanded form.

$$\begin{array}{r} 98 \\ -65 \end{array} \rightarrow \begin{array}{r|r} 90 & 8 \\ -60 & 5 \end{array}$$

STEP 2
Subtract the ones column.
Write 3 in the ones column.

$$\begin{array}{r|r} 90 & 8 \\ -60 & 5 \\ \hline & 3 \end{array}$$

STEP 3
Subtract the tens column.
Write 30 in the tens column.

$$\begin{array}{r|r} 90 & 8 \\ -60 & 5 \\ \hline 30 & 3 \end{array}$$

STEP 4
Combine and write the answer in standard form.

$$\begin{array}{r|r} 90 & 8 \\ -60 & 5 \\ \hline 30 & 3 \end{array}$$

$$30 + 3 = 33$$

The answer is 30 + 3 = 33.

Remembering the steps of expanded addition will help us complete expanded subtraction problems. We write problems in expanded form to see the value of each digit in the problem.

Let's try solving a problem using expanded subtraction. As in addition, we combine the parts of our answer to write it in standard form. The answer in subtraction is called the **difference** .

Example 1

Find the difference between 85 and 23 using expanded form.

$$
\begin{array}{r}
85 \\
-23
\end{array}
\rightarrow
\begin{array}{r|r}
80 & 5 \\
-20 & 3
\end{array}
$$

$$
\begin{array}{r|r}
80 & 5 \\
-20 & 3 \\
\hline
60 & 2
\end{array}
$$

$$
\begin{array}{r|r}
80 & 5 \\
-20 & 3 \\
\hline
60 & 2
\end{array}
\rightarrow 62
$$

The difference is 62.

We can also use expanded form to subtract three-digit numbers.

Example 2

Find the difference between 589 and 262 using expanded form.

$$
\begin{array}{r}
589 \\
-262
\end{array}
\rightarrow
\begin{array}{r|r|r}
500 & 80 & 9 \\
-200 & 60 & 2
\end{array}
$$

$$
\begin{array}{r|r|r}
500 & 80 & 9 \\
-200 & 60 & 2 \\
\hline
300 & 20 & 7
\end{array}
$$

$$
\begin{array}{r|r|r}
500 & 80 & 9 \\
-200 & 60 & 2 \\
\hline
300 & 20 & 7
\end{array}
\rightarrow 327
$$

The difference is 327.

Sometimes a number has digits that are zeros. When this happens in expanded subtraction, we need to use a placeholder.

Example 3

Find the difference between 479 and 204 using expanded form.

479		400	70	9		400	70	9
− 204	→	− 200	0	4		− 200	0	4
						200	70	5 → 275

Notice that there are 0 tens in 204. The 0 is written as a placeholder, and we subtract 70 − 0 in the tens place. The other digits are subtracted as usual.

The difference is 275.

Sometimes when we subtract, the amount of digits in each number is not the same. For example, we can subtract a two-digit number from a three-digit number.

Example 4

Find the difference between 586 and 61 using expanded form.

586		500	80	6		500	80	6
− 61	→	−	60	1		−	60	1
						500	20	5 → 525

There are no hundreds in 61, so we do not need to write a 0 in the hundreds place. The other digits are subtracted as usual.

The difference is 525.

POWER CONCEPT

Expanded subtraction helps us see place value.

 Apply Skills
Turn to *Interactive Text*, page 54.

 mBook **Reinforce Understanding**
Use the *mBook Study Guide* to review lesson concepts.

▶Problem Solving: **Analyzing Data Using Subtraction**

How do we find differences in data?

We used bar graphs to display data. Now we will use subtraction to analyze data in a bar graph. We use subtraction to find the difference between two pieces of data. The difference represents an increase or a decrease.

Look at the bar graph below. The graph displays the CD sales for the Scatter Plots from January through April.

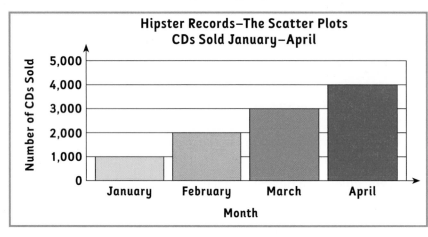

Suppose the Scatter Plots' manager wants to know how many more CDs were sold in April than in January. We subtract the data in the graph to determine the difference in sales between the months.

The graph shows that 1,000 CDs were sold in January.

It also shows that 4,000 CDs were sold in April.

We solve an extended subtraction fact to find the difference:

4,000 − 1,000 = 3,000.

The Scatter Plots sold 3,000 more CDs in April than January.

POWER CONCEPT

When we analyze data in a graph, it helps us to compare information by finding differences. The differences show an increase or decrease.

Problem-Solving Activity
Turn to *Interactive Text*, page 55.

mBook Reinforce Understanding
Use the *mBook Study Guide* to review lesson concepts.

Homework

Activity 1

Find the difference using expanded form. Then write the answer in standard form.

Model			

$$
\begin{array}{r} 76 \\ -53 \\ \hline \end{array} \rightarrow
\begin{array}{r|r} 70 & 6 \\ -50 & 3 \\ \hline 20 & 3 \end{array}
$$

$\rightarrow 20 + 3 = 23$

1. $\begin{array}{r} 98 \\ -64 \\ \hline \end{array}$

2. $\begin{array}{r} 77 \\ -15 \\ \hline \end{array}$

3. $\begin{array}{r} 275 \\ -53 \\ \hline \end{array}$

4. $\begin{array}{r} 353 \\ -31 \\ \hline \end{array}$

5. $\begin{array}{r} 436 \\ -125 \\ \hline \end{array}$

6. $\begin{array}{r} 397 \\ -265 \\ \hline \end{array}$

Activity 2

Use the bar graph to solve the problem.

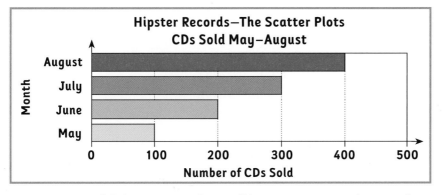

1. How many CDs did the Scatter Plots sell between May and August?

2. Compare the CD sales for May and June. What is the difference?

3. Compare the CD sales for July and August. What is the difference?

4. What were the total CD sales for May and June? July and August?

Activity 3 • Distributed Practice

Add.

1. $\begin{array}{r} 365 \\ +29 \\ \hline \end{array}$

2. $\begin{array}{r} 400 \\ +30 \\ \hline \end{array}$

3. $\begin{array}{r} 446 \\ +501 \\ \hline \end{array}$

4. $\begin{array}{r} 446 \\ +172 \\ \hline \end{array}$

5. $\begin{array}{r} 24 \\ +85 \\ \hline \end{array}$

6. $\begin{array}{r} 677 \\ +196 \\ \hline \end{array}$

Lesson **3** ▶Expanded Subtraction With Regrouping

Problem Solving:
▶Locating Information in a Table

▶**Expanded Subtraction With Regrouping**

What does regrouping look like in subtraction?

So far we have been working with subtraction problems that have not required regrouping. Just like with addition, sometimes we need to regroup. In subtraction, we regroup whenever a digit in the top number is less than the digit directly below it. Let's look at the problem 32 − 14.

In addition problems, coins are added to a set. When we subtract, coins are taken away. Let's subtract 14 from 32. Look at the ones column. We can't take 4 ones away from 2 ones, so we have to regroup.

To regroup, we must take one 10 from the tens column and regroup it into 10 ones.

Now we can subtract in the ones column. We take away 4 ones coins.

Finally, we can subtract in the tens column. We take away 1 tens coin.

We count the remaining coins to see the answer:
32 − 14 = 18.

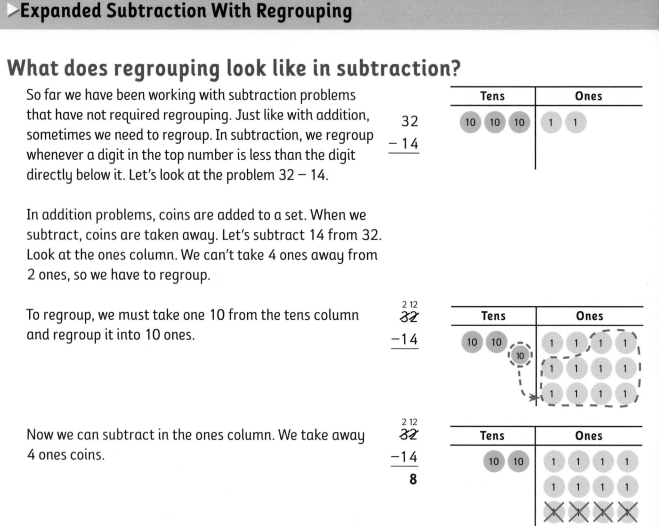

Expanded subtraction shows us how we regroup one 10 from the tens place. We turn it into ten 1s and put them in the ones place.

Example 1

Find the difference between 62 and 39 using expanded form.

STEP 1
Rewrite the problem in expanded form.
Notice that 2 is less than 9.
Regrouping is necessary.

$$\begin{array}{cc} 62 \\ -39 \end{array} \rightarrow \begin{array}{c|c} 60 & 2 \\ -30 & 9 \end{array}$$

STEP 2
Take a ten from the tens place.
We do this by rewriting 60 as 50 + 10.

$$\begin{array}{c|c} 50+10 & 2 \\ - \quad 30 & 9 \end{array}$$

STEP 3
Regroup.
Regroup the 10 to the ones place.

$$\begin{array}{c|c} 50 & 10+2 \\ -30 & 9 \end{array}$$

After regrouping, the ones digit in the top number is 10 + 2 = 12, which is greater than 9, so we can subtract.

STEP 4
Subtract the ones.

$$\begin{array}{c|c} 50 & 12 \\ -30 & 9 \\ \hline & 3 \end{array}$$

STEP 5
Subtract the tens.

$$\begin{array}{c|c} 50 & 12 \\ -30 & 9 \\ \hline 20 & 3 \end{array}$$

STEP 6
Write the answer in standard form.

The difference is 23.

$$\begin{array}{c|c} 50 & 12 \\ -30 & 9 \\ \hline 20 & 3 \end{array} \rightarrow 23$$

**%÷
=
<×** **Apply Skills**
Turn to *Interactive Text*,
page 57.

mBook **Reinforce Understanding**
Use the *mBook Study Guide*
to review lesson concepts.

▶Problem Solving: **Locating Information in a Table**

How do we locate information in a table?

A variety of information can be displayed in one table. To locate information in a table, we must look carefully at the rows and columns.

Follow these steps to find information in a table:

- Identify the row that contains the desired information.
- Identify the column that contains the desired information.
- Follow the row across and the column down to where the row and column meet.

The table below shows the roster for a soccer team. There is a lot of information in the table. We can identify all the different types of information by looking at the column and row headings.

Example 1

Find Tina's age.

The Ravens' Soccer Team Roster				
Player	**Dues paid?**	**Parents' Names**	**Age**	**Position**
Trinity	No	Mark and Tina	14	Forward
Bethany	Yes	James	13	Midfield
M.J.	Yes	Loretta	14	Defense
Tina	Yes	Lynn and Doug	13	Forward
April	No	Sue and Tom	13	Goalie
Jackie	Yes	Kerri and Jim	13	Midfield
Michelle	No	Bob	14	Defense

Once we locate information in a table, it is still important to ask, "Is this the correct information? Does it answer the question that is asked?"

Follow the steps for locating information in the table above:

- Find the row with Tina's name. This row is shaded.
- Find the column with the players' ages. This column is shaded.
- Follow the arrows across the row and down the column to where they meet. The information at this point is the answer to the question.

Tina is 13 years old.

 Problem-Solving Activity
Turn to *Interactive Text*, page 58.

 mBook **Reinforce Understanding**
Use the *mBook Study Guide* to review lesson concepts.

Activity 1

Find the difference using expanded subtraction. Then write the answer in standard form.

Model

$$\begin{array}{r} 76 \\ -57 \end{array} \rightarrow \begin{array}{r} 70 \mid 6 \\ -50 \mid 7 \end{array} \rightarrow \begin{array}{r} \cancel{70} \mid 6 \\ -50 \mid 7 \end{array} \rightarrow \begin{array}{r} 60+10 \mid 6 \\ - \quad 50 \mid 7 \end{array} \rightarrow \begin{array}{r} 60 \mid 10+6 \\ -50 \mid 7 \end{array}$$

$$\rightarrow \begin{array}{r} 60 \mid 16 \\ -50 \mid 7 \\ \hline 10 \mid 9 \end{array} \rightarrow 10+9=19$$

1.
$$\begin{array}{r} 69 \\ -21 \\ \hline \end{array}$$

2.
$$\begin{array}{r} 489 \\ -\ 11 \\ \hline \end{array}$$

3.
$$\begin{array}{r} 624 \\ -312 \\ \hline \end{array}$$

4.
$$\begin{array}{r} 62 \\ -35 \\ \hline \end{array}$$

5.
$$\begin{array}{r} 98 \\ -69 \\ \hline \end{array}$$

6.
$$\begin{array}{r} 729 \\ -105 \\ \hline \end{array}$$

Activity 2

Complete the basic or extended fact.

1. $1,700 - \underline{\hspace{1cm}} = 800$ **2.** $130 - \underline{\hspace{1cm}} = 80$ **3.** $12 - \underline{\hspace{1cm}} = 5$

4. $\underline{\hspace{1cm}} = 1,400 - 800$ **5.** $100 - \underline{\hspace{1cm}} = 90$ **6.** $\underline{\hspace{1cm}} = 140 - 70$

Activity 3

Find the missing value for the fact family. Then write the fact family for the group of numbers.

Model ?, 80, and 150
$70 + 80 = 150$ $150 - 80 = 70$
$80 + 70 = 150$ $150 - 70 = 80$

1. 40, ?, and 120

2. 400, 800, and ?

3. ?, 40, and 130

4. 900, 400, and ?

Activity 4 • Distributed Practice

Add.

1.
$$\begin{array}{r} 232 \\ +\ 52 \\ \hline \end{array}$$

2.
$$\begin{array}{r} 524 \\ +127 \\ \hline \end{array}$$

3.
$$\begin{array}{r} 209 \\ +126 \\ \hline \end{array}$$

4.
$$\begin{array}{r} 623 \\ +321 \\ \hline \end{array}$$

Lesson 4 ▶More Regroupings in Subtraction
Problem Solving:
▶Working With Tables and Graphs

How do we regroup more than one time?

We used place-value coins to see how subtraction problems with regrouping worked in the ones place. Now we'll look at regrouping in the tens place.

$$\begin{array}{r} 353 \\ -194 \\ \hline \end{array}$$

Hundreds	Tens	Ones
100 100 100	10 10 10 10 10	1 1 1

Let's use the coins to help us subtract 194 from 353. Because 4 ones is greater than 3 ones, we'll need to regroup before we can take away the ones.

$$\begin{array}{r} {}^{4\ 13} \\ 3\cancel{5}\cancel{3} \\ -194 \\ \hline \end{array}$$

Hundreds	Tens	Ones
100 100 100	10 10 10 10 (10)	1 1 1 1 1 / 1 1 1 1 / 1 1 1 1

Now we can subtract in the ones column. There are only 4 tens coins in the display, and we need to take away 9 tens, so we need to regroup from the hundreds coins.

$$\begin{array}{r} {}^{4\ 13} \\ 3\cancel{5}\cancel{3} \\ -194 \\ \hline 9 \end{array}$$

Hundreds	Tens	Ones
100 100 100	10 10 10 10	1 1 1 1 1 / 1 1 1 1 / ✗ ✗ ✗ ✗

One hundreds coin must be regrouped as 10 tens coins to subtract.

$$\begin{array}{r} {}^{14} \\ {}^{2\ 4\ 13} \\ 3\cancel{5}\cancel{3} \\ -194 \\ \hline 9 \end{array}$$

Hundreds	Tens	Ones
100 100 (100)	10 10 10 10 10 / 10 10 10 10 10 / 10 10 10 10	1 1 1 1 1 / 1 1 1 1

Now we can subtract in the tens column. We take away 9 tens coins. Then we subtract in the hundreds column.

$$\begin{array}{r} {}^{14} \\ {}^{2\ 4\ 13} \\ 3\cancel{5}\cancel{3} \\ -194 \\ \hline 159 \end{array}$$

Hundreds	Tens	Ones
100 ⊘100	10 10 10 10 10 / ✗✗✗✗✗ / ✗✗✗✗	1 1 1 1 1 / 1 1 1 1

The difference is 159.

$$159 \Big\{$$

Hundreds	Tens	Ones
100	10 10 10 10 10	1 1 1 1 1 / 1 1 1 1

Let's look at expanded subtraction problems with multiple regrouping.

Example 1

Find the difference between 325 and 147 using expanded form.

$$\begin{array}{r} 325 \\ -\ 147 \end{array} \rightarrow \begin{array}{c|c|c} 300 & 20 & 5 \\ -\ 100 & 40 & 7 \end{array}$$

STEP 1

Take a ten from the tens place.
Rewrite 20 as 10 + 10.

$$\begin{array}{c|c|c} 300 & 10 + 10 & 5 \\ -\ 100 & 40 & 7 \end{array}$$

STEP 2

Regroup.
Regroup the 10 to the ones place. Then subtract the ones.

$$\begin{array}{c|c|c} 300 & 10 & 10 + 5 \\ -\ 100 & 40 & 7 \end{array} \qquad \begin{array}{c|c|c} 300 & 10 & 15 \\ -\ 100 & 40 & 7 \\ & & 8 \end{array}$$

STEP 3

Take a hundred from the hundreds place.
Rewrite 300 as 200 + 100.

$$\begin{array}{c|c|c} 200 + 100 & 10 & 15 \\ - & 100 & 40 & 7 \\ & & 8 \end{array}$$

STEP 4

Regroup.
Regroup the 100 to the tens place. Then subtract the tens.

$$\begin{array}{c|c|c} 200 & 100 + 10 & 15 \\ -\ 100 & 40 & 7 \\ & & 8 \end{array} \qquad \begin{array}{c|c|c} 200 & 110 & 15 \\ -\ 100 & 40 & 7 \\ & 70 & 8 \end{array}$$

STEP 5

Subtract the hundreds.

$$\begin{array}{c|c|c} 200 & 110 & 15 \\ -\ 100 & 40 & 7 \\ \hline 100 & 70 & 8 \end{array}$$

STEP 6

Write the answer in standard form.

$$100 + 70 + 8 = 178$$

The difference is 178.

Apply Skills
Turn to *Interactive Text*, page 60.

mBook Reinforce Understanding
Use the *mBook Study Guide* to review lesson concepts.

▶**Problem Solving: Working With Tables and Graphs**

How do we represent data from a bar graph in a table?

Information can be displayed many ways. Sometimes it helps us solve a problem if the data are shown in a table instead of a bar graph. For these problems, we transfer data from a bar graph into a table to make them more readable.

Example 1

Problem:

The manager of the Scatter Plots wants to know how much money a competing band made on CD sales from May through August. She finds a bar graph that displays these data. How much money did the competing band make on CD sales from May through August?

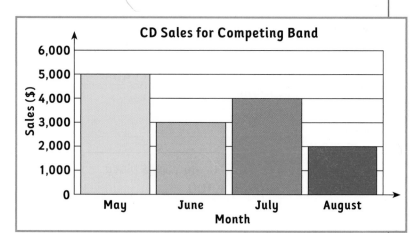

The total amount would be easier to compute if the data were displayed in a table.

The data from the graph are shown in the table below.

Each month is listed in a row with its sales next to it.

Month	Sales
May	$5,000
June	$3,000
July	$4,000
August	$2,000

Use the axis labels **Sales** and **Month** as column heads.

Just add the Sales column together to get the answer.

$5,000 + $3,000 + $4,000 + $2,000 = $14,000

The band made $14,000 on CD sales for May through August.

Problem-Solving Activity
Turn to *Interactive Text*, page 61.

Reinforce Understanding
Use the *mBook Study Guide* to review lesson concepts.

Lesson 4

Homework

Activity 1

Find the missing value for the fact family. Then write the fact family for the group of numbers.

Model 20, 90, and ?
$20 + 90 = 110$ $110 - 90 = 20$
$90 + 20 = 110$ $110 - 20 = 90$

1. 60, ?, and 130
2. 20, 30, and ?
3. 1, ?, and 60
4. 200, 700, and ?
5. 700, ?, and 1,600
6. ?, 900, and 1,800

Activity 2

Find the difference using expanded form. Then write the answer in standard form.

Model

$$\begin{array}{c} 176 \\ -\ 29 \end{array} \rightarrow \begin{array}{c|c|c} 100 & 70 & 6 \\ \hline & 20 & 9 \end{array} \rightarrow \begin{array}{c|c|c} 100 & \cancel{70} & 6 \\ \hline & 20 & 9 \end{array} \rightarrow \begin{array}{c|c|c} 100 & 60+10 & 6 \\ \hline & & 20 & 9 \end{array}$$

$$\rightarrow \begin{array}{c|c|c} 100 & 60 & 10+6 \\ \hline & 20 & 9 \end{array} \rightarrow \begin{array}{c|c|c} 100 & 60 & 16 \\ \hline & 20 & 9 \\ \hline 100 & 40 & 7 \end{array} \rightarrow 100+40+7 = 147$$

1. $\begin{array}{r} 718 \\ -522 \end{array}$
2. $\begin{array}{r} 856 \\ -\ 63 \end{array}$
3. $\begin{array}{r} 426 \\ -157 \end{array}$
4. $\begin{array}{r} 632 \\ -195 \end{array}$

Activity 3 • Distributed Practice

Add.

1. $\begin{array}{r} 237 \\ +898 \end{array}$
2. $\begin{array}{r} 572 \\ +489 \end{array}$
3. $\begin{array}{r} 653 \\ +757 \end{array}$

4. $\begin{array}{r} 999 \\ +312 \end{array}$
5. $\begin{array}{r} 176 \\ +845 \end{array}$
6. $\begin{array}{r} 483 \\ +268 \end{array}$

▶**Traditional Subtraction**

	Vocabulary
	traditional subtraction

What is traditional subtraction?

We know how traditional addition compares with expanded addition. Let's look at these two methods.

Expanded Addition	Traditional Addition

```
                    10
    55  →     50 | 5              1
  + 19      + 10 | 9             55
             ─────────         + 19
              70 | 4  = 74       ──
                                 74
```

We know the advantages and disadvantages of each of these methods. Traditional addition is more efficient, but it is easier to make a regrouping mistake. Expanded addition makes it easier to see regrouping, but it takes longer to do. Now we'll see how the same methods compare in subtraction.

Usually we solve problems using **traditional subtraction** . This is a shorthand method where we have to remember the value of each digit.

Steps for Using Traditional Subtraction

STEP 1
Check to see if we need to regroup.
Note that 4 is less than 9. We need to regroup.

```
  64
- 29
```

STEP 2
Regroup.
Regroup 1 ten to the ones column. Now there are 5 tens and 14 ones.

```
 5 14
  64
- 29
```

STEP 3
Subtract.

```
 5 14
  64
- 29
  ──
  35
```

The difference is 35.

How does regrouping compare in expanded and traditional subtraction?

The two methods of subtraction we learned are compared below.

Each method has its advantages and disadvantages when it comes to regrouping.

Expanded Subtraction

- Clearly shows regrouping.
- Shows the value of each digit.
- Takes longer to write all the steps.

Traditional Subtraction

- Shows regrouping in a shorthand way.
- Relies on memory to know the value of each digit.
- Takes less time to write the steps, so it is more efficient.

We want to subtract efficiently. This means working quickly and accurately. This is why most people use the traditional method of subtraction. In the lessons to come, we need to be efficient with computations so that we can focus on other concepts.

POWER CONCEPT

Expanded subtraction makes regrouping clear, but traditional subtraction is more efficient.

 Apply Skills
Turn to *Interactive Text*, page 63.

 Monitoring Progress
Quiz 1

mBook **Reinforce Understanding**
Use the *mBook Study Guide* to review lesson concepts.

Unit 2 • Lesson 5   **91**

Activity 1

Find the difference using traditional subtraction.

1. 78
    − 39

2. 538
    − 47

3. 62
    − 25

4. 891
    − 529

5. 271
    − 63

6. 919
    − 648

Activity 2

Describe what the circled number represents in the problem.

Model

$\overset{\text{⑥14}}{\cancel{74}}$
− 48
26

The circled 6 represents what is left in the tens place when we regroup one 10 from the tens to the ones. It has a value of six 10s, or 60.

1. $\overset{\text{7⑭}}{8\cancel{4}}$
    − 16
    68

2. $\overset{\text{④16}}{\cancel{56}}$
    − 18
    38

Activity 3

Find the difference using expanded form. Then write the answer in standard form.

Model

$$74 \quad \begin{array}{c|c} 70 & 4 \\ \hline -20 & 6 \end{array} \quad \begin{array}{c|c} \cancel{70} & 4 \\ \hline -20 & 6 \end{array} \quad \begin{array}{c|c} 60+10 & 4 \\ \hline -\quad 20 & 6 \end{array} \quad \begin{array}{c|c} 60 & 10+4 \\ \hline -20 & 6 \end{array}$$

$$\to \begin{array}{c|c} 60 & 14 \\ \hline -20 & 6 \\ \hline 40 & 8 \end{array} \to 40+8 = 48$$

1. 36
    − 19

2. 64
    − 25

3. 94
    − 77

4. 82
    − 17

Activity 4 • Distributed Practice

Add.

1. 679
    + 207

2. 847
    + 319

3. 495
    + 518

4. 187
    + 717

Lesson 6 ▶ Estimating Differences

Problem Solving:
▶ Finding Distances on a Map

▶ Estimating Differences

How do we use rounding to estimate differences?

Sometimes subtraction is like addition. There are times when we do not need to compute the exact number. We can estimate a close answer. To estimate a difference, we subtract numbers that are close to the numbers in the problem but that are easier to work with.

One way we estimate is by rounding. In this strategy, we round each number to the nearest ten, hundred, thousand, or greater place value.

Let's look at an example of how this strategy is used to estimate the difference between 68 and 41.

$$\begin{array}{r} 68 \\ -\ 41 \\ \hline \end{array}$$

First we round 68 to the nearest ten.

The number 68 is between 60 and 70. It is closer to 70 than 60. So 68 rounds up to 70. This is the nearest ten.

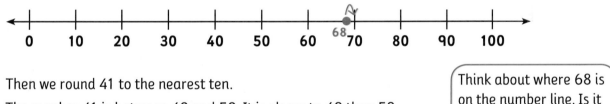

Then we round 41 to the nearest ten.

The number 41 is between 40 and 50. It is closer to 40 than 50. So 41 rounds down to 40. This is the nearest ten.

> Think about where 68 is on the number line. Is it closer to 60 or 70?

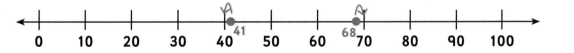

Finally, we subtract the rounded numbers: 68 − 41 rounds to 70 − 40.

> Think about where 41 is on the number line. Is it closer to 40 or 50?

$$\begin{array}{r} 68 \\ -\ 41 \\ \hline \end{array} \rightarrow \text{rounds to} \rightarrow \begin{array}{r} 70 \\ -\ 40 \\ \hline 30 \end{array}$$

The extended fact is 70 − 40 = 30.

The estimated difference is 30.

There is a simple way to decide whether to round a number up or down.

- **When rounding to the nearest ten**, if the number is halfway or more to the next ten, round up. If the number is less than halfway to the next ten, round down.
- **When rounding to the nearest hundred**, if the number is halfway or more to the next hundred, round up. If the number is less than halfway to the next hundred, round down.

Let's use the rounding strategy to estimate a difference by rounding to the nearest hundred.

Example 1

Estimate the difference between 472 and 213.
Round each number to the nearest hundred.
Round 472 to the nearest hundred.

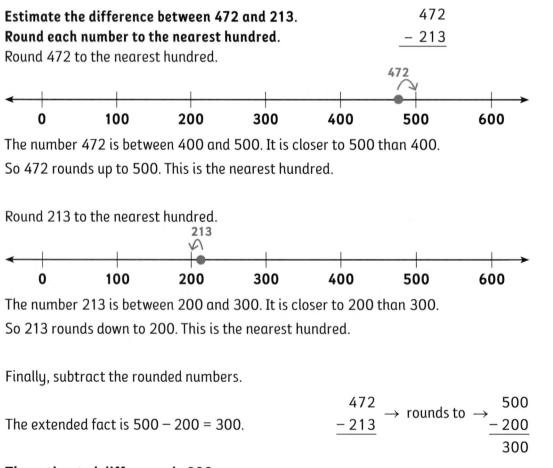

The number 472 is between 400 and 500. It is closer to 500 than 400.

So 472 rounds up to 500. This is the nearest hundred.

Round 213 to the nearest hundred.

The number 213 is between 200 and 300. It is closer to 200 than 300.

So 213 rounds down to 200. This is the nearest hundred.

Finally, subtract the rounded numbers.

The extended fact is 500 − 200 = 300.

$$\begin{array}{r} 472 \\ -\ 213 \\ \hline \end{array} \rightarrow \text{rounds to} \rightarrow \begin{array}{r} 500 \\ -\ 200 \\ \hline 300 \end{array}$$

The estimated difference is 300.

How do we determine which place value to round to?

When estimating differences, we follow these steps to round each number:

- Look at the lesser number.
- Round that number to its greatest place value.
- Round the other number to the same place value.

Let's look at an example of how this works.

Example 1

Estimate the difference between 12,100 and 8,860.

12,100
− 8,860

> The number 12,100 is between 12,000 and 13,000. It is less than halfway to 12,000, so it rounds down.

The number 8,860 is the lesser number. Its greatest place value is the thousands. So round both numbers to the nearest thousand.

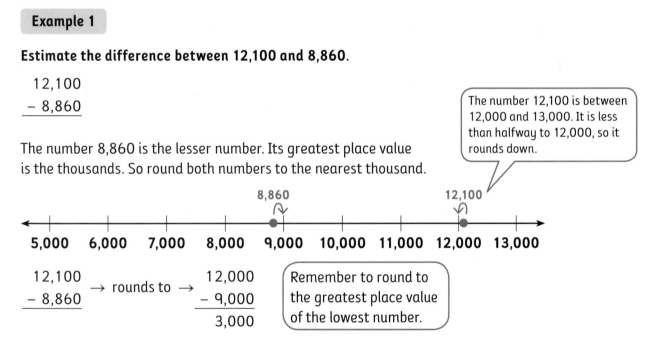

12,100
− 8,860 → rounds to → 12,000
− 9,000
3,000

> Remember to round to the greatest place value of the lowest number.

The estimated difference is 3,000.

 Apply Skills
Turn to *Interactive Text*, page 65.

 mBook Reinforce Understanding
Use the *mBook Study Guide* to review lesson concepts.

▶**Problem Solving: Finding Distances on a Map**

How do we use estimation to solve problems about distance?

We often use estimation when we determine driving distances. Most of the time, we do not need to know the exact distance from one place to another, so we use estimation.

The most common data displays for driving distances are maps. The map below shows the driving distances between three U.S. cities.

Example 1

Solve the word problem using estimation.

Problem:

The distance from Seattle to Phoenix is 1,508 miles. Rounded to the nearest hundred, the estimated distance is 1,500 miles. The distance from Seattle to San Francisco is 810 miles. Rounded to the nearest hundred, the estimated distance is 800 miles. About how much farther is the distance from Seattle to Phoenix than the distance from Seattle to San Francisco?

We can create an extended fact and subtract to find the estimated distance: 1,500 − 800 = 700.

POWER CONCEPT

Estimation is a good skill to use when reading maps because we usually do not need to know the exact distance.

The distance from Seattle to Phoenix is about 700 miles more than the distance from Seattle to San Francisco.

 Problem-Solving Activity
Turn to *Interactive Text*, page 66.

 Reinforce Understanding
Use the *mBook Study Guide* to review lesson concepts.

Homework

Activity 1

Find the difference using expanded form. Then write the answer in standard form.

Model

$$276 \quad \rightarrow \quad \begin{array}{c|c|c} 200 & 70 & 6 \\ \hline -100 & 50 & 7 \end{array} \quad \rightarrow \quad \begin{array}{c|c|c} 200 & \cancel{70} & 6 \\ \hline -100 & 50 & 7 \end{array} \quad \rightarrow \quad \begin{array}{c|c|c} 200 & 60+10 & 6 \\ \hline -100 & & 50 & 7 \end{array}$$

$$\rightarrow \quad \begin{array}{c|c|c} 200 & 60 & 10+6 \\ \hline -100 & 50 & 7 \end{array} \quad \rightarrow \quad \begin{array}{c|c|c} 200 & 60 & 16 \\ \hline -100 & 50 & 7 \\ \hline 100 & 10 & 9 \end{array} \rightarrow 100+10+9 = 119$$

1.	2.	3.	4.
53	429	697	78
− 27	− 352	− 368	− 59

Activity 2

Find the difference using traditional subtraction.

1.	2.	3.
375	291	515
− 128	− 78	− 124

Activity 3

Estimate the difference. Then use a calculator to compute the exact answer and compare.

Model

$$\begin{array}{r} 91 \\ -37 \\ \hline \end{array} \rightarrow \begin{array}{l} \text{91 rounds down to 90} \\ \text{37 rounds up to 40} \end{array} \rightarrow \begin{array}{r} 90 \\ -40 \\ \hline 50 \end{array}$$

The exact answer (using a calculator) is 91 − 37 = 54. Since 50 is close to 54, the answer is reasonable.

1.	2.	3.
98	593	582
− 57	− 257	− 319

Activity 4 • Distributed Practice

Add.

1.	2.	3.	4.
26	317	803	1,120
+ 25	+ 146	+ 902	+ 287

▸**Estimating to Check Answers**

How can we use estimation to check our answers?

One of the benefits of estimating differences is that it gives us a way to check our answers. When we use a calculator to subtract, we might accidentally enter the wrong numbers. A calculator will only compute the answer to the problem entered. It cannot tell whether we have entered the numbers correctly. An estimate helps us determine if we made a mistake. Let's see how this strategy helped a student correct a mistake.

Miguel had to find the difference between 472 and 213 on his calculator. When he entered the problem, he came up with the answer 529.

$$472$$
$$-\ 213$$

**Miguel's First
Calculator Answer**

$$529$$

Then Miguel checked his work by estimating. He estimated the difference by rounding 472 up to 500 and rounding 213 down to 200. The estimated difference was 300.

Miguel's Estimate

$$\begin{array}{c} 472 \\ -\ 213 \end{array} \rightarrow \text{rounds to} \rightarrow \begin{array}{c} 500 \\ -\ 200 \\ \hline 300 \end{array}$$

The estimated difference of 300 was not close to the calculator answer of 529. Miguel knew that there must be a mistake, so he entered the problem into his calculator again.

**Miguel's Second
Calculator Answer**

$$259$$

Now the estimate and calculator answer are close, so 259 is a reasonable answer. Miguel must have entered the problem into the calculator incorrectly the first time.

We also use estimates to check problems solved using paper and pencil. Errors made with paper and pencil are usually regrouping errors. We either forget to regroup or regroup incorrectly.

Improve Your Skills

It's easy to make mistakes when subtracting. We can check the answer with an estimate.

Traditional Subtraction		Estimate
732		700
− 591	**ERROR**	− 600
261		100

> The estimated difference of 100 is not close to the answer found using traditional subtraction. There must be a mistake.

Look at how the problem was solved using traditional subtraction. Look carefully at the tens column. Is it possible to subtract 9 from 3? No. We need to regroup. The problem is solved correctly below.

Traditional Subtraction		Estimate
6 13		
7̶3̶2		700
− 591	**CORRECT**	− 600
141		100

> Estimation is a good way to check if an answer is reasonable or if an error has been made.

Now the estimate and the answer found using traditional subtraction are close. Estimation helped us see that 141 is a reasonable answer.

 Apply Skills
Turn to *Interactive Text*, page 68.

 mBook Reinforce Understanding
Use the *mBook Study Guide* to review lesson concepts.

▶**Problem Solving: Checking Answers in Word Problems**

How can estimation help us in word problems?

Estimation is also important when solving word problems. It is especially useful when the word problems contain large numbers. We often use calculators when we work with large numbers. There is a chance we could enter the numbers incorrectly.

It is also easy to make an error when we use paper and pencil because there could be many regroupings in one problem. This makes estimation very important for checking the accuracy of our answers.

Example 1

Solve the word problem using estimation.

Problem:

You and your friends are going to see The Scatter Plots in concert. You bought the tickets for yourself and two of your friends. If you spent $117 total on the three tickets, and one ticket cost $39, what is the total amount you should get back from your friends?

One of your friends used the traditional method to subtract and then checked his answer by estimating.

Your Friend's Answer		Estimated Answer
$\begin{array}{r}\text{0 1017}\\ \cancel{117}\\ -\ 39\\ \hline 78\end{array}$	→ rounds to →	$\begin{array}{r}120\\ -\ 40\\ \hline 80\end{array}$

Your friend's answer and his estimate are very close, so he can assume that he calculated correctly.

 Problem-Solving Activity
Turn to *Interactive Text*, page 69.

 mBook Reinforce Understanding
Use the *mBook Study Guide* to review lesson concepts.

Homework

Activity 1

Find the difference using expanded form. Then write the answer in standard form.

Model

76		70 | 6		7̶0̶ | 6		60 + 10 | 6		60 | 10 + 6		60 | 16
− 58	→	− 50 | 8	→	− 50 | 8	→	− 50 | 8	→	− 50 | 8	→	− 50 | 8

$$10 \mid 8 \rightarrow 10 + 8 = 18$$

1. 73
   − 44

2. 71
   − 23

3. 95
   − 59

4. 55
   − 26

Activity 2

Find the difference using traditional subtraction.

1. 88
   − 39

2. 716
   − 127

3. 825
   − 253

Activity 3

Solve the word problems using (1) a calculator and (2) estimation. Then compare the numbers to check for reasonableness.

Central High School students were trying to decide on a band to play at their homecoming dance this year. They narrowed it down to three bands and had the students in each grade vote for their favorite band. The table below shows the outcome of the vote.

Grade	The Scatter Plots	One Later	The Hammerheads
Seniors	197	115	102
Juniors	175	108	125
Sophomores	105	95	230

1. Which band received the most votes?
2. What was the difference in votes between the first- and second-place bands? Check your answer by estimating.

Activity 4 • Distributed Practice

Add.

1. 1,108
   +   992

2. 2,429
   +   78

3. 1,004
   + 3,008

▶**Quarter Rounding**

Vocabulary
quarter rounding

What is another type of rounding?

We used number lines to help us round numbers to the nearest 10, 100, or 1,000. The number lines we used were marked in intervals of 10, 100, or 1,000 to help us locate the number and round it to the appropriate value.

Using this number line, we can see that 104 rounds to 100, 286 rounds to 300, 313 rounds to 300, and 470 rounds to 500.

We can also round to units of 25. These are called *quarters*, just like the quarter coin is worth 25 cents.

If we have 53 cents, we would have about 2 quarters. We have 3 pennies more than 2 quarters, but we are very close.

If we have 70 cents, we would have about 3 quarters. We are 1 nickel short of having 3 quarters, but we are very close.

If we have 92 cents, we would have about 4 quarters. We are 1 nickel and 3 pennies short, but we are very close.

This type of rounding is called **quarter rounding**. In quarter rounding, we round numbers to the nearest quarter: 25, 50, 75, 100, 125, and so on. For this strategy, we can also use number lines marked in intervals of 25 to help us round.

Let's look at an example of how we can use a number line when we do quarter rounding.

Example 1

Round the numbers 30 and 68 to the nearest quarter.

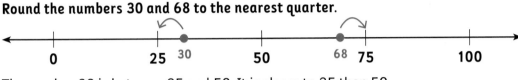

The number 30 is between 25 and 50. It is closer to 25 than 50. So 30 rounded to the nearest quarter is 25.

The number 68 is between 50 and 75. It is closer to 75 than 50.

So 68 rounded to the nearest quarter is 75.

How do we use quarter rounding to estimate differences?

The quarter rounding strategy is also used to estimate differences in subtraction. Sometimes we make a better estimate using this method than rounding to the nearest 10, 100, or 1,000.

Example 1

Use quarter rounding to estimate the difference between 73 and 47.
First, round 73 to the nearest quarter. The number 73 rounds up to 75.

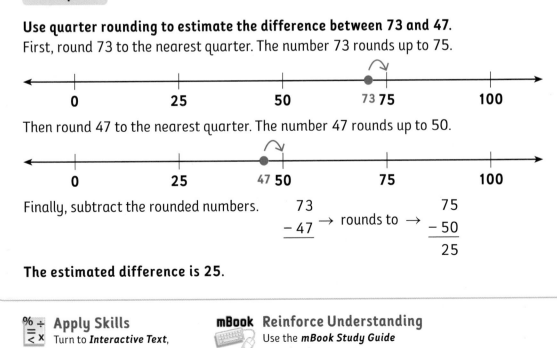

Then round 47 to the nearest quarter. The number 47 rounds up to 50.

Finally, subtract the rounded numbers.

$$\begin{array}{r} 73 \\ -47 \end{array} \rightarrow \text{rounds to} \rightarrow \begin{array}{r} 75 \\ -50 \\ \hline 25 \end{array}$$

The estimated difference is 25.

Apply Skills
Turn to *Interactive Text*, page 71.

mBook Reinforce Understanding
Use the *mBook Study Guide* to review lesson concepts.

▶**Problem Solving: Estimating in Word Problems**

When can we use estimation to solve word problems?

Sometimes we don't need an exact computation—an estimate is good enough. Computing with rounded numbers makes the computation easier.

Let's look at an example of a word problem where estimation alone is used to solve the problem.

Example 1

Solve the word problem using estimation.

Problem:

The Scatter Plots promised fans that every concert will last at least 150 minutes. The Scatter Plots played in Orlando, Florida, last night. The first set was 92 minutes long, and then there was a break. The second set lasted 81 minutes. Did the concert last at least 150 minutes as promised?

We only need to estimate the total time to see if it is more than 150 minutes. Because the greatest place value in each number is the tens, round both numbers to the nearest ten. The number 92 rounds down to 90. The number 81 rounds down to 80.

The extended fact is 90 + 80 = 170.

Because 170 minutes is much greater than 150 minutes, we can be confident that our estimate has sufficiently answered the problem.

Yes, the Scatter Plots' concert in Orlando lasted at least 150 minutes.

 Problem-Solving Activity
Turn to *Interactive Text*, page 72.

 mBook Reinforce Understanding
Use the *mBook Study Guide* to review lesson concepts.

Homework

Activity 1

Subtract using expanded form. Then write the answer in standard form.

Model

$$
\begin{array}{c}
44 \\
-19
\end{array}
\rightarrow
\begin{array}{c|c}
40 & 4 \\
-10 & 9
\end{array}
\rightarrow
\begin{array}{c|c}
\cancel{40} & 4 \\
-10 & 9
\end{array}
\rightarrow
\begin{array}{c|c}
30+10 & 4 \\
-10 & 9
\end{array}
\rightarrow
\begin{array}{c|c}
30 & 10+4 \\
-10 & 9
\end{array}
$$

$$
\rightarrow
\begin{array}{c|c}
30 & 14 \\
-10 & 9 \\
\hline
20 & 5
\end{array}
\rightarrow 20+5 = 25
$$

1. 56
  − 38

2. 75
  − 28

3. 47
  − 29

Activity 2

Find the difference using traditional subtraction.

1. 327
  − 39

2. 566
  − 328

3. 621
  − 240

Activity 3

Use quarter rounding to estimate the difference.

Model 48 − 23 Estimate: 50 − 25 = 25

1. 53 − 24   **2.** 78 − 29   **3.** 98 − 47

Activity 4 • Distributed Practice

Add.

1. 586
  + 273

2. 8,009
  + 678

3. 695
  + 365

Lesson 9 ▶More Estimating Differences

Problem Solving: ▶Using Estimation to Check a Bill

▶**More Estimating Differences**

Why are we learning to estimate?

Regrouping in traditional subtraction sometimes leads to many types of errors. This is one of the reasons we are learning how to estimate. If we know how to make good estimates, we are able to check for errors.

Let's look at the problem **4,021 − 2,987**. It can cause a lot of confusion when solved using traditional subtraction.

One mistake at any step in the problem will result in a wrong answer. It is a good idea to check the answer with an estimate.

$$\begin{array}{r} 4{,}021 \\ -\ 2{,}987 \\ \hline \end{array}$$

Example 1

Estimate the difference between 4,021 and 2,987 to check for errors.

$$\begin{array}{rll} 4{,}021 & \rightarrow \text{rounds down to} \rightarrow & 4{,}000 \\ -\ 2{,}987 & \rightarrow \text{rounds up to} \rightarrow & -\ 3{,}000 \\ \hline & & 1{,}000 \end{array}$$

The estimated difference is 1,000.

Check for errors by comparing the estimate to the traditional subtraction answer.

Estimate	Traditional Subtraction
	3 9 11 1
4,000	4,0̶2̶1
− 3,000	− 2,987
1,000 ⟶	1,034

The estimate is close to the answer, so the answer is reasonable.

 Apply Skills
Turn to *Interactive Text*, page 74.

 mBook Reinforce Understanding
Use the *mBook Study Guide* to review lesson concepts.

► **Problem Solving: Using Estimation to Check a Bill**

How do we use estimation to check a bill?

Sometimes we are in a hurry, and we need to quickly compute a sum or difference. We do not always have time to use the traditional method or a calculator. In these cases, the best option is to estimate. This situation might occur when we want to quickly check the bill at a restaurant.

Example 1

Solve the word problem using estimation.

Problem:

Two friends go out to dinner at a restaurant. The meal they order is $19. They also order a lemonade that costs $3. They figure the tax will be about $2. At the end of dinner, the server brings the bill, which is $50. The bill does not seem correct. How can they quickly check the bill?

They can quickly calculate an estimate that will tell them if the bill is reasonable.

Think: $19 is about $20.
    Together, the lemonade and tax are about $5.
    $20 + $5 = $25

The estimate of $25 is not close to $50, so the bill must be incorrect.

We can use estimation to quickly check a total amount we think might be incorrect.

Rounding is important in this type of situation. It helps us quickly estimate the actual cost of something so that we are not overcharged.

Problem-Solving Activity
Turn to *Interactive Text*, page 75.

mBook Reinforce Understanding
Use the *mBook Study Guide* to review lesson concepts.

Lesson 9

Homework

Activity 1

Complete the set of basic and extended facts.

Model $14 - 7 = 7$ $140 - 70 = 70$ $700 + 700 = 1,400$

1. $18 - 9 =$ _____ $90 +$ _____ $= 180$ $1,800 - 900 =$ _____

2. $75 -$ _____ $= 50$ $75 - 50 =$ _____ $500 = 750 -$ _____

3. _____ $+ 6 = 13$ $60 +$ _____ $= 130$ $1,300 - 600 =$ _____

Activity 2

Estimate the difference.

1. 368
   $- 192$

2. 368
   $- 199$

3. 754
   $- 386$

4. 908
   $- 104$

Activity 3

Solve the word problem using (1) a calculator and (2) estimation. Then compare the numbers to check for reasonableness.

1. The Scatter Plots performed three shows at a concert hall in New Jersey. The first show had an attendance of 1,058. The second show had an attendance of 959. The manager wants to know how many people attended the third show. The total attendance for all three shows was 3,128.

2. The Scatter Plots were looking at their total sales for January through March. They sold a total of 1,750 CDs over the 3-month period. They know that their sales for January were 575 CDs and their sales for March were 625 CDs. What were their sales for February?

Activity 4 • Distributed Practice

Add.

1. 499
   $+ 187$

2. 560
   $+ 370$

3. 500
   $+ 12$

4. 987
   $+ 105$

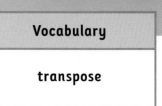

▸**Common Subtraction Errors**

Vocabulary
transpose

What are some common subtraction errors?

It is not unusual to make errors in subtraction because many problems require multiple steps with regrouping. This can be confusing, especially when there are zeros in the numbers.

Let's take a look at one common error.

Improve Your Skills

A student had to solve the following problem:

$$\begin{array}{r} 311 \\ -\ 102 \\ \hline \end{array}$$

What error did she make?

$$\begin{array}{r} 311 \\ -\ 102 \\ \hline 211 \end{array} \quad \textbf{ERROR}$$

The error the student made is in the ones place. The ones digit in the top number (1) is less than the digit below it (2), so regrouping is needed.

Instead of regrouping, the student switched the numbers around to subtract 2 − 1 = 1.

ERROR	CORRECT
311	3̸1̸1̸ (0 11)
− 102	− 102
211	209

This error happens when we **transpose** the numbers, or switch them around.

Another way to correct the error on the previous page is to use expanded subtraction. We use expanded subtraction because it is a clear way to see what is happening when we regroup.

Example 1

Find the difference between 311 and 102.

$$\begin{array}{r} 311 \\ -102 \end{array} \rightarrow \begin{array}{r|r|r} 300 & 10 & \mathbf{1} \\ -100 & 0 & \mathbf{2} \end{array}$$

$$\begin{array}{r|r|r} 300 & \mathbf{0 + 10} & 1 \\ -100 & 0 & 2 \end{array}$$

$$\begin{array}{r|r|r} 300 & 0 & \mathbf{1 + 10} \\ -100 & 0 & 2 \end{array}$$

$$\begin{array}{r|r|r} 300 & 0 & 11 \\ -100 & 0 & 2 \\ \hline 200 & 0 & 9 \end{array} \rightarrow 200 + 0 + 9 = 209$$

The difference is 209.

It is not unusual to transpose the numbers in a subtraction problem when regrouping. The most common errors in subtraction occur in the regrouping step. When there are regrouping errors in a problem, using the expanded form helps us find them. Expanded form shows the regrouping step very clearly.

Let's look at another type of error.

Improve Your Skills

Your friend had to solve the following problem:

$$
\begin{array}{r}
375 \\
-129 \\
\hline
\end{array}
$$

What error did he make?

$$
\begin{array}{r}
37\overset{15}{5} \\
-129 \\
\hline
256
\end{array}
$$

The error is in the tens place. Your friend regrouped in the ones column but then forgot to adjust the tens column. He subtracted $7 - 2 = 5$ instead of $6 - 2 = 4$.

$$
\begin{array}{r}
375 \\
-129 \\
\hline
256
\end{array}
$$

Let's use expanded form to help us understand this error and fix it.

$$
\begin{array}{r}
375 \\
-129
\end{array}
\rightarrow
\begin{array}{r|r|r}
300 & 70 & \mathbf{5} \\
-100 & 20 & \mathbf{9}
\end{array}
$$

$$
\begin{array}{r|c|c}
300 & \mathbf{60 + 10} & 5 \\
-100 & 20 & 9
\end{array}
$$

$$
\begin{array}{r|c|c}
300 & 60 & \mathbf{5 + 10} \\
-100 & 20 & 9
\end{array}
$$

$$
\begin{array}{r|r|r}
300 & 60 & 15 \\
-100 & 20 & 9 \\
\hline
200 & 40 & 6
\end{array}
\rightarrow 200 + 40 + 6 = 246
$$

The difference is 246.

Apply Skills
Turn to *Interactive Text*, page 77.

Monitoring Progress
Quiz 2

mBook **Reinforce Understanding**
Use the *mBook Study Guide* to review lesson concepts.

Activity 1

One of the problems contains an error. Use expanded form to find and fix the error. Explain.

Model

1. 468
    − 165
    ─────
    303

2. 382
    − 143
    ─────
    241

3. $\overset{6\ 18 12}{\cancel{792}}$
    − 495
    ─────
    297

Problem 2 has the error.

300	80	2
− 100	40	3

→

300	8̶0̶	2
− 100	40	3

→

300	70 + 10	2
− 100		40	3

→

300	70	10 + 2
− 100	40	3

→

300	70	12
− 100	40	3
200	30	9	→ 200 + 30 + 9 = 239

The problem was solved by transposing the numbers in the ones column instead of regrouping them. The ones digit in the top number is less than the digit below it, so regrouping is needed. I fixed the error by regrouping from the tens to the ones column. Now I can subtract in each place value.

1. 372
    − 347
    ─────
    35

2. 799
    − 482
    ─────
    317

3. $\overset{8\ 1}{9\!28}$
    − 635
    ─────
    293

Activity 2

Estimate the difference by quarter rounding. Then use a calculator to compute the exact answer and compare.

1. 351
    − 229

2. 889
    − 309

3. 391
    − 218

4. 672
    − 418

Activity 3 • Distributed Practice

Add.

1. 297
    + 45

2. 317
    + 498

3. 278
    + 189

4. 175
    + 397

▸**Using Addition to Check Subtraction**

How do we use addition to check subtraction?

Addition is used to check for subtraction errors by adding the answer we find to the bottom number in the problem. If we correctly solved the problem, these numbers will add up to the top number of the subtraction problem.

Let's see how this works by finding the difference between 328 and 165.

Here, we have subtracted incorrectly.

ERROR

$$\begin{array}{r} \overset{3}{\cancel{3}}28 \\ -\ 165 \\ \hline 263 \end{array}$$

Check Answer Using Addition

$$\begin{array}{r} 263 \\ +\ 165 \\ \hline 428 \end{array}$$

When we check our answer using addition, the answer and the bottom number do not add up to the top number. This answer is incorrect.

The answer is off by exactly 100. The error was made in the regrouping. The problem is solved correctly below.

CORRECT

$$\begin{array}{r} \overset{2\ 12}{\cancel{3}\cancel{2}8} \\ -\ 165 \\ \hline 163 \end{array}$$

Check Answer Using Addition

$$\begin{array}{r} 163 \\ +\ 165 \\ \hline 328 \end{array}$$

When we check our answer using addition the answer and the bottom number add up to the top number. The answer is correct.

The correct answer is 163.

Let's use this thinking to check the answer to a subtraction problem.

Example 1

Use addition to check the subtraction problem.

Does the subtraction problem contain an error? To check the answer, we need to see if 317 and 216 add up to 521.

$$
\begin{array}{r} 521 \\ -216 \\ \hline 317 \end{array}
\qquad
\begin{array}{r} 216 \\ +327 \\ \hline 543 \end{array}
\quad \textbf{ERROR}
$$

The numbers add up to 543, which is not equal to 521. This indicates there is an error. If we look closely, we see that the regrouping was not done correctly in the ones place.

> Remember: The commutative property states that we can add numbers in any order and get the same answer.

Let's solve the subtraction problem again and then check our new answer with addition.

$$
\begin{array}{r} {}^{1\ 11}\\ 5\cancel{2}\cancel{1} \\ -216 \\ \hline 305 \end{array}
\qquad
\begin{array}{r} 216 \\ +305 \\ \hline 521 \end{array}
\qquad
\begin{array}{r} 305 \\ +216 \\ \hline 521 \end{array}
$$

The numbers add up to 521, so 305 is the correct answer.

There are many different errors we can make when subtracting, especially for problems that require regrouping. *We must always check our answers using addition, expanded subtraction, or estimation to see if they are reasonable.*

Apply Skills
Turn to *Interactive Text*,
page 79.

mBook Reinforce Understanding
Use the *mBook Study Guide*
to review lesson concepts.

▶Problem Solving: **Understanding Income, Expenses, and Profit**

What is profit?

Bands in the music business such as the Scatter Plots make a lot of money, but they also have to spend a lot of money. Money earned is called **income**, and money spent is called **expenses**.

The Scatter Plots earns income from CD sales and concert performances. Some of the Scatter Plots' expenses while on tour include hotels, rental cars, gas, and food.

When we subtract the Scatter Plots' expenses from its income, we find its **profit**. Profit is the amount of money left after all the expenses are paid. Use the equation to determine profit.

Vocabulary
income
expenses
profit

Income − Expenses = Profit

Let's look at an example of how the Scatter Plots computes profit.

Example 1

Solve the word problem.

Problem:

The manager of the Scatter Plots wants to find the profit from its recent concert tour. The band spent $50,000 on hotels, rental cars, and food. It made $150,000 in ticket sales and merchandise sales. What was the band's profit?

To find profit, we must find the difference between income and expense. The band's income was $150,000. The band's expenses totaled $50,000. We can find the profit by calculating the answer to the following problem:

$150,000	Income
− $50,000	− Expenses
$100,000	Profit

The difference is $100,000.

The profit from the concert tour was $100,000.

 Problem-Solving Activity
Turn to *Interactive Text*, page 80.

 mBook Reinforce Understanding
Use the *mBook Study Guide* to review lesson concepts.

Activity 1

Use addition to check the answer to the subtraction problem.

1. $\begin{array}{r} 247 \\ -\ 39 \\ \hline 208 \end{array}$

2. $\begin{array}{r} 351 \\ -248 \\ \hline 103 \end{array}$

3. $\begin{array}{r} 901 \\ -790 \\ \hline 111 \end{array}$

Activity 2

Find the missing value for the fact family. Then write the fact family for the group of numbers.

Model   ?, 80, and 150 $70 + 80 = 150$ $150 - 80 = 70$
$80 + 70 = 150$ $150 - 70 = 80$

1. 7, ?, and 16

2. 20, ?, and 100

3. ?, 16, and 90

4. ?, 30, and 100

5. ?, 700, and 900

6. 500, ?, and 1,000

Activity 3

Choose the best method for solving the problem: (a) traditional subtraction or (b) estimation and a calculator. Then solve using the chosen method.

1. $\begin{array}{r} 689 \\ -222 \end{array}$

2. $\begin{array}{r} 897 \\ -198 \end{array}$

3. $\begin{array}{r} 6,012 \\ -\ 927 \end{array}$

4. $\begin{array}{r} 5,023 \\ -\ 834 \end{array}$

Activity 4 • Distributed Practice

Add.

1. $\begin{array}{r} 1,007 \\ +\ 289 \end{array}$

2. $\begin{array}{r} 3,018 \\ +\ 107 \end{array}$

3. $\begin{array}{r} 5,000 \\ +\ 500 \end{array}$

4. $\begin{array}{r} 6,000 \\ +\ 599 \end{array}$

Lesson 12 | ▶ Zeros in Subtraction
Problem Solving: ▶ Understanding Budgets

▶ **Zeros in Subtraction**

How do we avoid errors with zeros in subtraction?

Regrouping in a subtraction problem that has zeros can be shown with place-value coins. Let's model **100 − 16** with a hundreds coin.

$$\begin{array}{r} 100 \\ -\ 16 \\ \hline \end{array}$$

Hundreds	Tens	Ones
100		

Let's start with the ones: 0 − 6 cannot be subtracted. So we regroup. Look at the tens. The digit is 0. There is nothing to regroup from, so move to the hundreds. We have to regroup the hundred to the tens.

$$\begin{array}{r} {}^{0\ 10} \\ \cancel{100} \\ -\ 16 \\ \hline \end{array}$$

Hundreds	Tens	Ones
100	10 10 10 10 10	
	10 10 10 10 10	

Now there is something in the tens to regroup from. Next, we exchange 1 tens coin for 10 ones coins.

$$\begin{array}{r} {}^{\quad 9} \\ {}^{0\ 10\ 10} \\ \cancel{100} \\ -\ 16 \\ \hline \end{array}$$

Hundreds	Tens	Ones
	10 10 10 10 10	1 1 1 1 1
	10 10 10 10 10	1 1 1 1 1

Now we can subtract in the ones column. We take away 6 ones coins.

$$\begin{array}{r} {}^{\quad 9} \\ {}^{0\ 10\ 10} \\ \cancel{100} \\ -\ 16 \\ \hline 4 \end{array}$$

Hundreds	Tens	Ones
	10 10 10 10 10	1 1 1 1 ✗
	10 10 10 10	✗ ✗ ✗ ✗ ✗

Next, we can subtract in the tens column. We subtract 1 ten.

The difference is 84.

$$\begin{array}{r} {}^{\quad 9} \\ {}^{0\ 10\ 10} \\ \cancel{100} \\ -\ 16 \\ \hline 84 \end{array}$$

Hundreds	Tens	Ones
	10 10 10 10 10	1 1 1 1
	10 10 10 ✗	

For several lessons, we have discussed errors commonly made in subtraction. By far, the most troublesome part of subtraction involves zeros. When there are zeros in the top number, it usually means we have to regroup. Look at the problem below.

Example 1

Find the difference between 1,002 and 733 using expanded subtraction.

$$
\begin{array}{r}
1{,}002 \\
-\ \ 733
\end{array}
\ \rightarrow\
\begin{array}{r|r|r|r}
1{,}000 & 0 & 0 & 2 \\
-\quad\ \ & 700 & 30 & 3
\end{array}
$$

$$
\begin{array}{r|r|r|r}
\overset{0}{\cancel{1{,}000}} & \overset{1{,}000}{\cancel{0}} & 0 & 2 \\
- & 700 & 30 & 3
\end{array}
$$

$$
\begin{array}{r|r|r|r}
0 & \overset{900}{\underset{\cancel{1{,}000}}{0}} & \overset{100}{\cancel{0}} & 2 \\
- & 700 & 30 & 3
\end{array}
$$

$$
\begin{array}{r|r|r|r}
0 & 900 & \overset{90}{\cancel{100}} & 10+2 \\
- & 700 & 30 & \qquad 3
\end{array}
$$

$$
\begin{array}{r|r|r|r}
0 & 900 & 90 & 12 \\
- & 700 & 30 & 3 \\
\hline
 & 200 & 60 & 9
\end{array}
$$

200 + 60 + 9 = 269

The difference is 269.

We can use addition to check the answer.

$$
\begin{array}{r}
1{,}002 \\
-\ \ 733 \\
\hline
269
\end{array}
\qquad
\begin{array}{r}
{\scriptstyle 1\ 1} \\
269 \\
+\ 733 \\
\hline
1{,}002
\end{array}
$$

Yes, the answer 269 is correct.

Another common subtraction error happens most often in problems with zeros. This is when one place value is regrouped, but the regrouping in the other place value is forgotten.

Improve Your Skills

Look at the following subtraction problem. Do you know why the answer is incorrect?

ERROR

$$
\begin{array}{r}
{}^{9\ 1} \\
2,00\!\!\!/4 \\
-\quad 927 \\
\hline
2,977
\end{array}
$$

The answer is incorrect because the problem requires regrouping in each place value. However, only the ones and tens have been regrouped.

To subtract the ones column, we must regroup from the left until we reach a nonzero digit from which we can regroup.

CORRECT

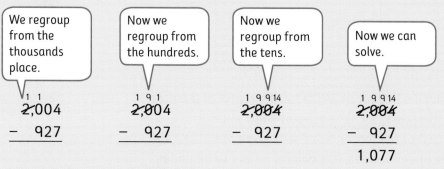

We regroup from the thousands place.

Now we regroup from the hundreds.

Now we regroup from the tens.

Now we can solve.

$$
\begin{array}{r}
{}^{1\ 1} \\
2,004 \\
-\ 927 \\
\hline
\end{array}
\qquad
\begin{array}{r}
{}^{1\ 9\ 1} \\
2,004 \\
-\ 927 \\
\hline
\end{array}
\qquad
\begin{array}{r}
{}^{1\ 9\ 9\,14} \\
2,004 \\
-\ 927 \\
\hline
\end{array}
\qquad
\begin{array}{r}
{}^{1\ 9\ 9\,14} \\
2,004 \\
-\ 927 \\
\hline
1,077
\end{array}
$$

The correct answer is 1,077.

 Apply Skills
Turn to *Interactive Text*, page 82.

 Reinforce Understanding
Use the *mBook Study Guide* to review lesson concepts.

▶ **Problem Solving: Understanding Budgets**

Vocabulary
budget

How do we determine if we are over or under budget?

In the music business, artists and bands need to keep track of their income and expenses. They create **budgets**, or estimates, of the amount of money they have to spend, to make sure they make a profit.

Let's look at an example of how the Scatter Plots used a budget.

Example 1

Compare the Scatter Plots' budget to their actual cost.

The Scatter Plots flew from Florida to Texas for the last leg of its concert tour. In Texas, the group played in Houston, San Antonio, Austin, Dallas, and El Paso. To get across Texas comfortably, the Scatter Plots rented a motor home in Houston and dropped it off in El Paso.

The following is a list of charges for renting the motor home from Easy Ride Motors.

The Scatter Plots' Budget		Motor Home Costs	
Motor Home	$900	One week rental fee	$645
		One-way drop off charge	$230
		Tax	$35
		Total	$910

The Scatter Plots planned a budget of $900 for the rental of a motor home. Because the actual cost, $910, is greater than $900, the group is over budget. If the cost of the motor home was less than $900, the Scatter Plots would be under budget. It is always better to be under budget because it means there is money left over.

 Problem-Solving Activity
Turn to *Interactive Text*, page 83.

mBook **Reinforce Understanding**
Use the *mBook Study Guide* to review lesson concepts.

Activity 1

Estimate the difference. Then use a calculator to compute the exact answer and compare.

1.
$$
\begin{array}{r}
397 \\
-209 \\
\hline
\end{array}
$$

2.
$$
\begin{array}{r}
721 \\
-432 \\
\hline
\end{array}
$$

3.
$$
\begin{array}{r}
7{,}027 \\
-2{,}139 \\
\hline
\end{array}
$$

4.
$$
\begin{array}{r}
575 \\
-399 \\
\hline
\end{array}
$$

Activity 2

Find the difference using expanded subtraction.

1.
$$
\begin{array}{r}
600 \\
-\ 47 \\
\hline
\end{array}
$$

2.
$$
\begin{array}{r}
705 \\
-\ 82 \\
\hline
\end{array}
$$

3.
$$
\begin{array}{r}
102 \\
-\ 63 \\
\hline
\end{array}
$$

4.
$$
\begin{array}{r}
400 \\
-135 \\
\hline
\end{array}
$$

5.
$$
\begin{array}{r}
803 \\
-244 \\
\hline
\end{array}
$$

6.
$$
\begin{array}{r}
729 \\
-468 \\
\hline
\end{array}
$$

Activity 3

Choose the best method for solving the problem: (a) traditional subtraction or (b) estimation and a calculator. Then solve using the chosen method.

1.
$$
\begin{array}{r}
5{,}555 \\
-1{,}100 \\
\hline
\end{array}
$$

2.
$$
\begin{array}{r}
8{,}014 \\
-1{,}925 \\
\hline
\end{array}
$$

3.
$$
\begin{array}{r}
477 \\
-226 \\
\hline
\end{array}
$$

Activity 4 • Distributed Practice

Add.

1.
$$
\begin{array}{r}
327 \\
+112 \\
\hline
\end{array}
$$

2.
$$
\begin{array}{r}
307 \\
+811 \\
\hline
\end{array}
$$

3.
$$
\begin{array}{r}
527 \\
+465 \\
\hline
\end{array}
$$

4.
$$
\begin{array}{r}
980 \\
+370 \\
\hline
\end{array}
$$

▶**Good Number Sense**

What is good number sense?

Let's think about how we would solve this problem using traditional subtraction:

$$62,000 \qquad \overset{\overset{9\ \ 9}{1\ 10\ 10\ 10}}{6\cancel{2},\cancel{0}\cancel{0}\cancel{0}}$$
$$-\,61,998 \qquad -\,61,998$$
$$ \qquad 2$$

We would do a lot of regrouping to finish the subtraction. We increase the chance of making an error when we do a lot of regrouping. So that we don't make these errors, we could use another method of finding the difference.

Using Estimation
We could solve the problem using estimation. Because both numbers round to 62,000, our estimated answer is zero. This tells us that the numbers are very close.

Using a Number Line
A simpler way to subtract is to find the small difference between the numbers on a number line. The number line below shows how close the numbers are.

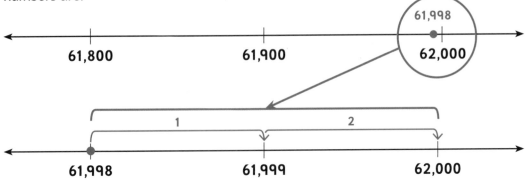

Sometimes we get so involved in the many steps of subtraction that we forget to use good number sense. Some problems that are difficult to solve using traditional or expanded subtraction have simple solutions if we think about them.

Let's look at an example where having good number sense is very important.

Example 1

Find the difference between 5,000,000 and 4,999,998 using traditional subtraction.

$$
\begin{array}{r}
\overset{4\ \ 9\ 9\ \ 9\ \ 9\ \ 9\,10}{\cancel{5,000,000}} \\
-\ 4,999,998 \\
\hline
2
\end{array}
$$

Notice that it takes six regroupings to get an answer of 2. We can avoid these regroupings by using good number sense to make observations about the numbers before we subtract.

> The best method for solving a subtraction problem depends on the numbers in the problem. Sometimes it is quickest to use traditional subtraction. Other times it is best to use mental math. There are also times when it is most efficient to use a calculator and an estimate.

Using Estimation
If we were to estimate this difference, we would round to the nearest million. Our estimate would be **5,000,000 – 5,000,000 = 0**. The rounded numbers are the same. This tells us that the numbers in the problem are very close, but does not tell us the difference.

Using a Number Line
We can count up from the lesser number to the greater one.

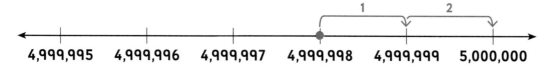

Think about how much we need to add to the lesser number to get the greater number.

4,999,998 + 2 = 5,000,000

We see that there is a difference of only 2 between the numbers. It is not necessary to go through all the regroupings to find this difference if we use good number sense.

%÷
≤× **Apply Skills**
Turn to *Interactive Text*, page 85.

 mBook **Reinforce Understanding**
Use the *mBook Study Guide* to review lesson concepts.

▶Problem Solving: **Solving With Estimation**

Can estimation alone solve a problem?

Sometimes a problem does not ask for an exact answer, so an estimate
might be good enough. We try to estimate first.

Example 1

Solve the word problem.

Problem:

Mr. Harvey has $228 in his wallet and $467 in his savings
account. Does he have enough money to buy a television that
costs $995, including tax?

The numbers in this problem are close to quarters, so
let's use quarter rounding to estimate.

$$\begin{array}{r} \$228 \\ + \$467 \end{array} \rightarrow \text{rounds to} \rightarrow \begin{array}{r} \$225 \\ + \$475 \\ \hline \$700 \end{array}$$

**Mr. Harvey has about $700. He does not have enough money to
buy the television. The amount $700 is much less than $995.**

In the example above, we could estimate to solve the problem because
the numbers we compared were not close. If the numbers being
compared are close, an estimate is not good enough.

Example 2

Solve the word problem.

Problem:

Mr. Harvey realizes he cannot afford the television
that costs $995. Now he is interested in buying
a television that costs $685, including tax. Does
Mr. Harvey have enough money to buy this television?

Mr. Harvey has about $700 to spend on a television.
This is very close to the cost of the television, which
is $685. Because the numbers are very close, it is
necessary to compute the exact answer.

**Mr. Harvey has $695, so he has enough money to buy
the television.**

Estimate

$$\begin{array}{r} \$228 \\ + \$467 \end{array} \rightarrow \text{rounds to} \rightarrow \begin{array}{r} \$225 \\ + \$475 \\ \hline \$700 \end{array}$$

Exact Answer

$$\begin{array}{r} \overset{1}{\$228} \\ + \$467 \\ \hline \$695 \end{array}$$

$695 is greater than $685

 Problem-Solving Activity
Turn to *Interactive Text*, page 86.

 mBook **Reinforce Understanding**
Use the *mBook Study Guide*
to review lesson concepts.

Homework

Activity 1

Solve the problem using good number sense and mental math.

Model $500 - 498 = \underline{2}$

485 486 487 488 489 490 491 492 493 494 495 496 497 498 499 500

1.   70
   $- 69$

2.   800
   $- 795$

3.   600
   $- 590$

Activity 2

Solve the problem using good number sense and mental math.

Model $17 - 1 = 16$ $170 - 10 = 160$ $1{,}700 - 100 = 1{,}600$

1. $10 - 1$
    $100 - 10$
    $1{,}000 - 100$

2. $15 - 1$
    $150 - 10$
    $1{,}500 - 100$

3. $12 - 1$
    $120 - 10$
    $1{,}200 - 100$

Activity 3

Find the difference using traditional subtraction.

1.   160
   $- 78$

2.   403
   $- 142$

3.   666
   $- 399$

4.   207
   $- 83$

Activity 4

Choose the best method for solving the problem: (a) traditional subtraction, (b) estimation and a calculator, or (c) mental math. Then solve using the chosen method.

1.   555
   $- 444$

2.   500
   $- 495$

3.   2,123
   $- 1{,}987$

4.   3,000
   $- 2{,}774$

Activity 5 • Distributed Practice

Add.

1.   5,000
   $+ 10$

2.   6,000
   $+ 100$

3.   7,000
   $+ 2{,}000$

4.   8,000
   $+ 50$

Lesson 14 ▶Writing About What We Have Learned

Problem Solving:
Writing Good Word Problems

▶**Writing About What We Have Learned**

How do we write about what we have learned?

An important part of mathematics is being able to explain our thinking in writing. Writing about math helps us better understand the concepts we learned. The following examples show how we can write about the subtraction methods we learned in this unit.

Explain Your Thinking

Explain how to find the difference between 6,068 and 1,279.

First, explain why this problem is difficult to solve using traditional subtraction.

> *"The hundreds, tens, and ones digits in the top number are less than those in the bottom number, so multiple regroupings are needed."*

Next, identify some strategies you can use to solve the problem.

- *Estimate the difference by rounding to the nearest thousand: 6,000 – 1,000 = 5,000.*
- *Use quarter rounding to estimate the difference: 6,075 – 1,275 = 4,800.*
- *Use a calculator to compute an exact answer.*

Then determine which estimate is closest to the exact answer.

> *"The estimate found using quarter rounding is closer to the exact answer: 6,068 – 1,279 = 4,789."*

Finally, you check the answer.

> *"We could check by adding the answer to the bottom number of the problem to make sure that the sum equals the top number."*

When we write about what we learned, we need to explain what we were thinking while we solved the problem.

Explain Your Thinking

Explain how to find the difference between 500 and 498.

First, explain why this problem is difficult to solve using traditional subtraction.

> *"The tens and ones digits in the top number are less than those in the bottom number, so multiple regroupings are needed."*

Next, find the best method to solve this problem.

> *"Mental math is the best method because I would not need to regroup with zeros."*

Finally, explain two ways to use mental math to solve this problem.

> *"I could count up from 498 to 500: 499, 500. I counted two numbers from 498 to reach 500, so the difference is 2. I could also think about what number can be added to 498 to equal 500: 498 + 2 = 500. The difference is 2."*

 Apply Skills
Turn to *Interactive Text*, page 88.

 mBook Reinforce Understanding
Use the *mBook Study Guide* to review lesson concepts.

▶Problem Solving: **Writing Good Word Problems**

Why is it important to know how to write a good word problem?

It is important for us to know how to write good word problems because it helps us look at them in a different way. Writing word problems helps us see things that we might not notice when we solve a problem. Let's look at an example.

Example 1

Write a word problem based on these data, then solve the problem.

| The Scatter Plots' Most Popular Songs ||
Song Title	Number of Weeks in Top 40
Golden Lines	19
Old-Time Modern	18
Going Away for Now	18
Rockin' Out Tonight	16
Water Mirage	15
Tree Hopping	13
Another Darling	10
Yellow Faces	10

The table shows the most popular songs by the Scatter Plots throughout the years.

- First, we need to decide what kinds of questions can be asked about the data.

- Next, we need to figure out what kinds of computations can be made.

Because we have been learning about subtraction in this unit, let's use the data to create a word problem that requires subtraction.

Word Problem:

How many more weeks was *Golden Lines* on the hits list than *Rockin' Out Tonight*?

Golden Lines was on the hits list for 3 more weeks than Rockin' Out Tonight: 19 − 16 = 3.

 Problem-Solving Activity
Turn to *Interactive Text*, page 89.

 mBook Reinforce Understanding
Use the *mBook Study Guide* to review lesson concepts.

Activity 1

Solve the problem using good number sense and mental math.

1. 500
    − 498

2. 600
    − 397

3. 9,500
    − 9,499

4. 8,000
    − 1,999

Activity 2

Solve the problem using estimation and a calculator.

1. Hipster Records sold 19,499 CDs last year. So far this year, the company has sold 20,000 CDs. How many more CDs has Hipster Records sold this year?

2. Kazoodle Records is competing against Hipster Records. Kazoodle sold 18,510 CDs last year and has sold 19,712 CDs so far this year. How many more CDs has Kazoodle Records sold this year?

3. Which record company, Kazoodle or Hipster, has sold the most CDs over the two-year period?

Activity 3

Find the difference using traditional subtraction.

1. 84
    − 68

2. 304
    − 105

3. 800
    − 149

4. 905
    − 145

Activity 4

Find the difference using expanded form. Then write the answer in standard form.

1. 304
    − 71

2. 521
    − 115

Activity 5 • Distributed Practice

Add.

1. 742
    + 199

2. 800
    + 58

3. 709
    + 101

▶**Subtraction**

What are different ways of thinking about subtraction?

One main focus of this unit has been the subtraction of whole numbers. We learned different ways to think about subtraction as well as the importance of place value.

Review 1

What are basic and extended subtraction facts?

$12 - 7 = 5$ $120 - 70 = 50$ $1,200 - 700 = 500$

Fact families

4, 5, and 9	$4 + 5 = 9$	$9 - 5 = 4$
	$5 + 4 = 9$	$9 - 4 = 5$

Understanding place value and expanded subtraction is especially helpful when we solve problems using traditional subtraction. The problem below compares these methods of subtraction.

Review 2

How is traditional subtraction different from expanded subtraction?

Subtraction Problem	Traditional Subtraction	Expanded Subtraction

Subtraction Problem:

$$\begin{array}{r} 742 \\ -315 \\ \hline \end{array}$$

Traditional Subtraction:

$$\begin{array}{r} \overset{3\ 12}{7\cancel{4}\cancel{2}} \\ -315 \\ \hline 427 \end{array}$$

Expanded Subtraction:

$$\begin{array}{rrr} & 30+\cancel{10} & 12 \\ 700 & \cancel{40} & \cancel{2}+\cancel{10} \\ -300 & 10 & 5 \\ \hline 400 & 20 & 7 \end{array}$$

$400 + 20 + 7 = 427$

Using strategies to round numbers is an important part of estimating differences. We have learned how to round numbers two different ways in this unit—the rounding strategy and quarter rounding. The examples below show how these two strategies are used to estimate answers to subtraction problems.

Review 3

How do we use rounding to estimate?

Rounding to the Nearest Ten		Quarter Rounding	
Exact answer	Estimate	Exact answer	Estimate
89	90	79	75
− 33	− 30	− 27	− 25
56	60	52	50

Here, the exact answer is 56. The estimate of 60 is very close to 56, so this is a good estimate.

Here, the exact answer is 52. The estimate for this problem is found using quarter rounding because the numbers in the problem are close to quarters. The estimate of 50 is very close to the exact answer, so this is also a good estimate.

It is easy to make mistakes when we subtract. Zeros are a source of many errors. The problem below shows how the expanded form of subtraction helps us find errors.

Review 4

What are common errors in subtraction?

ERROR

309
− 124   The tens digits were transposed to subtract.
225

Expanded subtraction shows the source of the error:

$$
\begin{array}{r|r|r}
200 + \cancel{100} & 100 & \\
\cancel{300} & \cancel{0 + 100} & 9 \\
- \quad 100 & 20 & 4 \\
\hline
100 & 80 & 5
\end{array}
$$

Answer: 100 + 80 + 5 = 185

 Apply Skills
Turn to *Interactive Text*, page 91.

 mBook Reinforce Understanding
Use the *mBook Study Guide* to review lesson concepts.

▶**Problem Solving: Working With Data**

How do we use information from tables and graphs to solve subtraction problems?

Tables and bar graphs are important sources of information for problem solving in math. Finding the right information in a table or graph takes time. We should always be careful that the information we locate is the correct information needed to solve the problem.

Review 1

How do we use tables and graphs to solve problems?

The town of Stewartville has become concerned about its increasing crime rates. The town decides to hire a new police chief to try to reduce the number of crimes in the town. The town's crime data for the police chief's first five years of service are shown in the table below.

New Police Chief's Year of Service	Burglaries	Computer Crimes	Stolen Cars
1	158	273	87
2	132	229	74
3	99	188	61
4	87	169	53
5	76	143	42

We can use the data in the table to answer a number of questions that involve subtraction.

How many fewer burglaries occurred in the police chief's second year of service than his first year?

Looking at the table, we see that there were 158 burglaries in the police chief's first year of service and 132 burglaries in the chief's second year. We can subtract to find the difference.

$$
\begin{array}{r}
158 \\
-132 \\
\hline
26
\end{array}
$$

There were 26 fewer burglaries.

 Problem-Solving Activity
Turn to *Interactive Text*, page 93.

mBook **Reinforce Understanding**
Use the *mBook Study Guide* to review lesson concepts.

BUT JIMMY DID INDEED START HIS OWN ROCK GROUP, AND HIS BAND "MÖTLEY KRILL" TOPPED THE CHARTS. MONEY AND FAME, JIMMY HAD IT ALL. BUT THE LITTLE FISH SOON DISCOVERED THAT MATH AND MULTIPLICATION STILL PLAYED A BIG ROLE IN HIS LIFE, EVEN AS A ROCK STAR!

15,000 T-SHIRTS AT $15 EACH EQUALS $225,000

2 MILLION CONCERT TICKETS AT $40 EACH EQUALS $80 MILLION

But then the band broke up!

Where are they now?

"DOC" LOBSTER, DRUMS — TOOK A JOB AS A HOST AT A SEAFOOD RESTAURANT NEAR BOSTON HARBOR.

GILL "TARTAR SAUCE," BASS GUITAR — COULD NOT BE REACHED BUT WAS RECENTLY SPOTTED HANGING AROUND A BAIT SHOP IN TULSA, OKLAHOMA.

JIMMY SOCKEYE, VOCALS, RHYTHM GUITAR — RETURNED HOME TO WORK WITH HIS DAD IN THE FAMILY ACCOUNTING BUSINESS.

I always knew you'd return home someday son. We salmon almost always do!

OBJECTIVES

Building Number Concepts

- Understand the relationship between basic and expanded multiplication

- Recognize and factor out powers of 10 from multiplication problems

- Estimate the solution to whole-number multiplication problems

Problem Solving

- Measure using common objects

- Measure objects using inches and metric units

- Use a variety of measurement strategies in real-world problems

▶**Basic and Extended Multiplication Facts**

Vocabulary

commutative property of multiplication

How do we use the commutative property in multiplication?

When we studied addition, we learned that we can change the order of the numbers being added without changing the answer. This is called the commutative property of addition. For each addition fact we know, we can use the commutative property to create another fact.

Commutative Property • Addition	
7 + 8 = 15 8 + 7 = 15	80 + 50 = 130 50 + 80 = 130

We can add numbers in any order and the answer stays the same.

The commutative property also works in multiplication. We can change the order of the factors without changing the answer. This is called the **commutative property of multiplication** .

Commutative Property • Multiplication	
7 × 8 = 56 8 × 7 = 56	9 × 3 = 27 3 × 9 = 27

POWER CONCEPT

Multiplication is similar to addition. You can change the order of the numbers in the problem without changing the answer.

What are extended multiplication facts?

We create extended multiplication facts by multiplying one or both of the numbers in a basic fact by a power of 10. Below, we are multiplying *one* number by a power of 10.

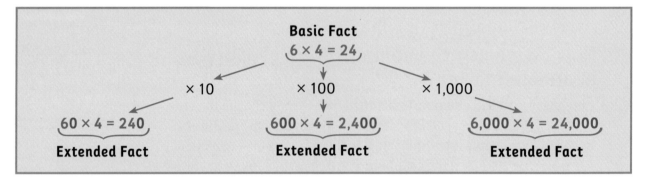

Basic Fact
6 × 4 = 24

× 10   × 100   × 1,000

60 × 4 = 240   600 × 4 = 2,400   6,000 × 4 = 24,000

Extended Fact   **Extended Fact**   **Extended Fact**

Look closely at the extended multiplication facts above. Notice that the basic fact 6 × 4 = 24 appears in each extended fact.

When we create extended multiplication facts, we need to pay close attention to the number of zeros in the answer. The number of zeros must be the same as the number of zeros in the numbers being multiplied.

Example 1

Write three extended facts for each of the basic multiplication facts below.

Basic Fact →	4 × 6 = 24	3 × 9 = 27	5 × 6 = 30
× 10	4 × 60 = 240	3 × 90 = 270	5 × 60 = 300
Extended Facts	40 × 6 = 240	30 × 9 = 270	50 × 6 = 300
× 100	400 × 6 = 2,400	300 × 9 = 2,700	500 × 6 = 3,000

% ÷ Apply Skills
Turn to *Interactive Text*,
page 95.

mBook Reinforce Understanding
Use the *mBook Study Guide*
to review lesson concepts.

▶**Problem Solving: Estimating Distances**

How do we estimate distance?

Sometimes we do not need to know exactly how far or long a distance is. We just find an estimate. One way we estimate length is to measure with an object whose length we are familiar with, such as a football or shoes. The object we use to measure other objects with is called the **unit of measurement** .

Standard units of measurement include feet, meters, and inches. In this lesson, we use nonstandard units of measurement to estimate distances.

A football is an object that most people are familiar with. Footballs are all roughly the same length. If we describe something as "about two footballs long," most people understand what we mean.

Example 1

Answer the question using estimation.

About how many footballs long is the distance from A to B?

A   B

We do not need to find the exact distance from A to B because the question uses the word **about** . The use of the word "about" in the question tells us we are going to find an estimate. The question also tells us that the unit of measurement is a football.

The distance from A to B is about three footballs long.

Nonstandard units of measurement are helpful when we estimate distance.

Problem-Solving Activity
Turn to *Interactive Text*, page 96.

mBook Reinforce Understanding
Use the *mBook Study Guide* to review lesson concepts.

Activity 1

Add or subtract to solve the basic or extended fact.

1. $7 + 9$
2. $70 + 90$
3. $13 - 8$
4. $1,300 - 800$
5. $8 + 7$
6. $800 + 700$
7. $17 - 9$
8. $170 - 90$
9. $1,700 - 900$

Activity 2

Multiply to solve the set of basic and extended facts.

1. 8×9
   8×90
   8×900
2. 9×8
   9×80
   9×800
3. 8×4
   8×40
   8×400

Activity 3

Write three extended facts for each of the basic multiplication facts.

1. 3×7
2. 4×8
3. 5×7

Activity 4 • Distributed Practice

Add or subtract.

1. $\begin{array}{r} 529 \\ + 186 \\ \hline \end{array}$
2. $\begin{array}{r} 257 \\ - 184 \\ \hline \end{array}$
3. $\begin{array}{r} 675 \\ + 129 \\ \hline \end{array}$
4. $\begin{array}{r} 5,402 \\ - 4,811 \\ \hline \end{array}$

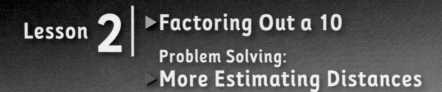

► Factoring Out a 10

Problem Solving:
► More Estimating Distances

► **Factoring Out a 10**

Vocabulary
factor
product

What does it mean to factor out a 10?

In multiplication facts, the numbers being multiplied are called **factors**. The answer is called the **product**.

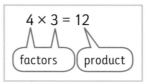

When we notice that 10 is a factor of a number, we identify what the other factor is by finding how many tens there are in the number.

Let's start with the number 50.

Count the tens on the number line. The number line shows that there are 5 tens in the number 50.

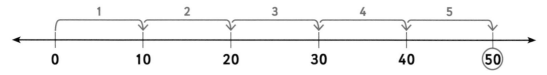

We see that 50 is the same as 5 tens. We write the number 50 as the product of the factors 5 and 10.

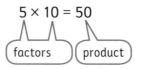

We learned that factors are the numbers being multiplied, but we also use the word factor to describe an action. We *factor* a number by writing it as the product of other numbers. We can factor out a 10 from any number that ends in zero.

Example 1

Factor out a 10 from the numbers 30, 70, and 90.

$30 = 3 \times 10$ $70 = 7 \times 10$ $90 = 9 \times 10$

Look at how we factored out a 10 from each number. We wrote each number as the product of 10 and another number.

Let's look at how we can do this with larger numbers.

Example 2

Factor out a 10 from the numbers 600, 6,000, and 60,000.

$600 = 60 \times 10$ $6,000 = 600 \times 10$ $60,000 = 6,000 \times 10$

Notice that the same number of zeros appear on each side of the equal sign when we factor out a 10. Counting the zeros is a good way to check that we have factored correctly.

 Apply Skills
Turn to *Interactive Text*, page 98.

 Reinforce Understanding
Use the *mBook Study Guide* to review lesson concepts.

▶**Problem Solving: More Estimating Distances**

How do we choose a unit of measurement?

We learned how to use everyday objects such as shoes and footballs to estimate distances. We used these items as nonstandard units of measurement instead of standard units, such as meters or centimeters.

When we are not given the unit of measurement in a problem, we have to decide what unit to use. Choosing an appropriate unit of measurement for an estimate is important.

It is important for us to select an appropriate unit of measurement for the length we are measuring. A unit of measurement that is too big will not be accurate. A unit of measurement that is too small can take a long time to calculate.

 Problem-Solving Activity
Turn to *Interactive Text*, page 99.

 mBook Reinforce Understanding
Use the *mBook Study Guide* to review lesson concepts.

Activity 1

Multiply to solve the basic fact.

1. 7×8 2. 8×7 3. 3×8

4. 8×3 5. 8×9 6. 9×8

7. 6×7 8. 7×6 9. 4×7

Activity 2

Multiply to solve the set of basic and extended facts.

1. 7×9 2. 8×6 3. 5×9
   7×90 8×60 5×90
   7×900 8×600 5×900

Activity 3

Factor out a 10 from the number.

Model $50 = 5 \times 10$ $500 = 50 \times 10$ $5{,}000 = 500 \times 10$

1. 70   2. 80   3. 300

4. 400   5. 8,000   6. 9,000

Activity 4 • Distributed Practice

Add or subtract.

1.
$$\begin{array}{r} 4{,}000 \\ -\ 2{,}000 \\ \hline \end{array}$$
2.
$$\begin{array}{r} 672 \\ +\ 987 \\ \hline \end{array}$$
3.
$$\begin{array}{r} 759 \\ +\ 827 \\ \hline \end{array}$$
4.
$$\begin{array}{r} 3{,}124 \\ +\ \ \ 519 \\ \hline \end{array}$$

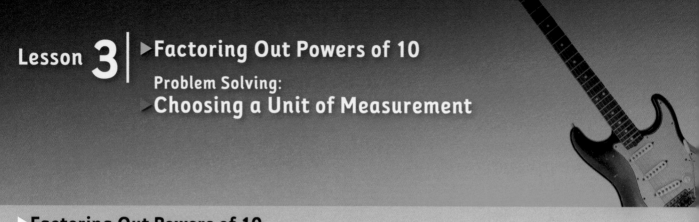

▶**Factoring Out Powers of 10**

Problem Solving:
▶**Choosing a Unit of Measurement**

▶**Factoring Out Powers of 10**

How do we factor out powers of 10 from numbers?

In Lesson 2, we learned how to factor out a 10 from numbers.

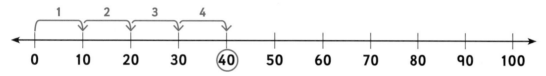

We see that there are 4 tens in 40, so $40 = 4 \times 10$.

Other Powers of 10

We can also factor out greater powers of 10 such as 100 and 1,000.

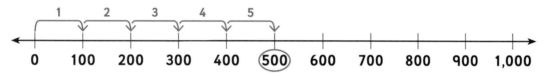

There are 5 hundreds in 500, so $500 = 5 \times 100$.

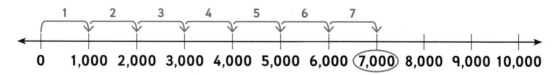

There are 7 thousands in 7,000, so $7,000 = 7 \times 1,000$.

Let's look more closely at factoring the powers of 10 from greater numbers.

We learned that we can factor out powers of 10 from any number that ends in zero. In large numbers, there are different powers of 10 that we can factor out.

Example 1

Factor out all powers of 10 possible from the numbers 500 and 7,000.

500 = 50 × 10   We can factor out 10.

500 = 5 × 100   We can factor out 100.

> Because the greatest place value in 500 is the hundreds, we factor out 10 and 100.

7,000 = 700 × 10   We can factor out 10.

7,000 = 70 × 100   We can factor out 100.

7,000 = 7 × 1,000   We can factor out 1,000.

> Because the greatest place value in 7,000 is the thousands, we factor out 10, 100, and 1,000.

Notice that there are the same number of zeros on both sides of the equal sign.

Another way to factor out a power of 10 is by using a table. A table helps us see patterns in our factors.

Example 2

Factor out 10, 100, and 1,000 from each number.

Number	? × 10	? × 100	? × 1,000
1,000	100 × 10	10 × 100	1 × 1,000
6,000	600 × 10	60 × 100	6 × 1,000
7,000	700 × 10	70 × 100	7 × 1,000

Look closely at the pattern of zeros in each row of the table. The total number of zeros in the factors always equals the number of zeros in the original number, no matter which power of 10 is factored out.

 Apply Skills
Turn to *Interactive Text*, page 101.

 mBook Reinforce Understanding
Use the *mBook Study Guide* to review lesson concepts.

▶**Problem Solving: Choosing a Unit of Measurement**

How do we choose a standard unit of measurement for an estimate?

We often make observations about lengths, heights, and distances using nonstandard units of measurement. For example, we might describe a tree as being about two stories tall.

TALES FROM PLANET TROON

PART TWO

YOU REMEMBER THE MUD PEOPLE FROM PLANET TROON. THEY DECIDED TO USE THEIR FEET AS A MEASURING DEVICE. HOWEVER, THEY REALIZED THEY DO NOT ALL HAVE THE SAME SIZE FEET.

WHEN MUD #1 AND MUD #2 MEASURED THE SAME THING, **THEY DID NOT HAVE THE SAME RESULTS!**

19   16

THEN— **ZOWIE— AN IDEA!**

THEY NEEDED TO CHOOSE **ONE FOOT SIZE** AS THE OFFICIAL UNIT OF MEASUREMENT.

THEY DECIDED TO USE MUD #1's FEET AS THE UNIT OF MEASUREMENT BECAUSE THEY WERE LARGER AND THERE WOULD BE LESS TO COUNT.

16

ALL'S WELL THAT ENDS WELL.

POWER CONCEPT

We can estimate a distance by comparing it to the length of a familiar object. This gives us a good sense of how long the distance is.

Problem-Solving Activity
Turn to *Interactive Text*, page 102.

mBook **Reinforce Understanding**
Use the *mBook Study Guide* to review lesson concepts.

Activity 1

Multiply to solve the basic or extended fact.

1. 4×6
2. 4×60
3. 6×40
4. 8×9
5. 8×90
6. 9×80

Activity 2

Factor out 10, 100, and 1,000 from each number.

Number	? × 10	? × 100	? × 1,000
1,000	100 × 10	10 × 100	1 × 1,000
2,000		20 × 100	
3,000	300 × 10		3 × 1,000
4,000	400 × 10		
5,000		50 × 100	
6,000			
7,000		70 × 100	7 × 1,000
8,000			8 × 1,000
9,000			

Activity 3

Complete the extended multiplication fact.

1. $2 \times 1{,}000 = \underline{\hspace{1cm}}$
2. $\underline{\hspace{1cm}} \times 10 = 2{,}000$
3. $20 \times 100 = \underline{\hspace{1cm}}$
4. $6{,}000 = 600 \times \underline{\hspace{1cm}}$
5. $6{,}000 = \underline{\hspace{1cm}} \times 1{,}000$
6. $6{,}000 = \underline{\hspace{1cm}} \times 100$
7. $\underline{\hspace{1cm}} = 8 \times 1{,}000$
8. $800 \times 10 = \underline{\hspace{1cm}}$
9. $\underline{\hspace{1cm}} = 80 \times 100$

Activity 4 • Distributed Practice

Add or subtract.

1. $\begin{array}{r} 547 \\ -\ 69 \end{array}$

2. $\begin{array}{r} 487 \\ +123 \end{array}$

3. $\begin{array}{r} 859 \\ -177 \end{array}$

4. $\begin{array}{r} 1{,}700 \\ -\ 645 \end{array}$

5. $\begin{array}{r} 875 \\ +925 \end{array}$

6. $\begin{array}{r} 9{,}000 \\ -2{,}000 \end{array}$

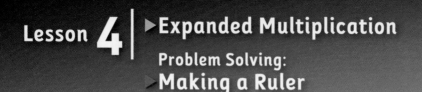

Lesson 4 | ▶Expanded Multiplication
Problem Solving:
▶ Making a Ruler

▶Expanded Multiplication

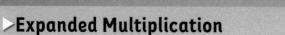

How do we use expanded form to multiply?

We learned how to write and solve addition and subtraction problems in expanded form. This helped us see place value clearly. We also apply the concept of expanded form to multiplication. This is called **expanded multiplication** .

Vocabulary
expanded multiplication

Let's look at the problem 21×3. We can write 21×3 in vertical or expanded form.

$$\begin{array}{r} 21 \\ \times\ 3 \end{array} \rightarrow \begin{array}{r} 20\ |\ 1 \\ \times\quad\ \ |\ 3 \end{array}$$

We use place-value charts to model the multiplication process.

We model 21 by placing 2 tens coins in the tens column and 1 ones coin in the ones column.

We model 21×3 by tripling the coins in each column. The problem 21×3 is the same as $21 + 21 + 21$. Let's start with the ones coins. There is 1 ones coin in the chart. To model 1×3, count one plus one plus one. The answer, 3, is part of the product.

$$\begin{array}{r} 20\ |\ 1 \\ \times\quad\ \ |\ 3 \\ \hline |\ 3 \end{array}$$

Now we repeat the process for the tens coins. Count twenty plus twenty plus twenty. This answer is the second part of the product.

$$\begin{array}{r} 20\ |\ 1 \\ \times\quad\ \ |\ 3 \\ \hline |\ 3 \end{array}$$

We add the two parts together to find the product.

The product is 63.

$$\begin{array}{r} 60 \\ \hline 63 \end{array}$$

Let's practice multiplying more numbers using expanded multiplication.

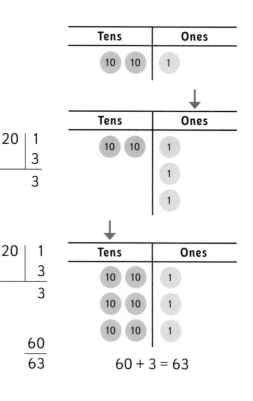

$60 + 3 = 63$

Expanded multiplication is similar to expanded addition and subtraction. In all three methods, the numbers are expanded first, then the operation is performed.

Example 1

Find the product of 86 and 6 using expanded multiplication.

$$\begin{array}{r} 86 \\ \times\ \ 6 \\ \hline \end{array}$$

STEP 1
Write the numbers in expanded form.

$$\begin{array}{r} 86 \\ \times\ \ 6 \end{array} \rightarrow \begin{array}{r|r} 80 & 6 \\ \times\quad & 6 \end{array}$$

STEP 2
Multiply the digits in the ones column.
$6 \times 6 = 36$

$$\begin{array}{r|r} 80 & 6 \\ \times & 6 \\ \hline & 36 \end{array}$$

STEP 3
Multiply the bottom digit by the tens column on top.
$6 \times 80 = 480$

$$\begin{array}{r|r} 80 & 6 \\ \times & 6 \\ \hline & 36 \\ 480 \end{array}$$

STEP 4

Add the products.

$$\begin{array}{r} 480 \\ +\ \ 36 \\ \hline 516 \end{array}$$

$36 + 480 = 516$

The product is 516.

In expanded form of multiplication, we find different parts of the product and then add the products together to find the actual product.

 Apply Skills
Turn to *Interactive Text*, page 104.

 mBook Reinforce Understanding
Use the *mBook Study Guide* to review lesson concepts.

▶Problem Solving: **Making a Ruler**

Vocabulary

U.S. customary units
standard unit of
measurement

How do we make a measuring device?

In Lesson 3, the mud people used a footprint as a measuring device to measure lengths and distances. A footprint is a good measuring device for distances.

A ruler is a good measuring device for the lengths of smaller objects because we can find an exact measurement.

An inch is a U.S. customary unit . The measurement of an inch became standard in England about 500 years ago. Feet, yards, and miles are also U.S. customary units. These units are the same for everyone who uses them. They are **standard units of measurement** .

The ruler is broken into parts. The second longest lines on the ruler mark half inches.

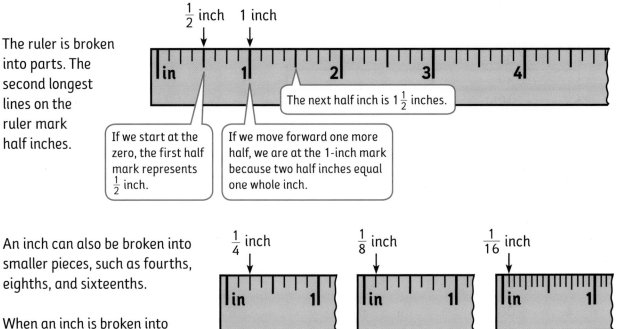

$\frac{1}{2}$ inch   1 inch

The next half inch is $1\frac{1}{2}$ inches.

If we start at the zero, the first half mark represents $\frac{1}{2}$ inch.

If we move forward one more half, we are at the 1-inch mark because two half inches equal one whole inch.

An inch can also be broken into smaller pieces, such as fourths, eighths, and sixteenths.

$\frac{1}{4}$ inch $\frac{1}{8}$ inch $\frac{1}{16}$ inch

When an inch is broken into fourths, this means there are four equal parts. Eighths indicate eight equal parts of one inch, and sixteenths indicate sixteen parts. The smaller the parts, the more accurate we can be when we measure length.

 Problem-Solving Activity
Turn to *Interactive Text*,
page 105.

mBook **Reinforce Understanding**
Use the *mBook Study Guide*
to review lesson concepts.

Activity 1

Multiply to solve the extended fact.

1. 3×50
2. 4×500
3. 6×900
4. 9×60
5. 300×5
6. 5×40

Activity 2

Find the product using expanded multiplication.

1. $\begin{array}{r} 42 \\ \times\ 4 \\ \hline \end{array}$
2. $\begin{array}{r} 33 \\ \times\ 2 \\ \hline \end{array}$
3. $\begin{array}{r} 62 \\ \times\ 3 \\ \hline \end{array}$

Activity 3

Complete the table.

Number	? × 10
30	3 × 10
40	
50	
60	
70	
80	

Activity 4 • Distributed Practice

Add or subtract.

1. $\begin{array}{r} 129 \\ +\ 237 \\ \hline \end{array}$
2. $\begin{array}{r} 307 \\ -\ 190 \\ \hline \end{array}$
3. $\begin{array}{r} 429 \\ -\ 168 \\ \hline \end{array}$

4. $\begin{array}{r} 5{,}001 \\ -\ 4{,}098 \\ \hline \end{array}$
5. $\begin{array}{r} 628 \\ +\ 189 \\ \hline \end{array}$
6. $\begin{array}{r} 1{,}498 \\ +\ 3{,}624 \\ \hline \end{array}$

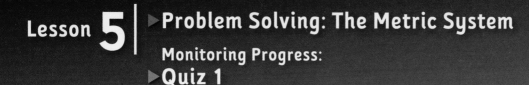

▶The Metric System

Vocabulary
metric system meter

What is the metric system?

We know we can measure the line below in different ways.

─

First, let's measure the line using a toothpick as the unit of measurement. Let's count how many toothpicks long the line is.

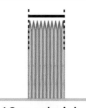

10 toothpicks

The answer is about 10 toothpicks. If we double the width of the line, the length is about 20 toothpicks.

Next, use the width of your little finger as the unit of measurement. Count how many finger widths the doubled line is.

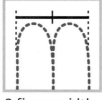

2 finger widths

The answer is about as wide as two fingers.

Let's look at the line at right.

This line is about 10 finger widths tall, or 100 toothpicks tall. Try it with your own fingers.

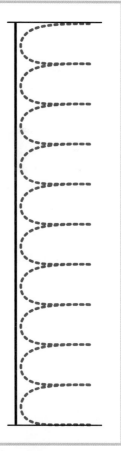

10 finger widths

We see a pattern using these units of measurement. The units of measurement seem to differ by a factor of 10. Let's look closely at a formal set of measurements that also differs by factors of 10.

In Lesson 4, we used rulers like the one below. This ruler measures objects using the U.S. customary system. Units of measurement like feet and inches are part of this system.

U.S. Customary Ruler

We learned that the U.S. customary system uses fractions to show measurements between whole numbers. For example, we might measure a paper clip that is $1\frac{1}{4}$ inches long or a dictionary that is $\frac{35}{16}$ inches thick. The U.S. customary ruler has many marks within each inch, which can be confusing.

Let's look at a different ruler. This ruler measures objects using the **metric system** . This system was developed in France about 200 years ago. Each unit of measurement in the metric system is based on the **meter** . One meter is about the length of a baseball bat.

The metric system of measurement is easy to use because it is based on powers of 10.

Metric Ruler

The metric system uses decimals to show measurements between whole units. For example, we might measure an eraser that has a length of 5.4 centimeters.

One of the greatest advantages of the metric system is its use of powers of 10. Some metric units of measurement are listed below. Notice how each unit is 10 times greater in length than the next shortest unit.

Metric Units	
meter (m)	1 meter = 10 decimeters
decimeter (dm)	1 decimeter = 10 centimeters
centimeter (cm)	1 centimeter = 10 millimeters
millimeter (mm)	1 millimeter = 0.1 centimeter

longest
↓
shortest

 Problem-Solving Activity
Turn to *Interactive Text*, page 107.

 Monitoring Progress
Quiz 1

 mBook Reinforce Understanding
Use the *mBook Study Guide* to review lesson concepts.

Homework

Activity 1

Use expanded multiplication to find the product.

Model

$$73 \times 7 \rightarrow$$

70	3
×	7
	21
+	490
	511

1. 61
× 8

2. 42
× 3

3. 21
× 9

Activity 2

Use a metric ruler to measure the line segment in the specified unit.

1. A is _____ mm long. **A** ____
2. B is _____ cm long. **B** _____
3. C is _____ mm long. **C** ____
4. D is _____ cm long. **D** _____

Activity 3

Factor out 10, 100, and 1,000 from each number.

Number	? × 10	? × 100	? × 1,000
1,000	100 × 10	10 × 100	1 × 1,000
3,000		30 × 100	
4,000	400 × 10		4 × 1,000
5,000			
7,000			
9,000			

Activity 4 • Distributed Practice

Add or subtract.

1. 587
+ 314

2. 10,420
+ 1,000

3. 6,107
− 1,982

4. 4,010
− 976

Lesson 6 ▸More Expanded Multiplication

Problem Solving:
▸Estimating Metric Measurements

▸**More Expanded Multiplication**

How do we use expanded form to multiply three- and four-digit numbers?

Let's review the steps of expanded multiplication using place-value coins.

$$\begin{array}{r} 122 \\ \times \quad 3 \end{array}$$

We start by modeling the number 122.

$$\begin{array}{r} 1\,22 \\ \times \quad 3 \end{array}$$

Hundreds	Tens	Ones
100	10 10	1 1

Because 122 is multiplied by 3, we triple the number of coins in each column.

$$\begin{array}{r} 122 \\ \times \quad 3 \end{array}$$

Hundreds	Tens	Ones
100	10 10	1 1
100	10 10	1 1
100	10 10	1 1

Because there are 3 hundreds coins, 6 tens coins, and 6 ones coins, the coins now represent the number 366. This is the product of 122 and 3.

Hundreds	Tens	Ones
100	10 10	1 1
100	10 10	1 1
100	10 10	1 1

} 366

This problem can also be solved using expanded multiplication.

$$\begin{array}{r} 122 \\ \times \quad 3 \end{array} \longrightarrow \begin{array}{r} 100 \mid 20 \mid \quad 2 \\ \times \qquad\qquad 3 \\ \hline 6 \\ 60 \\ +\qquad 300 \\ \hline 366 \end{array}$$

Lesson 6

We learned how to use expanded multiplication to multiply a two-digit number by a single-digit number. Expanded multiplication reminds us of the value of each digit when we multiply. Let's apply this thinking to larger numbers.

Example 1

Find the product of 745 and 3 using expanded multiplication.

$$\begin{array}{r} 745 \\ \times \quad 3 \end{array}$$

STEP 1
Write the numbers in expanded form.

$$\begin{array}{r} 745 \\ \times \quad 3 \end{array} \rightarrow \quad \begin{array}{r|r|r} 700 & 40 & 5 \\ \hline \times & & 3 \end{array}$$

STEP 2
Multiply the digits in the ones column.
$3 \times 5 = 15$

$$\begin{array}{r|r|r} 700 & 40 & 5 \\ \hline \times & & 3 \\ \hline & & 15 \end{array}$$

STEP 3
Multiply the bottom digit by the tens column on top.
$3 \times 40 = 120$

$$\begin{array}{r|r|r} 700 & 40 & 5 \\ \hline \times & & 3 \\ \hline & & 15 \\ & & 120 \end{array}$$

STEP 4
Multiply the bottom digit by the hundreds column on top.
$3 \times 700 = 2,100$

$$\begin{array}{r|r|r} 700 & 40 & 5 \\ \hline \times & & 3 \\ \hline & & 15 \\ & & 120 \\ & & 2,100 \end{array}$$

STEP 5
Add the products.
$15 + 120 + 2,100 = 2,235$

$$\begin{array}{r|r|r} 700 & 40 & 5 \\ \hline \times & & 3 \\ \hline & & 15 \\ & & 120 \\ + & & 2,100 \\ \hline & & 2,235 \end{array}$$

The product is 2,235.

Example 2

Find the product of 7,452 and 3 using expanded multiplication.

$$\begin{array}{r} 7{,}452 \\ \times\quad\ 3 \\ \hline \end{array}$$

STEP 1
Write the numbers in expanded form.

$$\begin{array}{r} 7{,}452 \\ \times\quad\ 3 \end{array} \rightarrow$$

7,000	400	50	2
×			3

STEP 2
Multiply the digits in the ones column.
$3 \times 2 = 6$

7,000	400	50	2
×			3
			6

STEP 3
Multiply the bottom digit by the tens column on top.
$3 \times 50 = 150$

7,000	400	**50**	2
×			3
			6
			150

STEP 4
Multiply the bottom digit by the hundreds column on top.
$3 \times 400 = 1{,}200$

7,000	**400**	50	2
×			3
			6
			150
			1,200

STEP 5
Multiply the bottom digit by the thousands column on top.
$3 \times 7{,}000 = 21{,}000$

7,000	400	50	2
×			3
			6
			150
			1,200
			21,000

STEP 6
Add the products.
$6 + 150 + 1{,}200 + 21{,}000 = 22{,}356$

The product is 22,356.

Notice that there are four partial products to add when we multiply with a four-digit number.

7,000	400	50	2
×			3
			6
			150
			1,200
+			21,000
			22,356

▶Problem Solving: Estimating Metric Measurements

Vocabulary
referent

How can we estimate measurements using the metric system?

In Lesson 5, we learned about different units of metric length. The table below lists these units of measurement.

The table also lists common objects we can use as **referents** for each unit of measurement. Referents are everyday objects we can refer to when we need to remember the approximate size of a unit of measurement. If we are told that a stack of DVDs is 5 centimeters high, we can mentally picture the height of the stack by imagining 5 widths of our little finger. The width of our little finger is a good referent for a centimeter.

	Metric Unit	Referent
longest	meter (m)	length of a baseball bat
↓	decimeter (dm)	length of your index finger from the tip of the finger to the base of the thumb
	centimeter (cm)	width of your little finger
shortest	millimeter (mm)	width of a pencil tip

Suppose we want to compare cell phones in different stores. One factor we would consider is the size of the phone. We would want to measure the height of each cell phone. If we do not have a ruler, we use a referent.

First, we have to select the most appropriate unit of measurement. Millimeters are too short and meters are too long. Decimeters or centimeters are the best choices to estimate the height of a cell phone because they are not too short or too long. Let's use centimeters because they will give us a more accurate measurement.

Example 1

Estimate the height of the cell phone in decimeters.

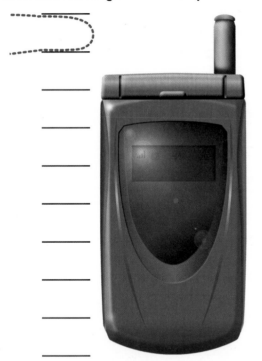

If the width of your little finger is 1 centimeter, then the cell phone is about 9 centimeters tall.

We know 10 centimeters = 1 decimeter, so this estimate tells us the height of the cell phone is about 1 decimeter.

We do not always have to measure using a ruler. Everyday *referents* like footballs and pencil tips help us estimate lengths.

 Problem-Solving Activity
Turn to *Interactive Text*, page 110.

 mBook Reinforce Understanding
Use the *mBook Study Guide* to review lesson concepts.

Homework

Activity 1

Multiply to solve the set of basic and extended facts.

1. 9×6 90×6 60×9 9×600

2. 7×8 70×80 700×8 800×7

3. 3×9 90×30 3×900 300×9

Activity 2

Find the product using expanded notation.

Model			
437	400	30	7
× 5 → ×			5
			35
			150
+			2,000
			2,185

1. $\begin{array}{r} 329 \\ \times\ \ 8 \\ \hline \end{array}$

2. $\begin{array}{r} 427 \\ \times\ \ 5 \\ \hline \end{array}$

3. $\begin{array}{r} 615 \\ \times\ \ 9 \\ \hline \end{array}$

Activity 3

Use a referent to estimate the length of the line segment in the specified unit.

1. A is about _____ cm long.   **A** _____

2. B is about _____ mm long.   **B** _____

3. C is about _____ cm long.   **C** _____

4. D is about _____ cm long.   **D** _____

Activity 4 • Distributed Practice

Add or subtract.

1. $\begin{array}{r} 598 \\ +\ 199 \\ \hline \end{array}$

2. $\begin{array}{r} 4,009 \\ -\ 3,999 \\ \hline \end{array}$

3. $\begin{array}{r} 5,107 \\ -\ \ \ 599 \\ \hline \end{array}$

4. $\begin{array}{r} 999 \\ +\ 111 \\ \hline \end{array}$

▶**Multiplying Two Multidigit Numbers**

How do we multiply two multidigit numbers?

When we multiply two multidigit numbers, we follow basic steps. These steps are just an extension of what we already learned.

Let's find the product of 231 and 75 using expanded multiplication.

Steps for Using Expanded Multiplication:

STEP 1

Write the numbers in expanded form.

$$231 \atop \times\ 75$$ →

200	30	1
×	70	5

STEP 2

Multiply the digits in the ones column.

200	30	1
×	70	5
		5

STEP 3

Multiply the ones digit on the bottom by the tens column on top.

200	**30**	1
×	70	5
		5
		150

STEP 4

Multiply the ones digit on the bottom by the hundreds digit on top.

200	30	1
×	70	5
		5
		150
		1,000

STEP 5

Multiply the tens digit on the bottom
by the ones digit on top.

```
      200 | 30 |    1
    ×      | 70 |    5
           |    |    5
                   150
                 1,000
                    70
```

STEP 6

Multiply the tens digit on the bottom
by the tens digit on top.

```
      200 | 30 |    1
    ×      | 70 |    5
           |    |    5
                   150
                 1,000
                    70
                 2,100
```

STEP 7

Multiply the tens digit on the bottom
by the hundreds digit on top.

```
      200 | 30 |    1
    ×      | 70 |    5
           |    |    5
                   150
                 1,000
                    70
                 2,100
    +            14,000
```

STEP 8

Add the products.

```
      200 | 30 |    1
    ×      | 70 |    5
           |    |    5
                   150
                 1,000
                    70
                 2,100
    +            14,000
                 17,325
```

In expanded multiplication, we multiply all of the numbers on the top
by both numbers on the bottom. Then we add the products together.

Example 1

Find the product of 82 and 63.

We start by writing the numbers in expanded form.
This step is the same as what we already learned,
except now we have two numbers in the tens column.

$$\begin{array}{r} 82 \\ \times\ 63 \end{array} \rightarrow \begin{array}{r|r} 80 & 2 \\ \times\ 60 & 3 \end{array}$$

Next, we multiply by the ones digit on the bottom. In this problem,
we find the products by multiplying each number on top by **3**. Just
like before, we write the products in the ones column.

$3 \times 2 = 6$ $3 \times 80 = 240$

$$\begin{array}{r|r} 80 & 2 \\ \times\ 60 & 3 \\ \hline & 6 \\ & 240 \end{array}$$

We start our new steps after we finish multiplying by the ones
column. We repeat the process that we just followed for the ones
column. Now we multiply each number on top by **60**.

$60 \times 2 = 120$ $60 \times 80 = 4,800$

$$\begin{array}{r|r} 80 & 2 \\ \times\ 60 & 3 \\ \hline & 6 \\ & 240 \\ & 120 \\ +\quad & 4,800 \end{array}$$

Finally, we add all the products together.
$6 + 240 + 120 + 4,800 = 5,166$

The product is 5,166.

$$\begin{array}{r|r} 80 & 2 \\ \times\ 60 & 3 \\ \hline & 6 \\ & 240 \\ & 120 \\ +\quad & 4,800 \\ \hline & 5,166 \end{array}$$

Remember that multiplying multidigit numbers is similar
to multiplying single-digit numbers.

Apply Skills
Turn to *Interactive Text*,
page 112.

mBook Reinforce Understanding
Use the *mBook Study Guide*
to review lesson concepts.

▶**Problem Solving: Estimating Measurements**

When do we need to estimate measurements?

We used a metric ruler to measure objects, but what if one is not available? It is important that we are able to estimate a measurement without using a ruler.

Suppose a car is approaching a school bus that makes a stop. A law states that the car has to stop 20 feet from the school bus. The driver of the car does not get out and measure this distance. Instead, the driver estimates 20 feet.

Approximately 20 feet

We make estimates about various types of measurements every day. The referents we learned for metric units help us make good estimates.

Example 1

Use referents to estimate.

What is the approximate length of an average housefly?

- **(a)** 1 millimeter (mm)
- **(b)** 1 centimeter (cm)
- **(c)** 1 decimeter (dm)
- **(d)** 1 meter (m)

Remember the referents we use to think about these metric units.

- If we choose 1 millimeter, we are estimating the length of a housefly as about the width of a pencil tip.

- If we choose 1 centimeter, we are estimating the length of a housefly as about the width of your little finger.

- If we choose 1 decimeter, we are estimating the length of a housefly as about the length of your index finger.

- If we choose 1 meter, we are estimating the length of a housefly as about the length of a baseball bat.

POWER CONCEPT

It is important to choose the most appropriate referent when we estimate a certain length or distance.

Think about the size of a housefly in comparison to each of the referents listed above. The best choice is 1 centimeter.

A housefly is about as long as the width of our little finger.

Problem-Solving Activity
Turn to *Interactive Text*, page 113.

mBook Reinforce Understanding
Use the *mBook Study Guide* to review lesson concepts.

Activity 1

Find the product using expanded multiplication.

1.   96
    × 3

2.   84
    × 4

3.   72
    × 9

Activity 2

Solve the problem using an extended multiplication fact. Write the fact you use.

1. RKRU is a radio station that plays long sets of commercial-free music. Each hour, they play 10 songs followed by 8 minutes of commercials. How many songs does the station play in 24 hours?

2. At RKRU, the Scatter Plots' most popular song gets requested about 30 times each day. About how many times will the song get requested in a week?

3. For 10 days, RKRU ran a contest in which the twelfth caller won dinner at a local restaurant. There was one winner each day. If the dinners were worth $75 each, what was the total value of the dinners the radio station gave away?

Activity 3 • Distributed Practice

Add or subtract.

1.   478
    − 289

2.   600
    − 398

3.   1,213
    − 767

4.   2,789
    + 1,321

5.   8,007
    + 2,993

6.   6,478
    + 1,986

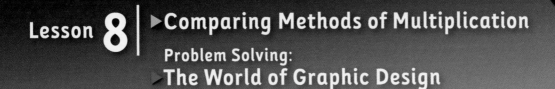

Lesson 8 ▸ Comparing Methods of Multiplication

Problem Solving:
▸ The World of Graphic Design

▸ **Comparing Methods of Multiplication**

Vocabulary
traditional multiplication

How do we compare methods of multiplication?

When we studied addition and subtraction, we compared the traditional methods with the expanded methods. We learned how each algorithm had advantages and disadvantages. As we look at the steps of **traditional multiplication**, we should remember expanded multiplication.

Let's find the product of 643 and 27 using traditional multiplication.

Steps for using traditional multiplication:

STEP 1
Write the problem vertically. Line up the place values.

$$\begin{array}{r} 643 \\ \times\ 27 \\ \hline \end{array}$$

STEP 2
Multiply the ones digit on the bottom by each digit on the top.

$$\begin{array}{r} {\scriptstyle 3\ 2} \\ 643 \\ \times\ 27 \\ \hline 4{,}501 \end{array}$$

STEP 3
Write a zero as a place holder.

$$\begin{array}{r} {\scriptstyle 3\ 2} \\ 643 \\ \times\ 27 \\ \hline 4{,}501 \\ 0 \end{array}$$

STEP 4
Multiply the tens digit on the bottom by each digit on the top.

$$\begin{array}{r} {\scriptstyle 3\ 2} \\ 643 \\ \times\ 27 \\ \hline 4{,}501 \\ 12{,}860 \end{array}$$

STEP 5
Add the products.

$$\begin{array}{r} {\scriptstyle 3\ 2} \\ 643 \\ \times\ 27 \\ \hline 4{,}501 \\ +12{,}860 \\ \hline 17{,}361 \end{array}$$

The product is 17,361.

Traditional multiplication is quick and efficient. Let's compare traditional multiplication with expanded multiplication.

Let's look at a problem using both traditional multiplication and expanded multiplication.

Example 1

Find the product of 325 and 64 using traditional multiplication and expanded multiplication.

Traditional Multiplication

Steps

1. Write vertically.

2. Multiply the ones digit on the bottom by the digits on the top.

3. Write a zero as a place holder, and multiply the tens digit on the bottom by the digits on the top.

4. Add the products.

$$
\begin{array}{r}
{\scriptstyle 1\ 3} \\
{\scriptstyle 1\ 2} \\
325 \\
\times\ \ 64 \\
\hline
1{,}300 \\
+\ 19{,}500 \\
\hline
20{,}800
\end{array}
$$

Expanded Multiplication

Steps

1. Write vertically in expanded form.

2. Multiply the number in the ones column on the bottom by each of the values on top. Write each value individually and stack them vertically.

3. Multiply the number in the tens column on the bottom by each of the values on top. Write each value individually and stack them below the first three products.

4. Add the six products.

$$
\begin{array}{r|r|r}
300 & 20 & 5 \\
\times & 60 & 4 \\
\hline
 & & 20 \\
 & & 80 \\
 & & 1{,}200 \\
 & & 300 \\
 & & 1{,}200 \\
+ & & 18{,}000 \\
\hline
 & & 20{,}800
\end{array}
$$

In Example 1, we found the same product using traditional multiplication and expanded multiplication. The steps are similar, but expanded multiplication requires many more steps. In expanded multiplication, we have to find and add six products. With traditional multiplication, we have to find and add two products.

Let's think about both methods and compare them:

Traditional Multiplication

- Has fewer steps
- Does not clearly show place value
- Is more efficient

Expanded Multiplication

- Has more steps
- Clearly shows place value
- Fewer mistakes likely to be made

POWER CONCEPT

Traditional multiplication is more efficient than expanded multiplication, especially when we multiply multidigit numbers. Expanded multiplication helps us keep track of the place value.

 Apply Skills
Turn to *Interactive Text*, page 115.

mBook Reinforce Understanding
Use the *mBook Study Guide* to review lesson concepts.

Why is measurement necessary in graphic design?

Many of the problems we have seen are about the music industry. Now we will learn about graphic design. The graphic design industry combines text and pictures to create many things. Over the next few lessons, we will learn how to use measurement to make our own designs.

Graphic designers create images that catch your attention and make it easy to locate information, such as:

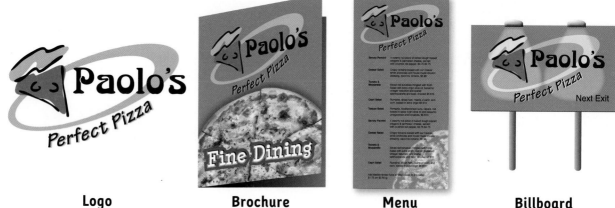

| Logo | Brochure | Menu | Billboard |

Graphic designers are also important because they design Web sites and the advertisements that go on those sites.

When a graphic designer creates an advertisement, he or she has to make sure all the elements of the design work well together. This includes making sure each element in the design is the correct size. All this creative work requires measurement.

 Problem-Solving Activity
Turn to *Interactive Text*, page 116.

 mBook Reinforce Understanding
Use the *mBook Study Guide* to review lesson concepts.

Lesson 8

Homework

Activity 1

Multiply to solve the set of basic and extended multiplication facts.

1.	7 × 8	80 × 70	700 × 8
2.	3 × 6	6 × 30	300 × 6
3.	9 × 7	70 × 90	900 × 7
4.	6 × 7	7 × 60	70 × 60

Activity 2

Factor out 10, 100, and 1,000 from each number.

Number	? × 10	? × 100	? × 1,000
2,000	200 × 10	20 × 100	2 × 1,000
5,000		50 × 100	
6,000	600 × 10		
8,000		80 × 100	
9,000			9 × 1,000
10,000			10 × 1,000

Activity 3

Use traditional multiplication to find the product.

1.	32	**2.**	451	**3.**	16	**4.**	98
	× 4		× 9		× 25		× 55

Activity 4 • Distributed Practice

Add or subtract.

1.	335	**2.**	425	**3.**	1,091
	+ 229		− 125		− 983

4.	558	**5.**	2,021	**6.**	7,462
	+ 670		− 608		+ 3,571

▶Estimating Products

Problem Solving:
▶Designing a Logo

▶Estimating Products

How do we estimate products?

We learned how to estimate sums and differences. In estimation, we round the numbers in a problem to numbers that are easier to work with. We learned how to use quarter rounding and how to round to the nearest 10; 100; and 1,000.

Look at the following problem. We round the numbers in the problem to estimate the product.

$$47$$
$$\times\ 39$$

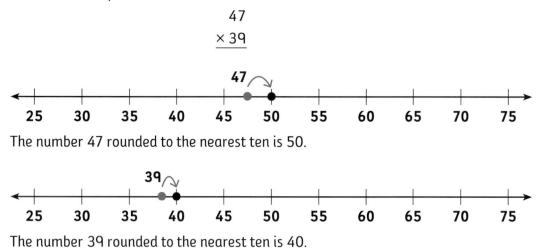

The number 47 rounded to the nearest ten is 50.

The number 39 rounded to the nearest ten is 40.

The product is about 2,000.

Remember that rounding can be very useful.

- Rounded numbers give us an answer that is close to the actual answer.
- Rounded numbers are easier to work with.
- We can solve problems mentally using rounded numbers.
- We do not always need an exact answer to solve a problem.

Let's practice rounding and estimation in multiplication.

Because we know the estimation techniques for addition and subtraction, it is easy to estimate in multiplication. Let's look at another example that shows how to estimate a product.

> To estimate a product, round the factors to create an extended fact that can be solved mentally.

Example 1

Estimate the product of 49 and 3.

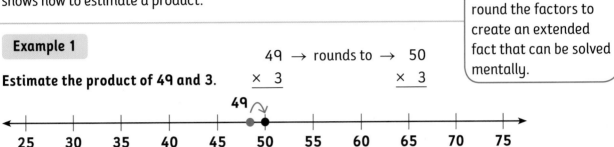

$$49 \to \text{rounds to} \to 50$$
$$\underline{\times \quad 3} \qquad \qquad \underline{\times \quad 3}$$

The factor 49 rounded to the nearest ten is 50. This creates the extended fact 50 × 3 = 150, which we can solve mentally. There is no need to round both numbers.

A good estimate of 49 × 3 is 150.

Let's see how a three-digit number being multiplied by a one-digit number is estimated.

Example 2

Estimate the product of 386 and 6.

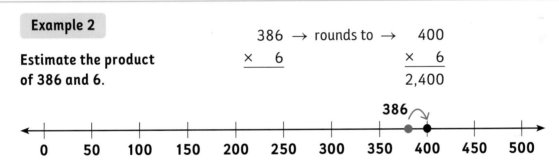

$$386 \to \text{rounds to} \to 400$$
$$\underline{\times \quad 6} \qquad \qquad \underline{\times \quad 6}$$
$$\qquad \qquad \qquad \qquad 2{,}400$$

The factor 386 rounded to the nearest hundred is 400. The other factor, 6, does not need to be rounded. These numbers create the extended fact 400 × 6 = 2,400, which can be solved mentally.

A good estimate of 386 × 6 is 2,400.

Using a calculator, we find that the exact product of 386 × 6 is 2,316. This is close to our estimated product of 2,400, so the answer is reasonable.

POWER CONCEPT

We can check an estimate if we compute it by hand or on a calculator. This helps us determine if the estimate is reasonable or if we have made an error.

In both examples above, we only rounded one factor. Because the bottom number is only one digit, we do not need to round it. Examples 1 and 2 show you that for numbers with more than one digit, we round each factor to the nearest ten or hundred.

How do we use estimation to solve word problems that require multiplication?

We can also use estimation to solve multiplication word problems that do not require an exact answer.

Example 1

Solve the word problem using estimation.

Problem:

The students in Ms. Randall's physics class are building bridges with plastic straws. The class is divided into 5 groups, and each group needs 85 straws. Ms. Randall has a box of 500 straws. Does she have enough straws for all of the groups?

Begin by asking the following questions:

- What is the problem asking for?
- What is the important information?

Because the problem asks us to compare two values, we do not need to find the exact number of straws Ms. Randall needs. Instead, we can estimate the number of straws she needs and compare it to the number of straws she has.

$$
\begin{array}{ll}
\begin{array}{r} 85 \\ \times\ 5 \\ \hline \end{array} \quad \rightarrow \text{rounds to} \rightarrow &
\begin{array}{r} 90 \\ \times\ 5 \\ \hline 450 \end{array}
\end{array}
$$

Ms. Randall needs about 450 plastic straws. This number is less than 500, so Ms. Randall has enough straws for all of the groups.

Apply Skills
Turn to *Interactive Text*,
page 118.

mBook Reinforce Understanding
Use the *mBook Study Guide*
to review lesson concepts.

▶**Problem Solving: Designing a Logo**

How does a graphic designer use measurement?

A logo is an image that uses words and pictures to represent a company, brand, or product. Graphic designers are hired to create logos that are appealing and will catch people's attention.

When graphic designers create logos, they use measurement just like when they design advertisements. A sample logo that a graphic designer might create for a pizza place is shown below.

A designer needs to consider:

- size of text
- size of image
- size of logo

We know that designing jobs require creativity, but designers must be able to use mathematics to measure.

 Problem-Solving Activity
Turn to *Interactive Text*,
page 119.

mBook **Reinforce Understanding**
Use the *mBook Study Guide*
to review lesson concepts.

Activity 1

Multiply to solve the set of basic and extended multiplication facts.

1. 5×5
   5×50
   5×500

2. 8×9
   8×90
   8×900

3. 7×4
   7×40
   7×400

Activity 2

Use traditional multiplication to find the product.

1. $\begin{array}{r} 64 \\ \times\ 2 \\ \hline \end{array}$

2. $\begin{array}{r} 87 \\ \times\ 5 \\ \hline \end{array}$

3. $\begin{array}{r} 962 \\ \times\ 4 \\ \hline \end{array}$

4. $\begin{array}{r} 729 \\ \times\ 5 \\ \hline \end{array}$

Activity 3

Estimate the product.

Model

$\begin{array}{r} 29 \\ \times\ 3 \\ \hline \end{array}$ $\begin{array}{r} 30 \\ \times\ 3 \\ \hline 90 \end{array}$

1. $\begin{array}{r} 67 \\ \times\ 5 \\ \hline \end{array}$

2. $\begin{array}{r} 21 \\ \times\ 2 \\ \hline \end{array}$

3. $\begin{array}{r} 45 \\ \times\ 7 \\ \hline \end{array}$

4. $\begin{array}{r} 685 \\ \times\ 6 \\ \hline \end{array}$

5. $\begin{array}{r} 495 \\ \times\ 3 \\ \hline \end{array}$

6. $\begin{array}{r} 241 \\ \times\ 6 \\ \hline \end{array}$

Activity 4 • Distributed Practice

Add or subtract.

1. $\begin{array}{r} 505 \\ -\ 29 \\ \hline \end{array}$

2. $\begin{array}{r} 9,100 \\ -\ 897 \\ \hline \end{array}$

3. $\begin{array}{r} 5,109 \\ +\ 2,981 \\ \hline \end{array}$

4. $\begin{array}{r} 6,000 \\ -\ 1,000 \\ \hline \end{array}$

5. $\begin{array}{r} 7,872 \\ +\ 387 \\ \hline \end{array}$

6. $\begin{array}{r} 777 \\ +\ 432 \\ \hline \end{array}$

Lesson 10 ▶Common Errors in Multiplication

Monitoring Progress:
▶Quiz 2

▶Common Errors in Multiplication

What are some common errors in multiplication?

When we studied addition and subtraction, we found that the traditional method was more efficient than the expanded method, but we were more likely to make errors. The same is true with traditional and expanded multiplication.

Let's look at the multiplication problem below. Let's try to identify and correct a mistake.

Improve Your Skills

ERROR	CORRECT
$\overset{4}{471}$	$\overset{1}{\overset{4}{471}} \longleftarrow$
$\times\ \ 26$	$\times\ \ 26$
$2{,}826$	$2{,}826$
$+\,1\,2{,}420 \longleftarrow$	$+\,9{,}420 \longleftarrow$
$15{,}246$	$12{,}246$

The person who solved this problem regrouped incorrectly. The 4 was regrouped as part of the first step of the problem. It was added again in the second step of the problem. Instead of the 4, a 1 should have been regrouped in the second step of the problem.

Be sure to regroup in each step if needed.

The product should be 12,246.

When we multiply numbers and have to regroup, there are many opportunities for error. If we make an error, it can be difficult to find where it occurred.

Let's look at another example of a problem that contains an error.

Improve Your Skills

Kelly solved the following problem. What error did Kelly make?

ERROR	CORRECT
$\overset{1}{\underset{}{}}$	
$\overset{2\ 1}{342}$	$\overset{2\ 1}{342}$
× 45	× 45
1,710	1,710
+ 12,680	+ 13,680
14,390	15,390

> Remember to add the regrouped number when multiplying.

Kelly forgot to add the regrouped 1 when she multiplied 4 × 3, so she wrote 12 instead of 13. The problem is solved correctly above.

The product is 15,390.

Estimation is a good tool for helping us catch errors.

Improve Your Skills

Deshawn solved the following problem. Use estimation to check his answer.

$$\overset{6\ 7}{218}$$
$$\times\ 9$$
$$\overline{2,412}$$

$$218 \rightarrow \text{rounds to} \rightarrow 200$$
$$\times\ 9 \qquad\qquad\qquad \times\ 9$$
$$\qquad\qquad\qquad\qquad \overline{1,800}$$

To estimate the product 218 × 9, we round 218 to the nearest hundred to create an extended fact.

> Remember to regroup the digit with the larger place value.

The estimated product is not close to Deshawn's answer 2,412. He made an error. When he multiplied 1 × 9, he remembered to add the regrouped 7 to get 16, but then he regrouped the 6 by mistake. He should have written 6 in the product and regrouped the 1.

The product is 1,962.

 Apply Skills
Turn to *Interactive Text*, page 121.

 Monitoring Progress
Quiz 2

mBook **Reinforce Understanding**
Use the *mBook Study Guide* to review lesson concepts.

Activity 1

Solve the set of basic and extended multiplication facts.

1. 7×8
    7×80
    7×800

2. 6×9
    6×90
    6×900

3. 5×4
    5×40
    5×400

Activity 2

Find and fix the error made in the problem. Explain.

Model

$$\begin{array}{r} \overset{1}{5}3 \\ \times\ 7 \\ \hline 362 \end{array}$$
Correct:
$$\begin{array}{r} \overset{2}{5}3 \\ \times\ 7 \\ \hline 371 \end{array}$$

The product $3 \times 7 = 21$ was written incorrectly. The 2 was written in the product and the 1 was regrouped. The 1 should have been written in the product and the 2 regrouped.

1. $$\begin{array}{r} 49 \\ \times\ 5 \\ \hline 254 \end{array}$$

2. $$\begin{array}{r} 78 \\ \times\ 8 \\ \hline 564 \end{array}$$

3. $$\begin{array}{r} 56 \\ \times\ 7 \\ \hline 374 \end{array}$$

Activity 3

Estimate the product.

Model

$$\begin{array}{r} 57 \\ \times\ 4 \\ \hline \end{array} \quad \begin{array}{r} 60 \\ \times\ 4 \\ \hline 240 \end{array}$$

1. $$\begin{array}{r} 79 \\ \times\ 9 \\ \hline \end{array}$$

2. $$\begin{array}{r} 36 \\ \times\ 4 \\ \hline \end{array}$$

3. $$\begin{array}{r} 85 \\ \times\ 5 \\ \hline \end{array}$$

4. $$\begin{array}{r} 417 \\ \times\ 3 \\ \hline \end{array}$$

5. $$\begin{array}{r} 599 \\ \times\ 9 \\ \hline \end{array}$$

6. $$\begin{array}{r} 627 \\ \times\ 7 \\ \hline \end{array}$$

Activity 4 • Distributed Practice

Add or subtract.

1. $$\begin{array}{r} 879 \\ -\ 192 \\ \hline \end{array}$$

2. $$\begin{array}{r} 603 \\ -\ 592 \\ \hline \end{array}$$

3. $$\begin{array}{r} 4,012 \\ +\ 5,978 \\ \hline \end{array}$$

4. $$\begin{array}{r} 8,246 \\ +\ 2,864 \\ \hline \end{array}$$

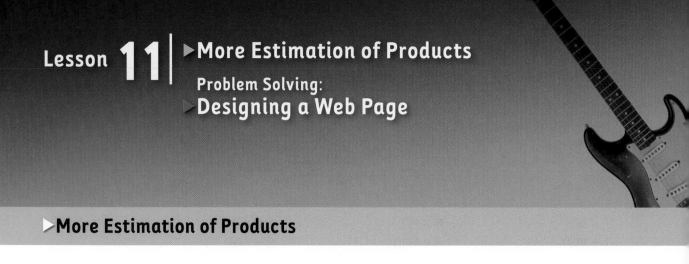

▸**More Estimation of Products**

How do we estimate the product of two multidigit numbers?

We know how to estimate the product of a one-digit number and a multidigit number. The multidigit number is rounded to the highest place value. The one-digit number does not need to be rounded. When multiplying two numbers that each have more than one digit, we round both of the numbers to their highest place value. Let's estimate the product of 398 and 82.

$$
\begin{array}{r}
398 \\
\times\ \ 82 \\
\hline
\end{array}
$$

First, we round the number 398. Hundreds is the highest place value in this number, so we round to the nearest hundred.

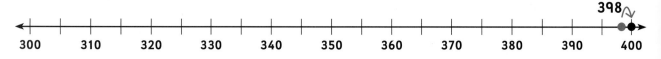

Next, we round the number 82. Tens is the highest place value in this number, so we round to the nearest ten.

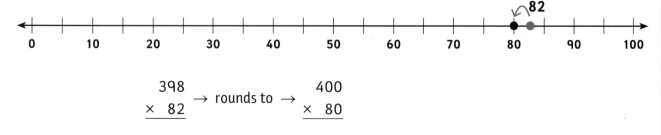

$$
\begin{array}{r}
398 \\
\times\ \ 82 \\
\hline
\end{array}
\ \rightarrow \text{ rounds to } \rightarrow\
\begin{array}{r}
400 \\
\times\ \ 80 \\
\hline
\end{array}
$$

Last, we multiply the rounded numbers. We can multiply $4 \times 8 = 32$ and add the zeros. There are two zeros in 400 and one zero in 80, which makes three zeros in all.

The product is about 32,000.

How does estimation help us check calculator answers?

Let's solve a problem using a calculator. We check that the answer is reasonable by quickly estimating. Comparing the calculator answer to the estimate will reveal any errors that we made inputting the problem.

Example 1

Use a calculator to find the product of 598 and 72. Estimate to check your answer.

STEP 1
Calculate.
Using a calculator, compute 598 × 72.

POWER CONCEPT

A good way to compute products of multidigit numbers is estimation and a calculator. Find the product using a calculator, then estimate the product to check that the calculator answer is reasonable.

STEP 2
Estimate.

The number 598 rounded to the nearest hundred is 600.

The number 72 rounded to the nearest ten is 70.

600 × 70 = 42,000

STEP 3
Compare.
The calculator answer, 43,056, and estimate, 42,000, are close.
So the calculator answer is reasonable.

The product is 43,056.

Even if we use traditional multiplication instead of a calculator, we can check our answer using estimation.

 Apply Skills
Turn to *Interactive Text*,
page 123.

 mBook Reinforce Understanding
Use the *mBook Study Guide*
to review lesson concepts.

▶**Problem Solving: Designing a Web Page**

How does a Web designer use measurement?

When designing a Web page, graphic designers create a layout of pictures and words to show how it will look. This task requires planning and good measurement skills.

The diagram below shows the layout of a Web page for The Hat Factory. This company wants to make its hats available to buyers online. Part of the layout is already complete. The designer will measure the space available to display hats. The space can be divided so that all of the hats can be seen on one page.

Customer Service
Special Features
More Shopping
Other Stores
Search

2 cm

|← - 2 cm - →|

Problem-Solving Activity
Turn to *Interactive Text*,
page 124.

mBook **Reinforce Understanding**
Use the *mBook Study Guide*
to review lesson concepts.

Activity 1

Use expanded multiplication to find the product.

Model

78	70	8
× 4 → ×		4
		32
+		280
		312

1. 65
    × 7

2. 25
    × 8

3. 44
    × 4

Activity 2

Use traditional multiplication to find the product.

1. 278
    ×   4

2. 329
    ×   4

3. 67
    × 87

Activity 3

Use a calculator and estimation to find the product.

Model

3 7 × 3 2 =

1,184

37	40
× 32	× 30
	1,200

The calculator answer and estimate are close, so the answer is reasonable.

1. 37
    × 19

2. 49
    × 81

3. 76
    × 91

Activity 4 • Distributed Practice

Add or subtract.

1. 4,096
    − 1,908

2. 3,875
    − 1,496

3. 700
    + 900

4. 9,025
    +   775

► **Problem Solving: Measuring to Design a Company Logo**

Vocabulary
specifications

How do we use measurement tools to create a logo?

Remember that a logo is a display that uses words and pictures to represent a company, brand, or product. Companies use logos to help consumers recognize their brand of product. This is an important sales technique.

It is important that a graphic designer use exact measurements to create a design that is just right. The exact measurements of a design are called **specifications**. When a company hires a graphic designer to make a logo for them, they will give the designer specifications for the logo.

Record Jams asked their designer to create a logo that uses a circle and a square for a background. They provided these specifications:

- The square should have sides that measure 5 centimeters. The square should be orange.
- The circle should fit inside the square, large enough to touch all four sides. The circle should be blue.

To create the background, we use a ruler to make a square with sides that are 5 centimeters long. Then we draw a circle inside the square.

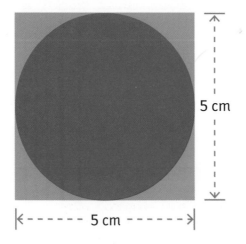

5 cm

5 cm

Record Jams wants their logo to have a guitar that runs diagonally across the background. We need to measure to find out how large the guitar should be.

We know that the guitar needs to be about 7 centimeters long.

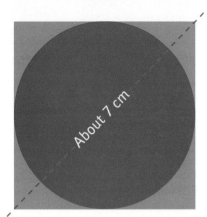

About 7 cm

Finally, we add the name. Record Jams would like their company name centered in the square. We need to divide the square into three equal parts so that the name is in the right place.

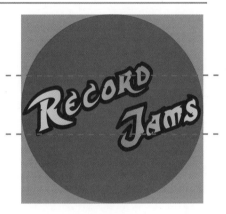

The name and guitar are placed into the logo. The logo is then delivered to Record Jams to be sure it meets their specifications.

Once the design is created, it is important to double-check that all of the specifications were met. Using measurement tools to check the specifications of the design is just as important as creating the design accurately.

 Problem-Solving Activity
Turn to *Interactive Text*, page 126.

 mBook Reinforce Understanding
Use the *mBook Study Guide* to review lesson concepts.

Activity 1

Multiply to solve the set of basic and extended facts.

1. 6×8
   6×80
   60×80

2. 7×9
   7×90
   70×90

3. 5×4
   5×40
   50×40

Activity 2

Use a metric ruler to measure the logo in the specified unit.

1. About how many millimeters wide is the Bolt Cola logo?

2. About how many centimeters wide is the Apollo Sports logo?

3. About how many millimeters wide is the Hometown Cinemas logo?

Activity 3

Use traditional multiplication to find the product.

1. $\begin{array}{r} 729 \\ \times \quad 8 \\ \hline \end{array}$

2. $\begin{array}{r} 64 \\ \times 72 \\ \hline \end{array}$

3. $\begin{array}{r} 81 \\ \times 35 \\ \hline \end{array}$

Activity 4 • Distributed Practice

Add or subtract.

1. $\begin{array}{r} 4{,}067 \\ + \quad 943 \\ \hline \end{array}$

2. $\begin{array}{r} 5{,}000 \\ - 1{,}999 \\ \hline \end{array}$

3. $\begin{array}{r} 4{,}123 \\ - 4{,}099 \\ \hline \end{array}$

▶More Estimation With Multidigit Factors
Problem Solving:
▶Scale Drawings

▶**More Estimation With Multidigit Factors**

How do we estimate the product of numbers in the thousands?

We know how to solve multiplication problems using estimation and a calculator. We have done this with one-, two-, and three-digit numbers. The same steps are used for greater numbers.

First, let's round the following four-digit numbers to their greatest place value.

5,689   6,001   4,500   9,758

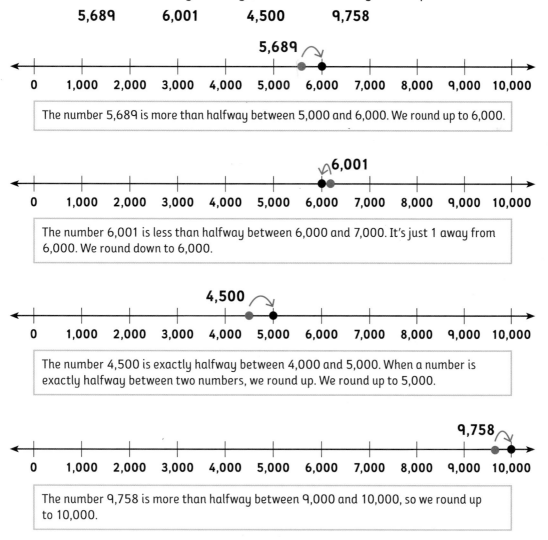

The number 5,689 is more than halfway between 5,000 and 6,000. We round up to 6,000.

The number 6,001 is less than halfway between 6,000 and 7,000. It's just 1 away from 6,000. We round down to 6,000.

The number 4,500 is exactly halfway between 4,000 and 5,000. When a number is exactly halfway between two numbers, we round up. We round up to 5,000.

The number 9,758 is more than halfway between 9,000 and 10,000, so we round up to 10,000.

To estimate the product of numbers in the thousands, we round the numbers before multiplying.

How does estimation help us check calculator answers for large numbers?

One method for solving a multiplication problem with factors that have more than two or three digits is to use a calculator then check the answer by estimating.

Example 1

Use a calculator to find the product of 5,689 and 6,001. Estimate to check your answer.

First, using a calculator, we find that $5,689 \times 6,001 = 34,139,689$.

Then we check the answer with estimation.

$$
\begin{array}{r}
5,689 \\
\times\ 6,001 \\
\hline
34,139,689
\end{array}
\quad \rightarrow \text{ rounds to } \rightarrow \quad
\begin{array}{r}
6,000 \\
\times\ 6,000 \\
\hline
36,000,000
\end{array}
$$

The calculator answer is close to the estimate, so it is reasonable.

When we estimate, the problem becomes an extended fact. We find the product using mental math, then we add all the zeros from both numbers to the end of the product.

Example 2

Use a calculator to find the product of 4,500 and 9,758. Estimate to check your answer.

First, using a calculator, we find that $4,500 \times 9,758 = 43,911,000$.

Then we check the answer with estimation.

$$
\begin{array}{r}
4,500 \\
\times\ 9,758 \\
\hline
43,911,000
\end{array}
\quad \rightarrow \text{ rounds to } \rightarrow \quad
\begin{array}{r}
5,000 \\
\times\ 10,000 \\
\hline
50,000,000
\end{array}
$$

The calculator answer is close to the estimate, so it is reasonable.

 Apply Skills
Turn to *Interactive Text*, page 128.

 mBook Reinforce Understanding
Use the *mBook Study Guide* to review lesson concepts.

▶**Problem Solving: Scale Drawings**

Vocabulary
scale drawing

What is a scale drawing?

Graphic designers are not the only professionals who use measurement. A large part of the job of an architect is to create designs. An architect is someone who designs buildings.

An architect uses blueprints. In a blueprint, everything in the design is a different size than it will be in real life but is the right size compared to everything else in the drawing. Because everything is drawn to a certain scale in a blueprint, they are called **scale drawings** . A scale drawing is a drawing that shows objects in a size related to their actual size.

Architects create scale drawings with precise measurements. Here is an example.

```
←- - - -14 feet - - - -→←6 feet→←- - 10 feet - →

  ┌─────────────┬────────┬──────────────┐  ↑
  │             │   B    │              │  |
  │   Bedroom   │   a    │   Bedroom    │  10 feet
  │             │   t    │              │  |
  │             │   h    │              │  ↓
  │             │   r    │              │
  ├────────┬────┤   o    ├──────────────┤  ↑
  │        │ E  │   o    │              │  |
  │        │ n  │   m    │              │  10 feet
  │ Kitchen│ t  ├────────┤  Living Room │  |
  │        │ r  │        │              │  ↓
  │        │ a  │        │              │
  │        │ n  │        │              │
  │        │ c  │        │              │
  │        │ e  │        │              │
  └────────┴────┴────────┴──────────────┘
←- - 12 feet - - -→←4 ft→←- - - -14 feet - - - -→
```

key
☐ = 2 feet

 Problem-Solving Activity
Turn to *Interactive Text*,
page 129.

 mBook Reinforce Understanding
Use the *mBook Study Guide*
to review lesson concepts.

Lesson 13

Homework

Activity 1

Solve the extended multiplication facts.

1. 7×900
2. 700×9
3. 70×90

4. 6×300
5. 60×30
6. 60×300

7. 5×700
8. 50×70
9. 50×700

Activity 2

Estimate the product.

Model $2{,}971 \times 312 \rightarrow 3{,}000 \times 300 = 900{,}000$

1. $4{,}912 \times 689$

2. $2{,}115 \times 437$

3. $2{,}973 \times 7{,}992$

Activity 3

Use traditional multiplication to find the product.

1. $\begin{array}{r} 68 \\ \times\, 56 \\ \hline \end{array}$

2. $\begin{array}{r} 309 \\ \times\ \ 42 \\ \hline \end{array}$

3. $\begin{array}{r} 611 \\ \times\ \ 23 \\ \hline \end{array}$

Activity 4 • Distributed Practice

Add or subtract.

1. $\begin{array}{r} 467 \\ +\,896 \\ \hline \end{array}$

2. $\begin{array}{r} 536 \\ +\,564 \\ \hline \end{array}$

3. $\begin{array}{r} 400 \\ +\,500 \\ \hline \end{array}$

4. $\begin{array}{r} 5{,}000 \\ -\,3{,}997 \\ \hline \end{array}$

5. $\begin{array}{r} 5{,}005 \\ -\,4{,}099 \\ \hline \end{array}$

6. $\begin{array}{r} 7{,}500 \\ -\ \ 500 \\ \hline \end{array}$

▶**Problem Solving: Comparing Amounts in a Bar Graph**

How do we describe changes in data using subtraction?

We worked with addition, subtraction, and multiplication in previous lessons. Now that we know how to use these algorithms, let's use them to work with data.

Companies often use bar graphs to compare the amounts of money they make from one month to another. These monthly comparisons help them make business decisions. Sometimes sales only increase or decrease by a small amount.

The following bar graph shows monthly sales for a company.

Use the graph to find how many more digital cameras were sold in April than in January.

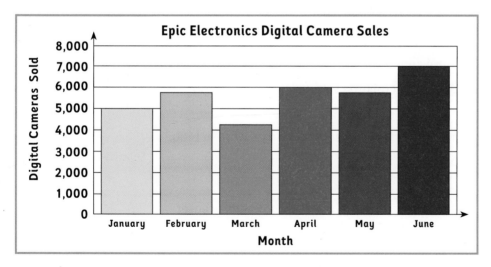

The graph shows:

- April—6,000 digital cameras sold
- January—5,000 digital cameras sold

We subtract to find the difference.

6,000 − 5,000 = 1,000

There were 1,000 more digital cameras sold in April than in January.

How do we describe changes in data using multiplication?

When we want to compare large changes in data, we use multiplication. This kind of comparison allows us to describe a sales figure as so many times greater than another. Let's look at an example.

Example 1

Use the graph to find how many times greater digital camera sales were in May than in February.

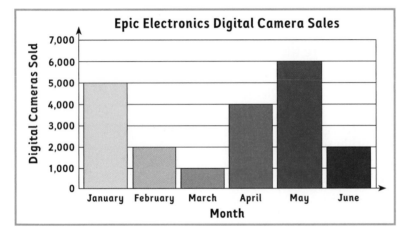

The graph shows:

- May—6,000 digital cameras sold
- February—2,000 digital cameras sold

We multiply to find how many times greater the sales were in May.

$2{,}000 \times \underline{\hspace{1cm}} = 6{,}000$

We know $2{,}000 \times 3 = 6{,}000$, so the answer is three times greater.

Digital camera sales in May were three times greater than digital camera sales in February.

When comparing amounts of change on a bar graph, make sure the amounts start at zero when determining how many times greater one amount is than another.

How do we describe changes in data using estimation?

Example 1

Use the graph to find about how many times greater digital camera sales were in January than in March.

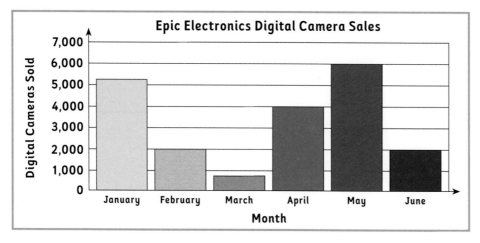

Epic Electronics Digital Camera Sales

Notice that the question asks for an estimate because it uses the word *about*.

The graph shows:

- January—*about* 5,000 digital cameras sold
- March—*about* 1,000 digital cameras sold

To answer the question "How many times greater were sales in January than in March?" we multiply 1,000 × _____ = 5,000.

We know 1,000 × 5 = 5,000, so the answer is about five times greater.

Digital camera sales in January were *about* five times greater than digital camera sales in March.

 Problem-Solving Activity
Turn to *Interactive Text*, page 131.

mBook **Reinforce Understanding**
Use the *mBook Study Guide* to review lesson concepts.

Activity 1

Multiply to solve the basic or extended fact.

1. 4×7
2. 40×7
3. 9×6
4. 9×600
5. 7×9
6. 70×90

Activity 2

Estimate the product.

1.
$$\begin{array}{r} 765 \\ \times\ \ 27 \\ \hline \end{array}$$

2.
$$\begin{array}{r} 901 \\ \times 316 \\ \hline \end{array}$$

3.
$$\begin{array}{r} 742 \\ \times 195 \\ \hline \end{array}$$

Activity 3

Use multiplication to compare information in the graph.

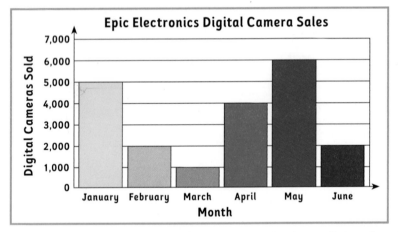

1. How many times greater were digital camera sales in April than in February?

2. How many times greater were digital camera sales in May than in March?

Activity 4 • Distributed Practice

Add or subtract.

1.
$$\begin{array}{r} 569 \\ +\ 241 \\ \hline \end{array}$$

2.
$$\begin{array}{r} 600 \\ +\ 400 \\ \hline \end{array}$$

3.
$$\begin{array}{r} 1,009 \\ -\ \ \ 999 \\ \hline \end{array}$$

4.
$$\begin{array}{r} 5,010 \\ -\ 1,099 \\ \hline \end{array}$$

Lesson 15 | Unit Review
▶Multiplication

Problem Solving:
▶Introduction to Measurement

▶Multiplication

What are different ways to think about multiplication?

Throughout this unit we focused on multiplication. We discussed different ways to think about multiplication and learned the importance of place value. Here are some examples of how place value is important.

Review 1

How does place value help us multiply?

Basic and Extended Multiplication Facts

$5 \times 7 = 35$ $50 \times 7 = 350$ $5 \times 70 = 350$ $500 \times 7 = 3,500$

If we think about these extended facts in relation to the basic fact 5×7, we can quickly compute the answers in our heads.

Expanded Multiplication

```
   452          400 | 50 |   2
 ×   6         ×     |    |   6
                         12
                        300
              +       2,400
                      2,712
```

Expanded multiplication helps us see place value. It also reduces the chance for error because we do not have to remember to add regrouped numbers written above the problem.

When using expanded multiplication, make sure that the products added together are lined up with the digits in the correct place value.

Now let's compare traditional multiplication and expanded multiplication. In the example below, two multidigit numbers are multiplied. We see that the traditional method is more efficient.

Review 2

How do expanded and traditional multiplication compare?

Multiplication Problem	Expanded Multiplication	Traditional Multiplication
$\begin{array}{r} 49 \\ \times\ 75 \\ \hline \end{array}$	$\begin{array}{rr} 40 & 9 \\ \times\ 70 & 5 \\ \hline & 45 \\ & 200 \\ & 630 \\ +\quad 2{,}800 \\ \hline & 3{,}675 \end{array}$	$\begin{array}{r} {}^{6}_{4} \\ 49 \\ \times\ 75 \\ \hline 245 \\ +\ 3{,}430 \\ \hline 3{,}675 \end{array}$

Another important concept we focused on is factoring out powers of 10. Any multidigit number that ends in a zero can be rewritten by factoring out one or more powers of 10. Let's look at how 4,000 is rewritten with 10, 100, and 1,000 as a factor.

Review 3

How do we factor out powers of 10 from numbers?

$4{,}000 = 400 \times 10 \qquad 4{,}000 = 40 \times 100 \qquad 4{,}000 = 4 \times 1{,}000$

Remember that we can check if we have factored correctly by counting the zeros on each side of the equal sign. The same number of zeros should appear on each side.

We use estimation to find how reasonable an answer is that we found using paper and pencil or a calculator. We also use estimation to solve some word problems instead of finding an exact answer. Let's look at some examples.

Review 4

How do we use estimation when we multiply?

Estimation

$$48 \longrightarrow \text{rounds to} \longrightarrow 50$$

$$\begin{array}{r} 48 \\ \times\ 7 \\ \hline \end{array} \qquad\qquad \begin{array}{r} 50 \\ \times\ 7 \\ \hline \end{array}$$

Exact answer: 336   Estimate: 350

We use extended facts to compute estimates. When we compare the exact answer with our estimate, the numbers are close, so the answer is reasonable.

Estimate Word Problems

Problem:

Rachel has $200. Does she have enough money to buy 3 sweaters that cost $38 each?

Sometimes estimation alone can be used to solve word problems. Let's try solving this problem using estimation.

$$38 \ \to \text{rounds to} \to\ 40$$

$$\begin{array}{r} 38 \\ \times\ 3 \\ \hline 114 \end{array} \qquad\qquad \begin{array}{r} 40 \\ \times\ 3 \\ \hline 120 \end{array}$$

The estimate of $120 is considerably less than $200, so Rachel has enough money.

 Apply Skills
Turn to *Interactive Text*, page 133.

 Reinforce Understanding
Use the *mBook Study Guide* to review lesson concepts.

▶**Problem Solving: Introduction to Measurement**

How do we think about measurement?

In this unit we learned how to use common objects, or *referents*, and units of measurement to estimate and measure lengths and distances. For example, we can:

- Estimate the length of a line segment using the tip of our little finger.
- Estimate a long distance using a city block as a unit of measurement.
- Measure the length of a small object using a ruler.

One of the key ideas for any measurement system is that large units of measurement can be converted into smaller units of measurement, making it possible to accurately measure all kinds of lengths and distances. The metric system uses powers of 10 to convert numbers between units of measurement.

Review 1

How do we use referents to estimate?

Use a referent to estimate the height of a two-story house.

We can think of the height of a two-story house with respect to the length of a baseball bat. Think about the height of 4 baseball bats stacked on top of each other. It would be about equal to the distance from the floor to the ceiling of one story. This means the height of a two-story house would be about equal to 8 baseball bats.

The height of a two-story house is about 8 meters.

Problem-Solving Activity
Turn to *Interactive Text*, page 135.

mBook Reinforce Understanding
Use the *mBook Study Guide* to review lesson concepts.

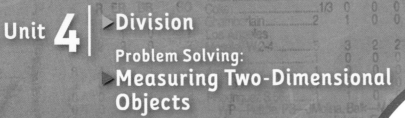

Take your height and divide by eight. That's the height of your head!

Everybody's body is different, but in general ...

1 head width

8 head lengths

1 head length

Measure the width of your shoulders. Divide by 3 to get your head width.

Measure the length of your elbow to your fingertip. Divide by 2 to get your head height.

Measure the length from your wrist to the fingertip of your middle finger. It should equal about 1 head length.

Measure the length from your feet to the top of your hips. Divide by 4 to get your head height.

OBJECTIVES

Building Number Concepts

- Understand the relationship between multiplication and division

- Solve problems using basic and extended division facts

- Represent whole-number division problems in a variety of ways

Problem Solving

- Use square units to measure the area of shapes

- Apply the concept of area to real-world situations

- Solve word problems using whole-number division

Problem Solving:
Measuring Square Units

▸**Multiplication and Division Fact Families**

What are multiplication and division fact families?

We studied fact families with addition and subtraction. We learned that addition and subtraction are opposites. Now we will look at the relationship between multiplication and division.

Let's review some basic division facts. We will use two different symbols for division. The following problems are the same, but they use a different division symbol.

$$56 \div 7 = 8 \quad \text{or} \quad 7\overline{)56}^{\,8}$$

Here are some basic division facts.

$72 \div 9 = 8$	$42 \div 7 = 6$	$35 \div 5 = 7$	$81 \div 9 = 9$

Multiplication and division are closely related. We write fact families for multiplication and division in much the same way as we write fact families in addition and subtraction. Let's see how the numbers 8, 9, and 72 make a fact family.

Fact Family for 8, 9, and 72	
$72 \div 9 = 8$ $72 \div 8 = 9$	$9 \times 8 = 72$ $8 \times 9 = 72$

The relationship between multiplication and division is similar to the relationship between addition and subtraction. Multiplication and division are opposite operations. Four facts are created by arranging three numbers in a different order. This knowledge of fact families helps us with division problems.

Let's look at some multiplication and division fact families.

Example 1

Write the fact family for 3, 7, and 21.

Multiplication Facts	Division Facts
$3 \times 7 = 21$	$21 \div 3 = 7$
$7 \times 3 = 21$	$21 \div 7 = 3$

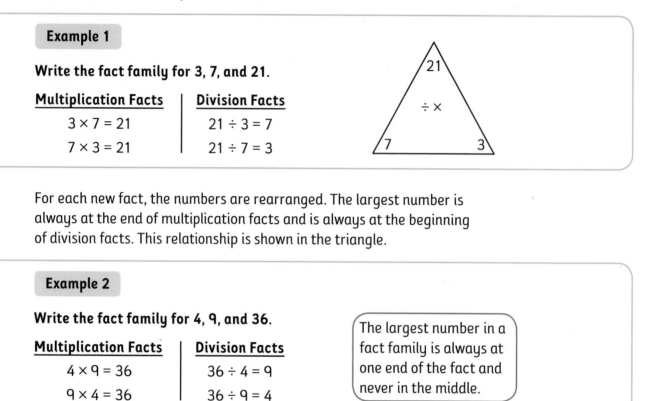

For each new fact, the numbers are rearranged. The largest number is always at the end of multiplication facts and is always at the beginning of division facts. This relationship is shown in the triangle.

Example 2

Write the fact family for 4, 9, and 36.

Multiplication Facts	Division Facts
$4 \times 9 = 36$	$36 \div 4 = 9$
$9 \times 4 = 36$	$36 \div 9 = 4$

The largest number in a fact family is always at one end of the fact and never in the middle.

Understanding the relationship between multiplication and division helps us to solve problems in the same fact family.

Example 3

Complete the division fact using a related multiplication fact.

$48 \div 6 = \underline{\hspace{1cm}}$

Think: $6 \times \underline{\hspace{1cm}} = 48$ so $48 \div 6 = \underline{\hspace{1cm}}$.
These are in the same fact family.

Since we know $6 \times 8 = 48$, we also know $48 \div 6 = 8$.
The complete division fact is $48 \div 6 = 8$.

 Apply Skills
Turn to *Interactive Text*, page 138.

 mBook **Reinforce Understanding**
Use the *mBook Study Guide* to review lesson concepts.

▶**Problem Solving: Measuring Square Units**

Vocabulary
square unit base height

How do we measure using square units?

In Unit 3, we learned about the measurement of length. We created and used a ruler. We call this one-dimensional measurement. In this unit, we will use square units . These units allow us to measure objects in two dimensions— base and height . The base is the bottom, or horizontal part of a shape. The height is the vertical part of a shape.

Let's measure the shape using square units.

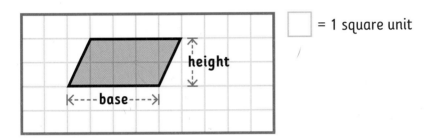

☐ = 1 square unit

Steps for using square units:

STEP 1

Start by counting the number of complete square units inside the object. There are six.

There are still some partial units left over.

STEP 2

Estimate by looking at the partial square units inside the shape. If we look closely, we see that on the left side of the object, there is a large part of a square unit and a small part of a square unit. Added together, they will be about the same size as one whole square unit. Do the same thing on the other side of the object.

> Don't forget to include the partial square units when finding the size of a shape on a grid.

STEP 3

Add all of the square units together.

6 + 1 + 1 = 8

The size of the shape is about 8 square units.

 Problem-Solving Activity
Turn to *Interactive Text*, page 139.

 mBook Reinforce Understanding
Use the *mBook Study Guide* to review lesson concepts.

Activity 1

Solve the basic division facts.

1. $49 \div 7$ 2. $27 \div 3$ 3. $24 \div 3$
4. $56 \div 7$ 5. $27 \div 9$ 6. $54 \div 6$
7. $36 \div 6$ 8. $42 \div 6$ 9. $18 \div 2$

Activity 2

Write fact families for each set of numbers.

Model	7, 8, and 56	$7 \times 8 = 56$	$56 \div 7 = 8$
		$8 \times 7 = 56$	$56 \div 8 = 7$

1. 9, 5, and 45   2. 8, 3, and 24   3. 6, 7, and 42

Activity 3

Write fact families for each set of numbers. Replace the "X" with the correct number.

Model	2, 5, and X	$5 \times 2 = 10$	$10 \div 2 = 5$
		$2 \times 5 = 10$	$10 \div 5 = 2$

1. X, 6, 24   2. 3, X, 21   3. 5, 4, X

Activity 4 • Distributed Practice

Solve.

1. 7,012   2. 672   3. 837
   $-$ 976 $-$ 465 $+$ 925

4. 67   5. 888   6. 26
   $\times$ 3 $\times$ 4 $\times$ 31

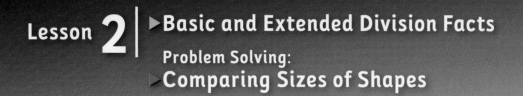

▶Basic and Extended Division Facts

Vocabulary
dividend divisor quotient

What are basic and extended division facts?

In Lesson 1, we learned that division is the opposite of multiplication. Because multiplication and division facts are in the same fact families, extended division facts are simply the opposite of extended multiplication facts. Let's look at some extended division facts.

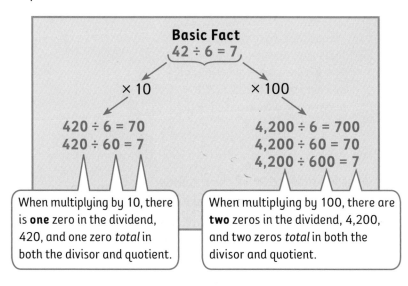

Basic Fact
42 ÷ 6 = 7

× 10

× 100

420 ÷ 6 = 70
420 ÷ 60 = 7

4,200 ÷ 6 = 700
4,200 ÷ 60 = 70
4,200 ÷ 600 = 7

When multiplying by 10, there is **one** zero in the dividend, 420, and one zero *total* in both the divisor and quotient.

When multiplying by 100, there are **two** zeros in the dividend, 4,200, and two zeros *total* in both the divisor and quotient.

In the next example, we will see that the amount of zeros in the **dividend** is equal to the amount of the zeros in the **divisor** and **quotient** combined. The divisor is the number dividing the dividend into parts, or the second number in the number sentence. The quotient is the answer to a division problem.

Example 1

Write three extended facts for the basic fact 63 ÷ 7 = 9.

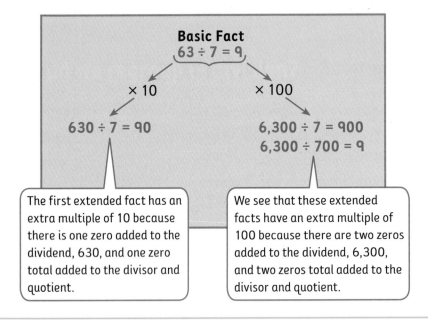

The first extended fact has an extra multiple of 10 because there is one zero added to the dividend, 630, and one zero total added to the divisor and quotient.

We see that these extended facts have an extra multiple of 100 because there are two zeros added to the dividend, 6,300, and two zeros total added to the divisor and quotient.

Knowing a basic division fact makes it simple to solve the extended fact. As in addition, subtraction, and multiplication, the extended division fact is a multiple of 10 of the basic fact. Let's see how to complete extended division facts using our knowledge of zeros.

Example 2

Use the basic facts to complete the extended division facts.

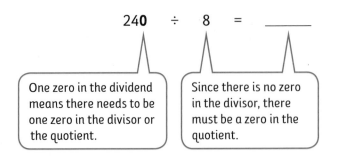

$$240 \div 8 = \underline{\hspace{1cm}}$$

One zero in the dividend means there needs to be one zero in the divisor or the quotient.

Since there is no zero in the divisor, there must be a zero in the quotient.

The complete extended division fact is 240 ÷ 8 = 30.

It is important to understand the pattern of zeros in division facts. Some basic division facts already contain a zero. In these cases, we need to balance the number of zeros added to the basic fact. Let's look at some examples of extended facts where there is already a zero in the basic division fact.

Example 3

Use the basic facts to complete the extended division facts.

Basic Fact: 30 ÷ 5 = 6

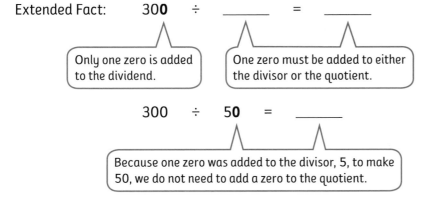

Extended Fact: 300   ÷ _____ = _____

Only one zero is added to the dividend.

One zero must be added to either the divisor or the quotient.

300   ÷   50   = _____

Because one zero was added to the divisor, 5, to make 50, we do not need to add a zero to the quotient.

The complete extended division fact is 300 ÷ 50 = 6.

Why do we have different symbols?

We have mostly been using the ÷ symbol for basic and extended facts. For more complicated division problems, it is sometimes easier to use another symbol. Let's look at some basic and extended facts using another division symbol.

$$27 \div 3 = 9 \text{ can also be written as: } 3\overline{)27}$$

$$270 \div 3 = 90 \text{ can also be written as: } 3\overline{)270}$$

$$270 \div 30 = 9 \text{ can also be written as: } 30\overline{)270}$$

Notice that when the division problems are written with the)‾ symbol, the number of zeros in the dividend is still equal to the number of zeros in the divisor and quotient combined.

 Apply Skills
Turn to *Interactive Text*, page 141.

mBook **Reinforce Understanding**
Use the *mBook Study Guide* to review lesson concepts.

Which shape is larger?

Sometimes, when we look at two shapes, we cannot tell which shape is larger. We have to explore it further. Look at the three different shapes. One shape is the tallest and another shape is the widest, but the third shape has the largest area.

Shape A is the widest shape.

Shape B is the tallest shape.
The area of both Shape A and Shape B is 10 square units.

Shape C is not the tallest or the widest, but it has the largest area. Its area is 15 square units. Looks can be deceiving.

We need to use our knowledge of square units to compare the sizes of many different shapes.

 Problem-Solving Activity
Turn to *Interactive Text*, page 142.

 mBook Reinforce Understanding
Use the *mBook Study Guide*
to review lesson concepts.

Homework

Activity 1

Solve the basic multiplication and division facts.

1. 8×9 2. 8×8 3. $24 \div 8$

4. 6×5 5. 3×4 6. $49 \div 7$

7. 3×9 8. $21 \div 3$ 9. $36 \div 9$

Activity 2

Solve the extended multiplication and division facts.

1. 7×90 2. 7×900 3. $640 \div 8$

4. $6,400 \div 80$ 5. $240 \div 4$ 6. $2,400 \div 400$

Activity 3

Write fact families for each set of numbers. Replace the "X" with the correct number.

Model X, 8, and 56 $7 \times 8 = 56$ $56 \div 7 = 8$
$8 \times 7 = 56$ $56 \div 8 = 7$

1. 9, X, and 45   2. 8, 3, and X   3. X, 7, and 42

Activity 4

Write three extended facts for each basic fact.

Model $24 \div 6 = 4$ $240 \div 6 = 40$
$240 \div 60 = 4$
$2,400 \div 60 = 40$

1. $20 \div 4$ 2. $18 \div 3$ 3. $81 \div 9$

Activity 5 • Distributed Practice

Solve.

1. $\begin{array}{r} 492 \\ + 267 \\ \hline \end{array}$ 2. $\begin{array}{r} 978 \\ - 109 \\ \hline \end{array}$ 3. $\begin{array}{r} 67 \\ \times \ 4 \\ \hline \end{array}$ 4. $\begin{array}{r} 983 \\ \times \ 7 \\ \hline \end{array}$

Lesson 3 ▶ Basic Division Facts on a Number Line

Problem Solving:
Same Shape, Different Size

| 1 | 2 | 3 | 4 | 5 | 6 | 7 | 8 | 9 |

▶ Basic Division Facts on a Number Line

Vocabulary
whole unit

What is division?

There are many situations when we use division naturally. For example, a class might need to break into equal groups for a class project. They would divide the total number of students in the class by the number of groups. This would show how many students to put in each group. When we divide, we are finding an equal amount of parts in a larger number.

Let's suppose the class that was doing group projects had to share a set of 54 colored pencils. If each of the groups got 9 colored pencils, we can figure out how many groups there were in the class. Look at the colored pencils to see how many groups there were.

Group 1   Group 2   Group 3   Group 4   Group 5   Group 6

There were 6 equal batches of 9 pencils. This means that there were 6 equal groups of 9. Since there were 6 groups of pencils, there were 6 groups of students.

We can also show how many groups of 9 there are in 54 on a number line.

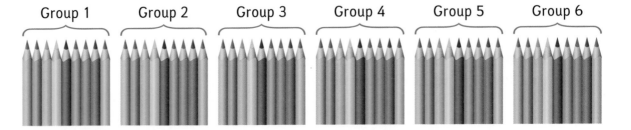

There are 6 groups of 9 in 54.

Division is about breaking up a larger number, or **whole**, into smaller, equal groups, or **units**.

208   Unit 4 • Lesson 3

One way to divide a whole is by breaking it into equal parts called units. The number in a unit is like the size of each of the parts. In the example, we will break 27 into units of 9.

Example 1

Show how 27 is broken into units of 9 on a number line.

In this problem, we want to know how many 9s are in 27 or how many units of 9 are in the whole. Let's take a look at this problem on a number line. To do this, we need the unit of 9 (drawn as a rectangle).

We need the number line.

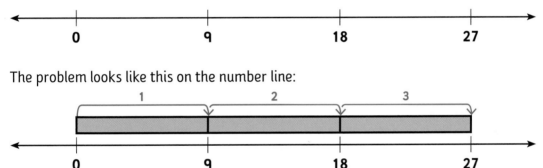

The problem looks like this on the number line:

We are able to place three of the rectangles, which are units of 9, on the number line. We see that 27 can be divided into three equal groups of 9.

There are 3 units of 9 in the number 27.

This is the same thing as saying $27 \div 9 = 3$.

Understanding what the whole is and how many units we want to divide it into is the key to division. This unit breaks up the whole into equal parts.

 Apply Skills
Turn to *Interactive Text*, page 144.

 mBook **Reinforce Understanding**
Use the *mBook Study Guide* to review lesson concepts.

▶**Problem Solving: Same Shape, Different Size**

Vocabulary

area

What is area?

Shapes can be the same size, but have different measurements. The total size inside a boundary is called the **area**.

Look at the diamonds. The area of the shape on the right is larger than the area of the shape on the left. Even though they are the same shape, their measurements are different.

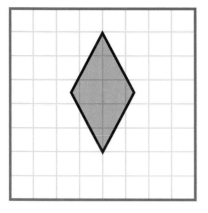

Approximate Number
of Square Units: 8

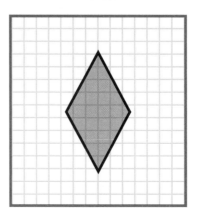

Approximate Number
of Square Units: 26

When we measure the area of shapes, it is important to pay attention to the size of the unit. The same shape can have different areas depending on the size of unit we use.

> When comparing the size of two shapes, we have to use the same size unit.

 Problem-Solving Activity
Turn to *Interactive Text*, page 145.

 mBook Reinforce Understanding
Use the *mBook Study Guide* to review lesson concepts.

Homework

Activity 1

Solve the basic multiplication and division facts.

1. 7×8
2. 9×4
3. 4×3
4. $56 \div 7$
5. $15 \div 3$
6. $36 \div 9$

Activity 2

Write the problem that the number line represents.

Model

3 times

0   3   6   9

What's the problem? $9 \div 3 = 3$

What's the problem?

1.

4 times

0   6   12   18   24   30   36   42   48   54

2.

6 times

0   7   14   21   28   35   42   49   56   63

3.

5 times

0   9   18   27   36   45   54   63   72   81

Activity 3

Find the area of the following two shapes.

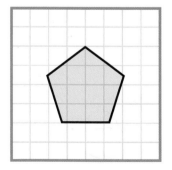 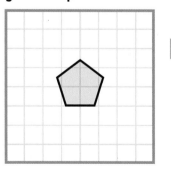

☐ = 1 square unit

Lesson 4 ▶ Extended Division Facts on a Number Line

Problem Solving:
Finding Area by Counting Squares

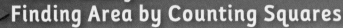

▶**Extended Division Facts on a Number Line**

What do extended facts look like on a number line?

We know what basic division facts look like on a number line. Let's show the fact **15 ÷ 5 = 3**.

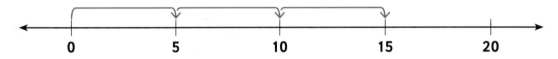

Since we want to divide 15 by 5, we count by fives from zero until we get to 15. That gives us 3 arrows. So, we have broken 15 into 3 units of 5. This means 15 ÷ 5 = 3.

We show extended division facts on a number line in the same way. Let's look at the extended fact **150 ÷ 5 = 30**.

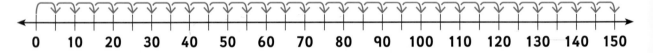

Since we want to divide 150 by 5, we count by fives from zero until 150. That gives us 30 arrows. So, we have broken 150 into 30 units of 5. This means 150 ÷ 5 = 30.

The equation 150 ÷ 5 = 30 is an extended division fact of the basic fact. Another extended fact from the same family is **150 ÷ 50 = 3**. Let's look at it on a number line.

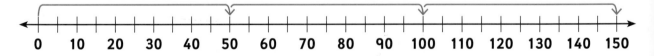

Since we want to divide 150 by 50, we count by 50s from zero until 150. That gives us 3 arrows. This means 150 ÷ 50 = 3.

Let's look at more extended division facts on a number line.

Showing extended division facts on a number line is very similar to showing basic division facts on a number line. Let's look at an example.

Example 1

Show the extended division fact 300 ÷ 50 on a number line.
In this problem, 50 is the unit and 300 is the whole. We want to know how many units of 50 there are in 300.

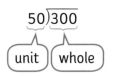

We need to represent a unit of 50 in the problem. The rectangle below extends from 0 to 50 on the number line. It represents the unit of 50.

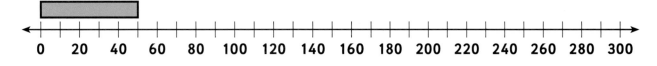

We need to see how many rectangles, or units of 50, we can fit into the number 300.

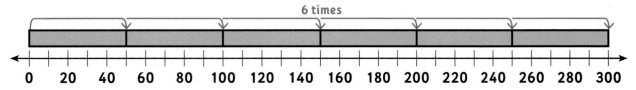

Notice how we placed six of the rectangles side by side above the number line.

We are counting by 50s: 50, 100, 150, 200, 250, 300.

It takes six of the units of 50 to make up the whole 300.

Solving a problem like this on a number line takes a long time. Instead, we need to solve problems like this using mental math.

Let's try to solve Example 2 using mental math. Because it is an extended fact, we can think about the basic fact and use our knowledge of zeros to solve it quickly.

Example 2

Solve the extended division fact $6\overline{)360}$ using mental math.

Notice that if we take off the zero in 360, it makes 36.

Think about the basic fact $36 \div 6 = 6$.

There is one zero added to the 36, so there should be one zero added to the quotient of $360 \div 6$.

$360 \div 6 = 60$

Using mental math is much more efficient than using number lines to solve extended division facts.

Improve Your Skills

Solve the problem $4,800 \div 60$ using mental math.
Lee's answer is 800.

800 is incorrect. Why?

> Remember that the dividend should have the same amount of zeros as the divisor and quotient combined.

Lee's Error
- Think about the basic fact $48 \div 6 = 8$.
- Look at the number of zeros in $4,800 \div 60$.
- There need to be two zeros total in the divisor and the quotient.
- Lee added two zeros to the quotient and made 800.

Add one zero to the quotient to make 80.

Correct
- Think about the basic fact $48 \div 6 = 8$.
- Look at the number of zeros in $4,800 \div 60$.
- There need to be two zeros total in the divisor and the quotient.
- Since there is already one zero in 60, only one zero needs to be added to the 8 in the quotient.

 Apply Skills
Turn to *Interactive Text*, page 147.

mBook Reinforce Understanding
Use the *mBook Study Guide* to review lesson concepts.

▶**Problem Solving: Finding Area by Counting Squares**

What are some strategies for finding area by counting squares in a bigger design?

We have been counting squares to find the area of simple designs. Now we will look at a more complex design and find its area. We use different strategies to find the area quickly.

Example 1

Find the area of the design.

We find the area of the design without counting all of the squares. Begin by looking carefully at the design. There are parts of the design that look the same. There are four squares and four rectangles.

The squares are the same. We only need to count one of them. There are four square units in each square. Multiply by 4. $4 \times 4 = 16$. There are 16 square units.

The rectangles are the same. We only need to count one of them. There are two square units in each rectangle. $4 \times 2 = 8$. There are 8 squares in the rectangles.

Add them together. $16 + 8 = 24$.

The area is 24 square units.

 Problem-Solving Activity
Turn to *Interactive Text*, page 148.

mBook **Reinforce Understanding**
Use the *mBook Study Guide* to review lesson concepts.

Homework

Activity 1

Solve the basic and extended multiplication and division facts.

1. 3×8
2. 5×4
3. $240 \div 3$
4. $45 \div 5$
5. 5×40
6. $24 \div 8$

Activity 2

Show the extended division facts on a number line.

Model

$$2\overline{)40} \quad 20$$

1. $8\overline{)160}$
2. $8\overline{)40}$
3. $40\overline{)320}$

Activity 3

Solve the extended division facts using mental math.

1. $6\overline{)120}$
2. $5\overline{)200}$
3. $4\overline{)160}$
4. $8\overline{)560}$

Activity 4

Find the area of the rectangle without counting every single square.

Activity 5 • Distributed Practice

Solve.

1. $\begin{array}{r} 456 \\ +\,987 \\ \hline \end{array}$

2. $\begin{array}{r} 1,500 \\ -\,800 \\ \hline \end{array}$

3. $\begin{array}{r} 46 \\ \times\ 3 \\ \hline \end{array}$

4. $\begin{array}{r} 389 \\ \times\ 4 \\ \hline \end{array}$

▶**Remainders**

Vocabulary
remainder decimal number

What is the remainder in division?

We know how to do division of basic and extended facts. Some division problems are not basic facts because they do not divide evenly. Look at the problem 13 ÷ 2. Let's use two different methods to solve this problem.

13 ÷ 2

Using a Number Line

The number line shows six units of 2. That makes 12. Adding another unit of 2 makes 14, but that is too much. The part left over on the number line is the remainder.

Using Long Division

In long division, we write the problem: $2\overline{)13}$.

The first step in long division is to figure out how many units of 2 there are in 13. From our number line, we know there are six complete units of 2. This means that 2 divides into 13 six times.

$$\begin{array}{r} 6 \\ 2\overline{)13} \end{array}$$

Since 6 × 2 = 12, we find what is left of the dividend by subtracting. After we subtract, we see that 2 cannot divide into 1. So, there is 1 leftover.

$$\begin{array}{r} 6 \\ 2\overline{)13} \\ -12 \\ \hline 1 \end{array}$$

The number that is left after dividing is called the **remainder** .

$$\begin{array}{r} 6 \text{ R1} \\ 2\overline{)13} \\ -12 \\ \hline 1 \end{array}$$

The quotient is 6 with a remainder of 1.

Let's look at other examples where the divisor does not divide the dividend evenly.

Example 1

Solve 21 ÷ 4 using long division.

The number 4 divides into 21 five times, or 4 × 5 = 20.
After we subtract 21 − 20, we see that 4 cannot divide into 1.
The remainder is 1.

In long division, the remainder is written as "R1."

$$\begin{array}{r} 5 \ \ \text{R1} \\ 4\overline{)21} \\ -20 \\ \hline 1 \end{array}$$

We found the remainder using long division, but we can also find a remainder using a calculator. Let's look at an example.

Example 2

Solve 21 ÷ 4 using a calculator.

We enter the following keystrokes into our calculator:

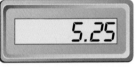

The calculator displays the following: | 5.25

When we divide on a calculator and there is a remainder, the quotient is a **decimal number**. Our quotient shows that there are five equal units of 4 in 21 and a remainder. In this case, the remainder is .25. When doing division on a calculator, the numbers to the right of the decimal point are always the remainder.

Decimal Number

5.25

Remainder

We see that the remainder looks different in long division than on a calculator. There are 5 equal units of 4 in the number 21, but there is "1" left over. What does the "1" mean?

In Example 3, we will look at a problem on a number line to get a better idea about what the remainder really means.

Example 3

Show 21 ÷ 4 on a number line.

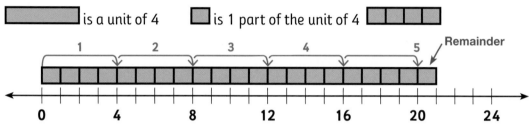

We see that the remainder of "1," or "R1," is 1 part of the unit of 4. See how the "1" is a smaller part of the 4.

One part of the unit of 4 is the fraction $\frac{1}{4}$. Our calculator also came up with a decimal remainder of 0.25. In future lessons, we will discuss how $\frac{1}{4}$ and 0.25 are equal.

Improve Your Skills

Celia solved this division problem using long division, but when she saw that the remainder was larger than the divisor, she knew she made a mistake.

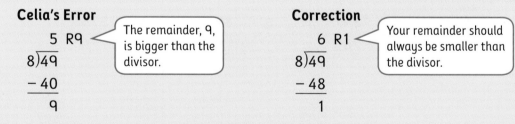

Celia had a remainder of 9. This means she should take one more 8 out of 49. The corrected problem shows one more 8, or six total 8s, taken out of 49 and the remainder is 1.

 Apply Skills
Turn to *Interactive Text*, page 150.

 Monitoring Progress
Quiz 1

 mBook Reinforce Understanding
Use the *mBook Study Guide* to review lesson concepts.

Activity 1
Solve the basic and extended division facts.

1. $9\overline{)270}$ 2. $3\overline{)15}$ 3. $3\overline{)150}$ 4. $7\overline{)21}$

5. $8\overline{)320}$ 6. $6\overline{)360}$ 7. $9\overline{)36}$ 8. $7\overline{)49}$

Activity 2
Solve using a calculator. Write the problem and the answer on your paper.
Put a box around the whole number, and a circle around the remainder.

Model

$\boxed{9}.\circled{5}$
$2\overline{)19}$

We enter 19 ÷ 2 = into our calculator. The calculator will display
9.5. We write down the problem and then draw a box around the
9 and a circle around the remainder, 5.

1. $4\overline{)31}$ 2. $6\overline{)21}$ 3. $2\overline{)17}$ 4. $8\overline{)36}$

Activity 3
Solve using long division. Show the remainder as "R and the number."

Model

    4 R3
$4\overline{)19}$
-16
    3

1. $4\overline{)31}$ 2. $6\overline{)21}$ 3. $2\overline{)17}$ 4. $8\overline{)36}$

Activity 4 • Distributed Practice
Solve.

1. $\begin{array}{r} 1{,}500 \\ -\ \ 900 \\ \hline \end{array}$
2. $\begin{array}{r} 397 \\ +285 \\ \hline \end{array}$
3. $\begin{array}{r} 80 \\ \times\ 6 \\ \hline \end{array}$
4. $\begin{array}{r} 375 \\ \times\ \ 9 \\ \hline \end{array}$

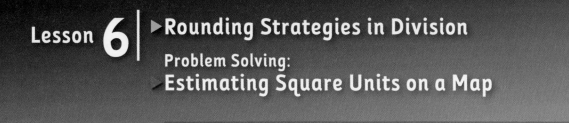

Lesson 6 ▶ Rounding Strategies in Division

Problem Solving:
Estimating Square Units on a Map

▶ **Rounding Strategies in Division**

How do we round when we have a remainder?

In Lesson 5, we learned that sometimes we get a quotient with a remainder. When we use a calculator, a quotient with a remainder is a decimal number. We often round decimal numbers to the nearest whole number.

Round 8.75.

The decimal number 8.75 is between the whole numbers 8 and 9. It is closer to 9. So the decimal number 8.75 rounded to the nearest whole number is 9.

Round 3.1.

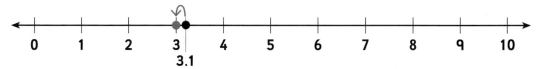

The decimal number 3.1 is between the whole numbers 3 and 4. It is closer to 3. So the decimal number 3.1 rounded to the nearest whole number is 3.

Round 0.8.

The decimal number 0.8 is between the whole numbers 0 and 1. It is closer to 1. So the decimal number 0.8 rounded to the nearest whole number is 1.

When we round decimal numbers to whole numbers, we look at the number to the right of the decimal point. We do this to decide if we should round up or down. If the number is 0 to 4, we round down. If the number is 5 to 9, we round up.

In real-life situations, it is common to use a calculator to solve difficult problems. When we use a calculator, the answers sometimes have a remainder. When the problem tells us to, we round the answer to the nearest whole number. Let's look at an example.

Example 1

Solve 17 ÷ 4. Round the quotient to the nearest whole number.

For the problem $4\overline{)17}$, we enter the following keystrokes into our calculator:

The calculator displays the following:

The answer is 4.25.

> The number to the right of the decimal point is less than 5, so we round down.

We round the quotient down to 4.

We look at the number to the right of the decimal point to decide if we should round up or down. If the number is 0 to 4, we round down. If the number is 5 to 9, we round up.

Example 2

Solve 19 ÷ 4. Round the quotient to the nearest whole number.

For the problem $4\overline{)19}$, we enter the following keystrokes into our calculator:

The calculator displays the following:

The answer is 4.75.

> The number to the right of the decimal point is more than 5, so we round up.

We round the quotient up to 5.

From these examples, we see that sometimes we round up and sometimes we round down. The rules for rounding are very simple. Let's look at Example 3 and decide if we should round up or down.

Example 3

Solve 13 ÷ 2. Round the quotient to the nearest whole number.

For the problem $2\overline{)13}$, we enter the following keystrokes into our calculator:

The calculator displays the following:

The number 6.5 is between 6 and 7.

> The number to the right of the decimal point is 5, so we round up.

We round the quotient to 7.

The rules for rounding decimal numbers are similar to the rules for rounding that we already learned.

 Apply Skills
Turn to *Interactive Text*,
page 152.

 mBook **Reinforce Understanding**
Use the *mBook Study Guide*
to review lesson concepts.

▶Problem Solving: Estimating Square Units on a Map

How do we use square units on a map?

We learned to find the area of shapes using square units. We can also use square units to measure on a map. The square units represent the actual size of an area. Let's look at the example to see how we use areas of maps to estimate.

Example 1

Estimate the population using a map.

Here is a map of the city of San Francisco, California. San Francisco is one of the most crowded cities in the United States. There are 32,471 housing units in the city. The land area of San Francisco is 46.7 square miles. Each full square contains about 26,400 people.

Count the squares to figure out the approximate population of San Francisco.

Marina
Fisherman's Wharf
Chinatown
Seacliff
Golden Gate Park
Fillmore
SAN FRANCISCO
Mission
St. Francis Wood
Bayview
Lake Merced
Hunters Point
Ocean View
Visitacion Park

P P P P P
P P F F F P
P F F F F P P
SAN FRANCISCO
P F F F F F P
P F F F F F P
P F F F F P P

= 26,400 People

There are 21 full (F) squares. When we combine the partial squares (P) to make full squares, there is a total of about 10 more squares.

San Francisco takes up about 30 squares on the map.

The number of people per square, 26,400, multiplied by 30 square units equals about 792,000 people in San Francisco.

Using square units on a map is helpful when we need to find distances and amounts on a map.

Problem-Solving Activity
Turn to *Interactive Text*, page 153.

mBook Reinforce Understanding
Use the ***mBook Study Guide*** to review lesson concepts.

Homework

Activity 1

Solve the basic and extended division facts.

1. $9\overline{)72}$
2. $7\overline{)490}$
3. $8\overline{)640}$
4. $6\overline{)48}$
5. $7\overline{)49}$
6. $5\overline{)350}$

Activity 2

Round the quotient to the nearest whole number.

Model

$29 \div 4$ $\boxed{7.25}$ Rounded Answer: 7

1. $1\ 7 \div 2 = \boxed{8.5}$

2. $3\ 3 \div 6 = \boxed{5.5}$

3. $7\ 6 \div 8 = \boxed{9.5}$

4. $2\ 9 \div 4 = \boxed{7.25}$

5. $2\ 3 \div 4 = \boxed{5.75}$

6. $5\ 8 \div 8 = \boxed{7.25}$

7. $1\ 3 \div 4 = \boxed{3.25}$

8. $6\ 4 \div 7 = \boxed{9.142857}$

Activity 3 • Distributed Practice

Solve.

1. 465×9

2. 37×48

3. $500 + 700$

4. $1,307 - 298$

Problem Solving:
Using Division in Everyday Life

▶**Near Fact Division**

Vocabulary
near fact

How do we use near facts to solve division problems?

We know that 27 ÷ 3 is a basic division fact. The number 3 divides evenly into 27 nine times.

Not all division problems will divide evenly into whole numbers.

$$27 ÷ 3 = 9$$

Let's look at some division facts that are slightly different than 27 ÷ 3 = 9. Try to find a pattern.

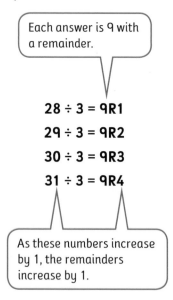

Each answer is 9 with a remainder.

$$28 ÷ 3 = 9R1$$
$$29 ÷ 3 = 9R2$$
$$30 ÷ 3 = 9R3$$
$$31 ÷ 3 = 9R4$$

As these numbers increase by 1, the remainders increase by 1.

These facts are close to the basic fact of 27 ÷ 3 = 9. Facts that are close to a basic fact are called **near facts** . The quotient of the near facts is 9 with a remainder.

Let's look at how to use near facts to estimate the quotient of division problems with remainders.

In Lesson 6, we rounded quotients to the nearest whole number. Another way to avoid remainders is to round the dividend to a whole number so that the near fact becomes a basic fact. The new dividend will be a number that can be divided evenly by the divisor.

Example 1

Estimate 31 ÷ 4 by rounding it to a near fact.

$$4\overline{)31}$$

The problem 31 ÷ 4 is not a basic fact because 4 does not divide evenly into 31. The answer will have a remainder.

We learned a couple of ways to solve a problem like this:

- Using a calculator, our answer is 7.75.

- Using long division, our answer is 7 R3.

$$
\begin{array}{r}
7 \text{ R3} \\
4\overline{)31} \\
-28 \\
\hline
3
\end{array}
$$

Another way to solve the problem is to find the nearest basic fact. Think about the facts with 4 as the divisor. Find the fact below that has a dividend close to the number 31:

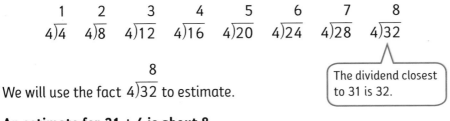

$$
\begin{array}{cccccccc}
1 & 2 & 3 & 4 & 5 & 6 & 7 & 8 \\
4\overline{)4} & 4\overline{)8} & 4\overline{)12} & 4\overline{)16} & 4\overline{)20} & 4\overline{)24} & 4\overline{)28} & 4\overline{)32}
\end{array}
$$

The dividend closest to 31 is 32.

We will use the fact $4\overline{)32}^{\,8}$ to estimate.

An estimate for 31 ÷ 4 is about 8.

Finding the near fact helps us solve the exact problem more quickly. This strategy helps when we want to estimate the answer to a problem. We also use this strategy to find the answer to larger division problems.

Let's look at another example of a near fact.

Example 2

Estimate 103 ÷ 10 by rounding it to a near fact.

$$10\overline{)103}$$

We know that 10 divides evenly into all numbers that end in zero.

Using powers of 10 to find a new fact makes it easy.

$$10\overline{)100} = 10$$

The near fact is 100 ÷ 10.

An estimate for 103 ÷ 10 is about 10.

We can use a calculator or long division to find the exact answer. If it is close to the near fact, we know that we worked the problem correctly.

Example 3

Compare rounding to using near facts.

$$10\overline{)103}$$

Enter the following keystrokes into the calculator:

The calculator displays the following:

Round the answer down to 10.

Our near fact gave us a very good estimate: 100 ÷ 10 = 10.

> **POWER CONCEPT**
>
> A very good way to get an estimate for a problem is to find a near fact.

Using near facts helps us estimate quotients and make sure our answers are reasonable.

 Apply Skills
Turn to *Interactive Text*, page 155.

 mBook Reinforce Understanding
Use the *mBook Study Guide* to review lesson concepts.

1   2   3   4   5   6   7   8

▶**Problem Solving: Using Division in Everyday Life**

How is division used in real-world contexts?

Any time we have a situation where a larger amount needs to be divided evenly into smaller parts, we use division.

Look at Example 1 to see how division is used in setting up for a concert.

Example 1

Solve the problem using division.

Problem:

We have 50 chairs for the concert tonight. If you want to make 5 rows, how many chairs will be in each row?

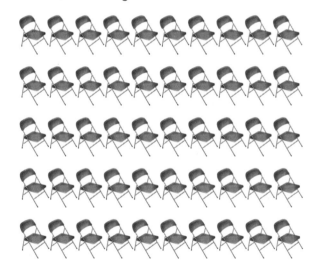

We know that 50 ÷ 5 = 10.

There will be 10 chairs in each row.

When we divide, the important thing to remember is to break the whole into equal amounts.

 Problem-Solving Activity
Turn to *Interactive Text*, page 156.

 mBook Reinforce Understanding
Use the *mBook Study Guide* to review lesson concepts.

Lesson 7

Homework

Activity 1

Solve the basic and extended multiplication and division facts.

1. 3×7
2. 6×8
3. $63 \div 9$
4. 3×70
5. 6×80
6. $630 \div 9$

Activity 2

Estimate by rounding to a near fact.

1. $9\overline{)75}$
2. $7\overline{)51}$
3. $3\overline{)23}$
4. $4\overline{)38}$
5. $8\overline{)66}$
6. $6\overline{)34}$
7. $4\overline{)17}$
8. $5\overline{)47}$

Activity 3

Use the table and division to solve the following problems.

The Scatter Plots' May Concert Tour in California		
Date	Concert	Profit
May 1	San Diego	$2,400
May 2	Anaheim	$1,440
May 8	Long Beach	$4,260
May 9	Riverside	$3,700
May 15	Los Angeles	$6,020
May 16	Santa Barbara	$4,040

1. The Scatter Plots had to pay their monthly bills by May 5. How much money had each of the four band members made by May 5?

2. The Scatter Plots made the most in Los Angeles. How much did each of the band members make?

3. Tickets at the Santa Barbara concert cost $40. If the band made $4,040, how many people attended?

Activity 4 • Distributed Practice

Solve.

1. $3,097 - 2,908$
2. 67×5
3. $4,769 + 5,231$
4. 891×4

▶**Place Value and Long Division**

Vocabulary
expanded division

What is the role of place value in long division?

We already know how to use place-value coins. Let's look at how place-value coins work in **expanded division** .

$$2\overline{)846}$$

First, we divide 2 into 8. We know the 8 in this problem stands for 800. We distribute eight hundreds coins equally in the two rows.

We have four hundreds coins in each row. They are divided into two rows equally.

Now we divide 2 into 4. We know the 4 stands for 40 in this problem. We distribute four tens coins equally in the two rows.

We have two tens coins in each row. They are divided into two rows equally.

Finally, we divide 2 into 6. We know the 6 stands for 6 ones in this problem. We distribute six ones coins equally in the two rows.

We have three ones coins in each row. They are divided equally in the two rows.

We add the coins in the top row by place value. The coins show us that 846 can be divided into 2 equal groups of 423.

Because the groups are equal, we know the quotient is 423.

Division is about one number breaking another number into equal groups.

A place-value table and expanded division help us see the role of place value in division.

Example 1

Solve 3)693 using expanded division.

$$3\overline{)693}$$

The place-value table is divided into the place values—hundreds, tens, and ones. It will show us how the divisor 3 will break up 693 into three groups.

We know the 6 in the dividend is worth 600. When we divide 3 into 600, we find there are three equal groups of 2 hundreds.

3)693

Hundreds	Tens	Ones
100 100		
100 100		
100 100		

Next, we divide 3 into the tens column. We know that the 9 is 90, so we find there are three equal groups of 3 tens in 90.

3)693

Hundreds	Tens	Ones
100 100	10 10 10	
100 100	10 10 10	
100 100	10 10 10	

Finally, we divide the ones column, or the 3. The 3 ones are split between the 3 rows.

3)693

Hundreds	Tens	Ones	
100 100	10 10 10	1	} 231
100 100	10 10 10	1	} 231
100 100	10 10 10	1	} 231

The place-value table shows us that 693 can be divided into 3 equal groups of 231.

The quotient is 231.

We know that division and multiplication are opposites. In Example 1, we learned that 693 ÷ 3 = 231. This means that there are three units of 231 in 693. Example 2 and Example 3 show more examples of how this works.

Example 2

Show 3⟌939 using expanded division. Find the related multiplication fact.

Hundreds	Tens	Ones	
100 100 100	10	1 1 1	} 313
100 100 100	10	1 1 1	} 313
100 100 100	10	1 1 1	} 313

313
3⟌939

939 ÷ 3 = 313

The expanded division shows us that there are three units of 313 in 939.

This means that 3 × 313 = 939.

Let's look at another example to see how numbers are divided.

Example 3

Show 4⟌848 using expanded division. Find the related multiplication fact.

Hundreds	Tens	Ones	
100 100	10	1 1	} 212
100 100	10	1 1	} 212
100 100	10	1 1	} 212
100 100	10	1 1	} 212

212
4⟌848

848 ÷ 4 = 212

The expanded division shows us that there are four units of 212 in 848.

This means that 4 × 212 = 848.

Long division seems like a series of confusing steps. When we think about long division in terms of place value, it makes sense. The divisor breaks the number into equal parts by place value.

%÷ **Apply Skills**
<× Turn to *Interactive Text*,
page 158.

 mBook **Reinforce Understanding**
Use the *mBook Study Guide*
to review lesson concepts.

▶**Problem Solving: Division in Word Problems**

How do we interpret remainders in word problems?

A remainder means different things in each word problem. We need to read the problem carefully to come up with the correct solution.

In Example 1, we don't need to worry about the remainder to come up with a solution.

Example 1

Interpret the remainder in the answer.

Problem:

You have 10 cookies and 4 friends. You want to divide the cookies evenly between your friends and yourself. How many cookies should everyone get?

Answer: 10 ÷ 4 = 2.5

Each person gets 2 whole cookies and there are 2 cookies left.

Break the extra 2 cookies in half to make four halves.

Each person gets 2 and $\frac{1}{2}$ cookies.

In Example 2, we round the remainder to come up with a solution.

Example 2

Interpret the remainder in the answer.

Problem:

There are 185 people going on a bus tour of a historic village. Each bus holds 30 people. How many buses will you need?

Answer: 185 ÷ 30 = 6.16666667

Normally, we would round the number down because the number to the right of the decimal is less than 1. But if we get 6 buses, there will be people left behind.

In this problem, the number to the right of the decimal point represents people, so we need to round up.

We need 7 buses for the bus tour.

 Problem-Solving Activity
Turn to *Interactive Text*, page 159.

 mBook **Reinforce Understanding**
Use the *mBook Study Guide* to review lesson concepts.

Homework

Activity 1

Estimate by rounding to a near fact.

1. $74 \div 9$ 2. $36 \div 5$ 3. $48 \div 7$

4. $66 \div 9$ 5. $43 \div 6$

Activity 2

Write fact families for the following. Replace the "X" with the correct number.

1. 7, 8, and X   2. X, 2, and 18   3. 4, X, and 24

4. 4, 3, and X   5. X, 6, and 30   6. X, 9, and 36

Activity 3

Solve using expanded division.

1. $2\overline{)468}$ 2. $3\overline{)369}$ 3. $2\overline{)882}$

4. $3\overline{)663}$ 5. $3\overline{)999}$ 6. $2\overline{)864}$

Activity 4

Solve the word problem. Think carefully about what to do with the remainder. Show your work.

Javier's English class had a party to celebrate the end of the year. One of his classmates brought in 21 candy bars. There are 10 students in the class. If all of the students get more than one candy bar, will there be enough for the teacher to have one as well?

Activity 5 • Distributed Practice

Solve.

1.
$$348 \times 8$$

2.
$$1,067 - 982$$

3.
$$1,600 - 800$$

4.
$$92 \times 13$$

▶**Regrouping in Division**

Problem Solving:
▶**Making Division Word Problems**

▶**Regrouping in Division**

How do we regroup in division?

Let's look at place-value coins and the division problem $3\overline{)159}$.

We will divide a place-value table into three rows to help us see how 3 divides into 159.

$$3\overline{)159}$$

First we need to divide 3 into 1. The 1 stands for 100. We cannot divide 1 hundreds coin among 3 hundreds rows. We have to move to the next column over.

$3\overline{)1\,59}$

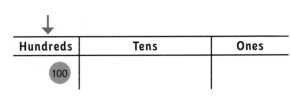

If we combine the 1 in the hundreds column and the 5 in the tens column, the value is 100 + 50 = 150. We can divide 150 by 3, but we must exchange the 1 hundreds coin for 10 tens coins: 10 tens coins + 5 tens coins = 15 tens coins. Fifteen tens coins divided into three rows gives us 5 tens coins in each tens row.

$$\begin{array}{r} 5 \\ 3\overline{)1\,5\,9} \\ -1\,5\,0 \end{array}$$

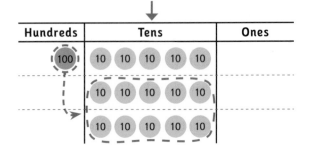

Next, we divide 3 into 9. The 9 stands for 9 ones. We can distribute 9 ones coins equally in the 3 ones rows.

$$\begin{array}{r} 53 \\ 3\overline{)1\,5\,9} \\ -1\,5\,0 \\ \hline 9 \\ -9 \\ \hline 0 \end{array}$$

Finally, we add the coins in each row by place value: 50 + 3 = 53.

The quotient is 53.

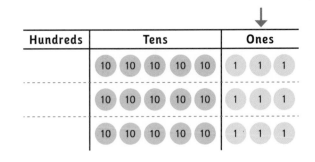

Using place-value coins helps us to understand the value of the digits we are dividing into. Place-value coins also help us to see that we are breaking the dividend into equal parts. Sometimes the divisor will not divide into the digits in a division problem. In this case, the digits have to be regrouped. We can use expanded division to regroup the digits.

Example 1

Solve $4\overline{)128}$ using expanded division.

$$4\overline{)128}$$

The number 4 cannot divide the digit 1, or 100, into equal hundreds. Instead, we will divide into the first two digits.

The 12 is 100 + 20 or 120 because 100 = 10 tens and 20 = 2 tens. We know that 120 ÷ 4 = 30 is an extended fact.

We can break the 12 tens into four equal groups of 3 tens.

$4\overline{)128}$

Hundreds	Tens	Ones
100	10 10 10	
	10 10 10	
	10 10 10	
	10 10 10	

The 4 divides the 8 ones into groups of 2.

$4\overline{)128}$

Hundreds	Tens	Ones	
	10 10 10	1 1	} 32
	10 10 10	1 1	} 32
	10 10 10	1 1	} 32
	10 10 10	1 1	} 32

There is nothing left to divide. We can see that the divisor 4 breaks 128 into 32 equal parts.

The quotient is 32.

 Apply Skills
Turn to *Interactive Text*, page 161.

 mBook Reinforce Understanding
Use the *mBook Study Guide* to review lesson concepts.

▶**Problem Solving: Making Division Word Problems**

How do we write division word problems?

We know that division is used in everyday life. Here are some situations where division is used:

- when a group of people is sharing things, such as food or supplies
- when one person needs to use equal amounts of something over a period of time, such as money
- any time a number of things will be split into equal parts

We can use our experiences to write our own division word problems.

Steps for Writing Division Word Problems:

STEP 1
Think of a situation where a large amount of items would need to be divided into equal parts.

Mr. Lopez's classes are taking the yearly statewide test. The school has provided a certain number of sharpened pencils for the students to use during the test. Mr. Lopez wants to make sure all of his students have a specific number of pencils so they will have spares if the lead breaks.

STEP 2
Choose reasonable amounts for the items and people in the word problem. This includes the answer that will be found.

- Mr. Lopez has a total of 125 students.
- He wants to make sure each of the students has at least 3 pencils.
- The school gave Mr. Lopez 380 pencils.

STEP 3
Write the word problem with the amounts and instructions. Be specific in your expectations.

Mr. Lopez's classes are taking the yearly statewide test. The school gave Mr. Lopez 380 sharpened pencils for the students to use during the test. If Mr. Lopez has 125 students, will each student get at least 3 pencils? Use division to solve the problem.

STEP 4

Work out the problem and write an explanation of how you solved it.

Mr. Lopez's classes are taking the yearly statewide test. The school gave Mr. Lopez 380 sharpened pencils for the students to use during the test. If Mr. Lopez has 125 students, will each student get at least 3 pencils? Use expanded division to solve the problem.

$$3\overline{)380}$$

Hundreds	Tens	Ones	
100	10 10	1 1 1 1 1 1	} 126
100	10 10	1 1 1 1 1 1	} 126
100	10 10	1 1 1 1 1 1	} 126
	10 10	1 1	} R2

- We want to know if all of the students will get 3 pencils if there are 380 pencils, so we divide 380 by 3.

- We know the answer must be at least 125 because there are 125 students.

- Our answer is 126 R2, so there will be at least 3 pencils for every student.

Creating division problems can be difficult. It is important to follow each step carefully. Keep in mind that we might need to go back to revise some of the steps if we find that our word problem will not work with the values we chose. Remember that our answer does not always have to be the quotient in a division problem. Sometimes the answer is also the remainder.

> When creating a division problem, don't forget to choose amounts that aren't too difficult to work with.

Problem-Solving Activity
Turn to *Interactive Text*, page 162.

mBook Reinforce Understanding
Use the *mBook Study Guide* to review lesson concepts.

Homework

Activity 1

Write extended fact families for each set of numbers. Replace the "X" with the correct number.

1. 3, 90, and X   **2.** 4, X and 280   **3.** X, 600 and 3,000   **4.** 8, 800 and X

Activity 2

Estimate by finding the near fact.

Model   9)80
Estimate: 9

1. 6)25   **2.** 8)54   **3.** 7)44

Activity 3

Solve using expanded division.

Model   2)186

Hundreds	Tens	Ones		Hundreds	Tens	Ones
(100)	10 10 10 10 10	1 1 1 1 1			10 10 10 10 10	1 1 1
	10 10 10	1			10 10 10	
	10 10 10 10 10				10 10 10 10 10	1 1 1
	10 10 10 10 10				10 10 10 10	

1. 2)148   **2.** 3)246   **3.** 4)312

Activity 4

Write a word problem that requires division to find the answer. Remember to follow all of the steps.

Activity 5 • Distributed Practice

Solve.

1.   347
       + 198

2.   1,400
       − 800

3.   47
       × 22

4.   400
       ×   3

▸**Traditional Long Division**

Vocabulary

traditional long
division

Why is traditional long division efficient?

We know the differences between traditional multiplication and expanded multiplication. We learned that traditional multiplication is faster and more efficient. Expanded multiplication shows the value of the digits as we multiply.

We will use the same thinking to see how **traditional long division** and expanded division compare. Let's solve a problem using the two methods.

Long Division

$$
\begin{array}{r}
21 \\
5\overline{)105} \\
-10 \\
\hline
05 \\
-5 \\
\hline
0
\end{array}
$$

Expanded Division

Hundreds	Tens		Ones	
	10	10	1	} 21
	10	10	1	} 21
	10	10	1	} 21
	10	10	1	} 21
100	10	10	1	} 21

- Since 5 will not divide into 1, we divide 5 into 10. 10 ÷ 5 = 2
- Subtract 10 − 10 = 0.
- Bring down the 5.
- Because 5 divides into 5 one time there is no remainder.
- The quotient is 21.

- We cannot break one hundred into 5 groups of hundreds, so we will have to regroup.
- 1 hundred = 10 tens. There is a 0 in the tens place, so 10 tens + 0 tens = 10 tens.
- We divide 10 tens into 5 groups of 2 tens each.
- We divide 5 ones into 5 groups of 1 ones.
- We add each row: 20 + 1 = 21
- The quotient is 21.

Traditional long division is more efficient. Expanded division helps us to understand what is happening with the digits. When working with larger division problems, traditional long division is easier to use.

Example 1 shows a problem where we use the traditional method for division. In this case, it is easier to use facts and near facts to work the problem. It is a shortcut because we do not have to think about place value.

Example 1

Solve 725 ÷ 5 using traditional long division.

We divide 5 into 7 without thinking about the value of 7. The number 5 goes into 7 one time, with 2 left over. Dividing 5 into 7 to get 1 is our near fact.

$$\begin{array}{r} 1 \\ 5\overline{)725} \\ -5 \end{array}$$

When dividing 22 by 5, 20 ÷ 5 = 4 is our near fact. Subtract 22 − 20 = 2.

$$\begin{array}{r} 14 \\ 5\overline{)725} \\ -5 \\ \hline 22 \\ -20 \end{array}$$

The equation 25 ÷ 5 = 5 is a basic fact. There is nothing left to divide.

The quotient is 145.

The traditional method tells us that 5 divides 725 into 145 equal parts. To check the answer, we multiply 5 × 145 = 725.

$$\begin{array}{r} 145 \\ 5\overline{)725} \\ -5 \\ \hline 22 \\ -20 \\ \hline 25 \\ -25 \\ \hline 0 \end{array}$$

The traditional method is faster than using place value. It uses shortcuts that let us think about facts and near facts. However, the traditional method makes it harder to see what the numbers stand for in the problem. Understanding where numbers go is the big difference between using place value or traditional long division to solve a problem.

 Apply Skills
Turn to *Interactive Text*, page 164.

 Monitoring Progress
Quiz 2

 mBook Reinforce Understanding
Use the *mBook Study Guide* to review lesson concepts.

Homework

Activity 1

Solve the basic and extended division facts.

1. $9\overline{)45}$ 2. $6\overline{)18}$ 3. $7\overline{)210}$

4. $8\overline{)48}$ 5. $3\overline{)120}$ 6. $5\overline{)250}$

Activity 2

Solve using traditional long division.

1. $9\overline{)387}$ 2. $7\overline{)469}$ 3. $8\overline{)632}$ 4. $6\overline{)354}$

Activity 3

Use the table to answer the questions about the Scatter Plots' CD sales.

The Scatter Plots' Monthly CD sales June–September	
Month	CD Sales
June	$24,000
July	$36,000
August	$18,000
September	$32,000

If there are 6 band members, and they all get the same amount:

1. How much will each get for June?

2. How much will each get for August?

3. If they add 2 more singers in September and still each get the same amount, how much will each get?

Activity 4 • Distributed Practice

Solve.

1. $\begin{array}{r} 400 \\ + 900 \\ \hline \end{array}$ 2. $\begin{array}{r} 63 \\ \times 48 \\ \hline \end{array}$ 3. $\begin{array}{r} 4,097 \\ - 2,884 \\ \hline \end{array}$ 4. $\begin{array}{r} 400 \\ \times 900 \\ \hline \end{array}$

▸Using Near Extended Facts to Estimate

Problem Solving:
Measurement in Architecture

▸**Using Near Extended Facts to Estimate**

Vocabulary
near extended fact

How do we estimate large numbers in division?

We know how to use near facts to estimate the answer to some division problems. For example:

$$82 \div 9 \text{ is close to the fact } 81 \div 9 = 9.$$

We use the same thinking to estimate the answers to division problems that have larger numbers. For these kinds of problems, we use **near extended facts**, or extended facts that are close to the larger division problems we are working with.

Let's compare a problem that uses a near fact with a problem that uses a near extended fact.

Near Fact
$82 \div 9$ is close to $81 \div 9 = 9$

In larger division problems, we look at the two digits with the highest place value. In this case, the digits are 82, and we think of a fact that is close to $82 \div 9$.

We know $81 \div 9 = 9$ is close, so we add a zero to 81 to find our near extended fact $810 \div 9 = 90$.

Near Extended Fact
$829 \div 9$ is close to $810 \div 9 = 90$

Let's use this thinking to help us use extended near facts to estimate and solve division problems.

$$591 \div 7 \text{ is close to the fact } 560 \div 7 = 80.$$
$$500 \div 7 \text{ is close to the fact } 490 \div 7 = 70.$$
$$553 \div 6 \text{ is close to the fact } 540 \div 6 = 90.$$
$$377 \div 5 \text{ is close to the fact } 350 \div 5 = 70.$$

Long division requires steps, which may result in errors. One way to find out if we made a mistake is to estimate the answer. Using near facts and near extended facts helps us to estimate.

Example 1

Solve 437 ÷ 7 using traditional long division.

First, we look to see if 7 divides into 4, but it does not.

Since 7 does not divide into 4, we try to divide 7 into the first two digits in the number, or 43.

We know 7 does not divide evenly into 43, but we can find a near fact. The closest basic fact is 7 × 6 = 42.

$$\begin{array}{r} 6 \\ 7\overline{)437} \\ -42 \\ \hline 17 \end{array}$$

After we subtract 43 − 42, we bring down the 7 to make 17. We know that 7 × 2 = 14 is the closest basic fact.

Finally, we subtract 17 − 14 = 3. Our remainder is 3.

$$\begin{array}{r} 62\ \text{R3} \\ 7\overline{)437} \\ -42 \\ \hline 17 \\ -14 \\ \hline 3 \end{array}$$

The quotient is 62 R3.

In Example 2, we see how near extended facts help us to estimate the answer to larger division problems.

Example 2

Find a near extended fact for 437 ÷ 7.

The divisor, 7, cannot divide into the digit in the hundreds place. We need to use the first two digits, 43. Since we know the basic fact 7 × 6 = 42, we think of the extended fact 7 × 60 = 420.

$$\begin{array}{r} 60 \\ 7\overline{)420} \end{array}$$

We know our answer is around 60.

When we compare our estimate with the long division answer, 62 R3, we see that we are close.

We estimate answers in long division by finding near facts or near extended facts.

 Apply Skills
Turn to *Interactive Text*, page 166.

 Reinforce Understanding
Use the *mBook Study Guide* to review lesson concepts.

▶Problem Solving: **Measurement in Architecture**

What does an architect do?

People need places in which to live, work, play, shop, and eat. Before building these places, an architect needs to design them. Architects need to know a lot about math, especially measurement and geometry. They use drawings called blueprints to help workers build the structure.

Look at the example of a blueprint. What does an architect consider when designing an apartment?

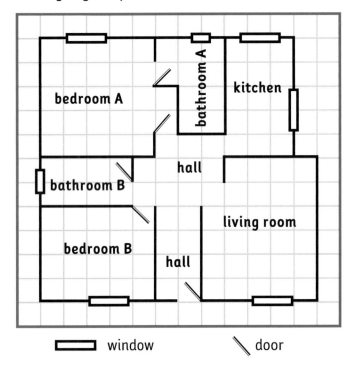

⬚⬚⬚ window   ＼ door

- Which are larger, bedroom A and bathroom A or bedroom B and bathroom B?
  Bedroom A and bathroom A are larger.

- Which is smaller, bedroom A or the living room?
  Bedroom A is smaller.

An architect needs to consider both length and area when designing an apartment.

 Problem-Solving Activity
Turn to *Interactive Text*, page 167.

 mBook Reinforce Understanding
Use the *mBook Study Guide*
to review lesson concepts.

Homework

Activity 1

Solve the basic and extended division facts.

1. $7\overline{)35}$
2. $9\overline{)360}$
3. $8\overline{)480}$
4. $6\overline{)540}$

Activity 2

Find a near fact for the problem. Then solve.

1. $9\overline{)28}$
2. $9\overline{)280}$
3. $7\overline{)23}$
4. $7\overline{)230}$
5. $8\overline{)18}$
6. $8\overline{)180}$

Activity 3

Solve using traditional long division.

1. $9\overline{)873}$
2. $7\overline{)434}$
3. $5\overline{)366}$
4. $6\overline{)396}$

Activity 4

Answer the questions based on the blueprint of a house.

1. How wide are the halls?

2. What rooms do not have a door?

3. Is bedroom A or bedroom B larger?

Activity 5 • Distributed Practice

Solve.

1.
$$\begin{array}{r} 5,600 \\ +\ \ 200 \\ \hline \end{array}$$

2.
$$\begin{array}{r} 1,400 \\ -\ \ 500 \\ \hline \end{array}$$

3.
$$\begin{array}{r} 1,700 \\ -\ \ 800 \\ \hline \end{array}$$

4.
$$\begin{array}{r} 60 \\ \times\ 4 \\ \hline \end{array}$$

Lesson **12** | ▸ **Estimating in Division**

Problem Solving:
Designing Your Own Floor Plan

| 1 | 2 | 3 | 4 | 5 | 6 | 7 | 8 | 9 |

▸**Estimating in Division**

How can we use near extended facts to estimate in division?

We saw patterns in extended division facts in previous lessons. The basic fact 27 ÷ 3 = 9 is in each of the extended facts below.

| 2,700 ÷ 3 = 900 | 270 ÷ 3 = 90 | 270 ÷ 30 = 9 | 2,700 ÷ 30 = 90 | 2,700 ÷ 300 = 9 |

The pattern is in the zeros. The amount of zeros added to the dividend should be equal to the amount of zeros added to the divisor and quotient combined. When we estimate in division, we can turn an extended fact into a basic fact by working with the zeros.

Let's say that [ ] is a unit of 3.

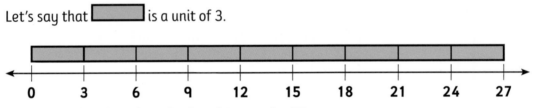

| 0 | 3 | 6 | 9 | 12 | 15 | 18 | 21 | 24 | 27 |

We see that it takes nine of units of 3 to make 27.

We extend the fact and see that 2,700 ÷ 300 = 9.

If [ ] is a unit of 300, then it also takes nine units of 300 to make 2,700.

| 0 | 300 | 600 | 900 | 1,200 | 1,500 | 1,800 | 2,100 | 2,400 | 2,700 |

$$\begin{array}{r} 9 \\ 300\overline{)2,700} \end{array}$$

The dividend 2,700 has two zeros. The divisor 300 has two zeros and the quotient 9 has no zeros. The number of zeros in the divisor and the quotient is the same as the number of zeros in the dividend.

> Understanding this relationship between basic and extended division facts helps us estimate answers to division problems.

Using near extended facts is a good way to estimate our answers to division problems. We discussed the concepts of tens. These tens also help us in division problems. We pull them out so we can find a basic or extended fact.

Example 1

Estimate the quotient of 239 ÷ 34 using near extended facts.

$$34\overline{)239}$$

STEP 1
Round the unit to the nearest ten.

Let's think about the unit of 34. In order to get a division fact, we need to round to the nearest ten. The nearest ten is 30.

$$34\overline{)239}$$
$$\downarrow$$
$$30\overline{)239}$$

STEP 2
Round the whole to create an extended fact.

Let's think about the whole 239. What's the nearest ten that makes an extended fact with 30? We think 8 × 3 = 24. We can round 239 to the nearest ten, which is 240.

$$30\overline{)240}$$

Now we have an extended fact: 240 ÷ 30.

STEP 3
Change the extended fact into a basic fact.

We look for the tens and remove them to get the basic fact. $$3\cancel{0}\overline{)24\cancel{0}}$$

STEP 4
Solve the basic fact.

Finally, we solve the basic fact: 24 ÷ 3 = 8.

$$3\overline{)24}^{\,8}$$

Since we know the relationship between basic and extended facts, we know that the answer to the near extended fact 240 ÷ 30 is also 8.

The quotient of 239 ÷ 34 is about 8.

When we work with large numbers by hand or with a calculator, we need a way to check our answers to see that they are correct. We can use estimation with near extended facts to check our answers to difficult division problems.

How do we pull out the tens when both numbers are two-digit numbers?

We know that the amount of extra zeros on the dividend should equal the amount of extra zeros on the divisor and quotient combined. Sometimes the zeros can get confusing in larger division problems. Let's look at another example of estimating using near extended facts.

Example 1

Estimate the quotient of 64 ÷ 27. $27\overline{)64}$

STEP 1
Round the unit to the nearest ten.

We start by rewriting the number we are using to divide into the nearest ten. The number 30 is the nearest ten.

$27\overline{)64}$
$\downarrow$
$30\overline{)64}$

STEP 2
Round the whole to create an extended fact.

Next, we round the bigger number to make a near extended fact.

$30\overline{)64}$
$\downarrow$
$30\overline{)60}$

STEP 3
Change the extended fact into a basic fact.

We eliminate the tens, and that gives us the basic fact.

$3 \times 10\overline{)6 \times 10}$

STEP 4
We solve the basic fact.

$3\overline{)6}$ with quotient 2

The quotient is about 2.

We use this thinking to find errors in division problems we've solved with a calculator or by hand.

 Apply Skills
Turn to *Interactive Text*, page 169.

 mBook **Reinforce Understanding**
Use the *mBook Study Guide* to review lesson concepts.

▶**Problem Solving: Designing Your Own Floor Plan**

How do you design your own floor plan?

In the past several lessons, we counted square units to measure the area of objects. We also discussed how an architect uses measurement to create blueprints for homes and other buildings. Now we are going to learn to design a space within a home or other building.

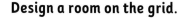
Example 1

Design a room on the grid.

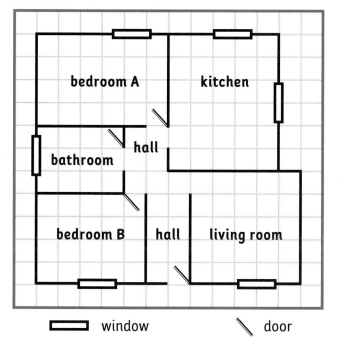

☐═══☐ window   ╲ door

> Designing a floor plan requires both measurement skills and creative thought.

There are several things we need to think about when designing the layout of a room:

- We should start with the largest items first.
- We should think about how much space we need around the pieces of furniture.
- We need to think about the amount of wall space each of the items needs.
- We need to think about the location of items in relation to other items, as well as the space in the room.

Problem-Solving Activity
Turn to *Interactive Text*, page 170.

mBook Reinforce Understanding
Use the *mBook Study Guide* to review lesson concepts.

Homework

Activity 1

Solve these basic and extended division facts.

1. $18 \div 3$ $180 \div 3$ $1,800 \div 3$

2. $36 \div 9$ $360 \div 9$ $3,600 \div 9$

Activity 2

Estimate the quotient.

Model
$$91\overline{)371} \rightarrow \overset{4}{90\overline{)360}}$$

1. $21\overline{)166}$ 2. $44\overline{)369}$ 3. $29\overline{)277}$

Activity 3

Solve using traditional long division.

1. $2\overline{)396}$ 2. $7\overline{)497}$ 3. $5\overline{)685}$

Activity 4

Use the floor plan to answer the questions.

Decide if all of the furniture listed below will fit comfortably into this living room. Explain your answer. Hint: Think about the wall space and walkways within the room.

- couch: 7×3
- couch table: 5×2
- 2 end tables: 3×2
- coffee table: 6×3
- book shelf: 10×2
- TV stand: 3×3

Living room

window

Activity 5 • Distributed Practice

Solve.

1. $\begin{array}{r} 3,047 \\ + 9,906 \\ \hline \end{array}$ 2. $\begin{array}{r} 5,106 \\ - 2,901 \\ \hline \end{array}$ 3. $\begin{array}{r} 467 \\ \times \quad 5 \\ \hline \end{array}$ 4. $\begin{array}{r} 5,000 \\ - 4,997 \\ \hline \end{array}$

Lesson 13 ▸Finding Division Errors

Problem Solving:
▸**Building Design**

▸Finding Division Errors

How do we know if we made a mistake?

We already know how to estimate the answer to a division problem using near facts and extended near facts. Let's look at a situation where we can use our knowledge to see calculator errors easily.

> ### Improve Your Skills

Three students—James, Manuel, and Li—each used their calculator to solve the problem $19\overline{)78}$, but each one came up with a different answer.

James' calculator showed:

0.2435897435

Manuel's calculator showed:

4.105263158

Li's calculator showed:

1.1666666667

Which one of them was correct?

We can find out using facts and near facts. Let's start by finding a near extended fact for $19\overline{)78}$.

- The near extended fact is $20\overline{)80}$.
- We pull out the 10s and get $2 \times 10\overline{)8 \times 10}$.
- This gives us a near fact of $2\overline{)8}$.

$$\begin{array}{r} 4 \\ 2\overline{)8} \end{array}$$

Our estimate is 4. Look again at the three answers the students got above. Manuel's answer is correct. The number 4.105263158 is close to our estimate of 4.

> It is important to enter each keystroke carefully.

Li and James each made a mistake calculating the answer. It is important to learn how to avoid common errors in division.

Let's look at a few more examples of common errors when using a calculator.

Improve Your Skills

What happens if we enter the numbers in reverse order?

We know that we should enter the following keystrokes into our calculator:

$$4 \overline{)17}$$

But what if we enter these keystrokes into our calculator the wrong way?

The calculator would display:  **ERROR**

The numbers cannot be switched around in division. If the dividend is bigger than the divisor, the answer will never be less than one. In the example above, we see that the numbers were entered the wrong way because the quotient is less than one.

Improve Your Skills

How can a near fact help us avoid errors?

One way to check a calculator answer is to estimate the answer using a basic fact. For $17 \div 4$, we round 17 to 16 so we can make a near fact.

$$\begin{array}{r} 4 \\ 4 \overline{)16} \end{array}$$

We see our answer should be about 4.

If we enter the numbers on a calculator correctly,

The calculator would display: 4.25 **CORRECT**

Our estimate tells us the quotient should be close to 4. Our calculator answer is correct.

 Apply Skills
Turn to *Interactive Text*, page 172.

 mBook Reinforce Understanding
Use the *mBook Study Guide* to review lesson concepts.

►**Problem Solving: Building Design**

What other areas of math do architects use?

We learned that architects use measurement and creativity to design buildings. Architects also use multiplication and division every day. Let's look at the example below to see how multiplication and division are used in architecture.

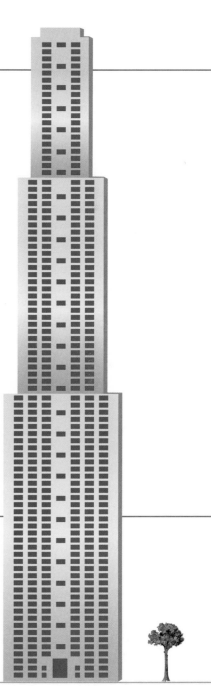

Example 1

When an architect designs a building, the client will set specific requirements. Some of those may be:

- The number of stories in a building.
  There are 89 stories in this building.

- The height of each of the stories in a building.
  To find the total height of the building, the height of each story is multiplied by the number of stories.

- The number, location, and size of windows in a building.
  Multiplication may be used to find how many windows of each size are needed for each floor or for the entire building.

- The number and size of rooms on each floor.
  The total area on one floor may need to be divided by the size of the rooms to find how many rooms will fit on that floor.

- The number of elevators or other similar things in a building.

There are many different parts of a building that require an architect to use multiplication and division.

 Problem-Solving Activity
Turn to *Interactive Text*, page 173.

 mBook Reinforce Understanding
Use the *mBook Study Guide* to review lesson concepts.

Activity 1

Solve the extended division facts.

1. $560 \div 70$
2. $270 \div 90$
3. $320 \div 40$
4. $420 \div 60$
5. $180 \div 30$
6. $150 \div 50$

Activity 2

Find the near extended fact. Do not solve the original problems.

Model

$$\overset{4}{61\overline{)245}} \quad 60\overline{)240}$$

1. $31\overline{)245}$
2. $49\overline{)256}$
3. $58\overline{)366}$

Activity 3

Choose the response that best describes the error in each situation.

1. Angela solved $7\overline{)429}$ on a calculator.

   She got the following answer: $\boxed{0.0163170163170163}$

   This answer is not correct. She must have:

   (a) Entered ⑦ ➕ ④ ② ⑨.

   (b) Entered ④ ② ⑨ ➗ ⑦.

   (c) Entered ⑦ ➗ ④ ② ⑨.

2. Seth solved $8\overline{)901}$ on a calculator.

   He got the following answer: $\boxed{0.008879}$

   This answer is not correct. He must have:

   He got the following answer:

   (a) Entered ⑧ ➗ ⑨ ⓪ ①.

   (b) Entered ① ⓪ ⑨ ➕ ⑧.

   (c) Entered ⑨ ⓪ ① ➗ ⑧.

Activity 4 • Distributed Practice

Solve.

1.
$$\begin{array}{r} 800 \\ +\ 700 \\ \hline \end{array}$$

2.
$$\begin{array}{r} 6{,}095 \\ -\ 4{,}807 \\ \hline \end{array}$$

3.
$$\begin{array}{r} 1{,}500 \\ +\ \ \ 900 \\ \hline \end{array}$$

4.
$$\begin{array}{r} 781 \\ \times\ \ \ \ 9 \\ \hline \end{array}$$

Lesson 14 ▶More Division Errors

Problem Solving:
Square Units and Triangular Units

▶More Division Errors

What are some common errors we can make in division?

In Lesson 13, we looked at a common error that can occur when we use a calculator—entering the numbers in reverse order. We should remember that even though using a calculator might seem like a good way to avoid errors, we still need to be cautious.

Improve Your Skills

There are many ways to make errors when using a calculator.

Let's look at one problem with several different answers. We can decide what error has been made for each one.

68)5,033

ERROR 1: The divisor and dividend were switched.

ERROR 2: The digits in 5,033 were entered out of order.

ERROR 3: A 7 instead of an 8 was entered for the number 68.

ERROR 4: The subtract button was entered instead of the divide button.

ERROR 5: The zero was hit twice instead of once in the number 5,033.

Let's practice checking our answers, identifying errors, and correcting errors once they have been identified.

One of the main errors in division on a calculator is to mix up some of the digits within a number.

Improve Your Skills

What happens if we enter the wrong number?

$$32\overline{)281}$$

What if we make a mistake and we enter these keystrokes instead?

The calculator would display the following: | 6.8125 | **ERROR**

This mistake is difficult to notice. That is why our estimation skills are very important in division. We need to be able to determine if our answer is reasonable. Let's look at a near extended fact for this problem.

How does an estimate help us avoid errors?

$$32\overline{)281}$$
$$\downarrow$$
$$30\overline{)270} \qquad 3 \times 10\overline{)27 \times 10} \qquad 3\overline{)27}^{\,9}$$

We see that the answer should be around 9. This is different than the answer we found on our calculator.

> Always double-check your work! Even though using estimation is a good way to find errors, sometimes errors are made in estimation.

If we find that our answer seems unreasonable, it is a good idea to enter the numbers into the calculator again. It is easy to switch the numbers around by mistake when using a calculator. We need to be very careful to enter the numbers correctly. If there is any doubt at all, we use estimation to check. If the estimate is not very close to our calculator answer, we enter the numbers into the calculator again.

 Apply Skills
Turn to *Interactive Text*, page 175.

 Reinforce Understanding
Use the *mBook Study Guide* to review lesson concepts.

▶**Problem Solving: Square Units and Triangular Units**

What are triangular units?

We worked with square units when measuring area. There is a different kind of unit we can use as well. It is called a triangular unit because it is in the shape of a triangle.

Look at the grid. It is divided into triangular units. A design has been placed on the grid for us to look at.

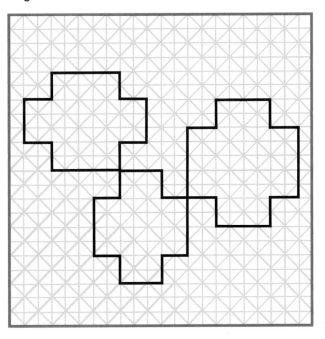

We see there are two triangles in every small square. This means the measurement for the area will be two times as large for triangular units versus square units.

We can estimate the area of the right shape in both square units and triangular shapes.

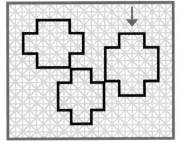

- square units: __56__
- triangular units: __112__

 Problem-Solving Activity
Turn to **Interactive Text**, page 176.

mBook **Reinforce Understanding**
Use the **mBook Study Guide**
to review lesson concepts.

Activity 1

Solve the basic and extended division facts.

1. $49 \div 7$
2. $270 \div 90$
3. $14 \div 2$
4. $420 \div 60$
5. $180 \div 3$
6. $250 \div 50$

Activity 2

Solve the original problems on a calculator. Check the answers by finding the near extended fact for each problem.

Model

$$61\overline{)245} \quad 60\overline{)240}^{\,4}$$

1. $89\overline{)644}$
2. $68\overline{)578}$
3. $49\overline{)399}$
4. $77\overline{)499}$

Activity 3

Choose the response that best describes the error in this situation.

Jesse solved $758 \div 86$ on a calculator.

He got the following answer: 6.7209302
This answer is not correct. He must have:

(a) entered $68 \div 578$

(b) entered $578 \div 86$

(c) entered $5788 \div 68$

Activity 4

Solve using traditional long division.

1. $6\overline{)47}$
2. $9\overline{)85}$
3. $3\overline{)279}$

Activity 5

Find the area of the left (L) shape and Bottom (B) shape in square units and triangular units.

1. **Left shape (L):**
   square units:
   triangular units:

2. **Bottom shape (B):**
   square units:
   triangular units:

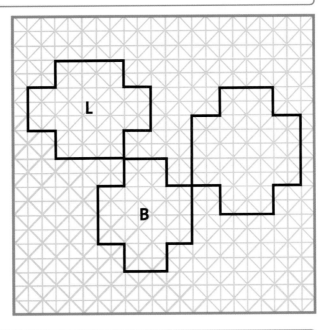

Activity 6 • Distributed Practice

Solve.

1.
$$3,605 \\ -\ \ 892$$

2.
$$1,700 \\ -\ \ 800$$

3.
$$479 \\ \times\ \ 6$$

4.
$$24 \\ \times 58$$

▶ **Division**

What are different ways to think about division?

Throughout this unit we focused on division of whole numbers. We emphasized the importance of place value as well as estimation in division, which are similar to place value and estimation in addition, subtraction, and multiplication. Here are some examples of how place value is important in division.

Review 1

How do we think about division?

Facts and Extended Facts		
$35 \div 5 = 7$	$350 \div 5 = 70$	$3,500 \div 5 = 700$

Fact Families for 5, 9, 45			
$9 \times 5 = 45$	$5 \times 9 = 45$	$45 \div 5 = 9$	$45 \div 9 = 5$

Expanded Division

Hundreds	Tens	Ones	
100	10 10	1	} = 121
100	10 10	1	} = 121
100	10 10	1	} = 121

The number 363 can be broken apart three times by 121. We can get the total amount of 363 by multiplying $3 \times 121 = 363$.

The next example shows traditional long division. Traditional long division is much more efficient than expanded division.

Review 2

Traditional Long Division

Solve 376 ÷ 4.

$$
\begin{array}{r}
94 \\
4\overline{)376} \\
-36 \\
\hline
16 \\
-16 \\
\hline
0
\end{array}
$$

We know that $4\overline{)360}$ with 90 above is a near extended fact.
This helps us to solve the problem more quickly.

We can put a 9 above the 7 and start the next steps.

**After subtracting, we see that $4\overline{)16}$ with 4 above is a basic fact.
We have no remainder.**

We need to remember to always double-check our work in division.
It is easy to make mistakes with difficult problems, even when using a calculator.

 Apply Skills
Turn to *Interactive Text*, page 178.

 mBook **Reinforce Understanding**
Use the *mBook Study Guide* to review lesson concepts.

▶**Problem Solving: Measuring Two-Dimensional Objects**

How do we measure two-dimensional objects?

A concept that we saw in this unit is the role of square units for measuring two-dimensional objects. Large square units are easy to count, but they may not give us as exact of a measurement as smaller square units.

Review 1

How do we measure a figure with square units?

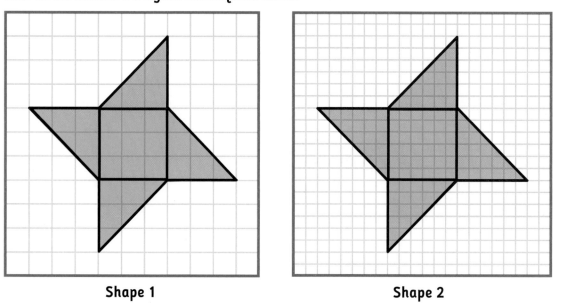

| Shape 1 | Shape 2 |

- The area of Shape 1 is about 30 square units.
- The area of Shape 2 is about 120 square units.

We see that the shapes are identical. However, if we find the area of each of them, we see that they are different because of the size of the square units.

Sometimes we can find the area of a shape by looking for patterns in the shape. This helps us avoid counting each square to find the area. Let's see how this works.

Review 2

How do patterns help us find area?

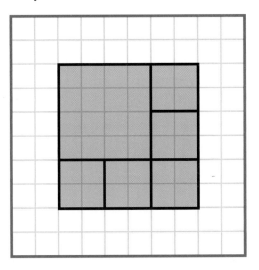

This shape is made up of six squares: one large square and five smaller squares that are all the same.

The area of one small square is 4 square units. There are 5 of these squares, so 5 x 4 = 20. There are 20 square units in the smaller squares.

The area of the large square is 4 x 4 = 16 square units.

The total area of the shape is 20 + 16 = 36 square units.

Looking for patterns in shapes helps us find areas.

Sometimes we need to use units other than square units when finding area. We can use triangular units to help us see area in a different way.

> **Review 3**
>
> **How do we use triangular units to find area?**
>
>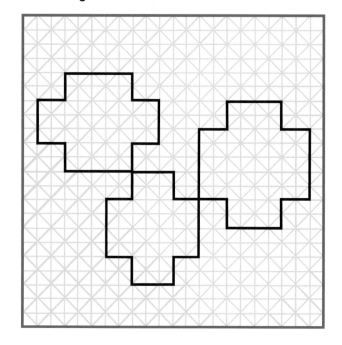
>
> On this grid, we see that every small square is divided into two triangles. This tells us that the number of triangular units in a shape will be two times the number of square units.
>
> Triangular units make it easier to find the area of shapes that are not squares or rectangles.

When finding the area of a shape, it is important to think about square units and to look for patterns.

 Problem-Solving Activity
Turn to *Interactive Text*, page 180.

 mBook Reinforce Understanding
Use the *mBook Study Guide* to review lesson concepts.

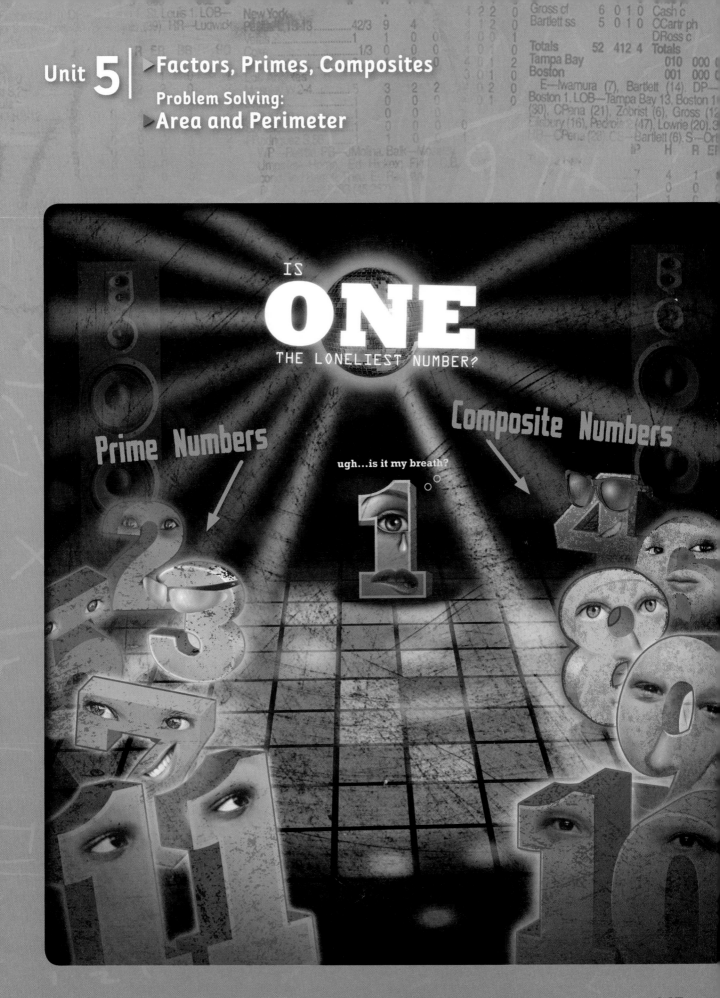

I do belong!

Building Number Concepts

- Factor whole numbers using a variety of methods

- Determine if a given number is prime or composite

- Find the prime factorization of a whole number

OBJECTIVES

Problem Solving

- Explore the relationship between perimeter and area of shapes

- Discover and use area formulas for triangles and parallelograms

- Find the area of irregularly shaped objects

▶Arrays of Numbers 1 to 25

Vocabulary
array

What is an array?

Another way to look at factors is by making an **array** . Arrays help us see factors and products visually. We can make an array for any set of factors and products.

For example, the array for **2 × 3 = 6** looks like this:

This array has 2 rows and 3 columns of squares. This means that the dimensions of this array are 2 × 3. There are 6 squares in the array, so the product is 6.

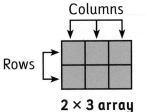

2 × 3 array

The factors of the problem determine the number of rows and columns. The total number of squares will always equal the product in the problem.

The array 2 × 3 is not the only way to show the product of 6. There is another array that has a total of 6 squares:

There are still 6 parts total, but they are arranged in 1 row and 6 columns. That means that the dimensions of this array are 1 × 6.

1 × 6 array

When we discuss arrays, we discuss them by listing the number of rows first, then the number of columns.

The product, 6, has 2 different arrays: a 2 × 3 array and a 1 × 6 array.

Arrays help us find the missing pieces in a multiplication problem. When we use an array to show a problem, it helps us visualize the products and factors.

Example 1

Create an array for the problem 3 × 4 = 12.
Let's look at the problem.

The first factor is 3. This tells us how many rows to make.

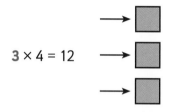

The next factor is 4. This tells us how many columns to make.

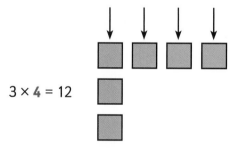

Now we have 3 rows and 4 columns.

To complete the array, we fill in the rows and columns so there are 3 complete rows and 4 complete columns.

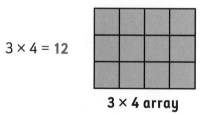

3 × 4 array

Count the squares in the array. There are 12 because 3 × 4 = 12.

In Example 1, we see that if we had not known the product, we could have found it by making a 3 × 4 array.

We can also find the factors of a product by making an array.

Example 2

Create an array for the product of 18.

Let's think of two numbers that can be multiplied to get a product of 18. We know that when we multiply 2 and 9 we get 18. We can show 18 by creating an array with 2 rows and 9 columns.

$2 \times 9 = 18$

There are other numbers we can multiply to get a product of 18. Remember that division is the opposite of multiplication. If we know that 18 can be divided by 3 evenly, then we can find the other factor by making an array. We do this by making 3 rows and adding new columns until we reach the product of 18.

$3 \times 6 = 18$

It takes 6 columns of 3 rows to make 18. This is a 3×6 array. Another array we can make for the product of 18 is 1×18.

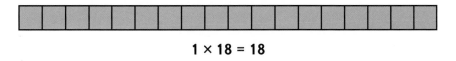

$1 \times 18 = 18$

Being able to tell the dimensions of an array helps us visualize multiplication problems.

 Apply Skills
Turn to *Interactive Text*, page 182.

 mBook Reinforce Understanding
Use the *mBook Study Guide* to review lesson concepts.

▶**Problem Solving: Irregularly Shaped Objects**

How do we estimate the area of irregularly shaped objects?

In Unit 4, we found areas using square units. In real life, most objects are not a regular shape like a rectangle, triangle, or circle. But, we can use a shape like a rectangle as a quick way to estimate the area of irregularly shaped objects. Let's see how this works.

To find the area of irregularly shaped objects, we draw one rectangle inside and one rectangle outside the shape. We can estimate that the area is between the two areas of the rectangles.

> We want our estimate to be accurate, so we make sure the regular shapes are as close to the irregular shapes as possible.

Once we draw the rectangles, we use multiplication to find the area.

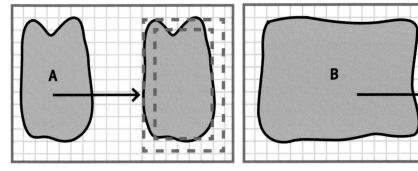

Area: Shape A	**Area: Shape B**

- The inner rectangle for A is $9 \times 5 = 45$.
- The outer rectangle for A is $11 \times 7 = 77$.
- The area of the shape A is between 45 and 77 square units.

- The inner rectangle for B is $8 \times 13 = 104$.
- The outer rectangle for B is $10 \times 15 = 150$.
- The area of the shape B is between 104 and 150 square units.

By drawing two regular shapes, we are able to estimate the area of an irregularly shaped object.

 Problem-Solving Activity
Turn to *Interactive Text*, page 183.

 Reinforce Understanding
Use the *mBook Study Guide* to review lesson concepts.

Homework

Activity 1

Solve these basic multiplication facts.

1. 2×8 2. 5×9 3. 7×8

4. 9×6 5. 3×8 6. 4×6

Activity 2

Tell the dimensions of each array.

Model The dimensions are 2×4.

1.
2.
3.
4.
5.

Activity 3 • Distributed Practice

Solve.

1. $\begin{array}{r} 297 \\ + 485 \end{array}$ 2. $\begin{array}{r} 789 \\ - 391 \end{array}$ 3. $\begin{array}{r} 72 \\ \times 49 \end{array}$ 4. $9\overline{)288}$

▶**Problem Solving: Area Formulas for Squares and Rectangles**

How do arrays help us understand area?

Area is the space inside an object. We began finding area in Unit 4 by counting the square units inside an object. One shape we have worked with is a rectangle.

Vocabulary
formula

Let's find the area of the rectangle:

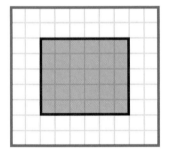

When we count all of the squares within the rectangle, we find there are 30 total.

In Lesson 1, we learned about arrays. We learned that the number of rows multiplied by the number of columns is equal to the total number of squares in the array. We can apply this to our rectangle above. Instead of counting the squares, we count the number of rows and columns. We multiply to find the total area in square units.

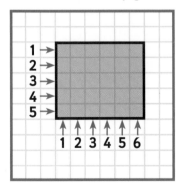

There are 5 rows and 6 columns.

5 × 6 = 30

The area is 30 square units.

We can think of a shape as an array. Multiplying to find an area is faster than counting all of the square units.

What is the area formula for squares and rectangles?

We can use a **formula**, or a rule shown with symbols, when finding the area of shapes like squares and rectangles.

When we found the area of the rectangle, we first counted the number of squares across the bottom of the shape. This is called the **base**. Then we counted the squares along the side that made up the **height** of the shape.

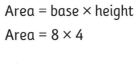

We know that multiplying is faster than counting, so we multiply the number of squares in the base by the number of squares in the height. This is a rule that we always follow:

Area = base × height

Showing a rule with symbols creates a formula. The formula above is the area formula for all rectangles and squares. Let's use the formula to find the area of a rectangle.

Example 1

Find the area of the rectangle.

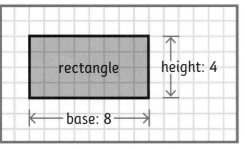

Area = base × height
Area = 8 × 4

The area is 32 square units.
We can count the squares to check that we multiplied correctly.

There are 32 squares in the rectangle. Our calculation is correct.

Example 2

Find the area of the shapes.

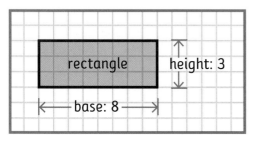

Base: 8 units

Height: 3 units

Area: 8 × 3 = 24 square units

The area of the rectangle is 24 square units.

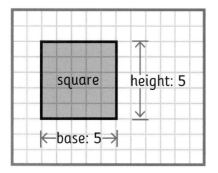

Base: 5 units

Height: 5 units

Area: 5 × 5 = 25 square units

The area of the square is 25 square units.

When we find the area of shapes, there is not always a grid with square units. That means it is hard to count square units to find the areas of the shape. This is another reason we need to know a formula. Formulas are one way to find the area of shapes, and it is important to understand why formulas work.

How is area used in everyday situations?

Contractors use blueprints to build houses and other buildings. They look at the blueprints to figure out how much material they will need. In the blueprint below, the rooms are rectangular. Let's look at how contractors use dimensions to find area.

Example 1

Use the dimensions in the blueprint to solve the problems.

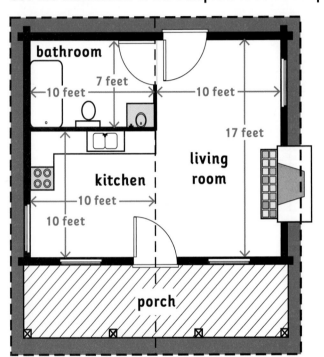

1. **How much carpet is needed for the living room?**
   The living room is 10 feet by 17 feet. 10 feet × 17 feet = 170 square feet. We need 170 square feet of carpet for the living room.

2. **How many square feet of tile is needed for the kitchen?**
   The kitchen is 10 feet by 10 feet. 10 feet × 10 feet = 100 square feet. We need 100 square feet of tile for the kitchen.

3. **How much vinyl flooring is needed for the bathroom?**
   The bathroom is 10 feet by 7 feet. 10 feet × 7 feet = 70 square feet. We need 70 square feet of vinyl flooring for the bathroom.

 Problem-Solving Activity
Turn to *Interactive Text*, page 185.

 mBook Reinforce Understanding
Use the *mBook Study Guide* to review lesson concepts.

Activity 1

Solve.

1. 3×9 2. 7×3 3. 3×4

4. 2×6 5. 3×8 6. 6×4

Activity 2

Write the dimensions for the arrays.

Model The dimensions are 3×4.

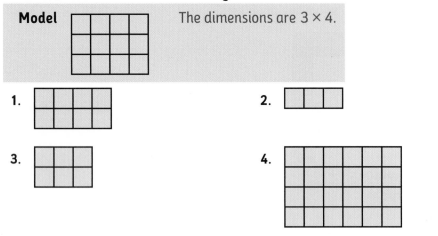

Activity 3

Find the area of each rectangle.

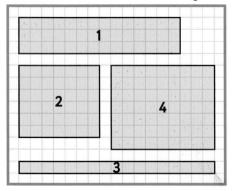

Activity 4 • Distributed Practice

Solve.

1. $\begin{array}{r} 1,400 \\ -700 \\ \hline \end{array}$ 2. $\begin{array}{r} 60 \\ \times 40 \\ \hline \end{array}$ 3. $9\overline{)360}$ 4. $\begin{array}{r} 7,012 \\ +5,981 \\ \hline \end{array}$

Lesson 3 ▸ From Arrays to Factors

Problem Solving:
Area Formulas for Triangles and Parallelograms

▶ **From Arrays to Factors**

Vocabulary
factor list

How do we use arrays to write a factor list?

In Lesson 1, we learned how arrays show factors. The dimensions of arrays are the factors of a number. Let's find the arrays for the number 24.

1 × 24

2 × 12

3 × 8

4 × 6

The dimensions of the arrays for **24** are **1 × 24, 2 × 12, 3 × 8**, and **4 × 6**. Each of these numbers is a factor of 24.

It is easier to see all of the factors if we write them in a **factor list**. To make a factor list, we use the numbers from the dimensions of the arrays. Each number is written once. The numbers are separated by commas.

The factors for 24 are 1, 2, 3, 4, 6, 8, 12, and 24.

This is our factor list.

Using arrays is a way to find the factors of a number. Arrays show multiplication problems. Once we have found the factors, writing them in a list is a good way to organize them.

Example 1

Write the factors for 16.

First, we use arrays to show the product 16.

1 × 16

2 × 8

4 × 4

The dimensions are all factors of 16. We put them in numerical order using commas: **1, 2, 4, 4, 8, 16.**

Last, we make sure there are no duplicated numbers. There are two 4s. After we remove one of the 4s, we have the factor list for 16.

The factors for 16 are 1, 2, 4, 8, and 16.

After we write a factor list, it is important to double-check these points:

- We found all arrays possible for the product.
- All dimensions from the arrays were recorded in the list.
- No numbers were duplicated.

Apply Skills
Turn to **Interactive Text**, page 187.

 mBook Reinforce Understanding
Use the **mBook Study Guide** to review lesson concepts.

▶**Problem Solving: Area Formulas for Triangles and Parallelograms**

What is the area formula for triangles?

We can use what we know about the area of squares and rectangles to find formulas for other shapes. We start by thinking about a rectangle or square and looking for a pattern. Let's see how this helps us find the area formula for a triangle.

The diagram shows that if a rectangle is cut in half from one corner to the other, it makes two triangles. If we pull out one of the triangles, we see that it is half the area of the rectangle. All triangles have half the area of a rectangle.

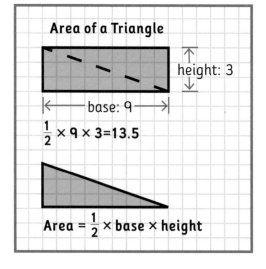

Area of a Triangle

height: 3

base: 9

$\frac{1}{2} \times 9 \times 3 = 13.5$

A triangle is half a rectangle. To find the area formula for triangles, we start with the area formula for rectangles: Area = base × height. If we multiply a rectangle's area formula by $\frac{1}{2}$, we find the area of a triangle.

$$\text{Area} = \frac{1}{2} \times \text{base} \times \text{height}$$

Area of a triangle = $\frac{1}{2}$ × base × height

Let's use the formula to find the area of a triangle.

Example 1

Find the area of the triangle.

We need to decide what the base and height are. The base is the length of the bottom line—8 units.

The height is the length of the vertical line—3 units.

Area of triangle = $\frac{1}{2}$ × base × height

$$\frac{1}{2} \times \underbrace{8 \times 3}$$

$$\frac{1}{2} \times 24$$

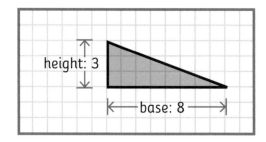

height: 3

base: 8

We start by multiplying the base by the height. Then we decide what half of the product is. Half of 24 is 12.

The area of the triangle is 12 square units.

What is the area formula for parallelograms?

We can use the same kind of thinking to find the area of a parallelogram.

A parallelogram is a four-sided shape like a rectangle, but its sides are slanted.

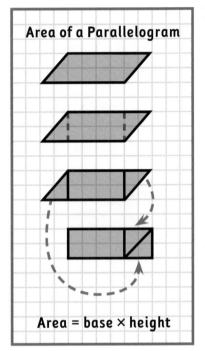

Area of a Parallelogram

Area = base × height

If we look closely, we see that a parallelogram is made up of a rectangle and two small triangles. If we move one of the triangles at the end of the parallelogram so that it is beneath the other triangle, we will have a rectangle with a base that is just as long as the original parallelogram. That means the area for a parallelogram is the same as the area for a rectangle.

Area of a parallelogram = base × height.

Let's use the formula to find the area of a parallelogram.

Example 1

Find the area of the parallelogram.

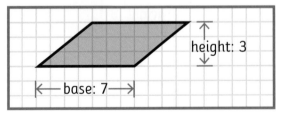

height: 3

base: 7

We only need the base and height.

    Base: 7 units

    Height: 3 units

    Area: **7 × 3 = 21**

The area of the parallelogram is 21 square units.

Problem-Solving Activity
Turn to *Interactive Text*, page 188.

mBook **Reinforce Understanding**
Use the *mBook Study Guide* to review lesson concepts.

Homework

Activity 1

Write fact families for the sets of numbers.

Model   2, 3, 6 $3 \times 2 = 6$ $2 \times 3 = 6$ $6 \div 2 = 3$ $6 \div 3 = 2$

1. 3, 9, 27
2. 4, 8, 32
3. 5, 4, 20
4. 9, 7, 63

Activity 2

Solve.

1. 3×7
2. 12×2
3. 8×2
4. 4×4
5. 6×5
6. 7×9

Activity 3

Write the factors for the following numbers.

1. 8
2. 15
3. 7
4. 25

Activity 4

Find the area of each shape.

1.

3

5

2.

4

7

3.

4

4

4.

4

6

Activity 5 • Distributed Practice

Solve.

1. $\begin{array}{r} 43 \\ \times\ 5 \\ \hline \end{array}$

2. $8\overline{)320}$

3. $\begin{array}{r} 5{,}000 \\ -\ \ 800 \\ \hline \end{array}$

4. $\begin{array}{r} 600 \\ +\,900 \\ \hline \end{array}$

Lesson 4 | ▶Factor Rainbows

Problem Solving:
▶Applying Area Formulas

▶**Factor Rainbows**

Vocabulary

factor rainbow

What is a factor rainbow?

In Lesson 3, we learned to write factor lists from the dimensions of arrays. We can also draw the factors of a number in a **factor rainbow**. A factor rainbow shows us how each of the factors are related. Let's look at a factor rainbow for the number 12.

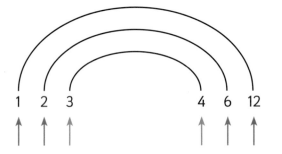

All the numbers in a factor rainbow are factors of a product. In this factor rainbow, the numbers are factors of 12.

Factor rainbows always start with the number 1 and end with the product of that factor rainbow. The outside numbers in this rainbow are 1 and 12. We know that 1 × 12 equals 12.

The numbers are in numerical order from left to right. This is true for every factor rainbow.

Each pair of numbers at the ends of an arc are factors of the product 12.

- 1 × 12 = 12
- 2 × 6 = 12
- 3 × 4 = 12

It is easy to create a factor list from a factor rainbow since the numbers are already written in numerical order.

The factor list for 12 is **1, 2, 3, 4, 6,** and **12.**

When finding the factors of a number, it helps to remember that division is the opposite of multiplication. Let's look at an example of this.

Example 1

Create a factor rainbow for 36.

We know that the number 1 divides evenly into every whole number.

1 × 36 = 36

- The outermost arc shows the numbers 1 and 36.

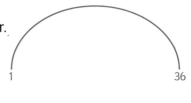

We want the numbers to move from left to right in numerical order. The number 2 can divide into 36.

2 × 18 = 36

- The next arc shows 2 and 18.

The next number we can divide evenly into 36 is 3. The number 3 divides into 36 twelve times.

3 × 12 = 36

- The third arc shows 3 and 12.

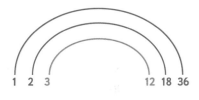

The number 4 also divides evenly into 36.

4 × 9 = 36

- The fourth arc shows 4 and 9.

The number 5 does not divide evenly into 36.

The number 6 divides evenly into 36.

6 × 6 = 36

- The last arc shows 6 and 6.

The factor list for 36 is 1, 2, 3, 4, 6, 9, 12, 18, and 36.

> The number 6 is shown two times in the factor rainbow, but only once in the factor list. This is because numbers should not be repeated in a factor list.

How do we know when we've found all the multiplication facts for a factor rainbow?

Listing multiplication facts with the smaller number first helps us know when we have found all the facts. The example shows us how to do this.

Example 1

Create a factor rainbow for 48.

To make sure that we include all the factors of 48 in our factor rainbow, we list all of the facts for 48. We start with the number 1 as a factor.

Our facts for this rainbow are:

1×48

2×24

3×16

4×12

5 does not divide evenly into 48.

6×8

7 does not divide evenly into 48.

The last arc shows 6 and 8. The numbers in this arc are closest in worth to each other. The only number between 6 and 8 is 7, which does not divide evenly into 48.

1 2 3 4 6   8 12 16 24 48

It's easy to find all the factors when we start with 1 and work our way up until the factors in an arc are so close that no number between them can divide into our product.

We are done with this factor rainbow because the two factors in the innermost arc are so close that no number between them will divide evenly into 48.

 Apply Skills
Turn to *Interactive Text*, page 190.

 Reinforce Understanding
Use the *mBook Study Guide* to review lesson concepts.

▶**Problem Solving: Applying Area Formulas**

How do we apply area formulas to irregular shapes?

Sometimes we need to find the area of a complex shape. We know area formulas for basic shapes. We can break a complex shape into smaller shapes, find their areas, and add them together.

Example 1

Find the area of the irregular shape.

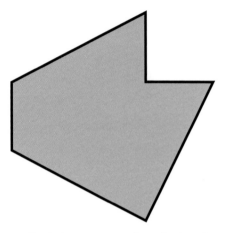
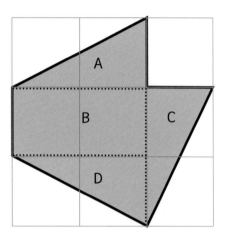

To find the area, we break the shape into shapes that we know. The dotted lines show where we can break the complex shape. We label the sections to make sure we have found the area of each part.

Here are the areas for each of the parts:

Triangle A: $\frac{1}{2} \times 2 \times 1 = 1$

Rectangle B: $2 \times 1 = 2$

Triangle C: $\frac{1}{2} \times 1 \times 2 = 1$

Triangle D: $\frac{1}{2} \times 2 \times 1 = 1$

> **Area Formulas**
>
> **Square and Rectangle:**
> Area = base × height
>
> **Triangle:**
> Area = $\frac{1}{2}$ × base × height
>
> **Parallelogram:**
> Area = base × height

We add the areas for each part to find the total area of the shape:

$1 + 2 + 1 + 1 = 5$.

The area of the irregular shape is 5 square units.

 Problem-Solving Activity
Turn to *Interactive Text*,
page 191.

 mBook **Reinforce Understanding**
Use the *mBook Study Guide*
to review lesson concepts.

Homework

Activity 1

Write fact families for the numbers.

Model   8, 9, 72 $8 \times 9 = 72$ $9 \times 8 = 72$ $72 \div 9 = 8$ $72 \div 8 = 9$

1. 4, 9, 36   **2.** 8, 7, 56   **3.** 6, 7, 42   **4.** 5, 9, 45

Activity 2

Create a factor rainbow for each number.

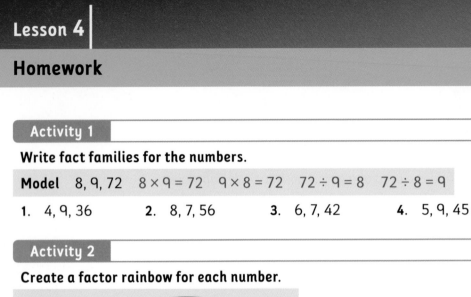

Model   6

1   2   3   6

1. 7   **2.** 12

3. 14   **4.** 24

5. 23   **6.** 36

Activity 3

Find the area of each shape.

1.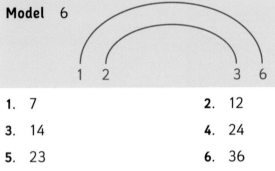
3
8

2.
10
3

Activity 4 • Distributed Practice

Solve.

1.   537
      × 8

2. $9\overline{)675}$

3.   700
      + 800

4.   1,200
       − 500

▶**Composite and Prime Numbers**

Vocabulary
composite numbers prime numbers

What are composite numbers?

In the last few lessons, we were finding factors. Most of the numbers that we looked at had several factors. We used arrays to show what these numbers look like.

Here are the arrays for the number **6**:

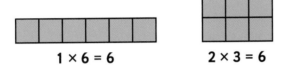

$1 \times 6 = 6$ $2 \times 3 = 6$

The factors for 6 are 1, 2, 3, and 6.

The number 6 has more than one array. That means it has more than two factors. We call a number with more than two factors a **composite number**. So 6 is a *composite number*.

The chart shows the factor lists for some composite numbers.

Examples of Composite Numbers	
Number	**Factor List**
6	1, 2, 3, 6
9	1, 3, 9
15	1, 3, 5, 15
18	1, 2, 3, 6, 9, 18
22	1, 2, 11, 22

Each composite number has more than two factors.

What are prime numbers?

The numbers below only have one array.

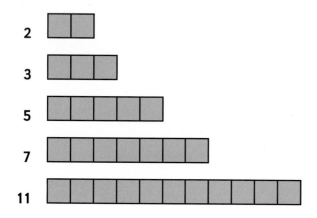

The list of numbers with only one array continues with 13, 17, 19, and 23. There is no end to this list of numbers. These numbers are called **prime numbers** . Each prime number has exactly two factors—1 and itself. There is no other way to arrange these numbers in an array. The arrays have only one row.

The only array for 11 has 1 row and 11 columns. The multiplication problem for this number is 1 × 11. Its only factors are 1 and 11.

The chart shows the factor lists for some prime numbers.

| Examples of Prime Numbers ||
Numbers	Factor List
17	1, 17
29	1, 29
53	1, 53
101	1, 101

- All prime numbers have exactly two factors.
- All composite numbers have more than two factors.

To tell the difference between prime and composite numbers, we need to know whether or not a number can be divided evenly by any number besides 1 and itself.

All even numbers can be divided by the number 2. Even numbers are numbers that end in 0, 2, 4, 6, or 8. All even numbers, other than the number 2, are composite.

Odd numbers end in 1, 3, 5, 7, or 9. Not all odd numbers can be divided evenly by other numbers. That makes several odd numbers prime. Let's see how to determine if a number is prime or composite.

Example 1

Use arrays to decide if the numbers are prime or composite.

29

We can only make one array. There are 2 factors: 1 and 29.
The number 29 is prime.

27

We can make 2 arrays. There are 4 factors: 1, 3, 9, and 27.
The number 27 is composite.

101

We can only make one array. There are 2 factors: 1 and 101.
The number 101 is prime.

There is only one row in the arrays of prime numbers. This is because we cannot divide them by any other number to create equal rows.

We can also use factor lists to see if a number is composite or prime.

Example 2

Use factor lists to decide if the numbers are prime or composite.

53

Only two factors: 1, 53

Nothing will evenly divide into 53 except 1 and itself.

The number 53 is prime.

30

More than two factors: 1, 2, 3, 5, 6, 10, 15, 30

The number 30 is an even number. It has eight factors.

The number 30 is composite.

42

More than two factors: 1, 2, 3, 6, 7, 14, 21, 42

The number 42 is an even number. It has eight factors.

The number 42 is composite.

15

More than two factors: 1, 3, 5, 15

The number 15 has four factors.

The number 15 is composite.

> The size of a number has nothing to do with whether it is prime or composite.

There are many, many numbers that are prime or composite. In fact, there is no end to these numbers. We can keep finding them forever.

 Apply Skills
Turn to *Interactive Text*, page 193.

 Monitoring Progress
Quiz 1

 mBook **Reinforce Understanding**
Use the *mBook Study Guide* to review lesson concepts.

Activity 1

List the factors for the numbers.

1. 5   **2.** 14   **3.** 17   **4.** 25

Activity 2

Use factor lists to decide if the number is prime or composite.

1. 6   **2.** 21   **3.** 31

4. 11   **5.** 27   **6.** 33

Activity 3

Write the dimensions for the arrays.

1.

2.

3.

Activity 4 • Distributed Practice

Solve.

1. $\begin{array}{r} 300 \\ \times\ \ 4 \\ \hline \end{array}$ **2.** $\begin{array}{r} 40 \\ \times 20 \\ \hline \end{array}$ **3.** $\begin{array}{r} 876 \\ + 295 \\ \hline \end{array}$ **4.** $4\overline{)372}$

▶**Understanding Prime Numbers**

Problem Solving:
▶**Perimeter**

▶**Understanding Prime Numbers**

Vocabulary
infinite

What are some interesting facts about prime numbers?

Prime numbers have fascinated mathematicians for centuries. About 2,300 years ago, the ancient Greeks proved that there were an **infinite**, or endless, number of prime numbers. They also noticed that there was no way to predict the distance between prime numbers. Prime numbers occur randomly.

Even though prime numbers occur randomly, there are common characteristics we notice about them. We know the common characteristics that define them:

- A prime number can only be divided by the number 1 and itself.
- A prime number has exactly two factors.

Let's look at the table of prime numbers from 1 to 1,000 to find some more characteristics.

Prime Numbers Between 0 and 1,000

2	3	5	7	11	13	17	19	23	29	31	37	41	43	47	53	59	61	67	71
73	79	83	89	97	101	103	107	109	113	127	131	137	139	149	151	157	163	167	173
179	181	191	193	197	199	211	223	227	229	233	239	241	251	257	263	269	271	277	281
283	293	307	311	313	317	331	337	347	349	353	359	367	373	379	383	389	397	401	409
419	421	431	433	439	443	449	457	461	463	467	479	487	491	499	503	509	521	523	541
547	557	563	569	574	577	587	593	599	601	607	613	617	619	631	641	643	647	653	659
661	673	677	683	691	701	709	719	727	733	739	743	751	757	761	769	773	787	797	809
811	821	823	827	829	839	853	857	859	863	877	881	883	887	907	911	919	929	937	941
947	953	967	971	977	983	991	997												

Notice the following:

- The number 2 is the only even number that is prime.
- The number 5 is the only prime number with a 5 in the ones place.
- The numbers 0 and 1 are not listed as prime.

Neither Prime nor Composite

The number 1 is not a prime number because it does not have exactly two factors—1 and itself. Instead of these two factors, it only has one factor—the number 1. It is a special case.

Where are the prime numbers?

Let's explore groups of prime numbers and look for patterns. The graph shows the number of prime numbers found from 1 to 10,000. They are grouped in sets of 2,500. The graph shows how many prime numbers occur in each of these groups. Let's use the graph to find patterns in the number of primes.

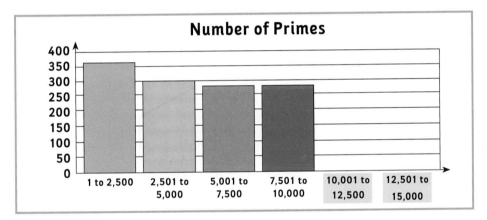

The amount of prime numbers in each group of 2,500 decreases as the numbers get larger. Putting this information in a table helps us see this better.

Number of Primes				
Group	1–2,500	2,501–5,000	5,001–7,500	7,501–10,000
Number of Primes	367	302	281	279
Decreases		65	21	2

⌄ points to the decrease in the number of prime numbers between groups of numbers.

 Apply Skills
Turn to *Interactive Text*, page 195.

 mBook Reinforce Understanding
Use the *mBook Study Guide* to review lesson concepts.

Unit 5 • Lesson 6   **295**

▶**Problem Solving: Perimeter**

Vocabulary

perimeter

What is perimeter?

We learned that if we want to know the size of the space inside an object, we need to find its area. We can also find the distance around a shape, or its **perimeter**. Perimeter is the length of the border around a shape.

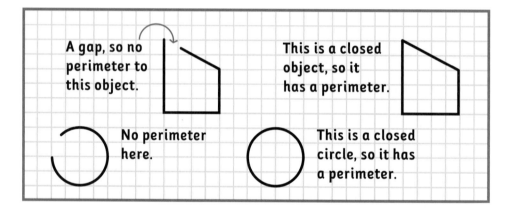

The border of the object must connect together, or be "closed," for the object to have a perimeter. The border cannot have any open spaces or gaps.

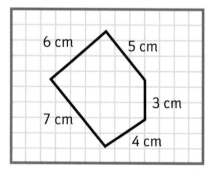

A gap, so no perimeter to this object.

This is a closed object, so it has a perimeter.

No perimeter here.

This is a closed circle, so it has a perimeter.

Finding Perimeter

To find the perimeter of an object, we add the lengths of all the sides.

6 cm + 5 cm + 3 cm + 4 cm + 7 cm = 25 cm

The perimeter of this shape is 25 centimeters.

How do we find the perimeter of rectangles and squares?

Let's use what we know about rectangles and squares to find their perimeters.

Perimeter of a Rectangle

We know that opposite sides of a rectangle are equal, so we add each side twice.

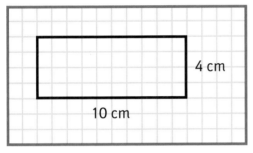

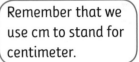

Remember that we use cm to stand for centimeter.

4 cm + 4 cm + 10 cm + 10 cm = 28 cm

A shortcut for finding the perimeter of a rectangle is to add the base and the height and then multiply the answer times 2.

10 cm + 4 cm = 14 cm

2 × 14 cm = 28 cm

The perimeter of the rectangle is 28 centimeters.

Perimeter of a Square

It's even easier to find the perimeter of a square. Because all four sides of the square are the same length, we just take the length of any side and multiply it times 4.

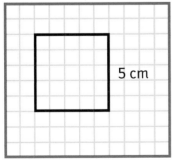

4 × 5 cm = 20 cm

The perimeter of the square is 20 centimeters.

Let's look at two more examples of finding perimeter.

Example 1

Find the perimeter of the rectangle.

To find the perimeter of a rectangle, add the lengths of all the sides, 6 cm + 6 cm + 10 cm + 10 cm = 32 cm
    or
add the base and the height and multiply times 2.

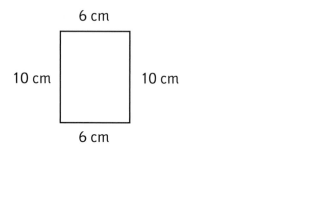

6 cm + 10 cm = 16 cm

2 × 16 cm = 32 cm

The perimeter is 32 centimeters.

Example 2

Find the perimeter of the square.

To find the perimeter of a square, we multiply the length of one side times 4.

4 × 4 cm = 16 cm

The perimeter is 16 centimeters.

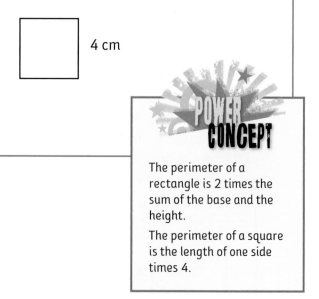

POWER CONCEPT

The perimeter of a rectangle is 2 times the sum of the base and the height.

The perimeter of a square is the length of one side times 4.

 Problem-Solving Activity
Turn to *Interactive Text*, page 196.

 mBook Reinforce Understanding
Use the *mBook Study Guide* to review lesson concepts.

Activity 1

List the factors for the numbers.

1. 7   2. 16   3. 21

4. 32   5. 50   6. 64

Activity 2

Use factor lists to decide if the number is prime or composite.

1. 5   2. 9   3. 17

4. 29   5. 33   6. 41

Activity 3

Find the perimeter and area of each shape.

1.

5
5

2.

4
9

3.

5
2

4.

3
3

Activity 4 • Distributed Practice

Solve.

1.
$$400 + 900$$

2.
$$1{,}600 - 700$$

3.
$$46 \times 93$$

4. $2\overline{)345}$

▸**Prime Factors**

What are prime factors?

One way to factor a number is to use **prime factors** . Prime factors are the most basic factors of a number.

Vocabulary
prime factors
prime factorization
prime factor tree

Let's use our knowledge of prime numbers and factors to understand what a prime factor is. We know that a prime number can only be divided by 1 and itself. The numbers 2, 3, 5, and 7 are all prime numbers. We also know that factors are the numbers we multiply to find a product.

Let's look at the factors of the number **24**.

Factors of 24
$$
\begin{cases}
1 \times 24 \\
2 \times 12 \\
3 \times 8 \\
4 \times 6
\end{cases}
$$

The factors of 24 are 1, 2, 3, 4, 6, 8, 12, and 24.

Now we're going to break down some of the factors of 24 further. Our goal is to break down all of the numbers in the factor list into *primes*.

Finding the prime factors of a number is called **prime factorization** . To do this, we use a special tool called a **prime factor tree.**

Here's how using prime factor trees works.

How do we use prime factor trees to find prime factors?

Using prime factor trees is an easy way to find the prime factors of a number. It allows us to use the numbers we know to break the products into factors. It is called a tree because it has branches on which we write the factors.

Let's make a prime factor tree for the number 24.

Steps for Making a Prime Factor Tree for the Number 24

STEP 1

Choose one multiplication fact that makes up the product. Let's choose 3 × 8 = 24. Write 24 first. Then write the factors 3 and 8 on the branches below it.

STEP 2

Decide if the first factors are prime.
We circle every prime number we find. If both the numbers are prime, then we are done factoring that number. The number 3 is prime, but 8 is not.

STEP 3

Find two factors for any composite numbers in the first step.
The number 8 is composite. Let's choose 2 × 4 = 8. Write 2 and 4 on the branches below the number 8.

STEP 4

Repeat Steps 2 and 3 for new factors until all of the factors at the bottom of the lines are prime.
The number 2 is a prime number.

The number 4 is composite, so we factor this to 2 × 2 = 4. Write 2 and 2 on the branches below the 4.

The number 2 is a prime number. All of the numbers are now prime.

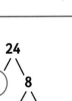

STEP 5

Rewrite all of the prime numbers in a multiplication problem to show the prime factors.

Our prime factorization of 24 is: 2 × 2 × 2 × 3.

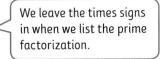
We leave the times signs in when we list the prime factorization.

We can use a prime factor tree to find the prime factors of any number. Let's look at some more examples of prime factor trees.

Example 1

Find the prime factors of 30 using a prime factor tree.
Think about the factors of 30. Choose two factors that multiply to get 30:

- 1 and 30
- 2 and 15
- 3 and 10
- 5 and 6

We do not want to choose the 1 and 30 because it does not break 30 into pieces. We will choose 2 and 15.

We circle 2 because it is prime.

Since 15 is composite, we need to choose two of its factors.

- 1 and 15
- 3 and 5

We will choose 3 and 5.

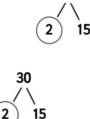

We circle both the 3 and the 5 because they are prime.

The prime factorization of 30 is 2 × 3 × 5.

To check our answer, we multiply the numbers together.

Multiply the first two numbers. Then we multiply the product of the first two numbers by the next number.

$$2 \times 3 = 6$$

$$6 \times 5 = 30$$

Our answer is 30, so our prime factorization is correct.

Apply Skills
Turn to *Interactive Text*, page 198.

mBook Reinforce Understanding
Use the *mBook Study Guide* to review lesson concepts.

▶**Problem Solving: Different Shapes, Same Perimeter**

Can different shapes have the same perimeter?

We learned how to find the perimeter of squares and rectangles. We added the lengths of all the sides to find the measurement. We use the same thinking to find the perimeters of other shapes.

Look at Shape A, Shape B, and Shape C.

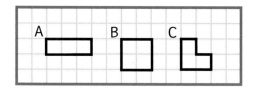

Shape A is a rectangle.

We find the perimeter by multiplying the length of the base and the height by 2 then adding.

• Length: 3 units $3 \times 2 = 6$

• Height: 1 unit $1 \times 2 = 2$

• $6 + 2 = 8$

The perimeter of Shape A is 8 units.

Perimeter = 8 units

Shape B is a square.

We find the perimeter of any square by multiplying the length of any side by 4.

• Length of one side: 2 units
  $2 \times 4 = 8$

The perimeter of Shape B is 8 units.

Perimeter = 8 units

Shape C is not a square or a rectangle.

We find the perimeter by adding the lengths of all the sides.

• The shape has six sides.

• Four of the sides are 1 unit long.

• Two of the sides are 2 units long.

• Add all of the lengths together.
  $1 + 1 + 1 + 1 + 2 + 2 = 8$

The perimeter of Shape C is 8 units.

Perimeter = 8 units

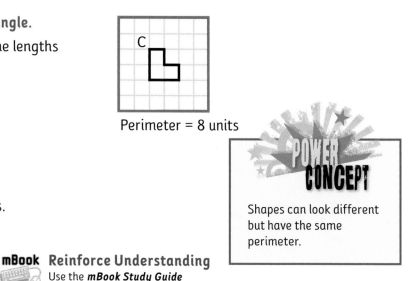

POWER CONCEPT

Shapes can look different but have the same perimeter.

 Problem-Solving Activity
Turn to *Interactive Text*, page 199.

 **Reinforce Understanding**
Use the *mBook Study Guide* to review lesson concepts.

Activity 1

List all the factors for the numbers.

1. 18

2. 22

3. 6

4. 30

5. 13

6. 4

Activity 2

Find the area and perimeter of each shape. Then answer the questions.

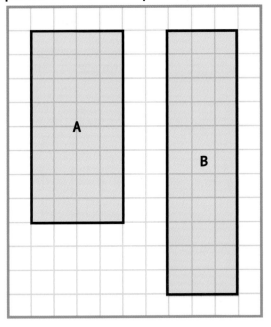

1. Which shape has the bigger area?

2. How much bigger is the area of the largest shape?

3. Which shape has the bigger perimeter?

4. How much bigger is the perimeter of the largest shape?

Activity 3

Fill in the missing numbers in these factor trees.

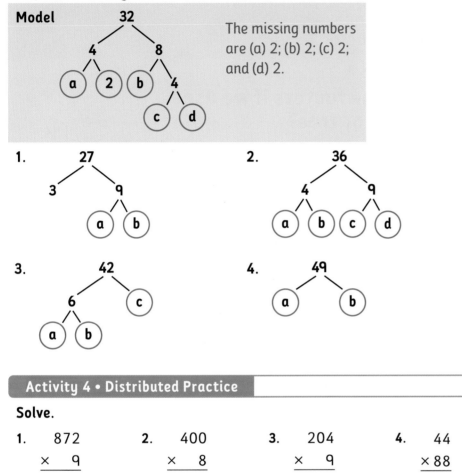

Model

32

4   8

(a)   (2)   (b)   4

(c)   (d)

The missing numbers are (a) 2; (b) 2; (c) 2; and (d) 2.

1.   27
   3   9
      (a) (b)

2.   36
     4   9
  (a) (b)   (c) (d)

3.   42
   6   (c)
(a) (b)

4.   49
  (a)   (b)

Activity 4 • Distributed Practice

Solve.

1. $\begin{array}{r} 872 \\ \times\ 9 \\ \hline \end{array}$

2. $\begin{array}{r} 400 \\ \times\ 8 \\ \hline \end{array}$

3. $\begin{array}{r} 204 \\ \times\ 9 \\ \hline \end{array}$

4. $\begin{array}{r} 44 \\ \times 88 \\ \hline \end{array}$

Problem Solving:
Same Perimeter, Different Area

▶**More Practice With Prime Factor Trees**

Will we get the same prime factors if we use different factors in a factor tree?

The good thing about prime factorization is that it lets us work with numbers we are comfortable with. When we use a prime factor tree, we can start with any combination of factors that equal our product. All of the factor combinations lead us to the same prime factors.

Let's look at some different factor combinations we can use to find the same prime factor list.

POWER CONCEPT

We only need to know one pair of factors to begin our factor tree.

Example 1

Use different factor combinations to find the prime factors of 40.

Start by thinking of what numbers can be multiplied to get 40.
One easy combination is 4 × 10.

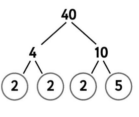

The prime factorization of 40 is 2 × 2 × 2 × 5.

Try another set of factors that can be multiplied to get 40. Using another set is a way to check that we did the prime factorization correctly the first time. We can use 2 × 20.

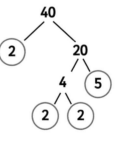

If we rearrange the prime factors from the tree, we see that the prime factorization of 40 still comes out to 2 × 2 × 2 × 5.

What are some strategies for factoring larger numbers?

When we see large numbers, we might think they are difficult to factor. Two strategies will help us: using basic facts and powers of 10.

Use Basic Facts

Let's find the prime factorization for 72.

We start with our knowledge of basic facts:
8 × 9 = 72.

We circle all of the primes.

The prime factorization of 72 is:
2 × 2 × 2 × 3 × 3.

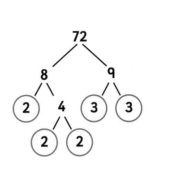

Use Powers of 10

Let's find the prime factorization for 70.

We start with a power of 10:
7 × 10 = 70.

The prime factorization of 70 is:
7 × 2 × 5.

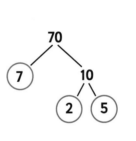

 Apply Skills
Turn to *Interactive Text*, page 201.

mBook Reinforce Understanding
Use the *mBook Study Guide* to review lesson concepts.

▶**Problem Solving: Same Perimeter, Different Area**

Can shapes with the same perimeter have different areas?

We know that different shapes can have the same perimeter. We used the three shapes below when we learned about perimeter. They all have the same perimeter of 8 units. Let's compare their areas and see if they are different.

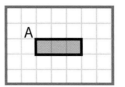

Shape A is a rectangle with a perimeter of 8 units.

The area of a rectangle is base × height.

base = 3 units

height = 1 unit

3 units × 1 unit = 3 square units

Shape A has an area of 3 square units.

A

Area = 3 sq. units

Shape B is a square with a perimeter of 8 units.

The area of a square is base × height.

The base and height are both 2 units.

2 units × 2 units = 4 square units

Shape B has an area of 4 square units.

B

Area = 4 sq. units

Shape C is not a rectangle or a square. It has a perimeter of 8 units.

We can find the area by adding together all of the square units inside the shape.

Shape C has an area of 3 square units.

- **Area of Shape A**: 3 square units
- **Area of Shape B**: 4 square units
- **Area of Shape C**: 3 square units

C

Area = 3 sq. units

The shapes have the same perimeter, but not the same area.

POWER CONCEPT

Shapes with the same perimeter can have different areas.

 Problem-Solving Activity
Turn to *Interactive Text*, page 202.

 mBook Reinforce Understanding
Use the *mBook Study Guide* to review lesson concepts.

Activity 1

List which of the numbers are composite.

1   4   7   23   30   100   1,000

Activity 2

List all of the factors for the numbers.

1. 10

2. 14

3. 16

4. 17

5. 24

6. 28

Activity 3

Fill in the missing numbers in these factor trees.

1.

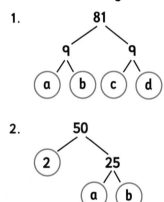

2.

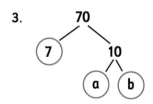

3.

Homework

Activity 4

Use factor trees to find the prime factorization of each number.

1. 80 **2.** 100 **3.** 75

4. 90 **5.** 36 **6.** 64

Activity 5 • Distributed Practice

Solve.

1. $\begin{array}{r} 3{,}697 \\ +\ 2{,}908 \\ \hline \end{array}$

2. $\begin{array}{r} 900 \\ +\ 600 \\ \hline \end{array}$

3. $\begin{array}{r} 30 \\ \times\ \ 4 \\ \hline \end{array}$

4. $6\overline{)500}$

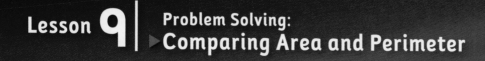

▶**Problem Solving: Comparing Area and Perimeter**

How do we compare area and perimeter?

We can find patterns that show what shapes have the greatest perimeter. Remember, area is the space that is measured inside an object. Perimeter is the border around the object. All of the objects shown here have both an area and a perimeter.

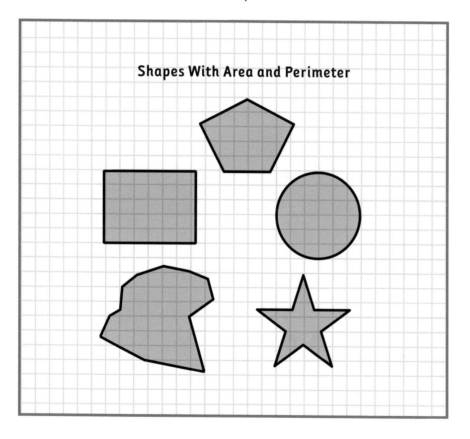

Shapes With Area and Perimeter

When we use both area and perimeter to describe shapes, we want to make sure that we do not confuse them.

Area measures the space inside an object. When we talk about area, we use square units.

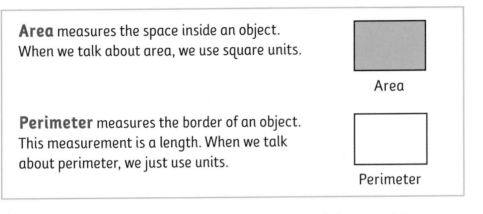

Area

Perimeter measures the border of an object. This measurement is a length. When we talk about perimeter, we just use units.

Perimeter

We sometimes compare the area and perimeter of shapes. While these comparisons can be useful, we need to remember that area and perimeter are measured in different units.

Let's look at an example.

Example 1

Compare the area and perimeter of a rectangle.

To find the *area* of a rectangle, we multiply the base times the height.

 3 cm

5 cm

Since 5 × 3 = 15, the area is 15 square centimeters.

To find the *perimeter* of the rectangle, we add 2 times the base and 2 times the height.

- Two times the base is 2 × 5 cm = 10 cm.
- Two times the height is 2 × 3 cm = 6 cm.

Since 10 cm + 6 cm = 16 cm, the perimeter is 16 centimeters.

The area of the rectangle is 15 square centimeters. The perimeter of the rectangle is 16 centimeters.

The area of the rectangle is smaller than its perimeter.

It is important to see relationships in mathematics. The area of the previous rectangle was smaller than its perimeter. Let's see if this is always true.

Example 2

Compare the area and perimeter of the rectangle.

The rectangle has a base of 7 cm and a height of 3 cm.

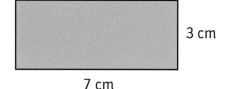

3 cm

7 cm

Find the area:
- Multiply the base times the height.
  7 cm × 3 cm = 21 square cm

The area is 21 square centimeters.

Find the perimeter:
- Two times the base is 2 × 7 cm = 14 cm.
- Two times the height is 2 × 3 cm = 6 cm.
- 14 cm + 6 cm = 20 cm.

The perimeter is 20 centimeters.

The area of the rectangle is 21 square centimeters.
The perimeter of the rectangle is 20 centimeters.

The area of the rectangle is larger than its perimeter.

When we look at this model, we know that either the area or perimeter of a rectangle can be larger.

Let's look at the perimeter and area of triangles.

Example 3

Compare the perimeter and area of triangle A.

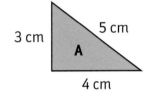

3 cm   5 cm   A   4 cm

Area: $\frac{1}{2} \times$ base $\times$ height

$\frac{1}{2} \times 4$ cm $\times 3$ cm $= 6$ square cm

Perimeter: base + height + diagonal

4 cm + 3 cm + 5 cm = 12 cm

The perimeter of the triangle is larger than its area.

Example 4

Compare the perimeter and area of triangle B.

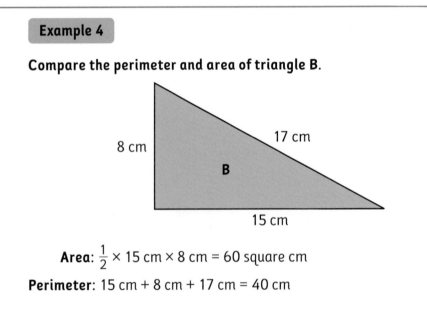

8 cm   17 cm   B   15 cm

Area: $\frac{1}{2} \times 15$ cm $\times 8$ cm $= 60$ square cm

Perimeter: 15 cm + 8 cm + 17 cm = 40 cm

The area of the triangle is larger than its perimeter.

Just like rectangles, the area or perimeter of a triangle can be larger.

 Problem-Solving Activity
Turn to *Interactive Text*,
page 204.

 mBook **Reinforce Understanding**
Use the *mBook Study Guide*
to review lesson concepts.

Homework

Activity 1

List all of the factors for each number.

1. 54
2. 50
3. 64
4. 75
5. 80

Activity 2

Fill in the missing numbers in these factor trees.

1.
```
            80
          /    \
         8      10
        / \    / \
      (2) (4) (c) (d)
          / \
        (a) (b)
```

2.
```
           90
         /    \
        9      10
       / \    / \
     (a) (b) (c) (d)
```

3.
```
           100
         /     \
        10      10
       / \     / \
     (a) (b) (c) (d)
```

Activity 3 • Distributed Practice

Solve.

1. $\begin{array}{r} 300 \\ \times\ \ 4 \\ \hline \end{array}$

2. $\begin{array}{r} 40 \\ \times 80 \\ \hline \end{array}$

3. $7\overline{)420}$

4. $7\overline{)476}$

▶**Common Errors in Prime Factorization**

Monitoring Progress:
▶**Quiz 2**

▶**Common Errors in Prime Factorization**

How do we avoid errors in prime factorization?

There are some common mistakes we sometimes make when we find the prime factorization of a number. Let's see how we can avoid these errors.

One error is forgetting to factor the numbers until only prime factors are left.

Improve Your Skills

Your friend used a prime factor tree to find the prime factors of 100.

ERROR

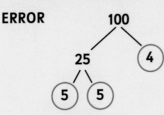

He says the prime factorization of 100 is **4 × 5 × 5**.

Your friend factored the 25 into prime factors, but forgot to factor the 4 into prime factors.

The correct factor tree looks like this:

CORRECT

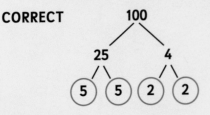

The prime factorization of 100 is **2 × 2 × 5 × 5**.

Let's look at another error that we might make.

Improve Your Skills

Your friend used a prime factor tree to find the prime factorization of 45.

ERROR

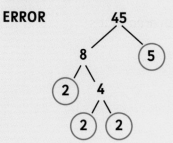

Your friend says the prime factorization of 45 is **2 × 2 × 2 × 5**.

She started her factor tree by factoring 45 into 8 and 5. The number 8 is not a factor of 45.

The correct basic fact for 45 is 9 × 5. Your friend should have started the factor tree by factoring 45 into 9 and 5.

CORRECT

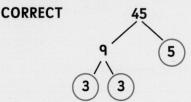

The prime factorization of 45 is **3 × 3 × 5**.

When we create prime factor trees, we need to be careful to avoid these common mistakes.

 Apply Skills
Turn to *Interactive Text*, page 206.

 Monitoring Progress
Quiz 2

 mBook Reinforce Understanding
Use the *mBook Study Guide* to review lesson concepts.

Activity 1

Draw prime factor trees for each number.

1. 15
2. 56
3. 64
4. 90

Activity 2

Select the best answer to each question.

1. All of these rectangles have a perimeter of 20. Which one has an area that's smaller than the perimeter?
    - (a) 3×7
    - (b) 2×8
    - (c) 5×5
    - (d) 4×6

2. The area and perimeter are the same for one of these rectangles. Which one?
    - (a) 4×4
    - (b) 2×2
    - (c) 9×9
    - (d) 7×7

3. All of these rectangles have an area of 24. Which has the largest perimeter?
    - (a) 4×6
    - (b) 8×3
    - (c) 2×12
    - (d) 1×24

Activity 3 • Distributed Practice

Solve.

1. $9\overline{)747}$

2. $\begin{array}{r} 1,999 \\ -999 \\ \hline \end{array}$

3. $\begin{array}{r} 600 \\ +800 \\ \hline \end{array}$

4. $\begin{array}{r} 99 \\ \times 88 \\ \hline \end{array}$

Lesson 11 ▸ Divisibility Rules for 2, 5, and 10

Problem Solving:
▸ Patterns in Area and Perimeter

▸ Divisibility Rules for 2, 5, and 10

Vocabulary
divisibility rules

What are the divisibility rules for 2, 5, and 10?

We used multiplication facts to find the factors for numbers. We also used powers of 10. When we have to factor much larger numbers, these strategies might not help us.

There is another strategy we can use to find the factors of larger numbers. **Divisibility rules** are rules that we sometimes use to divide numbers.

There are divisibility rules for the numbers 2, 5, 10, 3, and 6.
You already know some of these rules.

Divisibility Rule for 2

Look at the numbers in the table. These numbers are even numbers because they end in 2, 4, 6, 8, or 0.

Rule	Examples					
Divide by 2	8	12	66	302	1,000	3,954

We can divide a number by 2 if it ends with an even number.

What about the number 7,628?

It ends in an even number. We should be able to divide it by 2.

We can use a calculator to check:
7,628 ÷ 2 = 3,814

Since there is no remainder, 7,628 is divisible by 2.

Divisibility Rule for 10

Look at the numbers in the table. All of these numbers end with a zero.

Rule	Examples					
Divide by 10	10	50	110	300	5,000	30,150

We can divide a number by 10 if it ends with a zero.

What about the number 6,440?

It ends in 0. We should be able to divide it by 10.

We can use a calculator to check:

6,440 ÷ 10 = 644

Since there is no remainder, 6,440 is divisible by 10.

Notice that this rule works just like the powers of 10 rule. When a number ends in zero, we can pull out powers of 10.

Now let's look at the divisibility rule for 5.

Divisibility Rule for 5

Look at the numbers in the chart below. All of these numbers end in 5 or 0.

Rule	Examples					
Divide by 5	15	70	210	335	7,005	89,260

We can divide any number that ends in 5 or 0 by 5.

What about the number 79,465?

Can we divide by 5? The number ends in 5, so we should be able to divide it by 5.

We can use a calculator to check:

79,465 ÷ 5 = 15,893

Since there is no remainder, 79,465 is divisible by 5.

We found divisibility rules for 2, 5, and 10.

Divisibility Rules for 2, 5, and 10	
2	We can divide a number by 2 if it ends with an even number.
5	We can divide a number by 5 if it ends with a 5 or a 0.
10	We can divide a number by 10 if it ends with a 0.

Let's use the divisibility rules to learn more about the numbers in the following examples.

Example 1

Determine if 358 is divisible by 2.

- Is the last digit an even number?
- Yes, 8 is an even number.

Since 358 ends with an even number, 358 is divisible by 2.

By looking at the last digit of a number we can determine if it is divisible by 2, 5, or 10.

We can determine if a number is even and divisible by 2 by looking at the last digit of a number. We also look at the last digit for our divisibility rules for 10 and 5.

Example 2

Determine if 670 is divisible by 10.

- Does the number end with a 0?
- Yes, 670 ends with a 0.
- Since 670 ends with a 0, it is divisible by 10.

Determine if 1,425 and 3,670 are divisible by 5.

- Do the numbers end with a 5 or a 0?
- Yes, 1,425 ends with a 5 and 3,670 ends with a 0.

Since both numbers end with a 5 or 0, they are both divisible by 5.

We can determine whether numbers are divisible by other numbers when we use our divisibility rules. Later, we will find divisibility rules for the numbers 3 and 6.

 **Apply Skills**
Turn to *Interactive Text*,
page 208.

 mBook Reinforce Understanding
Use the *mBook Study Guide*
to review lesson concepts.

▶**Problem Solving: Patterns in Area and Perimeter**

Which type of rectangles have the largest area?

Let's look again at the relationship between perimeter and area. We learned that some rectangles have bigger perimeters than areas, and some have bigger areas than perimeters.

The perimeter of each of the rectangles below is the same, but the area of each rectangle is different.

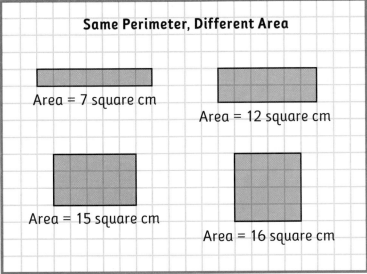

Same Perimeter, Different Area

Area = 7 square cm

Area = 12 square cm

Area = 15 square cm

Area = 16 square cm

If we look closely at these rectangles, we can make another observation. The rectangles that appear to be longer and thinner have smaller areas. This is a pattern.

Notice that the area is larger the closer the rectangle is to the shape of a square.

Our last rectangle is a square. It has the largest area.

POWER CONCEPT

Squares have a bigger area than any rectangle with the same perimeter.

 Problem-Solving Activity
Turn to *Interactive Text*, page 209.

 mBook Reinforce Understanding
Use the *mBook Study Guide* to review lesson concepts.

Homework

Activity 1

List all the factors for each number.

1. 10
2. 12
3. 14
4. 16
5. 18

Activity 2

Draw prime factor trees for each number.

1. 48
2. 54
3. 64

Activity 3

Determine if each number is divisible by 2, 5, or 10.

1. 212
2. 1,085
3. 5,010

Activity 4 • Distributed Practice

Solve.

1. $\begin{array}{r} 2{,}537 \\ + 3{,}879 \\ \hline \end{array}$

2. $\begin{array}{r} 6{,}002 \\ - 3{,}917 \\ \hline \end{array}$

3. $\begin{array}{r} 45 \\ \times 98 \\ \hline \end{array}$

4. $3\overline{)632}$

▶**Divisibility Rules for 3 and 6**

Problem Solving:
▶**Finding Area and Perimeter of Irregular Shapes**

▶**Divisibility Rules for 3 and 6**

What are the divisibility rules for 3 and 6?

We learned the divisibility rules for 2, 5, and 10. We found that we look at the last digit in a number to determine if it is divisible by these numbers. To know if a number is divisible by 3, we follow some simple rules and use division facts for 3.

Divisibility Rules for 3

Look at the numbers in the table.

Rule	Examples					
Divide by 3	84	114	261	339	3,003	56,112

- First, add up the digits in the number.
- If the sum can be divided by 3, then the original number can be divided by 3.

We can divide any number by 3 if the sum of its digits is divisible by 3.

Let's look at the number 84.

- Add the digits together: 8 + 4 = 12.
- Can 12 be divided by 3?
- Think of our basic facts: 3 × 4 = 12 or 12 ÷ 3 = 4.
- Since 12 can be divided by 3, the original number, 84, can be divided by 3.

We can use a calculator to check.

84 ÷ 3 = 28

Since there is no remainder, 84 is divisible by 3.

What about a larger number like 56,112? Can we divide it by 3?

- Add the digits together: $5 + 6 + 1 + 1 + 2 = 15$.
- Can 15 be divided by 3?
- Think of our basic facts: $3 \times 5 = 15$ or $15 \div 3 = 5$.
- Because 15 is evenly divided by 3, the original number 56,112 can be evenly divided by 3.

We can use a calculator to check.

$56,112 \div 3 = 18,704$

Since there is no remainder, 56,112 is divisible by 3.

$$18,704$$

Divisibility Rule for 6

Look at the numbers in the table.

Rule	Examples					
Divide by 6	96	390	462	756	6,120	45,018

To be divisible by 6, a number must be even and divisible by 3.

All of the numbers in the table are divisible by 6.

A number can be divided by 6 if it can be divided by 2 and 3.

Let's look at the number 96.

- The number 96 is even because it ends in an even number.
- If we add the digits together, we get $9 + 6 = 15$. We know that 15 is divisible by 3.

Since it is an even number and can be divided by 3, 96 can be divided by 6.

We now know divisibility rules for five numbers.

Divisibility Rules for 2, 3, 5, 6, and 10	
2	A number can be divided by 2 if it ends with an even number.
3	A number can be divided by 3 if the sum of its digits is divisible by 3.
5	A number can be divided by 5 if it ends with a 5 or a 0.
6	A number can be divided by 6 if it is divisible by both 2 and 3.
10	A number can be divided by 10 if it ends with a 0.

Let's use divisibility rules to determine if numbers are divisible by 3 and 6.

Example 1

Determine if 1,017 is divisible by 3.

- When we add the digits together, can the sum of the digits be divided by 3?
- Yes, 1 + 0 + 1 + 7 = 9.
- The number 9 is divisible by 3.

Since the sum of the digits is divisible by 3, the number 1,017 is divisible by 3.

Our divisibility rule tells us that a number can be divided by 6 if it is divisible by both 2 and 3.

Example 2

Determine if 570 is divisible by 6.

- Is the number even?
- Yes, the number 570 ends in 0, so the number is even.
- When we add the digits together, can the sum of the digits be divided by 3?
- Yes, 5 + 7 + 0 = 12.
- The number 12 is divisible by 3.

Because the number is even and the sum of the digits is divisible by 3, the number 570 is divisible by 6.

By looking at the last digit of a number or the sum of the digits in a number, we can determine if the number is divisible by 2, 3, 5, 6, or 10.

 Apply Skills
Turn to *Interactive Text*,
page 211.

 mBook Reinforce Understanding
Use the *mBook Study Guide*
to review lesson concepts.

How do we find the area of irregular shapes?

Sometimes it is hard to compare the area and perimeter of different shapes. The mind sometimes plays tricks on what we think we see.

Look at the three shapes below. We want to know:

"Do they have the same area?"

"Do they have the same perimeter?"

If we answer "No," then we are like most people. The shapes look like they have different areas, but the area for each shape is the same. They all have different perimeters.

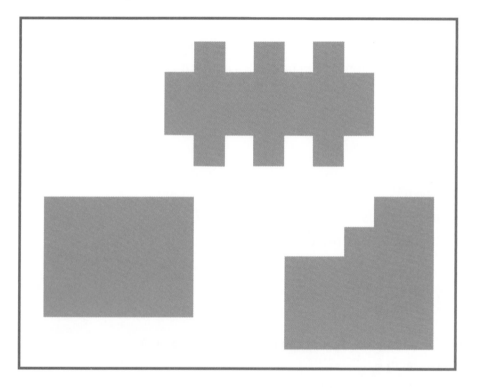

We can see why the shapes have the same area with different perimeters if we break the shapes into square units that are the same size. Let's use square units to count the area of each shape.

Breaking irregular shapes into square units makes it easier to compare their area. Even though all of our shapes have different perimeters, they all have the same area.

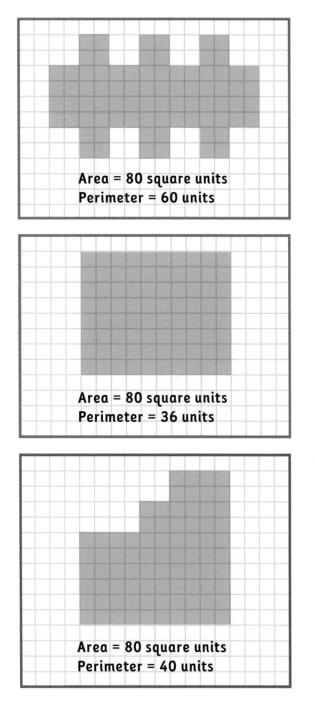

Area = 80 square units
Perimeter = 60 units

Area = 80 square units
Perimeter = 36 units

Area = 80 square units
Perimeter = 40 units

 Problem-Solving Activity
Turn to *Interactive Text*, page 212.

 mBook Reinforce Understanding
Use the *mBook Study Guide* to review lesson concepts.

Homework

Activity 1

Solve the basic multiplication facts.

1. 5×5
2. 8×7
3. 4×8
4. 3×9
5. 6×9
6. 9×7
7. 5×6
8. 8×3

Activity 2

Tell which divisibility rule or rules can be used to divide these numbers. Use your calculator to check your answers.

Model 984
       Answer: The 2, 3, and 6 rules.

1. 14
2. 93
3. 75
4. 150
5. 366
6. 5,420

Activity 3

Use divisibility rules to answer each of the questions.

1. What is a number that can be divided evenly by 2?

2. What is a number that can be divided evenly by 3?

3. What is a number that can be divided evenly by 5?

4. What is a number that can be divided evenly by 6?

5. What is a number that can be divided evenly by 10?

Activity 4 • Distributed Practice

Solve.

1. $\begin{array}{r} 800 \\ + 700 \\ \hline \end{array}$

2. $\begin{array}{r} 3{,}012 \\ - 987 \\ \hline \end{array}$

3. $\begin{array}{r} 17 \\ \times 48 \\ \hline \end{array}$

4. $9\overline{)369}$

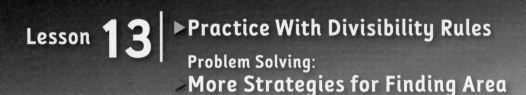

Lesson 13 ▶Practice With Divisibility Rules

Problem Solving:
▶More Strategies for Finding Area

▶**Practice With Divisibility Rules**

How can divisibility rules help us determine if a number is prime?

Divisibility rules give us new strategies for determining if numbers are prime or composite. If a number meets any of the divisibility rules, it has more than two factors. So the number is composite, not prime.

Let's look at the numbers from 0 to 50 in the table. We can use our divisibility rules to eliminate the numbers that are not prime.

First, we find all of the even numbers, because they are divisible by 2. We start with 4, because we know that 2 is prime. Numbers divisible by 2 are red.

Next, we find numbers that are divisible by 3. We start with 6 because 3 is prime. The number 6 is also divisible by 2, so we won't mark it again. The next number divisible by 3 is 9. These numbers are blue.

Now we find numbers that are divisible by 5. If a number is divisible by 5, it ends in a 5 or a 0. We start with 25 because 5 is prime and 10, 15, and 20 are already marked. These numbers are green.

Numbers that are divisible by 6 are also divisible by 2 and 3.
Numbers that are divisible by 10 are also divisible by 2 and 5.

There are no more numbers to mark. Look at the numbers 1 and 49. We know that the number 1 is neither prime nor composite. The number 49 is composite, because 7 × 7 = 49. We do not have a divisibility rule for 7, so we did not mark this number.

By checking numbers with our divisibility rules, we determine that certain numbers are composite. Sometimes we only need to use one divisibility rule. Sometimes we need to use several.

1	2	3	4	5
6	7	8	9	10
11	12	13	14	15
16	17	18	19	20
21	22	23	24	25
26	27	28	29	30
31	32	33	34	35
36	37	38	39	40
41	42	43	44	45
46	47	48	49	50

Let's use divisibility rules to determine whether numbers are composite or prime.

Example 1

Determine if 25 is prime or composite.

Is 25 divisible . . .

> **by 2?** The number 25 ends in a 5. The number 5 is not an even number.
> The number 25 is not divisible by 2.

> **by 3?** The sum of the digits of 25 is 7. The sum is not divisible by 3.
> The number 25 is not divisible by 3.

> **by 5?** The number 25 ends in a 5.
> The number 25 is divisible by 5.

The number 25 is divisible by 5. It is a composite number.

In the next example, we have a larger number. That does not always mean we have to use more divisibility rules.

Example 2

Determine if 53 is prime or composite.

Is 53 divisible . . .

> **by 2?** The number 53 ends in a 3. The last digit is not an even number.
> The number 53 is not divisible by 2.

> **by 3?** The sum of the digits of 53 is 8. The sum is not divisible by 3.
> The number 53 is not divisible by 3.

> **by 5?** The number does not end in 5 or 0.
> The number 53 is not divisible by 5.

The number 53 is not divisible by 6 or 10 because it is not divisible by 2, 3, or 5. The number is not divisible by 7, because $7 \times 7 = 49$ and 53 is only four greater than 49.

The number 53 is a prime number.

POWER CONCEPT

Any number that is divisible by another number is not a prime number.

 Apply Skills
Turn to *Interactive Text*, page 214.

 Reinforce Understanding
Use the *mBook Study Guide* to review lesson concepts.

►Problem Solving: **More Strategies for Finding Area**

What is the area of shapes with other shapes inside them?

We looked at finding the area of solid shapes. Now let's try to determine the area of shapes that have other shapes inside them.

Example 1

Find the area of the orange border of the tennis court.
The tennis team wants to repaint the orange part of the court. The entire court is 30 feet × 60 feet. The green part of the court is 20 feet × 40 feet.

What is the area of the part that needs to be painted?

First, we find the area of the **orange** part of the court, or the outside rectangle.

- The expression 30 × 60 is an extended fact.
- Since 3 × 6 = 18, we know that 30 × 60 = 1,800.
- The area of the large rectangle is 1,800 square feet.

Next, we find the area of the green part of the court, or the inside rectangle.

- The inside rectangle is 20 × 40. This is another extended fact.
- Since 2 × 4 = 8, we know that 20 × 40 = 800.
- The area of the small rectangle is 800 square feet.

Now we subtract the inside of the court (800 square feet) from the entire court (1,800 square feet).

The area of the orange border is 1,000 square feet.

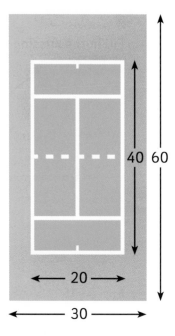

To find the answers for problems involving shapes within shapes, we have to subtract part of the area from the entire area.

 Problem-Solving Activity
Turn to *Interactive Text*, page 215.

 mBook Reinforce Understanding
Use the *mBook Study Guide* to review lesson concepts.

Activity 1

Use divisibility rules to determine if each number is prime or composite.

1. 36
2. 23
3. 45

Activity 2

Tell which divisibility rule or rules can be used to divide these numbers.

Model 84

Answer: The 2, 3, and 6 rules.

1. 88
2. 222
3. 156
4. 90
5. 105
6. 360

Activity 3

Fill in the missing numbers in these prime factor trees.

1. 16 → 4, 4 → (a)(b)(c)(d)
2. 36 → 6, 6 → (a)(b)(c)(d)
3. 49 → (a)(b)
4. 27 → (a), (b); a → (3)(3)
5. 15 → (a)(b)

Activity 4 • Distributed Practice

Solve.

1. 6,897
   + 2,185

2. 6,112
   − 1,987

3.   19
     × 98

4. 5)456

14 Prime Factorization for Large Numbers

Problem Solving:
Looking for Patterns

▶Prime Factorization for Large Numbers

How do we use divisibility rules to find the prime factorization of large numbers?

We use prime factor trees to find prime factorization. There is another method that we can use for larger numbers. We will use divisibility rules and a calculator.

Let's find the prime factorization using divisibility rules.

Example 1

Use a divisibility rule to find the prime factorization for 138.

Choose a divisibility rule.

Let's start with the divisibility rule for 3.

The sum of the digits of 138 is divisible by 3.

$138 \div 3 = 46$

The number 3 is a prime, but 46 is an even number.
We can divide it by 2.

$46 \div 2 = 23$

The numbers 2 and 23 are both primes.
So we're done.

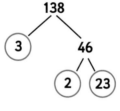

The prime factorization for 138 is 2 × 3 × 23.

Sometimes, more than one of our divisibility rules works for a number.
When this occurs, we select any of these divisibility rules and use it first.

Sometimes when a large number is first broken up, we still have two factors that have to be broken up further.

Example 2

Use divisibility rules to find the prime factorization of 270.

Choose a divisibility rule.

The number 270 ends in a 0. We can divide it by 10.

$270 \div 10 = 27$

The number 270 has two factors, 27 and 10. Neither of these factors is prime. We have to continue using divisibility rules with both of these factors. Let's start with the number 27.

Now we use our basic facts:

- for 27:

  $3 \times 9 = 27$

  The number 3 is prime.

- for 9:

  $3 \times 3 = 9$

  Both 3s are prime.

- for 10:

  $2 \times 5 = 10$

  Both 2 and 5 are prime.

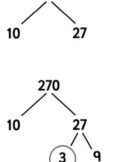

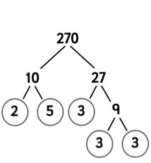

The prime factorization of 270 is $2 \times 3 \times 3 \times 3 \times 5$.

 Apply Skills
Turn to *Interactive Text*, page 217.

 mBook Reinforce Understanding
Use the *mBook Study Guide* to review lesson concepts.

▶**Problem Solving: Looking for Patterns**

How many squares are in this picture?

We have been looking at shapes and finding patterns when comparing their areas and perimeters. Finding patterns is an important skill. Sometimes answers to questions seem obvious, but we have to look closer to make sure that we get the correct answer.

Example 1

Determine the number of squares in the shape.

The shape contains a certain number of squares. The mind is tricked into seeing nine squares. Five of them are gray and the other four are white. But there is a big square that goes around the outside of the board. That makes 10. In fact, there are more than 10 squares.

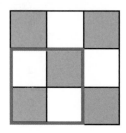

The bottom left four squares also form a larger square. Three more of these squares are made using the four squares in each corner.

We now know that there are:

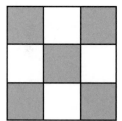

  9 small squares

  4 larger squares

  1 big square

There are 14 squares.

By looking closely, we see that the pattern of squares within squares reveals a different answer than we might have thought.

 Problem-Solving Activity
Turn to *Interactive Text*,
page 218.

 mBook **Reinforce Understanding**
Use the *mBook Study Guide*
to review lesson concepts.

Activity 1

List the factors for each number.

1. 22

2. 13

3. 28

4. 33

Activity 2

Tell which divisibility rule or rules can be used to divide these numbers.

Model 80,105

Answer: The 5 rule.

1. 633   2. 12,406   3. 12,408

4. 190   5. 33,875   6. 600

Activity 3

Draw a prime factor tree for each of the numbers.

Model 16

Answer:

1. 207   2. 185   3. 250   4. 320   5. 666

Activity 4 • Distributed Practice

Solve.

1. $\begin{array}{r} 4,017 \\ + 6,928 \end{array}$ 2. $\begin{array}{r} 7,950 \\ - 2,825 \end{array}$ 3. $\begin{array}{r} 98 \\ \times 76 \end{array}$ 4. $3\overline{)537}$

▶**Factors, Primes, and Composites**

How do we think about factoring numbers?

Any number can be broken into factors. At the beginning of this unit, we learned two ways to visualize factors for numbers: arrays and factor rainbows. In the examples below for the number 16, the factor lists do not have duplicate numbers. While the number 16 has a 4 × 4 array, we only use the number 4 once in the factor list.

Review 1

What are the arrays and factor rainbow for 16?

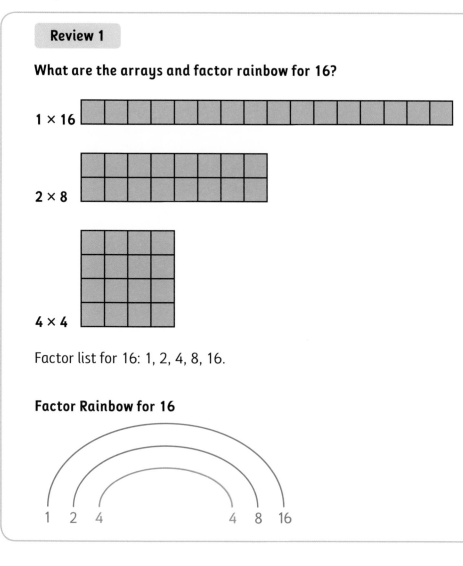

1 × 16

2 × 8

4 × 4

Factor list for 16: 1, 2, 4, 8, 16.

Factor Rainbow for 16

1 2 4   4 8 16

Prime numbers are numbers that only have two factors—1 and themselves. Let's look at arrays for prime numbers.

Review 2

How do arrays help us see prime numbers?

7

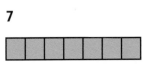

Factor list: 1, 7

13

Factor list: 1, 13

29

Factor list: 1, 29

Primes are important because all numbers can be broken down through prime factorization. We can use a prime factor tree to break 44 into primes. Notice that there can be duplicates in the prime factors of a number. In this example, 2 is repeated.

Review 3

How do we find the prime factorization of a number?

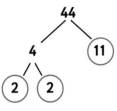

The prime factorization of 44 is 2 × 2 × 11.

Divisibility rules help us break down large numbers. Finding the prime factors for 44 is relatively easy. But, breaking down larger numbers into prime factors is much more difficult.

Review 4

How do divisibility rules help with prime factorization?

Find the prime factorization for 612 using divisibility rules.

• Since 6 + 1 + 2 = 9, the number 612 can be divided by ③.

There are two factors, 3 and 204.

• Since 2 + 0 + 4 = 6, the number 204 can be divided by ③.

• Since 68 ends in an even number, it can be divided by ②.

• Since 34 ends in an even number, it can be divided by ②.

The number ⑰ is a prime number, so we can stop.

All of the circled numbers are part of our prime factorization.

The prime factorization of 612 is 2 × 2 × 3 × 3 × 17.

 Apply Skills
Turn to *Interactive Text*, page 220.

 Reinforce Understanding
Use the *mBook Study Guide* to review lesson concepts.

What is the relationship between area and perimeter?

Perimeter measures the distance around the outside of a shape. It measures only one dimension: length. The space inside of the perimeter is the area of a shape. It is measured in two dimensions and is described in square units.

We find the perimeter of a rectangle by multiplying the base by 2 and the height by 2 and adding the products together.

We find the area of a rectangle by multiplying its base by its height.

Review 1

How do we find the area and perimeter of a rectangle?

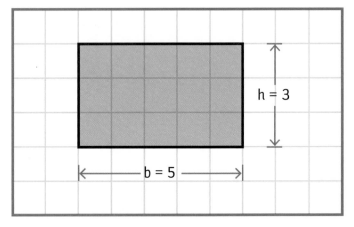

- To find the perimeter, multiply its base by 2 and its height by 2. Then add the products together.

$$5 \times 2 = 10$$
$$3 \times 2 = 6$$
$$10 + 6 = 16$$

We can also add the sides together. $3 + 5 + 5 + 3 = 16$

The perimeter of the rectangle is 16 units.

- Area formula for a rectangle = base × height

$$5 \times 3 = 15$$

The area of the rectangle is 15 square units.

We know that the area of a rectangle is base times height. We use this relationship to understand the area of a triangle as well as the area of a parallelogram.

Review 2

What is the area formula for triangles?

The area of a triangle is half the area of a rectangle with the same base and height.

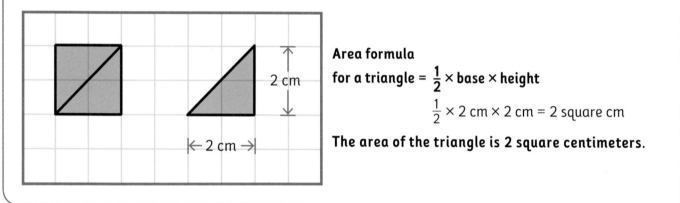

Area formula

for a triangle $= \frac{1}{2} \times$ base $\times$ height

$\frac{1}{2} \times 2$ cm $\times 2$ cm $= 2$ square cm

The area of the triangle is 2 square centimeters.

If we think about one side of the parallelogram forming a triangle, we can move it to the other side to form a rectangle. The area formula for a parallelogram is the same as the area formula for a rectangle.

Review 3

What is the area formula for parallelograms?

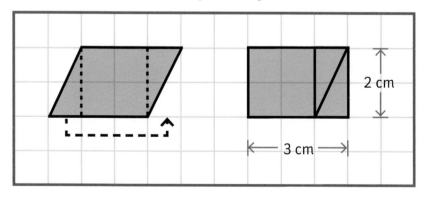

Area formula for a parallelogram = base × height

3 cm × 2 cm = 6 square cm

The area of the parallelogram is 6 square centimeters.

The relationship between area and perimeter is complicated if we change the shape but keep the perimeter the same.

Review 4

What is the relationship between area and perimeter?

Shape A

Perimeter = 24 units

Area = 20 square units

Shape B

Perimeter = 24 units

Area = 36 square units

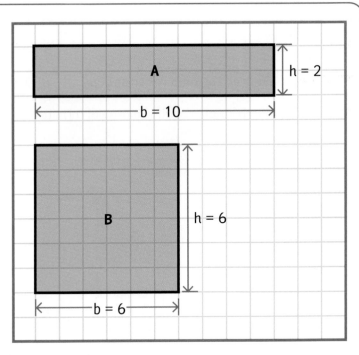

Another relationship occurs when we keep the area the same but change the shape.

Shape C

Perimeter = 30 units

Area = 30 square units

Shape D

Perimeter = 22 units

Area = 30 square units

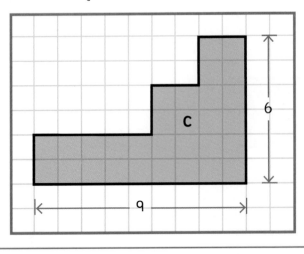

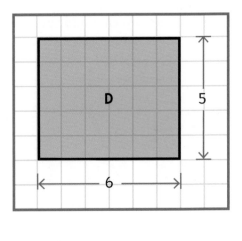

 Problem-Solving Activity
Turn to *Interactive Text*,
page 222.

 mBook Reinforce Understanding
Use the *mBook Study Guide*
to review lesson concepts.

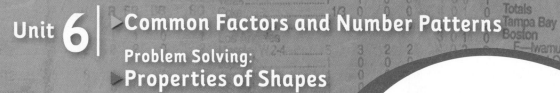

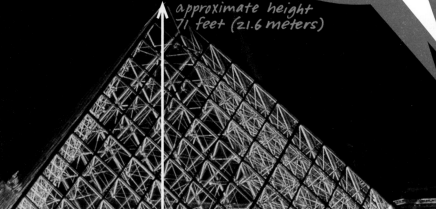

"Math, it's a puzzle to me. I love figuring out puzzles."

Maya Lin, artist and architect; designer of the Vietnam Veterans Memorial in Washington, D.C.

Louvre Museum Entrance

Paris, France   Completed in 1989

approximate height
71 feet (21.6 meters)

approximate length of base: 116 feet (35.4 meters)

Number of diamond-shaped panes of glass: 603
Number of triangle-shaped panes of glass: 70

The Burj Dubai

Location: Dubai, United Arab Emirates
Height: 2,684 feet (818 meters)
Number of floors: 162
Cost: $4.1 billion

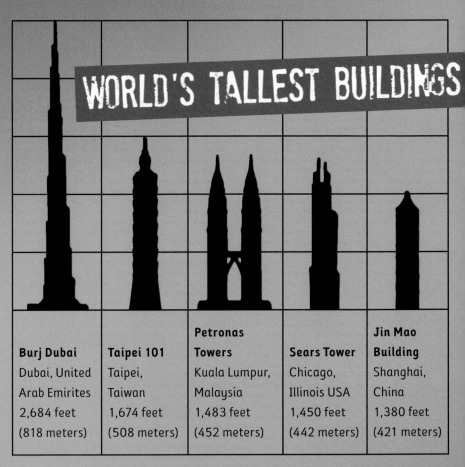

WORLD'S TALLEST BUILDINGS

Burj Dubai	Taipei 101	Petronas Towers	Sears Tower	Jin Mao Building
Dubai, United Arab Emirites	Taipei, Taiwan	Kuala Lumpur, Malaysia	Chicago, Illinois USA	Shanghai, China
2,684 feet (818 meters)	1,674 feet (508 meters)	1,483 feet (452 meters)	1,450 feet (442 meters)	1,380 feet (421 meters)

OBJECTIVES

Building Number Concepts

- Find common factors for whole numbers using a variety of methods

- Identify the greatest common factor for two or more whole numbers

- Explore patterns in odd, even, and square numbers

Problem Solving

- Group shapes based on common properties

- Explore congruence and similarity of shapes

- Expand and contract shapes on a grid

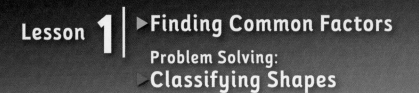

Lesson 1 ▶Finding Common Factors

Problem Solving: ▶Classifying Shapes

▶**Finding Common Factors**

Vocabulary

common factor

How do we find the common factors of two numbers?

Factors that two or more numbers share are called **common factors** . By listing all the factors of two numbers, we find the common factors.

First, we think about multiplication facts to identify all of the factors. To find common factors, we list all of the factors for the numbers. Then we look for factors that are the same in both lists.

Let's find the common factors for the numbers 12 and 16.

Steps for Finding Common Factors

STEP 1
List all the factors of 12 and 16.

Factors of 12: 1, 2, 3, 4, 6, 12
Factors of 16: 1, 2, 4, 8, 16

STEP 2
Line up the factors.

Factors of 12	1	2	3	4	6		12	
Factors of 16	1	2		4		8		16

STEP 3
Circle the common factors.

Factors of 12	1	2	3	4	6		12	
Factors of 16	1	2		4		8		16

The common factors of 12 and 16 are 1, 2, and 4.

Knowing multiplication facts will help us identify all the factors.

Example 1

Find the common factors of 18 and 27.

STEP 1

List all the factors of 18 and 27.

Factors of 18: 1, 2, 3, 6, 9, 18
Factors of 27: 1, 3, 9, 27

STEP 2

Line up the factors.

Factors of 18
| 1 | 2 | 3 | 6 | 9 | 18 | |

Factors of 27
| 1 | | 3 | | 9 | | 27 |

STEP 3

Circle the common factors.

Factors of 18
| 1 | 2 | 3 | 6 | 9 | 18 | |

Factors of 27
| 1 | | 3 | | 9 | | 27 |

The common factors of 18 and 27 are 1, 3, and 9.

We find all the factors of both numbers so that we do not miss any common factors.

Let's use the same method to identify the factors of two prime numbers. Prime numbers only have two factors, 1 and themselves.

Example 2

Find the common factors of 7 and 13.

STEP 1
List all the factors of 7 and 13.
Because 7 and 13 are prime, they only have two factors.

Factors of 7: 1, 7
Factors of 13: 1, 13

STEP 2
Line up the factors.

Factors of 7	1	7	
Factors of 13	1		13

STEP 3
Circle the common factors.

Factors of 7	1	7	
Factors of 13	1		13

The common factor of 7 and 13 is 1.

The number 1 is a common factor of all numbers, but it is the only common factor for two or more prime numbers.

%÷ Apply Skills
=<x Turn to *Interactive Text*,
page 225.

 mBook Reinforce Understanding
Use the *mBook Study Guide*
to review lesson concepts.

▶**Problem Solving: Classifying Shapes**

What are different ways to classify shapes?

We classify shapes by identifying how they are alike and how they are different.

Look at the shapes below. We can classify them in many different ways.

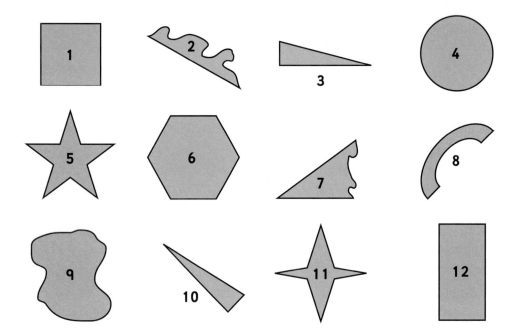

We put these shapes into groups by identifying which ones have at least one characteristic in common.

Some of the shapes are made up of curved lines and can be grouped.

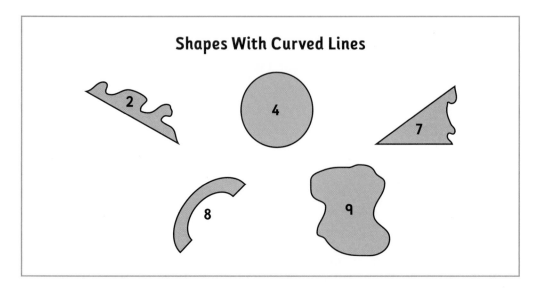

Shapes With Curved Lines

Some of the shapes are triangles.

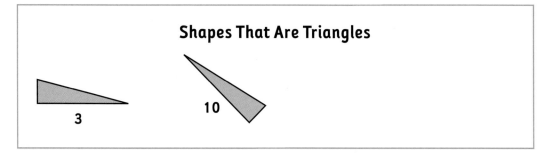

Shapes That Are Triangles

3

10

All of the shapes are closed. There are no openings in their perimeters.

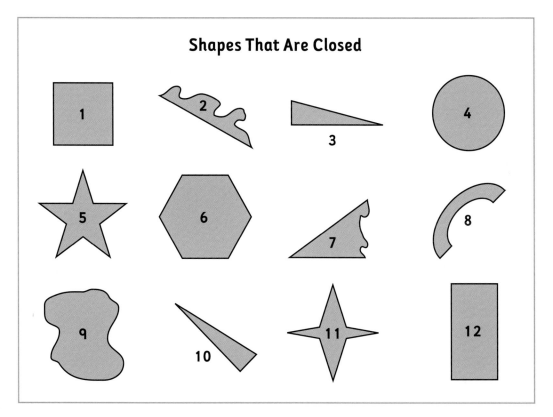

Shapes That Are Closed

1

2

3

4

5

6

7

8

9

10

11

12

These are only a few of the characteristics of shapes. Shapes can be classified in many other ways. As we learn more about shapes, we will find more ways that shapes are similar and different.

 Problem-Solving Activity
Turn to *Interactive Text*,
page 226.

 mBook **Reinforce Understanding**
Use the *mBook Study Guide*
to review lesson concepts.

Homework

Activity 1

List the factors.

1. 45
2. 27
3. 40
4. 60

Activity 2

Tell which divisibility rule or rules can be used to divide each number.

Model   3,672   Answer: The 2, 3, and 6 rules.

1. 750
2. 1,416
3. 955
4. 652

Activity 3

Find common factors for each of the following pairs of numbers.

1. 8 and 10
2. 3 and 4
3. 6 and 9
4. 12 and 18

Activity 4 • Distributed Practice

Solve.

1. $\begin{array}{r} 400 \\ +\,800 \\ \hline \end{array}$

2. $\begin{array}{r} 1,500 \\ -\ \ 700 \\ \hline \end{array}$

3. $\begin{array}{r} 43 \\ \times\,72 \\ \hline \end{array}$

4. $\begin{array}{r} 958 \\ \times\ \ \ 2 \\ \hline \end{array}$

5. $50\overline{)450}$

► **More Practice Finding Common Factors**

Problem Solving:
► **Reclassifying Shapes**

►**More Practice Finding Common Factors**

How do divisibility rules help us find the common factors for more than two numbers?

One way to find common factors is to use divisibility rules. Let's use divisibility rules to find the common factors of the numbers 16, 20, and 24.

Divisibility Rule	16 20 24
2	All the numbers end with even digits—**2** *is a* common factor.
3	The sum of the digits of each of the numbers is not divisible by 3—**3** *is not* a **common factor.**
5	All the numbers do not end with 5 or 0—**5** *is not* a common factor.
6	All the numbers are not divisible by 2 and 3—**6** *is not* a common factor.
10	All the numbers do not end with 0—**10** *is not* a common factor.

All of the numbers are divisible by 2, so 2 is a common factor of 16, 20, and 24. Remember that all numbers have a common factor of 1.

Some of the common factors of 16, 20, and 24 are 1 and 2.

Using divisibility rules may not always give us all of the common factors, but it is a good way to think about some of the common factors before writing a factor list.

How do we find the common factors for more than two numbers?

The process for finding the common factors of more than two numbers is still the same as before. In addition to using divisibility rules to get started, we create factor lists to identify the common factors.

Let's find the common factors for the numbers 16, 20, and 24.

Steps for Finding Common Factors for More Than Two Numbers

STEP 1
List all the factors of 16, 20, and 24.

Factors of 16: 1, 2, 4, 8, 16
Factors of 20: 1, 2, 4, 5, 10, 20
Factors of 24: 1, 2, 3, 4, 6, 8, 12, 24

STEP 2
Line up the factors.

Factors of 16	1	2		4			8			16		
Factors of 20	1	2		4	5			10			20	
Factors of 24	1	2	3	4		6	8		12			24

STEP 3
Circle the common factors.

Factors of 16	1	2		4			8			16		
Factors of 20	1	2		4	5			10			20	
Factors of 24	1	2	3	4		6	8		12			24

The common factors of 16, 20, and 24 are 1, 2, and 4.

When we used divisibility rules, we missed 4 as a common factor. We do not have a divisibility rule for the number 4.

Notice that 16 and 24 have a common factor of 8. However, our task is to find common factors for all three numbers. That means the factor needs to be in each factor list.

Let's find the common factors of 20, 25, 30, and 35. The first thing we notice before we write factor lists is that all of the numbers are divisible by 5. That means 5 will be one of the common factors. We also know that all numbers greater than 0 will have a common factor of 1.

Example 1

Find the common factors of 20, 25, 30, and 35.

STEP 1
List all the factors of 20, 25, 30, and 35.

Factors of 20: 1, 2, 4, 5, 10, 20
Factors of 25: 1, 5, 25
Factors of 30: 1, 2, 3, 5, 6, 10, 15, 30
Factors of 35: 1, 5, 7, 35

STEP 2
Line up the factors.

Factors of 20	1	2		4	5			10		20			
Factors of 25	1				5						25		
Factors of 30	1	2	3		5	6		10	15			30	
Factors of 35	1				5		7						35

STEP 3
Circle the common factors.

Factors of 20	1	2		4	5			10		20			
Factors of 25	1				5						25		
Factors of 30	1	2	3		5	6		10	15			30	
Factors of 35	1				5		7						35

We see from our lists that all four numbers have 1 and 5 as factors.

The common factors of 20, 25, 30, and 35 are 1 and 5.

We also use divisibility rules to find common factors. Remember the divisibility rules from earlier lessons:

Divisibility Rules	
Divisibility by 2	Ends with 2, 4, 6, 8, or 10.
Divisibility by 3	The sum of the digits is divisible by 3.
Divisibility by 5	Ends with 5 or 0.
Divisibility by 6	Divisible by 2 and 3.
Divisibility by 10	Ends with 0.

Example 2

Find the common factors of 6, 15, and 24 using divisibility rules.

Divisibility Rule	6 15 24
2	All of the numbers do not end with even digits—**2 is not a common factor.**
3	The sum of the digits of each of the numbers is divisible by 3—3 is a common factor.
5	All of the numbers do not end with 5 or 0—**5 is not a common factor.**
6	All of the numbers are not divisible by 2 and 3—**6 is not a common factor.**
10	None of the numbers end with 0—**10 is not a common factor.**

All of the numbers are divisible by 3. The number 3 is a common factor of 6, 15, and 24. Remember that all numbers have a common factor of 1.

The common factors of 6, 15, and 24 are 1 and 3.

If we check our answer by using factor lists, we find that we have discovered all of the common factors.

> We can use factor lists and divisibility rules to find common factors for as many numbers as we want.

 Apply Skills
Turn to *Interactive Text*, page 228.

 mBook Reinforce Understanding
Use the *mBook Study Guide* to review lesson concepts.

What characteristics can we use to describe how shapes are alike?

It is easy to compare shapes by looking at one characteristic. It is more difficult to find multiple ways that two or more shapes are alike.

Look at the following four shapes. Think about ways to put these shapes in a group.

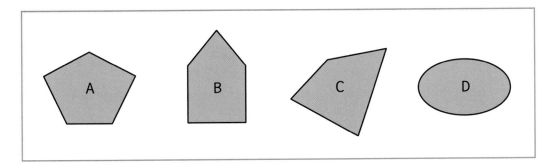

Observations:

- Shapes A, B, and C all have straight sides.

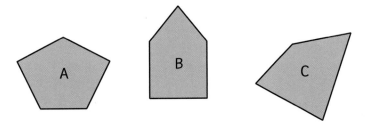

- Shapes A and B both have five corners.

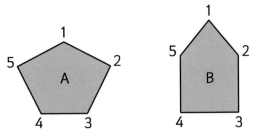

- Shapes A, B, C, and D all have closed space on the inside with no gaps in their perimeters.

We identified three ways that Shapes A and B are alike.
Shapes A and B both:

- Have straight sides.
- Have five corners.
- Are closed shapes.

When comparing shapes, there are many ways that they can be alike.
Shapes can have the same length, area, number of sides, etc. Look
closely at shapes when finding similarities.

 Problem-Solving Activity
Turn to *Interactive Text*,
page 229.

 Reinforce Understanding
Use the *mBook Study Guide*
to review lesson concepts.

Activity 1

List the common factors.

1. 8 and 10   **2.** 12 and 14   **3.** 9, 12, and 15   **4.** 3, 6, 8, and 12

Activity 2

Tell which divisibility rule or rules can be used to divide each number.

Model   663

Answer: The 3 rule.

1. 1,042   **2.** 963   **3.** 141   **4.** 180,000

Activity 3

Look at the pairs of shapes in each problem and tell what properties they have in common.

The properties are:

(a) straight lines
(b) curved lines
(c) 4-sided
(d) 3-sided

Write a, b, c, or d on your paper.
Note: The shapes may have more than one property in common.

1.

2.

3.

4.

Activity 4 • Distributed Practice

Solve.

1. 500
      + 600

2. 4,097
      − 1,892

3. 4)876

4. 600
      ×   4

5. 7)1,400

| ▶**Greatest Common Factor**

Problem Solving:
▶**Tessellations**

▶**Greatest Common Factor**

Vocabulary
greatest common factor (GCF)

What is the greatest common factor?

We learned how to break a number into factors and how to find common factors. Now we are going to find the greatest common factor. The **greatest common factor**, or **GCF**, is the largest of all the common factors.

We've already found common factors for two or more numbers using factor lists. We will use factor lists to find the greatest common factor of 12 and 18.

Steps for Finding the Greatest Common Factor, or GCF

STEP 1
Find all of the common factors.

Factors of 12	1	2	3	4	6		12	
Factors of 18	1	2	3		6	9		18

The common factors of 12 and 18 are 1, 2, 3, and 6.

STEP 2
Look for the greatest common factor.

Factors of 12	1	2	3	4	6		12	
Factors of 18	1	2	3		6	9		18

The number 6 is the biggest, or *greatest*, common factor.

The greatest common factor, or GCF, of 12 and 18 is 6.

By finding all of the common factors, we can identify the greatest common factor. Now we can use this process to find the greatest common factor of other sets of numbers.

Example 1

Find the greatest common factor, or GCF, of 10 and 15.

STEP 1
Create factor lists and identify the common factors.

Factors of 10	1	2		5	10	
Factors of 15	1		3	5		15

The common factors of 10 and 15 are 1 and 5.

STEP 2
Identify the greatest common factor.

Factors of 10	1	2		5	10	
Factors of 15	1		3	5		15

The number 5 is the biggest of these factors.

The greatest common factor, or GCF, of 10 and 15 is 5.

Example 2

Find the GCF of 12 and 22.

Factors of 12	1	2	3	4	6		12	
Factors of 22	1	2				11		22

The common factors of 12 and 22 are 1 and 2.

Factors of 12	1	2	3	4	6		12	
Factors of 22	1	2				11		22

The number 2 is the biggest of the common factors.

The greatest common factor of 12 and 22 is 2.

POWER CONCEPT

Making sure that the GCF identified is the biggest factor will help prevent errors when working with factors.

 Apply Skills
Turn to *Interactive Text*, page 231.

 mBook Reinforce Understanding
Use the *mBook Study Guide* to review lesson concepts.

What are tessellations?

A design using the same shapes repeatedly is called a **tessellation**.
We can use many different shapes to make a tessellation.

Look at this tessellation that is made of triangles.

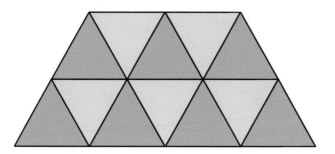

Look at some of the properties of this triangle that allow us to make
a tessellation.

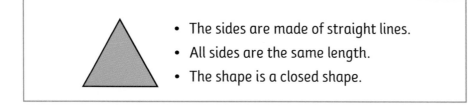

- The sides are made of straight lines.
- All sides are the same length.
- The shape is a closed shape.

Since the sides of the triangle are all straight lines and the same length,
the shape fits together without any spaces. Tessellations can also
combine two shapes with similar properties. Let's look at an example
of a tessellation using more than one shape.

Example 1

Identify properties of the tessellation.

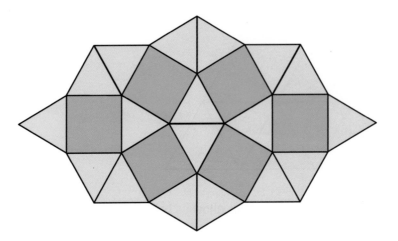

This tessellation is made up of triangles and squares. Both the triangles and squares in the tessellation have sides of the same length. This is often true when more than one shape is used in a tessellation, and it allows the pieces to fit together without any spaces.

Properties of Tessellations

- Shapes must be closed.
- Shapes must fit together without any spaces or gaps.
- Shapes often have sides that are the same length.

 Problem-Solving Activity
Turn to *Interactive Text*,
page 232.

 mBook Reinforce Understanding
Use the *mBook Study Guide*
to review lesson concepts.

Homework

Activity 1

Tell which divisibility rule or rules can be used to divide each number.

Model   984

Answer: The 2, 3, and 6 rules.

1. 10,984   **2.** 665   **3.** 850

4. 15   **5.** 36   **6.** 54

Activity 2

Find the common factors for each pair of numbers.

1. 12 and 20

2. 18 and 50

3. 9 and 30

4. 24 and 30

Activity 3

Tell the GCF for these pairs of numbers.

1. 18 and 21

2. 25 and 35

3. 24 and 36

4. 19 and 23

Activity 4 • Distributed Practice

Solve.

1.   5,698
     + 2,017

2.   23
       × 15

3.   800
        ×   4

4. $80\overline{)3,200}$

▸**More Practice With the GCF**

How do we find the GCF for more than two numbers?

We can find the greatest common factor (GCF) for as many numbers as we want by using the methods we have learned.

Use Factor Lists

Factor lists are the safest way to find the greatest common factor for a set of numbers. Let's find the greatest common factor for 20, 25, and 30 using this method.

Factors of 20	1	2		4	5		10		20		
Factors of 25	1				5					25	
Factors of 30	1	2	3		5	6	10	15			30

The common factors of 20, 25, and 30 are 1 and 5. The GCF is 5.

Look for Patterns

Another method for finding the GCF is to look for patterns in the numbers. For instance, are they all part of the same multiplication or division fact family?

Let's find the GCF for 14, 21, and 28 using this method. When we look at these numbers, we see a pattern. The numbers are all part of the multiplication and division facts for 7.

Multiplication Facts for 7		
$7 \times 2 = 14$	$7 \times 3 = 21$	$7 \times 4 = 28$

Division Facts for 7		
$14 \div 7 = 2$	$21 \div 7 = 3$	$28 \div 7 = 4$

We check by creating factor lists to see if 7 is the largest factor.

Factors of 14	1	2			7	14	
Factors of 21	1		3		7		21
Factors of 28	1	2		4	7	14	28

The common factors for 14, 21, and 28 are 1 and 7.

The GCF of 14, 21, and 28 is 7.

Use Divisibility Rules

Another way to find the GCF of two or more numbers is to use divisibility rules. Let's find the GCF of 18, 24, and 36 using this method.

Divisibility Rule	18　　24　　36
2	All of the numbers end with even digits—**2** *is a* **common factor.**
3	The sum of the digits of each of the numbers is divisible by 3—**3** *is a* **common factor.**
5	None of the numbers end with 5 or 0—**5** *is not* a **common factor.**
6	All of the numbers are divisible by 2 and 3—**6** *is a* **common factor.**
10	None of the numbers end with 0—**10** *is not* a **common factor.**

All of the numbers are divisible by 2, 3, and 6. The numbers 2, 3, and 6 are all factors of 18, 24, and 36. The number 6 is the greatest common factor.

Now we can check this by looking at the factor lists for the three numbers.

Factors of 18	1	2	3		6		9		18		
Factors of 24	1	2	3	4	6	8		12		24	
Factors of 36	1	2	3	4	6		9	12	18		36

The GCF of 18, 24, and 36 is 6.

Using factor lists, finding patterns, and looking at divisibility rules are all ways to find the greatest common factor.

Example 1

Find the GCF of 15, 21, and 33.

These numbers are all part of the multiplication and division facts for the number 3.

Multiplication Facts for 3		
$3 \times 5 = 15$	$3 \times 7 = 21$	$3 \times 11 = 33$

Division Facts for 3		
$15 \div 3 = 5$	$21 \div 3 = 7$	$33 \div 3 = 11$

We think that 3 might be the greatest common factor of these numbers. Let's check by creating factor lists for 15, 21, and 33.

Factors of 15	1	3	5			15	
Factors of 21	1	3		7			21	
Factors of 33	1	3			11			33

The common factors of 15, 21, and 33 are 1 and 3.

The number 3 is the greatest common factor.

The GCF of 15, 21, and 33 is 3.

 Apply Skills
Turn to *Interactive Text*, page 234.

 mBook **Reinforce Understanding**
Use the *mBook Study Guide* to review lesson concepts.

When are shapes congruent?

Both shapes below have the same number of sides, and their corresponding sides are the same length. When two shapes are exactly the same, they are **congruent** .

Vocabulary
congruent

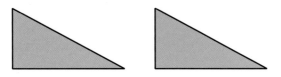

Shapes may be turned sideways, upside down, or flipped over, and still be considered congruent.

Congruent Triangles

Congruent Rectangles

Congruent Parallelograms

The three shapes in each group are all the same size and shape. They are just turned, rotated, or moved in some way. If the shapes are still the same size and all of their sides are the same, they are congruent.

 Problem-Solving Activity
Turn to *Interactive Text*, page 235.

 mBook Reinforce Understanding
Use the *mBook Study Guide* to review lesson concepts.

Homework

Activity 1

Tell which divisibility rule or rules (2, 3, 5, 6, or 10) can be used to divide each number.

1. 15,782
2. 651
3. 486,795
4. 587,920
5. 735,714

Activity 2

Find the greatest common factor (GCF) for the numbers.

1. 18, 27, 363
2. 4, 8, 12
3. 6, 9, 18
4. 15, 20, 25, 30

Activity 3

Select the shape that is NOT congruent to the other shapes in the group. Write the letter (a, b, c, or d) on your paper.

1. (a)   (b)   (c)   (d)

2. (a)   (b)   (c)   (d)

3. (a)   (b)   (c)   (d)

4. (a)   (b)   (c)   (d)

Activity 4 • Distributed Practice

Solve.

1. $\begin{array}{r} 4,000 \\ -\,2,987 \\ \hline \end{array}$
2. $\begin{array}{r} 4,870 \\ +\,5,950 \\ \hline \end{array}$
3. $\begin{array}{r} 539 \\ \times\quad 8 \\ \hline \end{array}$
4. $6\overline{)180}$
5. $5\overline{)181}$

▶**Prime Factor Trees and the GCF**

How do factor trees help us find the GCF?

Another way to find greatest common factors is to use prime factor trees for each number.

Here we use prime factor trees to find the GCF for 42 and 36.

Steps for Using Factor Trees

STEP 1
Find two factors for each number.

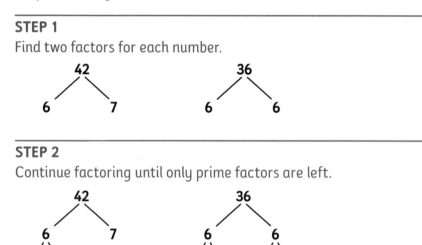

STEP 2
Continue factoring until only prime factors are left.

STEP 3
Circle the prime factors.

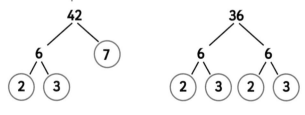

STEP 4
Find the GCF.

Both 42 and 36 have 2 and 3 as common prime factors. To find the greatest common factor for 42 and 36, we multiply these two prime factors: **2 × 3 = 6.**

The GCF for 42 and 36 is 6.

Let's look at another example.

Example 1

Find the greatest common factor for 14 and 56 using prime factor trees.

STEP 1
Find two factors for each number.

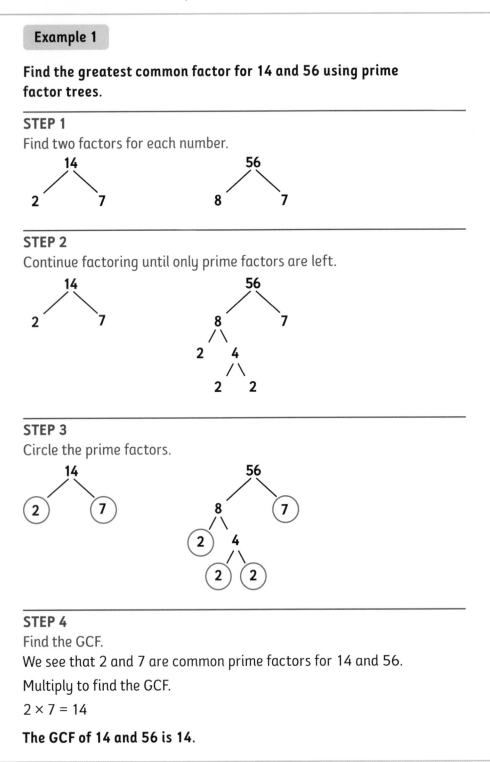

STEP 2
Continue factoring until only prime factors are left.

STEP 3
Circle the prime factors.

STEP 4
Find the GCF.
We see that 2 and 7 are common prime factors for 14 and 56.

Multiply to find the GCF.

$2 \times 7 = 14$

The GCF of 14 and 56 is 14.

⅟× Apply Skills
Turn to *Interactive Text*,
page 238.

📈 Monitoring Progress
Quiz 1

mBook Reinforce Understanding
Use the *mBook Study Guide*
to review lesson concepts.

Homework

Activity 1

Tell which divisibility rule or rules (2, 3, 5, 6, or 10) can be used to divide each number.

1. 4,685   **2.** 1,350   **3.** 57,912   **4.** 45,402   **5.** 179,031

Activity 2

Find the GCF for each pair of numbers by drawing prime factor trees.

Model   12 and 20

$2 \times 2 = 4$ GCF = 4

1. 4 and 16   **2.** 32 and 36

3. 18 and 24   **4.** 16 and 30

Activity 3 • Distributed Practice

Solve.

1. 5,000   **2.** 6,978   **3.** 50   **4.** 6)200   **5.** 7)454
    − 4,999   + 3,482   × 50

▶More Practice With Prime Factor Trees and the GCF

How do we find the greatest common factor of large numbers?

In Lesson 5, we learned to use prime factor trees to find the greatest common factor of two numbers. Prime factor trees are especially helpful when we work with large numbers. Using other methods, such as fact families and divisibility rules, can make it easier to find common factors, but not necessarily the greatest common factor.

Let's look at how we use prime factor trees to find the greatest common factor for two large numbers, 80 and 100.

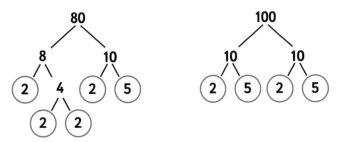

The numbers 80 and 100 have three prime factors in common: **2, 2,** and **5.**

We multiply the three prime numbers together: **2 × 2 × 5 = 20.**

The GCF of 80 and 100 is 20.

Using prime factor trees can help us feel confident that we have found the greatest common factor for two large numbers.

It's easy to make mistakes when we're trying to find the common factors for large numbers. Prime factor trees allow us to break down the numbers and make them easier to work with. We use our knowledge of fact families and divisibility rules to break down the numbers.

Example 1 shows us how to use divisibility rules to get us started with a prime factor tree.

Example 1

Find the greatest common factor for 65 and 75.

Both numbers end in 5. The divisibility rules tell us that all numbers ending in 5 or 0 are divisible by 5. We can find a multiplication fact for both of the numbers by starting with 5 as one of the factors. Then we continue with the factor tree until all the numbers are prime.

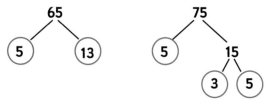

The numbers 65 and 75 have one prime factor in common: 5. We do not need to multiply since there is only one common factor.

The GCF of 65 and 75 is 5.

How does knowledge of extended fact families help us find the GCF?

It is important to know different strategies to start prime factor trees. Using extended fact families can help us divide numbers more quickly since we will use bigger numbers.

Example 1

Find the greatest common factor for 560 and 630. Start by using knowledge of extended fact families.

Since both numbers end with a zero, we know we can use extended fact families to find factors.

- We know that $7 \times 8 = 56$, so the extended fact is $70 \times 8 = 560$.
- We know that $7 \times 9 = 63$, so the extended fact is $7 \times 90 = 630$.

We choose one fact family to begin each of the factor trees.

Continue factoring until only prime factors are left.

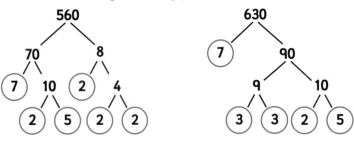

The common prime factors of 560 and 630 are 2, 5, and 7.

$2 \times 5 \times 7 = 70$

The GCF of 560 and 630 is 70.

> Using a combination of all methods and strategies we have learned helps us have good number sense when it comes to solving math problems.

 Apply Skills
Turn to *Interactive Text*, page 240.

 mBook Reinforce Understanding
Use the *mBook Study Guide* to review lesson concepts.

How many congruent shapes can we make within one shape?

In Lesson 4, we learned about congruency. We find congruent shapes within single shapes by breaking them into smaller pieces.

Example 1

Divide the square into smaller congruent shapes.

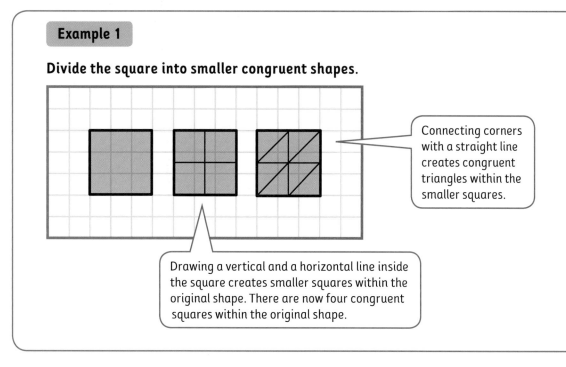

Connecting corners with a straight line creates congruent triangles within the smaller squares.

Drawing a vertical and a horizontal line inside the square creates smaller squares within the original shape. There are now four congruent squares within the original shape.

Example 2

Divide the parallelogram into triangles that are congruent.

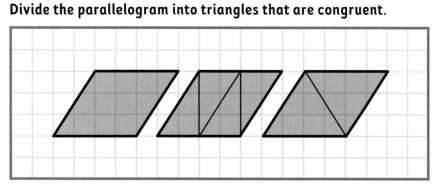

By adding lines, we create smaller shapes within the parallelogram.
- There are four congruent triangles within the middle parallelogram.
- There are two congruent triangles within the right parallelogram.

 Problem-Solving Activity
Turn to *Interactive Text*, page 241.

 mBook **Reinforce Understanding**
Use the *mBook Study Guide* to review lesson concepts.

Activity 1

List the common factors for the following numbers.

1. 18 and 20   **2.** 20 and 22   **3.** 20 and 25   **4.** 25 and 30

Activity 2

Draw a factor tree to find the GCF for each pair of numbers.

Model   63 and 75

The GCF is 3.

1. 44 and 108

2. 190 and 210

3. 64 and 120

Activity 3 • Distributed Practice

Solve.

1.   700
       + 800

2.   3,802
       − 1,999

3.   479
       ×   3

4. $9\overline{)864}$

5. $9\overline{)999}$

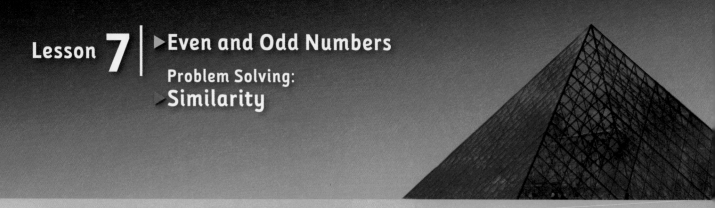

▶**Even and Odd Numbers**

What are even and odd numbers?

We already know some rules about even and odd numbers. We know that all even numbers can be divided into two equal whole numbers, but odd numbers cannot. When we try to divide odd numbers into two equal whole numbers, there is always something left over.

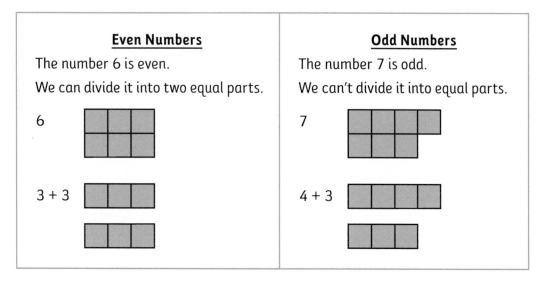

Even Numbers

The number 6 is even.

We can divide it into two equal parts.

6

3 + 3

Odd Numbers

The number 7 is odd.

We can't divide it into equal parts.

7

4 + 3

What are some patterns we see when we add even and odd numbers?

Let's look at some rules for adding even and odd numbers. Arrays can help us.

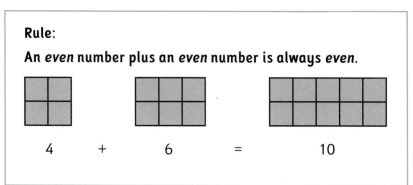

Rule:

An *even* number plus an *even* number is always *even*.

4   +   6   =   10

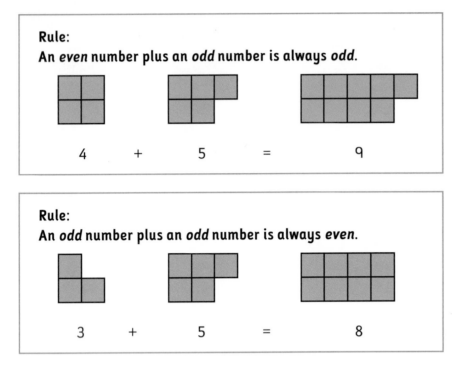

Rule:

An *even* number plus an *odd* number is always *odd*.

4   +   5   =   9

Rule:

An *odd* number plus an *odd* number is always *even*.

3   +   5   =   8

We can summarize the addition patterns like this:

- **Even + Even = Even**
- **Even + Odd = Odd**
- **Odd + Odd = Even**

Example 1

Without solving these addition problems, tell whether the answers will be even or odd numbers.

2 + 5

11 + 12

8 + 22

Let's look at the patterns.

2 + 5   even + odd = ?
11 + 12   odd + even = ?
8 + 22   even + even = ?

The patterns tell us whether the answer will be even or odd.

2 + 5   even + odd = odd
11 + 12   odd + even = odd
8 + 22   even + even = even

What are some patterns we see when we multiply even and odd numbers?

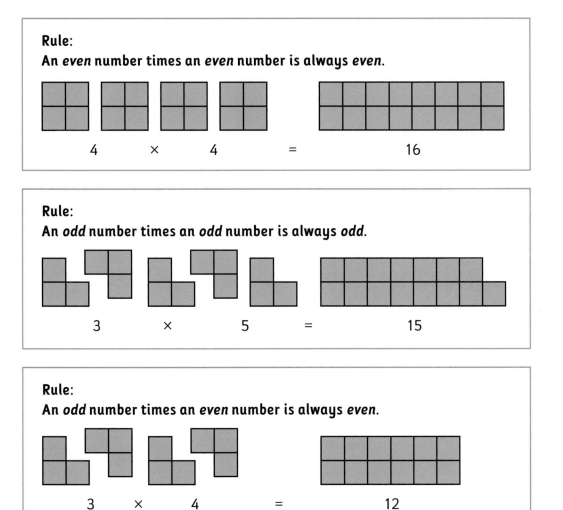

Rule:
An *even* number times an *even* number is always *even*.

4 × 4 = 16

Rule:
An *odd* number times an *odd* number is always *odd*.

3 × 5 = 15

Rule:
An *odd* number times an *even* number is always *even*.

3 × 4 = 12

We can summarize the multiplication patterns like this:

- Even × Even = Even
- Odd × Odd = Odd
- Odd × Even = Even

Example 1

Without solving the multiplication problems, tell whether the answer will be an even or an odd number.

2 × 6

3 × 9

7 × 6

Let's look at the patterns.

2 × 6   even × even = ?

3 × 9   odd × odd = ?

7 × 6   odd × even = ?

The patterns tell us whether the answer will be even or odd.

2 × 6   even × even = even

3 × 9   odd × odd = odd

7 × 6   odd × even = even

When we added two even numbers, the result was an even number. When we multiplied an even and an odd number, the result was an even number. The results will always be the same. There is a pattern for each of the combinations.

 Apply Skills
Turn to *Interactive Text*, page 244.

 mBook Reinforce Understanding
Use the *mBook Study Guide* to review lesson concepts.

▶**Problem Solving: Similarity**

What is similarity?

Let's look at the design below. Moving from the center of the design out, the squares **expand** . This means they get bigger. If we start at the outermost square and move in, the squares **contract** . This means they get smaller.

Vocabulary
expand contract scale

Expanding and contracting are ways to change an object and make similar objects. Similarity is when we have two shapes that are the same except one is an enlargement or contraction of another.

Mathematicians call this expanding and contracting of objects scaling. When we **scale** an object, we make it bigger or smaller by a certain amount.

For example, we can make a square with sides that are *twice as big*.

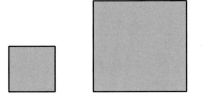

We can also make a square with sides that are *half as big*.

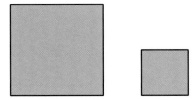

We can use grids to help us expand or contract an object *exactly*. Suppose we wanted to draw a rectangle and then make a copy of it that was half as big. We could draw a rectangle on a grid, and then draw another one with the sides half as long (or divided by 2).

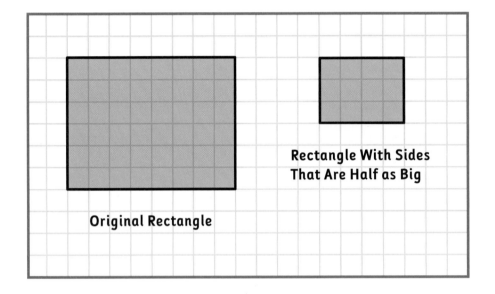

Rectangle With Sides That Are Half as Big

Original Rectangle

The sides of the small rectangle are half as long as the sides of the original rectangle.

The sides of the original object were divided by 2 to find the sides of the contracted rectangle.

Original Rectangle	Contracted Rectangle
Length: 8	Length: 4
Height: 6	Height: 3

We say that the second rectangle is similar. It is drawn to scale because we made the sides smaller by the same amount.

 Problem-Solving Activity
Turn to *Interactive Text*, page 245.

 mBook Reinforce Understanding
Use the *mBook Study Guide* to review lesson concepts.

Homework

Activity 1

List the GCF for each pair of numbers.

1. 2 and 15   **2.** 20 and 24

Activity 2

Find the odd numbers in this list.

2, 897, 32, 466, 268, 444, 137, 598, 87, 640, 201,
16, 822, 423, 217, 953, 305, 316, 500, 792

Activity 3

Without solving the addition problems, tell whether the answers are going to be odd or even.

Model   39 + 42   odd

1. 64 + 82   **2.** 129 + 377

3. 468 + 599   **4.** 1,987 + 9,888

Activity 4

Without solving the multiplication problems, tell whether the answers are going to be odd or even.

Model   39 × 42   even

1. 78 × 44   **2.** 137 × 141

3. 528 × 603   **4.** 5,111 × 8,222

Activity 5 • Distributed Practice

Solve.

1.   1,800   **2.**   5,061   **3.**   597   **4.** $8\overline{)313}$ **5.** $8\overline{)496}$
       − 900   + 3,989   ×   8

▶**Square Numbers**

Vocabulary

square number
consecutive

What are square numbers?

In this unit, we use arrays to study patterns of numbers. Another pattern we will look at is **square numbers** . The array for a square number always has an equal number of rows and columns. Since it has equal sides, it forms a square. That is why the number is called a *square number*.

The number 9 is a square number.

It has 3 rows and 3 columns.

The easiest way to find square numbers is to multiply numbers by themselves. The arrays show that the numbers are square.

1

4

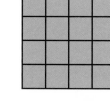
9

16

$1 \times 1 = 1 \quad \rightarrow \quad$ 1 is a square number
$2 \times 2 = 4 \quad \rightarrow \quad$ 4 is a square number
$3 \times 3 = 9 \quad \rightarrow \quad$ 9 is a square number
$4 \times 4 = 16 \quad \rightarrow \quad$ 16 is a square number

We can continue finding square numbers this way indefinitely.

What are the consecutive square numbers from 1 to 100?

When we list square numbers in order, we are writing **consecutive** square numbers. *Consecutive* means "in order."

The consecutive square numbers from 1 to 100 are:

1, 4, 9, 16, 25, 36, 49, 64, 81, and 100.

Let's look at an interesting pattern involving square numbers. The pattern has to do with the distance between consecutive square numbers. Remember: consecutive means "in order." The pattern is predictable. That means there is always a way to find the next square number.

Look at this picture. It shows how we add on to a square number to make the next square number. The pattern looks like this:

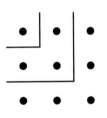

The distance between square numbers looks like this:

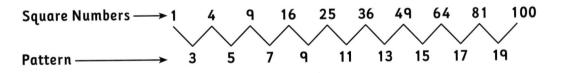

We add consecutive odd numbers to the square numbers to find the consecutive square numbers.

%÷ Apply Skills
**≦× ** Turn to *Interactive Text*,
page 247.

 mBook Reinforce Understanding
Use the *mBook Study Guide*
to review lesson concepts.

How does expanding and contracting help us see the pattern in square numbers?

An interesting way to investigate square numbers is through geometry. In Lesson 7, we learned to expand and contract rectangles and squares.

The shape of a square is a demonstration of a square number. Let's think of the square number 4. In an array it has two rows and two columns. Different square numbers are expanded or contracted versions of each other.

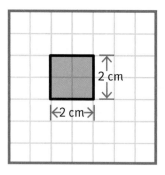

We contract this square by looking at the consecutive square numbers list and choosing a number that is smaller.

Consecutive square numbers from 1 to 100 are 1, 4, 9, 16, 25, 36, 49, 64, 81, and 100.

In this case, the only number that is smaller is 1.

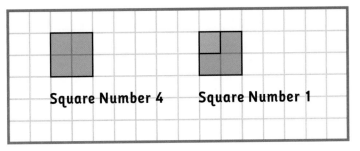

Square Number 4   Square Number 1

To contract the square number 4 (2 × 2) to the square number
1 (1 × 1), we subtract 1 unit from each of the sides. This leaves us
with a difference of 3 square units.

If we look back at the pattern of distance between square numbers,
we see that the difference in the size of the squares is the same as the
distance between the square numbers.

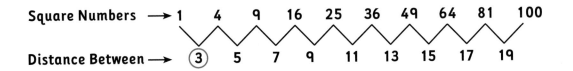

Square Numbers → 1   4   9   16   25   36   49   64   81   100

Distance Between → ③   5   7   9   11   13   15   17   19

We also see this pattern when we expand to a larger square number.
Let's choose 16.

We expanded the 1 × 1 square by adding 3 units to each of the sides.
This left us with a difference of 15 square units. If we look at the pattern
of distance between square numbers, we can add the distances between
the square numbers 1 and 16 to find the same difference in the size of
the square shape: 3 + 5 + 7 = 15.

 Problem-Solving Activity
Turn to *Interactive Text*,
page 248.

mBook Reinforce Understanding
Use the *mBook Study Guide*
to review lesson concepts.

Homework

Activity 1

List common factors for each of the following.

1. 16 and 20
2. 18, 20, and 24
3. 25 and 50
4. 27, 36, and 72
5. 140 and 160
6. 56, 64, and 72

Activity 2

Find the square numbers in this list.

3   4   7   9   12   16   25   32   36   49   56   81

Activity 3

Find the next square number in each list.

1. 4, 9, 16
2. 36, 49, 64
3. 100, 121, 144

Activity 4 • Distributed Practice

Solve.

1. $\begin{array}{r} 5{,}555 \\ -\ 4{,}879 \\ \hline \end{array}$
2. $\begin{array}{r} 800 \\ +\ 700 \\ \hline \end{array}$
3. $\begin{array}{r} 66 \\ \times\ 55 \\ \hline \end{array}$
4. $\begin{array}{r} 333 \\ \times\ \ \ 5 \\ \hline \end{array}$
5. $8\overline{)808}$

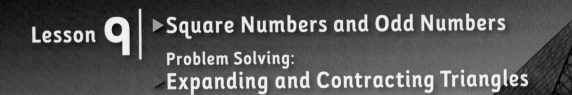

Lesson 9 ▸ Square Numbers and Odd Numbers

Problem Solving:
Expanding and Contracting Triangles

▸ **Square Numbers and Odd Numbers**

How can we see the connection between square numbers and odd numbers?

In Lesson 8, we found a pattern in the square numbers. When listed in order, the distance between the square numbers starts at 3 and continues through the odd numbers. This tells us there is a connection between square numbers and odd numbers.

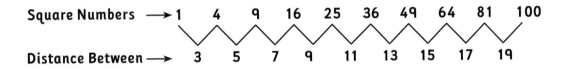

Let's see what this looks like in geometry.

The first square number is 1: $1 \times 1 = 1$.

The array is a square. It has 1 row and 1 column.

1×1

The next square number is 4: $2 \times 2 = 4$.

The array is also shaped like a square. It has 2 rows and 2 columns.

Let's compare the arrays for 1 and 4.

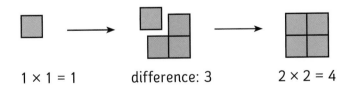

$1 \times 1 = 1$ ⟶ difference: 3 ⟶ $2 \times 2 = 4$

To make the array for 4, we added 3 units.

The next square number is 9: 3 × 3 = 9.

To create this array, we start with the previous 2 × 2 square and add 5 more units to make it a 3 × 3 square.

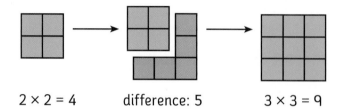

2 × 2 = 4   difference: 5   3 × 3 = 9

The next time, we would add 7 more squares. Why 7? It is the next consecutive odd number. That would make the area of the array 16. Yes, 4 × 4 = 16.

Geometry helps us see the connection between square numbers and odd numbers. When we add "the next consecutive odd number" of squares to a square array, we get the next consecutive square number. We will look more closely at this pattern by examining the changes in the arrays as they move from square number to square number.

This shows how helpful a picture is in mathematics. When we can see a mathematical relationship in a picture, we are able to understand it better.

POWER CONCEPT

The difference between two consecutive square numbers is an odd number.

We are starting to see the pattern of consecutive odd numbers. Let's look at a few more examples.

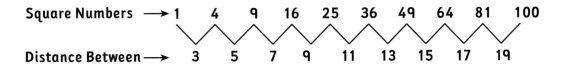

The next square number is 16: $4 \times 4 = 16$.

To create its array, we start with the previous 3×3 square and add 7 more squares to it to get a 4×4 square.

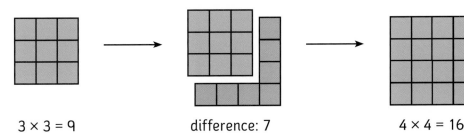

$3 \times 3 = 9$ difference: 7 $4 \times 4 = 16$

The next square number is 25: $5 \times 5 = 25$.

To create its array, we start with the previous 4×4 square and add 9 more squares to it to get a 5×5 square.

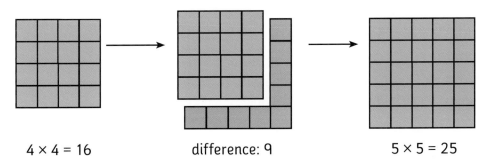

$4 \times 4 = 16$ difference: 9 $5 \times 5 = 25$

This time we added 9 more squares to make the 5×5 square that represents 25.

The pattern becomes very clear when we use geometry and draw the squares. We see that for the next square number, we would add one more row, one more column, and one extra square in the corner. It's because of the one extra square that we get an odd number of squares when we add each time.

%÷ Apply Skills
≦× Turn to *Interactive Text*,
page 250.

 mBook Reinforce Understanding
Use the *mBook Study Guide*
to review lesson concepts.

▶Problem Solving: **Expanding and Contracting Triangles**

How do we expand and contract triangles?

In Lesson 7, we learned how to expand and contract rectangles and squares. We can also expand and contract triangles. Let's look at some examples.

Example 1

Find an expanded version of the triangle.

We expand the triangle by multiplying the height and base by the same amount. In this case, we multiplied the base and height of the triangle by 2 to find an expanded triangle.

Original Triangle	Expanded Triangle
Base: 3	Base: 6
Height: 6	Height: 12

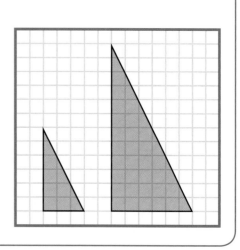

Example 2

Find a contracted version of the triangle.

We contract the triangle by dividing the height by the same amount as the base. In this case, we divide both the base and height of the triangle by 3 to find a contracted triangle.

Original Triangle	Contracted Triangle
Base: 6	Base: 2
Height: 9	Height: 3

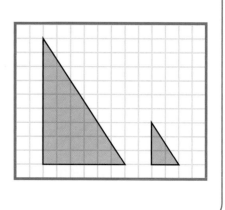

The process of expanding and contracting triangles is very similar to the process we use with squares and rectangles. In both cases, we have to use the same operation and number when working with the measurements of the shape to find a similar figure.

 Problem-Solving Activity
Turn to **Interactive Text**,
page 251.

 Reinforce Understanding
Use the **mBook Study Guide**
to review lesson concepts.

Homework

Activity 1

Find the square numbers in this list.

11   12   16   24   25   37   48   64   81   111   121   144

Activity 2

Find the GCF for the numbers by drawing prime factor trees.

Model

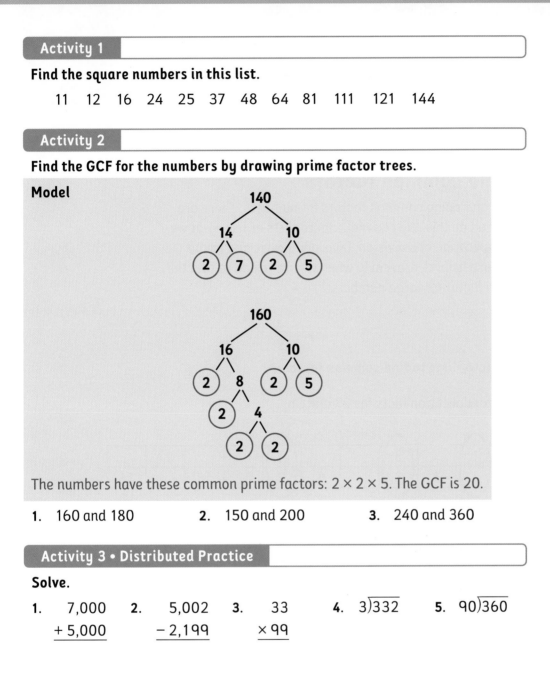

The numbers have these common prime factors: $2 \times 2 \times 5$. The GCF is 20.

1.   160 and 180   2.   150 and 200   3.   240 and 360

Activity 3 • Distributed Practice

Solve.

1. $\begin{array}{r} 7,000 \\ + 5,000 \\ \hline \end{array}$
2. $\begin{array}{r} 5,002 \\ - 2,199 \\ \hline \end{array}$
3. $\begin{array}{r} 33 \\ \times 99 \\ \hline \end{array}$
4. $3\overline{)332}$
5. $90\overline{)360}$

▶**Common Factors and Number Patterns**

How do we find common factors?

This unit focused on finding common factors for numbers. There are several ways we can do this. We can make factor lists or use what we know about multiplication and division. Divisibility rules and prime factor trees are also helpful, especially when we are trying to find the greatest common factor for large numbers.

Review 1

How do we use factor lists to find common factors?

Think about the multiplication facts for 27 and 36.

Factors of 27	1		3			9			27	
Factors of 36	1	2	3	4	6	9	12	18		36

Numbers that are part of both lists are common factors.

The common factors of 27 and 36 are 1, 3, and 9.

How do we find the greatest common factor (GCF)?

Factor lists help us identify common factors of two or more numbers. We use those factors to find the greatest common factor, or GCF. The GCF is the biggest factor of all of the numbers in the set.

Review 1

How do we use factor lists to find the GCF?

List the factors of 27 and 36 so that they can be easily compared.

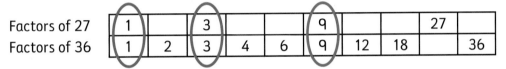

| Factors of 27 | 1 | | 3 | | | 9 | | | 27 | |
| Factors of 36 | 1 | 2 | 3 | 4 | 6 | 9 | 12 | 18 | | 36 |

The common factors are 1, 3, and 9. The greatest common factor is 9.

The GCF of 27 and 36 is 9.

Review 2

How do we use prime factor trees to find the GCF?

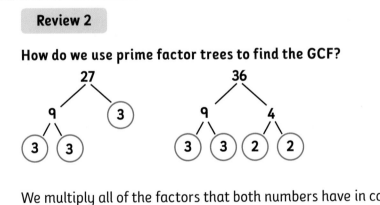

We multiply all of the factors that both numbers have in common to find the GCF. Both numbers have two 3s in common: $3 \times 3 = 9$

The GCF of 27 and 36 is 9.

Prime factor trees are a good way to find the GCF for two or more numbers. They are particularly useful with large numbers.

What are the patterns for odd, even, and square numbers?

Odd, even, and square numbers have interesting patterns that we can see if we use arrays. When we look at addition and multiplication, it is easy to see the rules.

Review 1

What are the rules for addition and multiplication?

(a) An even plus an even number—it is always even.

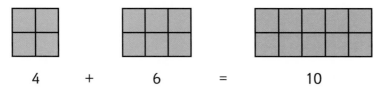

4   +   6   =   10

(b) An even plus an odd number—it is always odd.

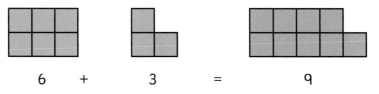

6   +   3   =   9

(c) An odd plus an odd number—it is always even.

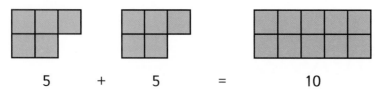

5   +   5   =   10

(d) An even times an even number—it is always even.

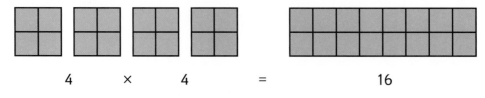

4   ×   4   =   16

(e) An odd times an odd number—it is always odd.

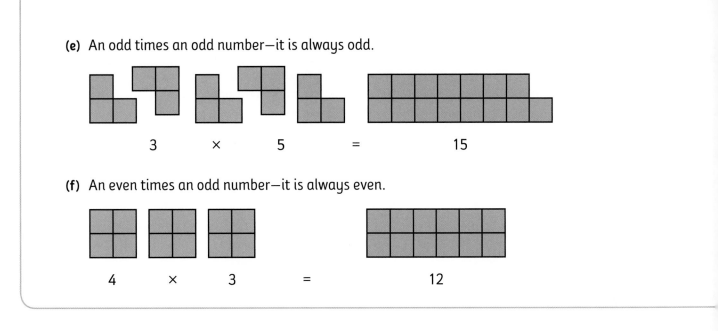

3   ×   5   =   15

(f) An even times an odd number—it is always even.

4   ×   3   =   12

Finally, the square numbers have several interesting patterns. One is that the distance between square numbers is predictable. It is a growing series of odd numbers.

Review 2

What are some patterns in square numbers?

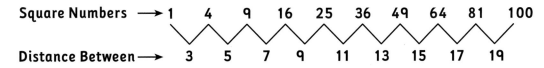

Square Numbers ⟶ 1   4   9   16   25   36   49   64   81   100

Distance Between ⟶   3   5   7   9   11   13   15   17   19

One pattern found with square numbers is in the distance between the numbers. The distance between consecutive square numbers is an odd number.

 Apply Skills
Turn to *Interactive Text*, page 253.

 Reinforce Understanding
Use the *mBook Study Guide* to review lesson concepts.

What are common properties of shapes?

We can identify a number of different properties for shapes. We can label these properties using math terms, or we can make up our own terms. A more challenging task is to put different shapes in groups based on their properties because some shapes can be put into more than one group.

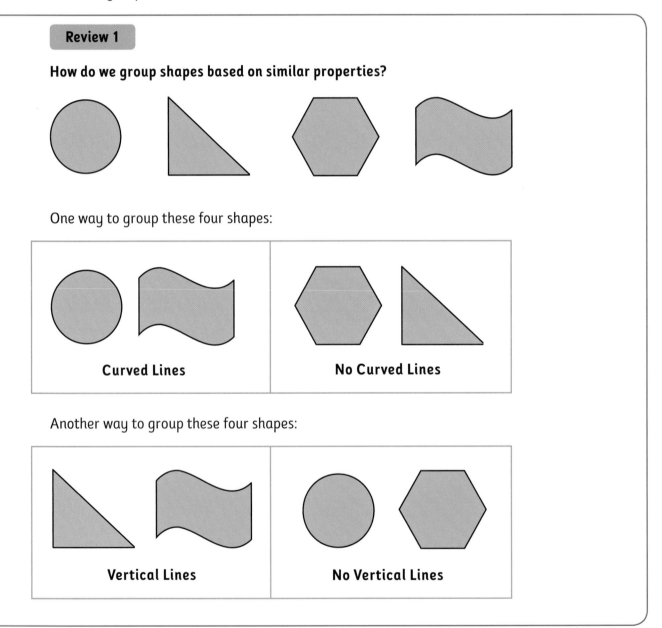

Review 1

How do we group shapes based on similar properties?

One way to group these four shapes:

Curved Lines	**No Curved Lines**

Another way to group these four shapes:

Vertical Lines	**No Vertical Lines**

What are congruence and similarity?

The concept of congruence is important in geometry. We will use it more as we continue to study math. Congruent shapes are shapes that are exactly the same. Even if they are moved, rotated, or flipped, the length of their sides and their angles stays the same.

Review 1

Congruent Triangles

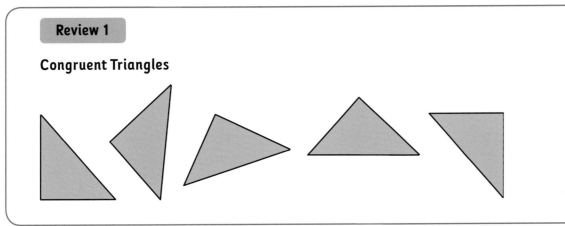

Similarity, on the other hand, involves scaling. We can expand or contract a shape by the same amount. This makes the two shapes similar. Grids help us see the measure of each side of the shape. The example shows two similar rectangles. The one on the right is two times as wide and tall as the one on the left.

Review 2

Similar Rectangles

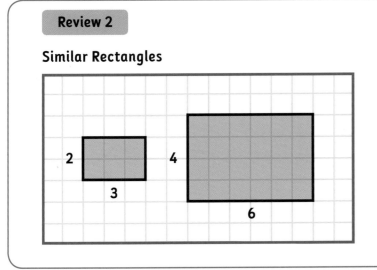

How do we expand and contract shapes?

When we expand or contract a shape, we make it larger or smaller. It is important to remember to multiply or divide all of the lengths by the same number.

Review 1

How do we find the expanded version of a triangle?
We multiply the base and the height by the same amount. In this case, we multiply by 3 to find the expanded triangle.

Original Triangle	Expanded Triangle
Base: 3	Base: 9
Height: 4	Height: 12

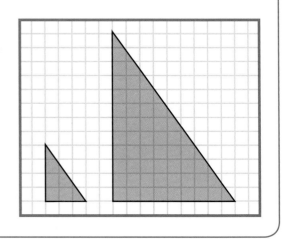

To find the expanded version of a shape, we multiply. To find the contracted version of a shape, we divide.

 Problem-Solving Activity
Turn to *Interactive Text*, page 255.

 mBook **Reinforce Understanding**
Use the *mBook Study Guide* to review lesson concepts.

Math in Motion...

SLIDES

FLIPS

TURNS

Geometry on the dirt track. Awesome!

FUN FACTS

The first bicycle with steering was manufactured in 1817. This boneshaker was built mostly of wood.

The longest jump on a bicycle was accomplished in 2006 by Jason Rennie when he cleared a 133-foot, 6-inch span between two ramps. (To get up to speed, he was towed behind a motorcycle.)

In 1962, French biker Jose Meiffret reached a world-record speed of 127.243 miles per hour.

OBJECTIVES

Building Number Concepts

- Understand the relationships between triangular and square numbers

- Use exponents to show repeated multiplication

- Identify common multiples of two or more whole numbers

Problem Solving

- Recognize slides, flips, and turns in shapes

- Use tangrams to explore the properties of shapes

- Understand reflection and rotational symmetry

►**Triangular Numbers**

Vocabulary
triangular numbers

What are triangular numbers?

Patterns are one of the most interesting things about math. Mathematicians use patterns to make rules about how our number system works. Look at the pattern below.

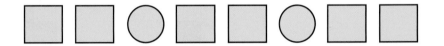

The pattern is two squares and a circle, two squares and a circle, two squares. The next shape would be a circle.

Let's look at some patterns involving numbers.

We learned that a square number can be represented by an array that is a perfect square. The first three square numbers are made of 1, 4, and 9 square units. These are the first three square numbers.

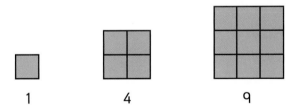

A **triangular number** is a number that has an array that looks like a triangle. Here are the first three triangular numbers, starting with the number 1.

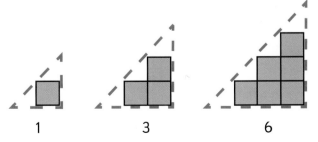

Triangular numbers form a pattern. Let's take a closer look.

What are some patterns of triangular numbers?

If we start with one block, then add a row below it that is one block longer than the first row, we have made the array for the next triangular number, 3.

To create the array for the next triangular number, we add another row that is one block longer than the row above.

This continues for each triangular number. We add another row that is one block longer.

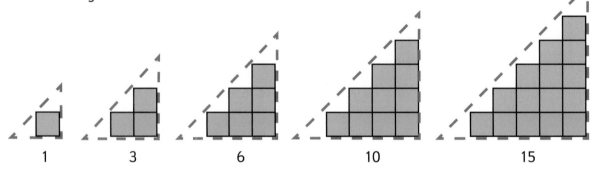

| 1 | 3 | 6 | 10 | 15 |

We see the same pattern when we use numbers to represent what we did with the arrays. When we add each row to create the next array, it is the same as adding the next number in the sequence to find the next triangular number.

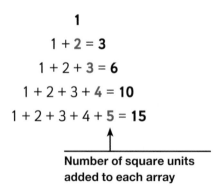

$$1$$
$$1 + 2 = 3$$
$$1 + 2 + 3 = 6$$
$$1 + 2 + 3 + 4 = 10$$
$$1 + 2 + 3 + 4 + 5 = 15$$

Number of square units added to each array

We find more triangular numbers when we follow this pattern.

The next three triangular numbers are 21, 28, and 36.

How are triangular numbers connected to square numbers?

What makes the triangular number pattern interesting is a rule that most people don't know. We can take any triangular number, multiply it by 8, and add 1 to get a square number. Here's an example using the number 3.

STEP 1
Take the triangular number 3.
Multiply it by 8.

STEP 2
Add 1 more.

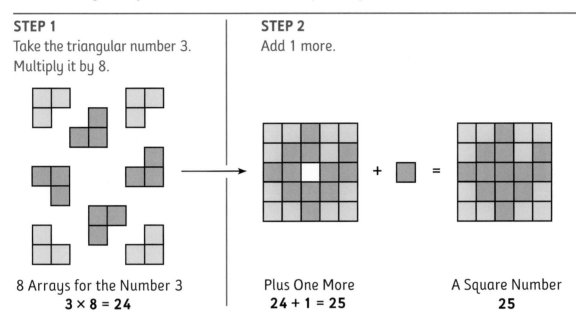

8 Arrays for the Number 3
$3 \times 8 = 24$

Plus One More
$24 + 1 = 25$

A Square Number
25

Let's try this with another number.

Example 1

Use the steps above to find a square number using the triangular number 6.

STEP 1
Take the triangular number 6.
Multiply it by 8. $6 \times 8 = 48$

STEP 2
Add 1 more. $48 + 1 = 49$

The answer 49 is a square number.

 Apply Skills
Turn to *Interactive Text*,
page 258.

mBook Reinforce Understanding
Use the *mBook Study Guide*
to review lesson concepts.

▶Problem Solving: Tangrams

Vocabulary
tangrams

How do we build complex designs from simple shapes?

One way to learn about geometry and the properties of shapes is to build complex designs from simple shapes. A **tangram** provides an opportunity to do this. A tangram is a puzzle made from a square that is divided into seven shapes. Look at the tangram below.

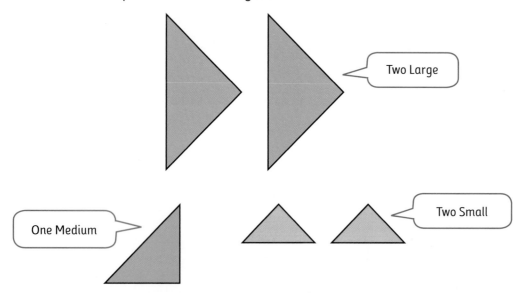

Five of the shapes are similar triangles:

Two Large

One Medium

Two Small

There is one small square and one small parallelogram.

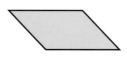

When the shapes are cut out, they can be moved in different ways to make pictures or designs.

The shapes in the tangram are very simple. However, we can form hundreds of tangram designs with them.

Example 1

Make a complex design with the tangram.
All seven of the tangram pieces are used in a tangram design. The outlines for all of the tangram pieces are shown in our examples.

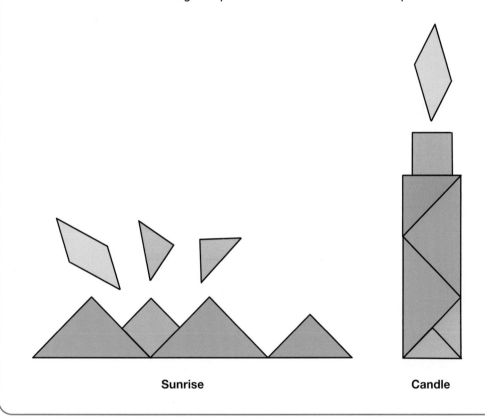

Sunrise   Candle

These are just two designs that can be formed. Sometimes we cannot see the outlines of all of the individual pieces. When the outlines are not shown, it can be more difficult to see where each piece is used. We will look at other designs later in this unit.

 Problem-Solving Activity
Turn to *Interactive Text*, page 259.

mBook **Reinforce Understanding**
Use the *mBook Study Guide* to review lesson concepts.

Activity 1

Which of the numbers are square numbers?

15   25   35   49   64   81   100   112   121   134   144

Activity 2

Look at the number line. What is the counting pattern? Complete the pattern.

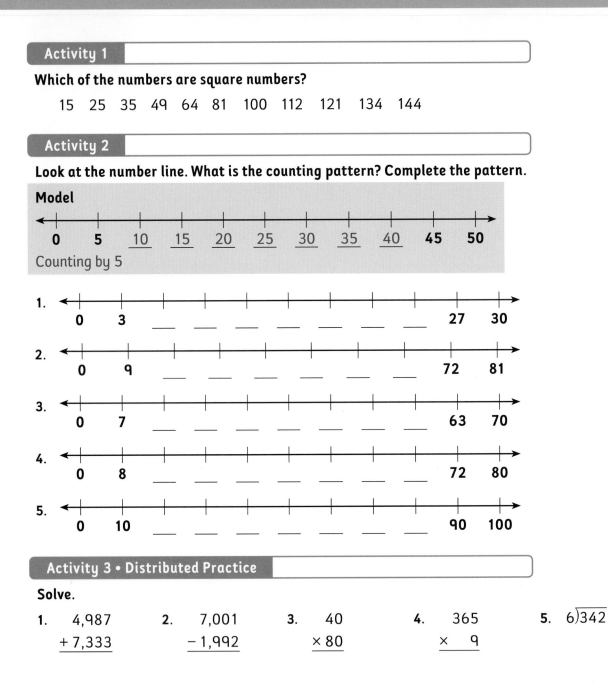

Model

0   5   10   15   20   25   30   35   40   **45**   **50**

Counting by 5

1.   0   3   __   __   __   __   __   __   __   27   30

2.   0   9   __   __   __   __   __   __   72   81

3.   0   7   __   __   __   __   __   __   63   70

4.   0   8   __   __   __   __   __   __   72   80

5.   0   10   __   __   __   __   __   __   90   100

Activity 3 • Distributed Practice

Solve.

1.   4,987   2.   7,001   3.   40   4.   365   5. 6)342
    + 7,333   − 1,992   × 80   ×   9

▸**Exponents**

Vocabulary
base exponent power

What are exponents?

We worked with prime factor trees to find the prime factorization of numbers. Often there are factors that repeat in a prime factorization.

We circled all of the prime numbers in the prime factor tree. There are four 3s. **The prime factorization for 81 is 3 × 3 × 3 × 3.**

We can write repeated multiplication like this in a different way. We multiply all the 3s together and write the number this way: 3^4.

A more efficient way to write $3 \times 3 \times 3 \times 3$ is 3^4.

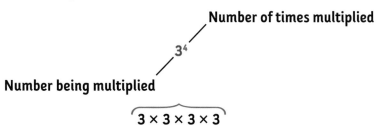

In our new way of writing, the 3 is called the **base** . It is the number that is being multiplied repeatedly. The 4 is called the **exponent** . It tells us how many times to multiply the base.

Exponent

3^4

Base

The base and exponent together are called a **power** . This number is read "three to the fourth power." The number 3^4 is equal to the number we started with—81.

How do we write numbers as powers?

Powers make repeated multiplication problems easier to work with. We know that the number 81 can be written $3 \times 3 \times 3 \times 3$, or 3^4. We can write other numbers as powers too.

Many large numbers can be written as powers of 10. There is a pattern to how we write these numbers.

- The number **100** has two zeros, so it is written as a multiplication problem with two 10s—**10 × 10**.
- The number 1,**000** has three zeros, so it is written **10 × 10 × 10**.
- The number 1**0,000** has four zeros, so it is written **10 × 10 × 10 × 10**.

This is the pattern: a 10 is added to the repeated multiplication for each zero in the number. Let's write the next number in our pattern as a power of 10.

Example 1

Write 100,000 as a power of 10.

The number **100,000** has five zeros. We can write it as repeated multiplication using 10s.

$$10 \times 10 \times 10 \times 10 \times 10 = 100,000$$

The number 10 is the number being multiplied—it is our base. There are five 10s, so 5 is our exponent.

$$10 \times 10 \times 10 \times 10 \times 10 = 10^5$$

The number 100,000 is 10^5, or 10 to the fifth power.

How do we use powers to write large numbers so they are easier to read?

Using exponents makes large numbers easier to read. Let's look at how we rewrite the distance from the Earth to the Sun, which is 93,000,000 miles.

Example 1

Use powers of 10 to simplify the number 93,000,000.

- Start with the number 93,000,000.
- Pull out the 10s.

$$93 \times \underbrace{10 \times 10 \times 10 \times 10 \times 10 \times 10}_{10^6}$$

- Don't forget the 93.

$$93 \times 10^6$$

A more efficient way to write 93,000,000 is 93×10^6.

Using powers is a more efficient way to write large numbers.

 Apply Skills
Turn to *Interactive Text*, page 262.

mBook Reinforce Understanding
Use the *mBook Study Guide* to review lesson concepts.

What are some other tangram designs?

We can make many designs with tangram pieces. Tangram designs are challenging when only the outline of the design is given. Let's try to recreate the design of a cat.

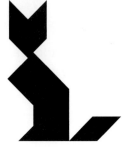

This design resembles a cat. It uses all seven pieces of the tangram. However, none of the individual pieces are outlined.

First we try to identify the easy pieces. Look at the tail of the cat. It's clear that the tail is the parallelogram. It's the only piece that is not a square or a triangle.

Now look at the cat's head. The ears seem to be small triangles. If we use the two small triangles for the ears, we can place the square at an angle for the head.

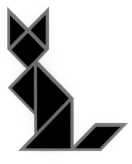

We still have the two large triangles and the medium triangle to form the body of our cat. Here is our completed cat with all of the pieces outlined.

Constructing a tangram design can be difficult. It often takes many tries to figure out how to assemble all seven pieces correctly.

When we solve a tangram puzzle, we look for the easy-to-see pieces first and place them where we think they should go. Then we use the remaining pieces to finish the puzzle.

 Problem-Solving Activity
Turn to *Interactive Text*, page 263.

 mBook **Reinforce Understanding**
Use the *mBook Study Guide* to review lesson concepts.

Lesson 2

Homework

Activity 1

Look at the number line. What is the counting pattern? Complete the pattern.

Model

```
←+——+——+——+——+——+——+——+——+——+——+——+——+→
  0    2    4    6    8   10   12   14   16   18   20   22   24
```

Counting by 2

1.
```
←+——+——+——+——+——+——+——+——+——+——+→
  0    6    __   __   __   __   __   __   __   54   60
```

2.
```
←+——+——+——+——+——+——+——+——+——+——+→
  0    5    __   __   __   __   __   __   __   45   50
```

3.
```
←+——+——+——+——+——+——+——+——+——+——+→
  0    20   __   __   __   __   __   __   __   180  200
```

Activity 2

Rewrite using exponents.

Model

$10 \times 10 \times 10$

Answer: 10^3

1. 10×10

2. $5 \times 5 \times 5$

3. 7×7

4. $10 \times 10 \times 10 \times 10 \times 10$

Activity 3

Rewrite each power using repeated multiplication.

Model 10^3 Answer: $10^3 = 10 \times 10 \times 10$

1. 10^2

2. 2^3

3. 3^3

4. 10^6

Activity 4 • Distributed Practice

Solve.

1. $\begin{array}{r} 500 \\ + 700 \\ \hline \end{array}$

2. $\begin{array}{r} 3,678 \\ - 1,899 \\ \hline \end{array}$

3. $\begin{array}{r} 40 \\ \times 60 \\ \hline \end{array}$

4. $6\overline{)366}$

▶**Patterns With Exponents**

How do we multiply powers?

Below are several ways to show 7^{10} with repeated multiplication. The left side of the problem changes, but the right side is always 7^{10}.

$$7 \times 7 \times 7 \times 7 \times 7 \times 7 \times 7 \times 7 \times 7 \times 7 = 7^{10}$$

$$7^2 \times 7 \times 7 \times 7 \times 7 \times 7 \times 7 \times 7 \times 7 = 7^{10}$$

$$7^3 \times 7 \times 7 \times 7 \times 7 \times 7 \times 7 \times 7 = 7^{10}$$

$$7^4 \times 7 \times 7 \times 7 \times 7 \times 7 \times 7 = 7^{10}$$

To create this pattern, we used powers of 7. In the second problem, we substituted 7^2 for 7×7. In the third problem, we substituted 7^3 for $7 \times 7 \times 7$. In the fourth problem, we substituted 7^4 for $7 \times 7 \times 7 \times 7$. All of the problems still equal 7^{10}.

We can do other substitutions, too. These problems create another pattern.

$$7^2 \times 7^8 = 7^{10}$$

$$7^3 \times 7^7 = 7^{10}$$

$$7^4 \times 7^6 = 7^{10}$$

The problems in this pattern also equal 7^{10}. We continue this pattern until we get to $7^{10} = 7^{10}$. In each case, we add the exponents on the left side of the equal sign to find the exponent on the right side.

$$7^4 \times 7^6 = 7^{10}$$

The sum of the exponents on the left equals the exponent on the right.

This kind of pattern is the basis for rules about exponents. Mathematicians are always looking for patterns. When they find a pattern, they use it to make a rule. This pattern gives us a rule to remember about exponents.

> **Rule: Multiplying Exponents**
> When we multiply powers with the same base, we can add the exponents.

In order for this rule to work, we need to look for two things:

- We must be multiplying.
- The base must be the same.

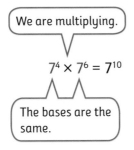

We are multiplying.

$$7^4 \times 7^6 = 7^{10}$$

The bases are the same.

Let's use this rule to solve a multiplication problem.

Example 1

Multiply the powers $3^4 \times 3^5$.
We know the rule for multiplying powers with the same base. Since 3^4 and 3^5 have the same base, we find the answer by adding the exponents.

$$3^{4+5} = 3^9$$

The product is 3^9.

We use other patterns to create more rules about exponents.

 Apply Skills
Turn to *Interactive Text*, page 265.

 mBook Reinforce Understanding
Use the *mBook Study Guide* to review lesson concepts.

▶**Problem Solving: Slides, Flips, and Turns**

Vocabulary
transformation
slide
flip
turn

How can shapes be changed?

When we make designs for objects, we sometimes take the same shape and move it or change it in different ways. Look at the design of the door. The window at the top of the door uses a series of triangles that are turned slightly. That is one kind of change called a **transformation**.

Let's look at three kinds of transformations: a **slide**, a **flip**, and a **turn**. Here is an example of each using a triangle.

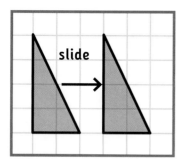

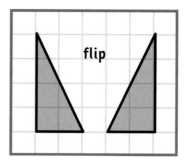

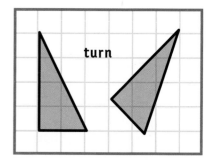

Slide

In a slide, we move the object in one direction. Everything else about the shape stays the same.

Flip

In a flip, we take the object and flip it over. It can be flipped over from front to back or from top to bottom.

Turn

In a turn, we rotate the object so that it rests at a new angle. The door above features several versions of the same triangle that have been turned again and again.

 Problem-Solving Activity
Turn to *Interactive Text*, page 267.

 mBook Reinforce Understanding
Use the *mBook Study Guide* to review lesson concepts.

Activity 1

Write each of the following using exponents.

Model $10^2 \times 10 \times 10$ Answer: 10^4

1. $9 \times 9 \times 9 \times 9 \times 9 \times 9 \times 9$
2. $7^5 \times 7 \times 7 \times 7$
3. $10^3 \times 10 \times 10 \times 10 \times 10 \times 10$
4. $3^6 \times 3 \times 3 \times 3$
5. $2^7 \times 2$

Activity 2

Write each power using repeated multiplication.

Model 4^9 Answer: $4 \times 4 \times 4 \times 4 \times 4 \times 4 \times 4 \times 4 \times 4$

1. 5^9
2. 7^2
3. 8^6
4. 2^6
5. 10^4

Activity 3

Multiply the powers.

Model $2^4 \times 2^4$ Answer: $2^{4+4} = 2^8$

1. $2^3 \times 2^6$
2. $3^2 \times 3^3$
3. $5^8 \times 5^2$
4. $10^2 \times 10^2$

Activity 4 • Distributed Practice

Solve.

1. $\begin{array}{r} 3,067 \\ -\ 1,987 \\ \hline \end{array}$
2. $\begin{array}{r} 700 \\ +\ 900 \\ \hline \end{array}$
3. $\begin{array}{r} 600 \\ \times\ \ \ 3 \\ \hline \end{array}$
4. $\begin{array}{r} 69 \\ \times\ 55 \\ \hline \end{array}$
5. $7\overline{)4,249}$

Lesson 4 | ▸More Exponent Patterns

Problem Solving:
▸Symmetry

▸**More Exponent Patterns**

What are some other exponent patterns?

There is another rule that comes from exponent patterns. We looked at exponents from 2 to 10. The exponent 1 is a special exponent. We know that 7^1 is the same as 7 to the first power, or 7.

The exponent 1 is special because any power with an exponent of 1 is equal to the base number.

We know that:
$$7 \times 7 \times 7 \times 7 \times 7 \times 7 \times 7 \times 7 \times 7 \times 7 = 7^{10}$$

If we rewrite each 7 as 7^1, the answer stays the same.
$$7^1 \times 7^1 \times 7^1 \times 7^1 \times 7^1 \times 7^1 \times 7^1 \times 7^1 \times 7^1 \times 7^1 = 7^{10}$$

We know that we add the exponents when we multiply powers with the same base. The problem above is the same as:
$$7^{1+1+1+1+1+1+1+1+1+1} = 7^{10}$$

The numbers 7 and 7^1 are the same thing. So we don't need to write the exponent 1. This rule applies to any number with an exponent of 1.

> **Rule: Exponents With the Power of 1**
> Any power with an exponent of 1 is equal to the base number.
>
> $5^1 = 5$ $\qquad$ $1^1 = 1$ $\qquad$ $324^1 = 324$ $\qquad$ $1,893^1 = 1,893$

Let's use this thinking to work with more complex powers.

Example 1

Multiply the powers $100^1 \times 10^{24}$.

Using our power of 1 exponent rule, we know that 100^1 is the same as 100. We also know that 100 is the same as 10×10 or 10^2.

So we can rewrite our problem $10^2 \times 10^{24}$.

Now that we have two powers with the same base, we use our multiplication rule for exponents: When we multiply powers with the same base, we add the exponents.

$10^2 \times 10^{24} = 10^{2+24} = 10^{26}$

The product is 10^{26}.

Having good number sense and understanding patterns helps us figure out complex problems.

Improve Your Skills

Your friend multiplied the powers $9^4 \times 9^2$.

$9^4 \times 9^2 = 9^8$ **ERROR**

His answer was incorrect. What was his mistake?

Your friend didn't remember the rule: When we multiply powers with the same base, we **add** the exponents.

Your friend **multiplied** the exponents instead.

$9^4 \times 9^2 = 9^6$ **CORRECT**

> Remember to add the exponents when multiplying powers with the same base.

 Apply Skills
Turn to **Interactive Text**, page 271.

mBook Reinforce Understanding
Use the **mBook Study Guide** to review lesson concepts.

► **Problem Solving: Symmetry**

Vocabulary
properties reflection symmetry line of symmetry

When does a shape display symmetry?

Looking at different shapes, we notice many things about them. They might have straight edges or curves. They might have four sides or three. In mathematics, these different characteristics are called **properties** . Different shapes can have many properties in common.

One important property of shapes is **reflection symmetry** . Objects have symmetry, or are symmetrical, when they are balanced. This means that they have two halves that are exactly the same. If a symmetrical shape is folded in half, one half folds exactly on top of the other half. The two halves have the identical shape and outline. This is a symmetrical shape.

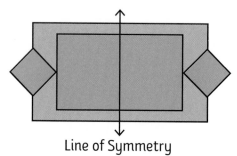

Line of Symmetry

One way to tell if an object is symmetrical is by drawing a line of symmetry. A **line of symmetry** divides an object in half so that the two halves are mirror images of each other. The line in the shape above divides it in half. This is a line of symmetry.

Some shapes have more than one line of symmetry. We can draw a second line of symmetry that divides the shape into identical top and bottom parts.

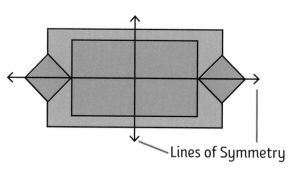

Lines of Symmetry

Sometimes lines appear to divide a shape into nearly equal parts, but they are not lines of symmetry.

Example 1

Determine which shape has a line of symmetry.

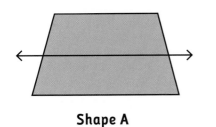

Shape A

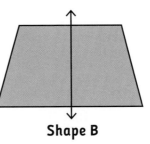

Shape B

- **Shape A and Shape B** are identical, but they have different lines drawn through them.

- **Shape A** is divided into two parts with a line going from left to right. The top part is smaller than the bottom part. The line does not divide the shape into two identical parts. This is not a line of symmetry.

- **Shape B** is divided into two parts with a line from top to bottom. The two sides are mirror images of each other. This is a line of symmetry.

Shape B shows a line of symmetry.

Symmetry is a property we use to describe shapes. It is closely connected to congruence. A line of symmetry can divide a shape into congruent parts.

 Problem-Solving Activity
Turn to *Interactive Text*, page 272.

 mBook Reinforce Understanding
Use the *mBook Study Guide* to review lesson concepts.

Homework

Activity 1

Multiply powers.

Model $2^4 \times 2^4 = 2^8$ **1.** $2^3 \times 2$ **2.** $3^2 \times 3^3$

                                    3. $5^8 \times 5^2$ **4.** $10^2 \times 10^2$

Activity 2

Rewrite each of the following using exponents.

Model $10 \times 10 \times 10$ Answer: 10^3

1. $2 \times 2 \times 2 \times 2$ **2.** $3 \times 3 \times 3 \times 3 \times 3 \times 3$

3. $5 \times 5 \times 5$ **4.** $10 \times 10 \times 10 \times 10 \times 10 \times 10 \times 10 \times 10 \times 10 \times 10 \times 10$

Activity 3

Look at the line in each shape. Determine if the line is a line of symmetry. List the letters of the shapes that show a line of symmetry.

(a)   (b)   (c)   (d)   (e)

(f)   (g)   (h)   (i)   (j)

Activity 4 • Distributed Practice

Solve.

1. 500   **2.** 7,890   **3.** 500   **4.** $5\overline{)246}$
   $+ 700$ $- 1,209$ $\times \quad 4$

▶Common Multiples

Vocabulary
multiples common multiples

What are common multiples?

When we think about the multiplication facts for a number, we are thinking about **multiples** . Multiples of a number are all the products of that number and another whole number. Below are the first four multiples of the number 6.

a number × a whole number = its multiple

	Multiples of 6
6 × 1 = 6 6 × 2 = 12 6 × 3 = 18 6 × 4 = 24	6, 12, 18, 24

Another way to think about multiples is counting by numbers on a number line. The number line below shows all the multiples of 6 up to 6 × 7, or 42.

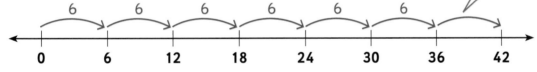

multiples of 6

0   6   12   18   24   30   36   42

In this lesson we will work with **common multiples** . Common multiples of two numbers are multiples that are the same for both numbers.

Let's compare the multiples of 4 with the multiples of 6 on two number lines. The common multiples are the multiples that are the same for both 4 and 6.

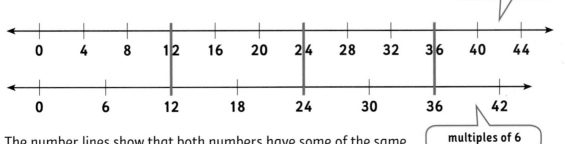

multiples of 4

0   4   8   12   16   20   24   28   32   36   40   44

0   6   12   18   24   30   36   42

multiples of 6

The number lines show that both numbers have some of the same multiples. Three common multiples of 4 and 6 are 12, 24, and 36.

How do we find common multiples for more than two numbers?

We found common multiples of two numbers by comparing number lines. We use the same process to find the common multiples for more than two numbers. Let's find the common multiples for 4, 6, and 8.

Example 1

Find common multiples of 4, 6, and 8.

First, we construct number lines by counting by the number.

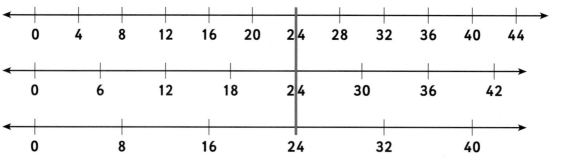

The number lines show that for numbers up to 44, the only common multiple of 4, 6, and 8 is the number 24.

A common multiple of 4, 6, and 8 is 24.

When we compared the multiples of 4 and 6, we found that 12 was a common multiple. The number 12 is part of two number lines in the example, but because it is not a part of all three number lines, it is not a common multiple for all three numbers.

There are other common multiples for these three numbers, but they are larger than the numbers on our number lines.

A common multiple is a multiple shared by two or more numbers.

 Apply Skills
Turn to *Interactive Text*,
page 274.

 Monitoring Progress
Quiz 1

 mBook Reinforce Understanding
Use the *mBook Study Guide*
to review lesson concepts.

Homework

Activity 1

Rewrite the following powers as repeated multiplication.

Model

5^4 $5 \times 5 \times 5 \times 5$

1. 6^2
2. 10^4
3. 7×10^2
4. 2×3^5

Activity 2

Multiply the powers.

Model

$2^4 \times 2^6$ 2^{10}

1. $3^2 \times 3^4$
2. $3^4 \times 3^8$
3. $10^2 \times 10^3$
4. $10^9 \times 10$
5. $6^8 \times 6^2$
6. $5^2 \times 5^3$

Activity 3

Use the lists of multiples in each problem to identify common multiples.

Model What are some common multiples of 6 and 3? Answer: 6, 12, 18, and 24

Multiples of 6		6		12		18		24	
Multiples of 3	3	6	9	12	15	18	21	24	27

1. What are some common multiples of 5 and 10?

Multiples of 5	5	10	15	20	25	30	35	40
Multiples of 10		10		20		30		40

2. What are some common multiples of 4 and 8?

Multiples of 4	4	8	12	16	20	24	28	32
Multiples of 8		8		16		24		32

3. What are some common multiples of 2, 4, and 8?

Multiples of 2	2	4	6	8	10	12	14	16	18
Multiples of 4		4		8		12		16	
Multiples of 8				8				16	

Activity 4 • Distributed Practice

Solve.

1.
$$\begin{array}{r} 1{,}700 \\ -800 \\ \hline \end{array}$$

2.
$$\begin{array}{r} 9{,}898 \\ +2{,}112 \\ \hline \end{array}$$

3.
$$\begin{array}{r} 90 \\ \times 90 \\ \hline \end{array}$$

4.
$$\begin{array}{r} 678 \\ \times2 \\ \hline \end{array}$$

Lesson 6 ▸Least Common Multiple (LCM)

Problem Solving:
▸Symmetry and Mobiles

▸**Least Common Multiple (LCM)**

<table>
<tr><td>Vocabulary</td></tr>
<tr><td>least common multiple (LCM)</td></tr>
</table>

How do we find the least common multiple?

Finding common multiples is very important when working with other numbers, such as fractions. When we look for common multiples, we usually need to find the **least common multiple**, or **LCM**. The least common multiple is the smallest multiple that two or more numbers have in common.

Here are two number lines with the multiples of both 3 and 4.

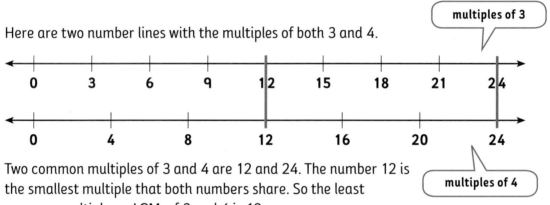

Two common multiples of 3 and 4 are 12 and 24. The number 12 is the smallest multiple that both numbers share. So the least common multiple, or LCM, of 3 and 4 is 12.

Sometimes it's a lot of work to make number lines and to get the numbers to line up correctly. We can also use organized lists to find common multiples.

Here are the multiples of 3 and 4 in a list.

	×1	×2	×3	×4
Multiples of 3	3	6	9	12
Multiples of 4	4	8	12	

We find the multiples for our list by thinking about multiplication facts. The first column in the list is 3 and 4 multiplied by 1. The next column is 3 and 4 multiplied by 2. We can continue until we get to the first number that matches. This number is the least common multiple. In this case, that number is 12.

Let's use this thinking to find the least common multiple of 2, 4, and 6.

Example 1

Find the least common multiple of 2, 4, and 6 using lists of multiples.
We start by multiplying each number by 1.

$$2 \times 1 = 2 \qquad 4 \times 1 = 4 \qquad 6 \times 1 = 6$$

We use these products to fill in the first column in our list. Then we continue by multiplying each number by 2, 3, and so on.

	×1	×2	×3	×4	×5	×6
Multiples of 2	2	4	6	8	10	12
Multiples of 4	4	8	12	16	20	24
Multiples of 6	6	12				

We can stop writing multiples once we have found a multiple that all of the numbers share. The number 12 is the smallest common multiple.

The LCM of 2, 4, and 6 is 12.

Another way to write multiplication

In Example 1, we wrote the multiplication facts $2 \times 1 = 2$, $4 \times 1 = 4$, and $6 \times 1 = 6$, using the × to mean times. Another way to show that we are multiplying is to use the · symbol. This symbol means the same as ×, or times. We use · when we are working in horizontal multiplication problems. It helps us better separate multiplication from other functions. The list of facts below shows basic facts for 2 using the · symbol.

$2 \cdot 1 = 2$

$2 \cdot 2 = 4$

$2 \cdot 3 = 6$

$2 \cdot 4 = 8$

$2 \cdot 5 = 10$

$2 \cdot 6 = 12$

> From now on, we will use the · symbol when we are multiplying horizontally.

 Apply Skills
Turn to *Interactive Text*, page 276.

mBook Reinforce Understanding
Use the *mBook Study Guide* to review lesson concepts.

What is a mobile?

Mobiles were popularized by an American artist named Alexander Calder many years ago. His idea was to create a hanging wire sculpture that had moving parts. Many other artists have created mobiles. As mobiles move in the air, their appearance changes. Mobiles are works of art that are always changing shape.

Alexander Calder holding *21 Feuilles Blanches* in Paris, 1954. Agnès Varda.

We can use mobiles to explore some of the geometry concepts that we have learned so far. One of those concepts is symmetry.

Objects are symmetrical if they have two halves that are the same. Let's look at the mobiles in the examples and determine if they have symmetry.

Example 1

Determine if a mobile has reflection symmetry.

We know that one way to determine symmetry is by using a line of symmetry. Let's look at Mobile A.

There is no place to draw a line so that we have two identical halves. Mobile A does not have a line of symmetry. So it does not display symmetry.

Mobile A is not symmetrical.

Mobile A

Example 2

Determine if the mobile has reflection symmetry.

Our first mobile was not symmetrical. Look at Mobile B.

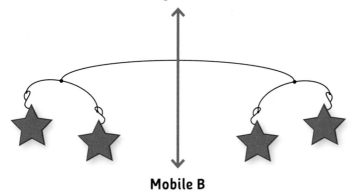

Mobile B

Mobile B has a line of symmetry that divides it into two identical halves.
It displays symmetry.

Mobile B is symmetrical.

Reflection symmetry is not just a characteristic of geometric shapes.
Being able to determine symmetry is important for creating art,
working on designs, and completing other tasks.

Problem-Solving Activity
Turn to *Interactive Text*,
page 277.

mBook **Reinforce Understanding**
Use the *mBook Study Guide*
to review lesson concepts.

Homework

Activity 1

Rewrite the following using exponents.

Model	1. $7 \cdot 7 \cdot 7 \cdot 7$	2. $10 \cdot 2 \cdot 2 \cdot 2 \cdot 2$
$4 \cdot 10 \cdot 10 \cdot 10 \quad 4 \cdot 10^3$	3. $8 \cdot 9 \cdot 9 \cdot 9 \cdot 9 \cdot 9$	4. $68 \cdot 10 \cdot 10 \cdot 10$

Activity 2

Multiply the powers.

Model	1. $2^4 \cdot 2^6$	2. $3^2 \cdot 3^2$
$10^2 \cdot 10^3 \quad 10^5$	3. $10 \cdot 10^4$	4. $7^2 \cdot 7^2$

Activity 3

Find the least common multiple (LCM) for the pairs of numbers in each problem.

1. What is the least common multiple of 4 and 2?

4	4	8	12	16	20	24	28	32	36	40
2	2	4	6	8	10	12	14	16	18	20

2. What is the least common multiple of 7 and 6?

7	7	14	21	28	35	42	49	56	63	70
6	6	12	18	24	30	36	42	48	54	60

3. What is the least common multiple of 6 and 9?

6	6	12	18	24	30	36	42	48	54	60
9	9	18	27	36	45	54	63	72	81	90

4. What is the least common multiple of 8 and 12?

8	8	16	24	32	40	48	56	64	72	80
12	12	24	36	48	60	72	84	96	108	120

5. What is the least common multiple of 6 and 8?

6	6	12	18	24	30	36	42	48	54	60
8	8	16	24	32	40	48	56	64	72	80

Activity 4 • Distributed Practice

Solve.

1.	7,897	2.	4,892	3.	53	4.	$3\overline{)303}$
	$-\,5,299$		$+\,6,218$		$\times\,69$		

▶**Problem Solving: Creating Mobiles**

How do we use symmetry to create mobiles?

We looked at mobile designs that displayed reflection symmetry. Let's use what we learned about symmetry and mobiles to create our own. The example shows how a mobile is built.

Example 1

Create a mobile that displays reflection symmetry.

Only the left half of the mobile is drawn, along with the line of symmetry.

Because there is a line of symmetry, we know the right half of the mobile has to be a mirror image of the left half.

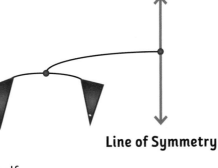

Line of Symmetry

We start where the left half of the design touches the line of symmetry.

STEP 1

Draw a line on the right side that begins on the line of symmetry at the same place as the line on the left side. Draw the line so that it has the same length and shape.

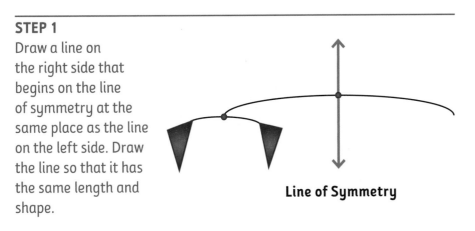

Line of Symmetry

STEP 2

Place a circle at the end of our new line just like on the left side. The circle shows that a new line will begin at that point.

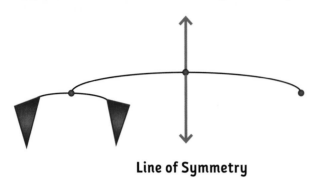

Line of Symmetry

We drew the first line on the right to match the left side.

STEP 3

Add the second line at our new circle. Make sure the line is the same length and shape. It should be a mirror image of the matching line on the left.

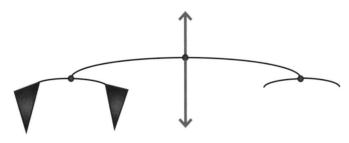

Line of Symmetry

We now have lines on the right side to match all the lines on the left.

STEP 4

Add the two triangles. Draw the triangles the same size. Draw the triangles the same shape. Draw the triangles pointing in the same direction.

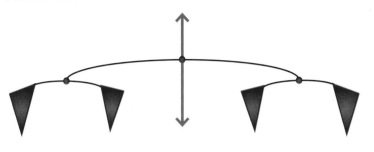

Line of Symmetry

We added everything needed to the right side. We can check to make sure that it looks the same as the left side.

The mobile is symmetrical.

Since both sides of our mobile are the same, we have created a figure that displays reflection symmetry, and our line of symmetry is drawn correctly.

Let's take these ideas and apply them to creating our own mobiles. Remember to use symmetry.

 Problem-Solving Activity
Turn to *Interactive Text*, page 279.

 mBook Reinforce Understanding
Use the *mBook Study Guide* to review lesson concepts.

Activity 1

Rewrite the following powers as repeated multiplication.

Model 5^4 $5 \cdot 5 \cdot 5 \cdot 5$

1. 6^3
2. 10^2
3. 8^1
4. $4 \cdot 10^3$
5. $5 \cdot 10^{10}$

Activity 2

Multiply the powers.

Model $10^2 \cdot 10^3$ 10^5

1. $10 \cdot 10^3$
2. $4^2 \cdot 4^3$
3. $3^3 \cdot 3^4$
4. $6^7 \cdot 6^9$

Activity 3

Find the least common multiple (LCM) for the pairs of numbers in each problem.

1. What is the LCM of 3 and 8?
2. What is the LCM of 6 and 8?
3. What is the LCM of 5 and 8?
4. What is the LCM of 4 and 6?

Activity 4 • Distributed Practice

Solve.

1. $\begin{array}{r} 4,000 \\ -\ 1,879 \\ \hline \end{array}$

2. $\begin{array}{r} 600 \\ \times\ \ \ 8 \\ \hline \end{array}$

3. $7\overline{)469}$

4. $\begin{array}{r} 19 \\ \times 81 \\ \hline \end{array}$

▸**Applications of LCM**

What do wheels inside a cuckoo clock have to do with math?

We have been finding LCMs, or least common multiples. When finding the LCM, we used both number lines and lists. Now we are going to find least common multiples in a very different way. We are going to use a specially made cuckoo clock.

At right is a cuckoo clock. Normally, the figure of a bird comes out of a door in the clock once an hour and sings. However, in this special clock the figure of the bird comes out and sings, but not every hour. We are going to work with the wheels on the back of the clock to find out when the bird appears.

Inside the clock are two gear wheels. One is gold, and the other is white. Notice the clip on each wheel.

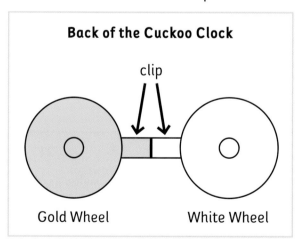

Back of the Cuckoo Clock

clip

Gold Wheel   White Wheel

The wheels both turn clockwise at different speeds. That means that the clips will touch at various times. Every time the clips touch, the bird comes out of the clock and sings.

The gold wheel makes one full turn clockwise every two hours, and the white wheel makes one full turn clockwise every three hours. The clips start out touching. Let's look at where the clips are every hour for the next six hours.

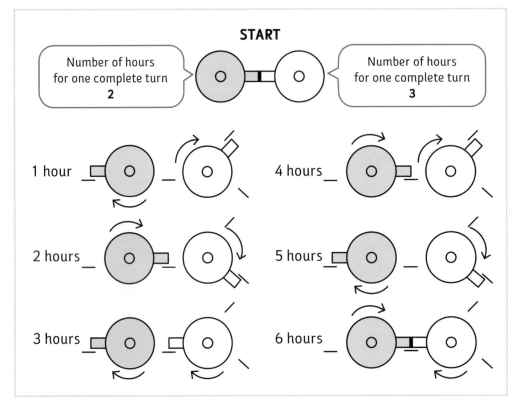

Notice that it takes six hours for the clips to touch and the bird to come out of the clock. We can show this mathematically. Let's use number lines.

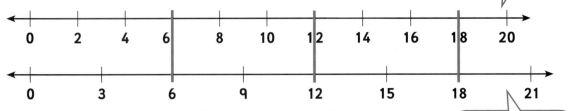

Some of the common multiples for the numbers 2 and 3 are 6, 12, and 18. The least common multiple for 2 (the number of hours for a complete turn of the gold wheel) and 3 (the number of hours for the white wheel) is 6. This is how we know that the bird will come out of the clock every six hours.

By finding when the clips would touch, we found the LCM of two numbers. The turning wheels are another way of showing how least common multiples work, and how they can be used.

Let's look at another cuckoo clock problem where the wheels turn at other speeds. This time, the gold wheel makes one complete turn every two hours, and the white wheel makes one complete turn every four hours.

Example 1

Determine when the bird will come out of the clock.

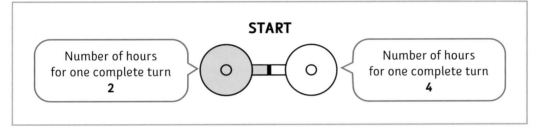

The gold wheel makes one full turn clockwise every two hours. The white wheel makes one full turn clockwise every four hours. We need to find the least common multiple of 2 and 4.

We create a multiple list.

	×1	×2
2	2	4
4	4	

Just like with greatest common factors, the LCM is sometimes one of the original numbers.

The number 4 is the smallest common multiple. This means that the clips touch after four hours. Look at the wheels below to see how the wheels for this clock work.

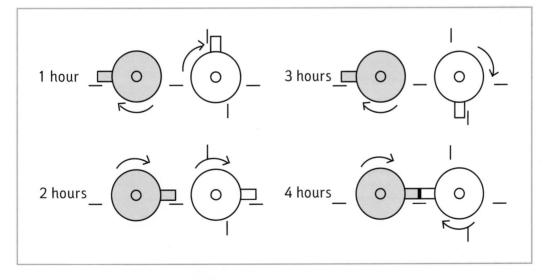

Apply Skills
Turn to *Interactive Text*, page 281.

mBook Reinforce Understanding
Use the *mBook Study Guide* to review lesson concepts.

▶**Problem Solving: Rotational Symmetry**

What is rotational symmetry?

Look at the shapes below. We can draw a line of symmetry to divide these shapes into similar halves. This type of symmetry is also called *reflection symmetry*.

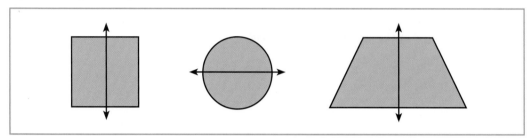

There is another kind of symmetry. Objects like the pinwheel below still look the same when turned. We call this **rotational symmetry**.

All three pictures below are of the same pinwheel. The arrows show how the pinwheel has been turned.

Even though the pinwheel has moved, it still looks the same. This pinwheel has rotational symmetry.

Here is another example of rotational symmetry. The design contains rectangles that are turned around a center point. When we rotate the object slightly, it still looks the same.

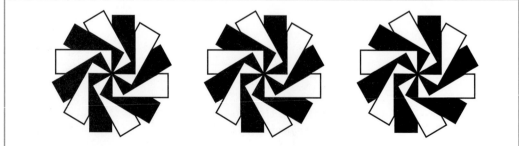

We identified a square as symmetrical using reflection symmetry. Let's see if a square also has rotational symmetry.

Example 1

Determine if a square has rotational symmetry. Look at the square to the right. The dot at the top right helps show the rotation of the square as it moves clockwise.

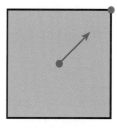

We rotate the square clockwise around its center so that the top right corner becomes the bottom right corner. The square still looks the same.

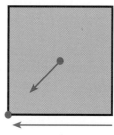

We rotate the square again to see if it still appears the same. Now the bottom right corner becomes the bottom left corner. The square still looks the same.

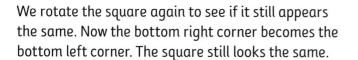

When we rotate the square one more time, we see that the square still looks the same.

Since we rotated the square and it still looked the same, it has rotational symmetry.

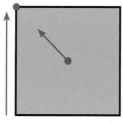

A square has rotational symmetry.

The square looks the same after we rotate it. Let's see if a trapezoid has rotational symmetry.

Example 2

Determine if a trapezoid has rotational symmetry.
Look at the trapezoid to the right.

We rotate the trapezoid one-quarter turn clockwise around its center.

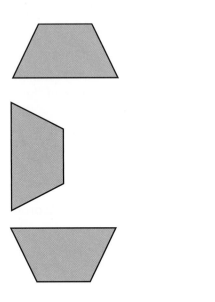

The new trapezoid does not look the same. Instead of the longest side being on the bottom, the longest side is now on the left of the trapezoid.

We can rotate it another quarter turn. The trapezoid does not appear exactly the same.

A trapezoid does not have rotational symmetry.

The trapezoid looks different when we rotate it. Of the two shapes, only the square has rotational symmetry.

Objects that are rotated and do not look the same do not have rotational symmetry.

 Problem-Solving Activity
Turn to *Interactive Text*,
page 282.

 mBook Reinforce Understanding
Use the *mBook Study Guide*
to review lesson concepts.

Activity 1

Rewrite the following using exponents.

Model $10 \cdot 10 \cdot 10 \cdot 10 \cdot 10$ 10^5

1. $2 \cdot 2 \cdot 2 \cdot 2 \cdot 2 \cdot 2 \cdot 2 \cdot 2$

2. $3 \cdot 3 \cdot 3 \cdot 3$

3. $4 \cdot 4 \cdot 4 \cdot 10$

4. $6 \cdot 10 \cdot 10 \cdot 10 \cdot 10 \cdot 10 \cdot 10 \cdot 10$

Activity 2

Find the least common multiple (LCM) for the numbers in each problem.

1. What is the LCM of 10 and 12?

2. What is the LCM of 7 and 11?

3. What is the LCM of 6, 9, and 12?

4. What is the LCM of 4 and 5?

Activity 3

Determine which picture in each pair shows a line of symmetry.

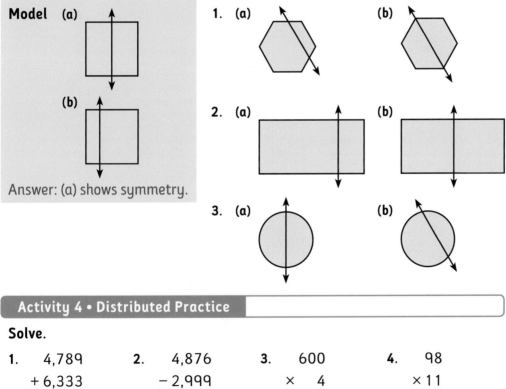

Answer: (a) shows symmetry.

Activity 4 • Distributed Practice

Solve.

1.   4,789
    + 6,333

2.   4,876
    − 2,999

3.   600
    ×   4

4.   98
    × 11

▶**Properties of Numbers**

What properties have we learned about numbers?

We have learned a lot about numbers. We get a sense of how much we have learned just by thinking about the properties of numbers and the many ways we can describe them. Think about how we could describe these numbers.

Speaking of Math

1	2	3	4	5	6	7	8	9	10
11	12	13	14	15	16	17	18	19	20
21	22	23	24	25	26	27	28	29	30
31	32	33	34	35	36	37	38	39	40
41	42	43	44	45	46	47	48	49	50
51	52	53	54	55	56	57	58	59	60
61	62	63	64	65	66	67	68	69	70
71	72	73	74	75	76	77	78	79	80
81	82	83	84	85	86	87	88	89	90
91	92	93	94	95	96	97	98	99	100

Here are some of the ways we have learned to talk about numbers.

even
odd

We learned that numbers are either even or odd.

- Numbers divisible by 2 are even numbers.
  The numbers 2, 4, and 6 are even numbers.

- Numbers not divisible by 2 are odd numbers.
  The numbers 1, 15, and 325 are odd numbers.

divisibility rules

We learned about divisibility rules. These rules tell us what numbers another number can be divided by.

- We know divisibility rules for the numbers 2, 3, 5, 6, and 10.
  The number 15 is divisible by 5 because it ends with a 5.

prime
composite

We learned about prime and composite numbers.

- Prime numbers are only divisible by 1 and themselves.
  The numbers 3, 7, and 19 are prime numbers.
- Composite numbers can be divided by more than two numbers.
  The numbers 6, 12, and 40 are composite numbers.

factors
multiples

We learned about factors and multiples.

- Factors are numbers that can be multiplied to get a number.
  The numbers 2 and 5 are factors of 10.
- Multiples are the result when we multiply a number by other numbers.
  The numbers 14 and 21 are multiples of 7.

GCF
LCM

We learned about greatest common factors (GCF) and least common multiples (LCM).

- The GCF of two or more numbers is the largest factor that those numbers share.
  The number 3 is the greatest common factor of 6 and 9.
- The LCM of two or more numbers is the smallest multiple that those numbers share.
  The number 20 is the least common multiple of 4 and 5.

triangular numbers
square numbers

We learned about triangular numbers and square numbers.

- Triangular numbers can be represented by a triangular array.
  The numbers 1, 3, 6, and 10 are the first four triangular numbers.

- Square numbers can be represented by a square array.
  The numbers 1, 4, 9, and 16 are the first four square numbers.

exponents

We learned about exponents.

- Exponents represent repeated multiplication.
  The numbers $6 \cdot 6 \cdot 6 \cdot 6$ can be written as 6^4.

We can use all the properties we have learned when talking about numbers. The two numbers below can be described by many of our properties.

Example 1

Describe the properties of the numbers 3 and 4.

The number 3	The number 4
• odd	• even
• divisible by 3	• divisible by 2
• prime	• composite
• a triangular number	• a square number
• factors: 1 and 3	• factors: 1, 2, and 4
• multiples: 3, 6, 9, and 12	• multiples: 4, 8, and 12
Both numbers 3 and 4	
• The LCM of 3 and 4 is 12. • The GCF of 3 and 4 is 1.	

 Apply Skills
Turn to *Interactive Text*, page 284.

 Reinforce Understanding
Use the *mBook Study Guide* to review lesson concepts.

▶**Problem Solving: More Rotational Symmetry**

What other shapes have rotational symmetry?

Many shapes and objects have rotational symmetry. They can be rotated and still appear exactly the same. The objects below all display rotational symmetry.

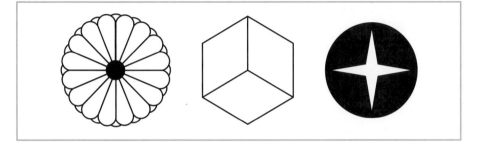

All three objects can be rotated and still appear the same.

Look at the partial propeller blades below. In the first picture, look at the blade pointing to the left. We rotate the propeller so that the blade is pointing up.

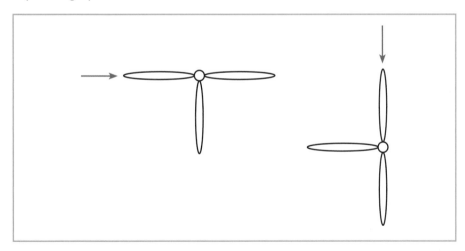

The two propeller pictures do not appear identical. The propeller does not have rotational symmetry.

Let's change the shape to give it rotational symmetry.

Example 1

Give the propeller rotational symmetry.
When we turned the propeller with three blades, it did not look the same. We need to balance the shape so that when it is turned it looks the same. Let's add a fourth blade.

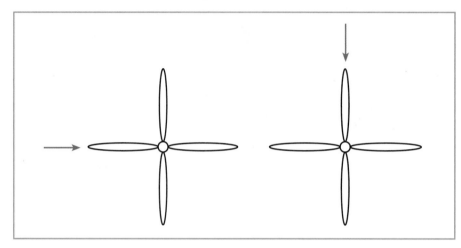

By adding a fourth blade to our propeller, we give it rotational symmetry.

The propeller and a square can be turned four times and appear identical after every turn. A triangle with all sides the same length can be rotated three times.

 Problem-Solving Activity
Turn to *Interactive Text*,
page 285.

 mBook Reinforce Understanding
Use the *mBook Study Guide*
to review lesson concepts.

Activity 1

Rewrite the following with exponents.

Model $4 \cdot 4 \cdot 4 \cdot 4$ Answer: 4^4

1. 6
2. $6 \cdot 6 \cdot 6$
3. $6 \cdot 10 \cdot 10 \cdot 10 \cdot 10 \cdot 10 \cdot 10$
4. $3 \cdot 3 \cdot 3 \cdot 3 \cdot 3 \cdot 5$

Activity 2

Multiply the powers.

Model $10^2 \cdot 10^3$ Answer: 10^5

1. $4^2 \cdot 4$
2. $10^3 \cdot 10^6$
3. $5 \cdot 5^4$
4. $6^9 \cdot 6$

Activity 3

Find the least common multiple (LCM) for the pairs of numbers in each problem.

1. What is the LCM of 20 and 40?
2. What is the LCM of 8 and 12?
3. What is the LCM of 10 and 20?
4. What is the LCM of 9 and 10?

Activity 4 • Distributed Practice

Solve.

1. $\begin{array}{r} 5{,}000 \\ -2{,}500 \\ \hline \end{array}$

2. $\begin{array}{r} 750 \\ +850 \\ \hline \end{array}$

3. $\begin{array}{r} 46 \\ \times 89 \\ \hline \end{array}$

4. $9\overline{)909}$

▸More Number Patterns and Common Multiples

Problem Solving:
▸Slides, Flips, Turns, and Symmetry

▸More Number Patterns and Common Multiples

What are number patterns for triangular numbers and exponents?

Triangular numbers have a relationship with square numbers. They are connected by a pattern. The best way to understand this pattern is to use blocks. The example below shows how we represent triangular numbers by using a block pattern.

Review 1

What is the relationship between triangular numbers and square numbers?

STEP 1
Multiply a triangular number by 8.
$3 \cdot 8 = 24$

STEP 2
Add 1 to the product.
$24 + 1 = 25$

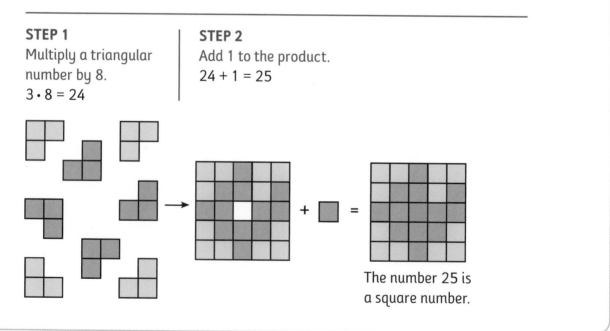

The number 25 is a square number.

Exponents give us a simple way of writing repeated multiplication. If we did not have exponents, the equations that are used in higher math would be much more difficult to read and use.

Review 2

How do we use exponents?

Repeated multiplication can be written using exponents.

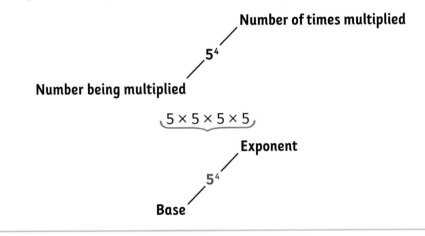

Rule: Multiplying Exponents

When we multiply powers with the same base, we add the exponents to find the exponent in our answer.

$$4 \cdot 4 \cdot 4 \cdot 4 \cdot 4 \cdot 4 \cdot 4 = 4^7$$
$$4^2 \cdot 4 \cdot 4 \cdot 4 \cdot 4 \cdot 4 = 4^7$$
$$4^2 \cdot 4^5 = 4^{2+5} = 4^7$$

Rule: Multiplying Bases Without Exponents

When we multiply powers and one base has no exponent, we use an exponent of 1 if the bases are the same.

$$4 \cdot 4 \cdot 4 \cdot 4 \cdot 4 \cdot 4 \cdot 4 = 4^7$$
$$4^6 \cdot 4 = 4^7$$
$$4^6 \cdot 4^1 = 4^{6+1} = 4^7$$

What are common multiples for numbers?

An important way to think about numbers is to think about common multiples. We will use this idea in later units when we add and subtract fractions.

The least common multiple (LCM) is the first multiple that is common to two or more numbers. The example below shows some of the common multiples for 6 and 10.

Review 1

What are common multiples and the LCM?

We use number lines or lists of multiples to find common multiples, including the LCM.

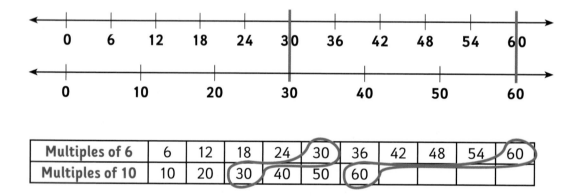

Multiples of 6	6	12	18	24	30	36	42	48	54	60
Multiples of 10	10	20	30	40	50	60				

Two common multiples for 6 and 10 are 30 and 60.

The LCM of 6 and 10 is 30.

What are some number concepts we learned?

Whole Number Concepts	Examples
Place Value	$93 = 90 + 3$
Powers of 10	$50 = 5 \cdot 10$

Composite and Primes	Examples
Composite Numbers	$24 = 6 \cdot 4$
Prime Numbers	17

Divisibility Rules	Examples
Divide by 2	46
Divide by 3	81
Divide by 5	65
Divide by 6	78
Divide by 10	90

Number Patterns	Examples
Even Numbers	88
Odd Numbers	89
Square Numbers	4, 9, 16, 25
Triangular Numbers	6, 10, 15, 21

Exponents and Multiples	Examples
Exponents	$8 = 2 \cdot 2 \cdot 2$ or 2^3
Multiples	4, 8, 12, 16

% ÷ Apply Skills
Turn to *Interactive Text*,
page 287.

mBook Reinforce Understanding
Use the *mBook Study Guide*
to review lesson concepts.

How do we describe shapes that move?

The example below shows three ways a triangle is moved. In all cases, the triangles are congruent. We use three terms to describe the movements, or transformations: slides, flips, and turns.

Review 1

What are slides, flips, and turns?

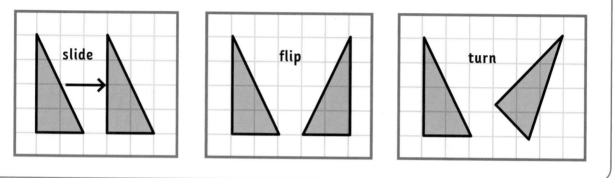

We use these shape transformations to create designs called tangrams.

Review 2

What are tangrams?
By using transformations, we take a collection of simple shapes and create complex designs.

What is symmetry?

We learned about two kinds of symmetry: reflection symmetry and rotation symmetry. We see these kinds of symmetry in many different objects. It is important to be able to recognize both kinds of symmetry. Look at the shapes in the example below. We have drawn a line of symmetry for each. We see that the shapes on each side of the line are congruent. This means that the shapes are symmetrical.

Review 1

How do we know if a shape has reflection symmetry?

We show that shapes have reflection symmetry using lines of symmetry. If we flip the shape over the line of symmetry, it will look the same.

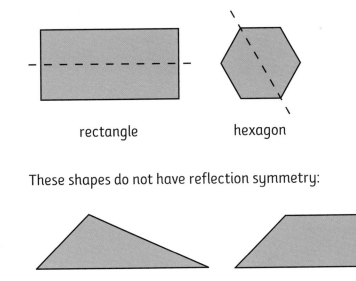

rectangle   hexagon

These shapes do not have reflection symmetry:

The hexagon is a special shape. If we turn it just a little bit, it will look the same. This means that it has rotational symmetry.

Review 2

How do we know if a shape has rotational symmetry?

We have an arrow pointing to one of the sides so that we can see the rotational symmetry more clearly. Notice how the first and last hexagons appear identical.

There are other shapes that also have rotational symmetry. Here are a few examples of these other special shapes.

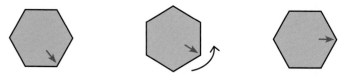

 Problem-Solving Activity
Turn to *Interactive Text*,
page 289.

 mBook **Reinforce Understanding**
Use the *mBook Study Guide*
to review lesson concepts.

Every month, we throw away enough bottles and jars to fill up a giant skyscraper. Most of these containers are recyclable.

Now THAT's scary!!!

- Gallons of bottled water consumed by Americans each year: 8,000,000,000.

- Plastic bottles recycled in the U.S. each year: about 1 out of 5.

- Number of years for a plastic bottle to naturally degrade: 1,000.

- Number of plastic bags Americans throw away each year: 100 billion.

- Amount of solid garbage the U.S. tosses out each year: 254 million tons.

- Portion of the average junked car that is recycled: $\frac{3}{4}$.

- Estimated number of computers and TVs Americans throw out each year: 100,000,000.

- Portion of Americans who recycle: about 9 out of 10.

- Portion of U.S. garbage that is recycled: about $\frac{3}{10}$.

- Portion of paper products in U.S. made with recycled materials: about $\frac{1}{2}$.

Think recycling is a waste of time?

CHECK THIS OUT:

Recycling 1 aluminum can saves...

...enough energy to run your TV for over 3 hours...

...or enough energy to burn a 100-watt light bulb for four hours!

OBJECTIVES

Building Number Concepts

- Recognize common fractions between whole numbers

- Represent fractions using shapes and fraction bars

- Find equivalent fractions

Problem Solving

- Find the mean, median, and range of a set of data

- Use tables to organize data

- Read and create line plots and stem-and-leaf plots

▸**Fractional Parts on a Number Line**

Vocabulary
infinite
fractional parts

What is between the whole numbers on a number line?

A good way to visualize numbers is to look at them on a number line.

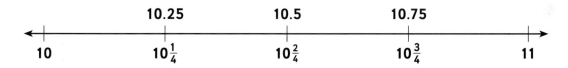

We know that the numbers on a number line are always in order. The arrows at the ends of the line tell us that the number line goes on **infinitely**, or forever. Even though we only see 0, 1, and 2, the numbers never stop in either direction.

Something that we have not discussed, however, is the gaps between the whole numbers on the number line. The numbers that go in those gaps are parts of whole numbers. We divide the sections between the whole numbers into fractional parts.

The number line shows that we write the fractional parts in decimal or fraction form. The number 10.5, or $10\frac{2}{4}$, is between the whole numbers 10 and 11. It is 10 plus part of a whole.

In our lives, we are constantly exposed to fractions and decimal numbers. We talk about fractions any time we divide something into equal parts.

- We order pizza and ask for $\frac{1}{2}$ plain and $\frac{1}{2}$ with extra cheese.

- We say that we'll meet a friend in about $\frac{1}{4}$ of an hour.

- We talk about decimal numbers in our money system—a pair of jeans costs $34.99.

What are some fractional parts between whole numbers?

Fractional parts of whole numbers are what go in the gaps between whole numbers on a number line. There are many fractional parts between any two whole numbers. Let's look at some examples that show fractions and decimal numbers.

Example 1

Look at a number line divided into *fourths*.

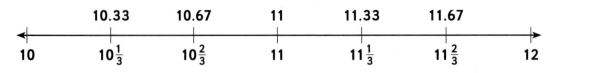

We see that one way to divide the gap between 10 and 11 is to divide it into equal parts called fourths. This is just one way to divide the gap between 10 and 11. It's divided into fractional parts called *fourths*.

Let's look at some other fractional parts between the whole numbers 10 and 11.

Example 2

Look at the number line divided into *thirds*.

The number line shows another way to divide the gap between 10 and 11. It is divided into fractional parts called *thirds*.

Let's look at one more way to divide the gap between 10 and 11 using fractions and decimal numbers.

Example 3

Look at a number line divided into *halves*.

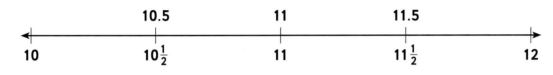

Here the gap has been divided into fractional parts called *halves*.

Notice that in these examples the gap is always divided into equal parts. The concept of equal parts is a very important concept when working with fractions.

There are many more numbers in the gaps between whole numbers. We have just shown a few of the fractional parts between the numbers 10 and 12. Here are some examples showing a variety of fractional parts between different whole numbers.

Example 4

Look at the fractional parts between larger numbers.
The gap between 40 and 41 is divided into thirds.

The gap between 110 and 111 is divided into halves.

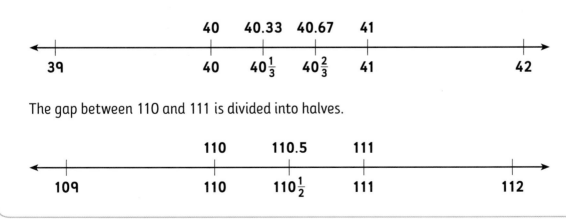

Just as there are infinitely many whole numbers on the number line, there are infinitely many fractional parts between the whole numbers. Here's an example showing just a few of the fractional parts between 10 and 11.

```
              10.25  10.33      10.5      10.67  10.75
   ←——————+————+————+————————+————————+————+——————————→
     10        10¼   10⅓      10½      10⅔   10¾        11
```

Notice the order of the fractional parts on the number line. They appear in a certain order. For example:

- The fraction $10\frac{1}{4}$ is smaller than $10\frac{1}{3}$, so it comes before.

- The decimal number 10.75 is larger than 10.5, so it comes after.

The gaps between whole numbers on a number line are not always divided into equal parts.

Speaking of Math

Here's how we can explain our thinking when we find missing fractions and decimal numbers on a number line.

- *First, I look at the number line to see how many equal parts there are between whole numbers.*

- *Then I look at any information that is already on the number line.*

- *Finally, I fill in the missing fractions or decimal numbers by adding the fractional part to the whole number.*

 Apply Skills
Turn to *Interactive Text*, page 291.

 Reinforce Understanding
Use the *mBook Study Guide* to review lesson concepts.

►**Problem Solving: Finding Averages**

What are averages?

One basic idea when working with **averages** is that over time, the numbers that make up a specific set of data even out. A basketball player may score 16 points in one game and 20 points in the next game. But over time, if we look at all the player's scores, we see that they even out to make an average.

Let's take a look at some averages. The table shows data for the number of points scored in six different games.

Game	Points
1	14
2	10
3	18
4	16
5	15
6	11

The next three graphs show how the numbers that make up the data set even out to make an average. The first graph shows points per game for the six games described in the table.

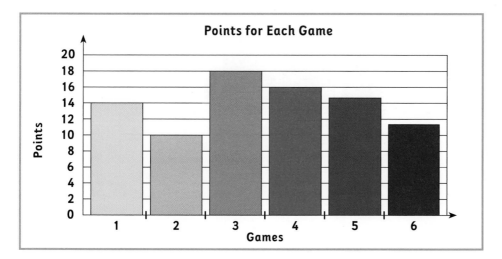

The next graph shows how we can restack, or move each bar, so that all the bars come out as evenly as possible.

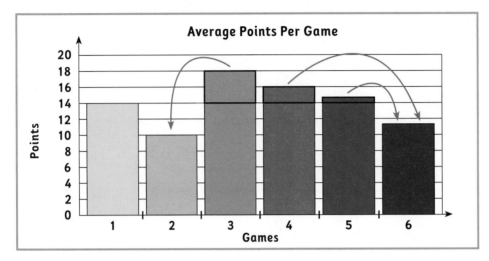

The final graph shows how the points all even out, and we have an average score of 14 points per game.

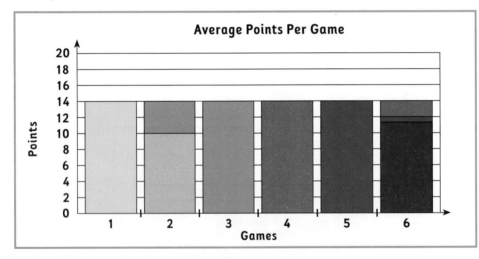

By restacking the bars we are able to find the average score.

POWER CONCEPT

Being able to find averages helps us to understand numbers and make predictions in our daily lives.

 Problem-Solving Activity
Turn to *Interactive Text*, page 292.

 mBook Reinforce Understanding
Use the *mBook Study Guide* to review lesson concepts.

Homework

Activity 1

Find the missing whole numbers on the number lines. For each problem, write the letters and the correct answers on your paper.

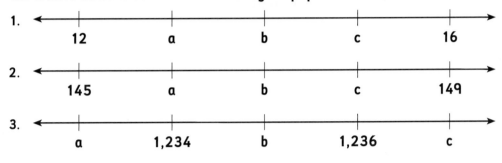

1. 12   a   b   c   16

2. 145   a   b   c   149

3. a   1,234   b   1,236   c

Activity 2

Find the missing fractions, decimal numbers, and whole numbers on the number lines.

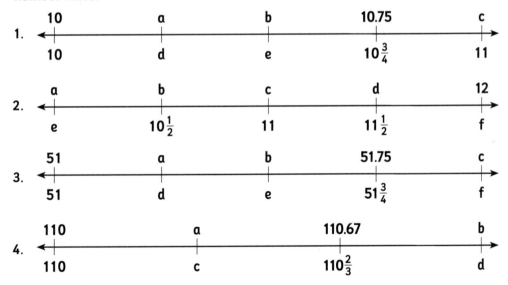

1. 10   a   b   10.75   c
   10   d   e $10\frac{3}{4}$ 11

2. a   b   c   d   12
   e $10\frac{1}{2}$ 11 $11\frac{1}{2}$ f

3. 51   a   b   51.75   c
   51   d   e $51\frac{3}{4}$ f

4. 110   a   110.67   b
   110   c $110\frac{2}{3}$ d

Activity 3

Use the number line to answer the questions.

1. Is $10\frac{1}{2}$ greater than or less than $10\frac{3}{4}$?

2. Is 10.67 greater than or less than 10.25?

3. Is $10\frac{1}{3}$ closer to 10 or to 11?

4. Is 10.75 closer to 10 or to 11?

5. Which is closer to $10\frac{1}{2}$: $10\frac{1}{4}$ or $10\frac{1}{3}$?

Activity 4 • Distributed Practice

Solve.

1.	2.	3.	4.	5.
900 + 300	1,400 − 900	12 × 34	895 × 7	$9\overline{)846}$

Problem Solving:
▶**Estimating Averages**

▶**Fractional and Decimal Parts Between 0 and 1**

What are the fractional parts between 0 and 1?

In Lesson 1, we learned that fractions and decimal numbers occur between any two whole numbers on the number line. But most of the time when people talk about fractions, they are talking about the fractional parts between 0 and 1. These fractional parts are all less than one whole, like parts of one pizza or one pie.

Let's look at some of these fractional parts on number lines.

We can divide one whole into two halves.

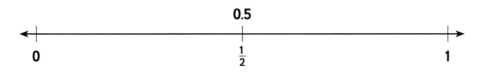

We can divide one whole into four fourths.

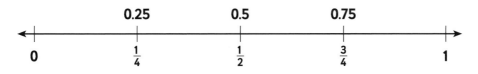

We can divide one whole into three thirds.

Notice that when we choose a fractional part such as $\frac{1}{2}$, we are dividing the distance 1 into two equal parts. With $\frac{1}{3}$, 1 is divided into three equal parts.

Here are some fractions between 0 and 1 that we often see in our everyday lives:

$$\frac{1}{2} \qquad \frac{1}{3} \qquad \frac{1}{4} \qquad \frac{2}{3} \qquad \frac{3}{4}$$

Here are some decimal numbers we might see in everyday life, especially when we work with money:

$$0.25 \qquad 0.50 \qquad 0.75 \qquad 0.99$$

These fractional parts appear between all whole numbers on the number line, not just between 0 and 1.

All the fractions and decimal numbers between 0 and 1 (and between other whole numbers) can appear on the number line at the same time. Let's take a look at several fractions that are together on one number line.

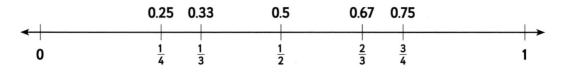

We see that many types of fractions and decimal numbers appear at the same time on a number line, and that they are in a certain order. For instance:

- $\frac{1}{2}$ is bigger than $\frac{1}{4}$

- $\frac{2}{3}$ is bigger than $\frac{1}{2}$

- 0.5 is bigger than 0.33

- 0.75 is bigger than 0.5

What are some places where we see fractions and decimal numbers between 0 and 1 in everyday life? For fractions, think about a measuring cup and a ruler. Think about a calculator and cash register for decimal numbers.

POWER CONCEPT

The space between two whole numbers can be divided into an infinite number of equal fractional parts.

Apply Skills
Turn to *Interactive Text*, page 294.

mBook **Reinforce Understanding**
Use the *mBook Study Guide* to review lesson concepts.

▶**Problem Solving: Estimating Averages**

How do we estimate averages?

In the last lesson, we used bar graphs to estimate averages. The average is a measure of the middle. Bar graphs are a good tool for showing averages. We take from some bars and add to other bars. This makes the bars all the same height.

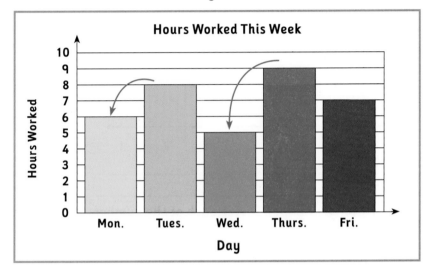

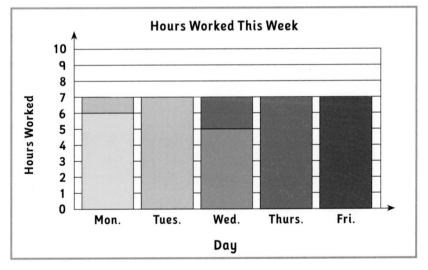

In this graph, we see that we can make all of our bars the same height. This helps us see that the average is 7 hours per day.

 Problem-Solving Activity
Turn to *Interactive Text*, page 295.

mBook **Reinforce Understanding**
Use the *mBook Study Guide* to review lesson concepts.

Activity 1

Figure out the missing fractions and decimal numbers on the number lines.

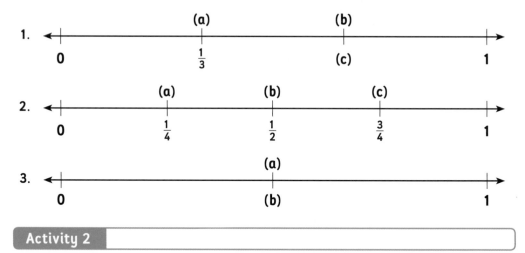

Activity 2

Draw three number lines from 0 to 1 on your paper. Divide each of the number lines evenly in this way:

1. Divide 1 into halves.

2. Divide 1 into fourths.

3. Divide 1 into thirds.

Activity 3

Look at the number line. Then answer the questions.

1. Which fraction is bigger: $\frac{1}{4}$ or $\frac{1}{3}$?

2. Which decimal number is smaller: 0.25 or 0.5?

3. Name a decimal number between 0 and 1 that is bigger than $\frac{1}{3}$.

4. Name a fraction between 0 and 1 that is smaller than 0.75.

Activity 4 • Distributed Practice

Solve.

1. $\begin{array}{r} 5{,}007 \\ +\ 2{,}903 \\ \hline \end{array}$

2. $\begin{array}{r} 6{,}005 \\ -\ 4{,}872 \\ \hline \end{array}$

3. $7\overline{)475}$

4. $\begin{array}{r} 66 \\ \times\ 97 \\ \hline \end{array}$

5. $\begin{array}{r} 300 \\ \times\ \ \ 9 \\ \hline \end{array}$

Lesson 3 ▸ Fair Shares

Problem Solving:
▸ Computing the Mean and the Range

▸Fair Shares

Vocabulary
fair share

What are fair shares?

Many times people only think of circles or pies as representing fractions, but all sorts of different shapes can represent fractions. When we divide shapes into equal fractional parts, each of the parts is the same size. These parts are called **fair shares** .

Let's look at two triangles that have been divided into parts.

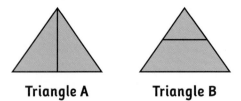

Triangle A   **Triangle B**

Look at Triangle A. The two sides are equal in size. If we split the triangle at the dividing line and flip one side over, we would see that both sides are fair shares.

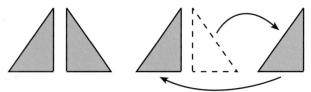

This triangle demonstrates the fractional part $\frac{1}{2}$.

Now look at Triangle B. The two sides are not equal in size. If we split the triangle in two at the dividing line, then put the two pieces side by side, we would see that they are not fair shares.

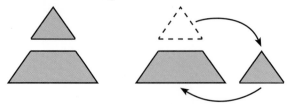

Triangle B is not broken into fair shares. The parts in the triangle are not equal in size.

Remember that when we represent fractions in different shapes, each part must be the same size. They must be *fair shares*.

Here are some different shapes that can be broken up into fractional parts. Notice that each shape is divided into parts and each of the parts is the same size. The parts are fair shares.

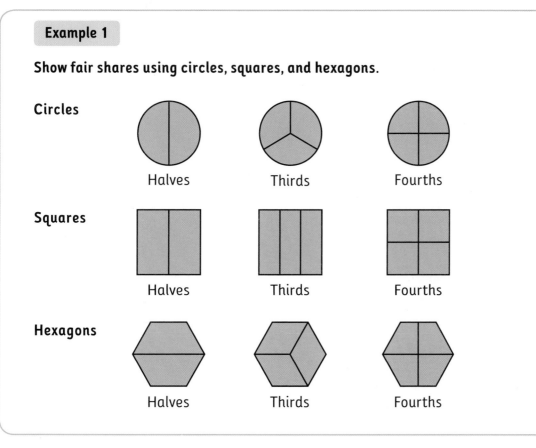

Example 1

Show fair shares using circles, squares, and hexagons.

Circles

Halves   Thirds   Fourths

Squares

Halves   Thirds   Fourths

Hexagons

Halves   Thirds   Fourths

We can use different shapes to show the same fractional part. Here are three examples of halves.

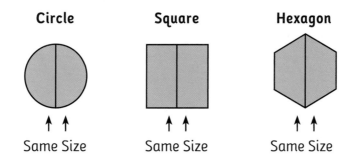

Circle   **Square**   **Hexagon**

Same Size   Same Size   Same Size

The most important thing to notice is that each fractional part in the shape is a fair share. That means that each part is the same size.

We cannot call something a fractional part if the shape is not divided into fair shares. Doing so is a common mistake people make when they first learn about fractions. Here are some examples.

Example 2

Notice that the hexagon on the right is not divided into equal parts. One part is bigger than the other. We cannot call these parts halves.

This is a correct representation of halves.   **This is not.**

Let's look at another example.

Example 3

The square on the right is not divided into equal parts. Each of the three parts is a different size. We cannot call these parts thirds.

This is a correct representation of thirds.   **This is not.**

When we work with fractions, the parts must be fair shares.

 Apply Skills
Turn to *Interactive Text*, page 298.

 mBook Reinforce Understanding
Use the *mBook Study Guide* to review lesson concepts.

▶**Problem Solving: Computing the Mean and the Range**

Vocabulary

mean
range
minimum
maximum

How do we compute the mean and the range?

In earlier lessons, we worked with averages by moving sections of bars in bar graphs. But there is an easier way to find averages.

The information in bar graphs is based on data from some kind of research, like a survey. Averages can be computed directly from the data. Another word for average is **mean** . From now on, we will use the word mean instead of average. Let's find the mean of some data.

Steps for Computing the Mean

STEP 1

Add the data.

$$
\begin{array}{r}
12 \\
15 \\
10 \\
11 \\
20 \\
8 \\
14 \\
8 \\
+\ 10 \\
\hline
108
\end{array}
$$

STEP 2

Count how many numbers are in the data and divide the sum by that number.

$$9)\overline{108} \quad 12$$

In this case, there are 9 numbers. Divide the answer, 108, by the number 9.

The mean is 12.

When we add up all of the numbers in a set of data and then divide by how many numbers there are in the set, we get the mean. People use the mean to make predictions about data. If we know the mean, we can predict what kind of numbers to expect if we go collect more data.

The mean is one important statistic. Let's take a look at another important statistic, the **range** . The range shows the difference between the biggest number and the smallest number in a data set. Let's look at how we find the range.

To compute the range of a set of data, subtract the smallest number from the largest number in the data set.

$20 - 8 = 12$

Using the data from the previous page, 8 is the smallest number and 20 is the largest number.

The range is 12.

The smallest number in the data is called the **minimum** . The largest number in the data is called the **maximum** .

The range is important because it tells us how much the data are spread out. When there is a big range, it means there is a big difference between the highest and lowest number in the data. The opposite is true when there is a small range.

Let's say we go to the public library. If we go near the magazines, the oldest person looking at the magazines might be 72 years old and the youngest might be 12. The range is $72 - 12 = 60$. A range of 60 years is relatively large. If we go to the children's section of the library where kids are looking at books, the oldest child might be 9 and the youngest might be 4 years old. The range is $9 - 4 = 5$. A range of 5 is relatively small.

Let's look at the mean, range, maximum, and minimum for two sets of data.

Data Set A		Data Set B
1	◄—— minimum ——►	8
2		9
8		10
19		11
+ 20	◄—— maximum ——►	+ 12
50		50

$$\begin{array}{r} 10 \\ 5\overline{)50} \end{array} \quad \longleftarrow \text{mean} \longrightarrow \quad \begin{array}{r} 10 \\ 5\overline{)50} \end{array}$$

$$\begin{array}{r} 20 \\ -\ 1 \\ \hline 19 \end{array} \quad \longleftarrow \text{range} \longrightarrow \quad \begin{array}{r} 12 \\ -\ 8 \\ \hline 4 \end{array}$$

In this data, both the totals and the means are exactly the same, but the ranges for the two sets of numbers are very different.

- The range of Data Set A is relatively large.
- The range of Data Set B is relatively small.

Even though the means are the same, we know that the numbers in Data Set A are more spread out.

The four terms we have discussed are described below, and examples of each are given for this set of data:

8   8   10   10   11   12   14   15   20

Key Terms	Example
Mean—the average of the numbers	12
Minimum—the smallest of the numbers	8
Maximum—the largest of the numbers	20
Range—the maximum minus the minimum	20 − 8 = **12**

 Problem-Solving Activity
Turn to *Interactive Text*, page 299.

 mBook Reinforce Understanding
Use the *mBook Study Guide* to review lesson concepts.

Activity 1

Fill in the missing numbers on the number lines. Use the letters to label your answers.

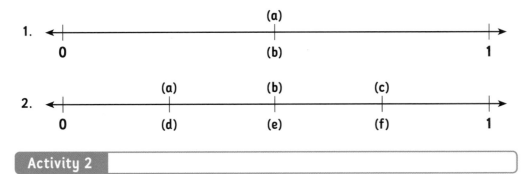

1.

(a)

0   (b)   1

2.

(a)   (b)   (c)

0   (d)   (e)   (f)   1

Activity 2

Use the number line to help answer the questions.

$$0.25 \quad 0.33 \qquad 0.5 \qquad 0.67 \quad 0.75$$

$$0 \qquad \frac{1}{4} \quad \frac{1}{3} \qquad \frac{1}{2} \qquad \frac{2}{3} \quad \frac{3}{4} \qquad 1$$

1. Is $\frac{1}{2}$ greater than or less than $\frac{2}{3}$?

2. Is $\frac{1}{3}$ greater than or less than $\frac{1}{4}$?

3. Which is closer to 1: $\frac{1}{3}$ or $\frac{3}{4}$?

4. Which is closer to 0: $\frac{1}{4}$ or $\frac{1}{3}$?

5. Which is larger: 0.33 or 0.5?

6. Which is smaller: 0.75 or 0.67?

Activity 3

Draw these shapes on your paper. Divide the circle into halves. Divide the rectangle into thirds. Divide the square into fourths.

1.   2.   3.

Lesson 3

Homework

Activity 4

Which of the following shapes is divided correctly into fourths? Write the letter(s) on your paper.

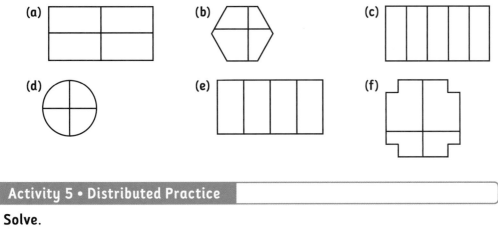

Activity 5 • Distributed Practice

Solve.

1. 5,678
    − 1,986

2. 5,010
    + 2,998

3.   40
    × 30

4.   600
    ×   8

5. 9)‾9‾0‾8‾

Numerator and Denominator

Problem Solving:
The Median in Data

▶**Numerator and Denominator**

Vocabulary

numerator
denominator

How do we write fractions?

There are two numbers in a fraction: the **numerator** and the **denominator** . Here's an easy way to remember these two words: The **numerator** is the <u>n</u>umber on top of the line; the **denominator** is the number <u>d</u>own below the line.

Here are a few examples of common fractions.

$$\frac{1}{2} \qquad \frac{1}{3} \qquad \frac{1}{4} \qquad \frac{1}{6} \qquad \frac{3}{4} \begin{array}{l} \leftarrow \text{numerator} \\ \leftarrow \text{denominator} \end{array}$$

Let's look closer at the different parts of a fraction.

The Denominator

The denominator (the number <u>d</u>own below) tells the total number of parts in a shape. We call this the **total parts**.

Example 1

Find the total parts for the fraction $\frac{1}{3}$.

Look at the denominator. $\frac{1}{3}$ ← denominator

Total Parts: 3

There are 3 total parts.

Here, we are working with the fractional part "thirds."

We see the total parts by looking at shapes with fair shares made up of thirds. Each shape has three total parts.

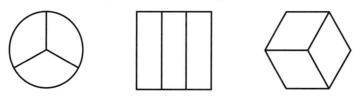

The Numerator

The numerator (the **n**umber on top) tells us how many **parts we have**.

Example 2

Find the parts we have for the fraction $\frac{1}{3}$.

The denominator tells us we have 3 total parts.

How many parts do we have?

Look at the numerator.

$$\frac{1}{3} \leftarrow \text{numerator}$$

Parts: 1

We have 1 part.

We see this in the figures. The shaded part in each figure tells us how many parts we have.

  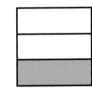

Each of these shapes represents the fraction $\frac{1}{3}$.

> **POWER CONCEPT**
>
> In a fraction, the denominator represents the total number of parts in a whole and the numerator represents the pieces we have out of that total.

Example 3

Find the meaning of the fraction.

$$\frac{3}{4}$$

Let's figure out the denominator (the number **d**own below). Remember that the denominator is the total number of parts.

Denominator → $\frac{3}{\textbf{4}}$

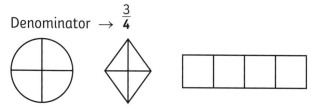

Now let's look at the numerator (the **n**umber on top). Remember that the numerator is how many parts we have.

Numerator → $\frac{\textbf{3}}{4}$

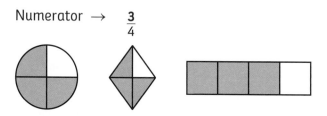

We have 3 out of 4 total parts.

Improve Your Skills

Joy looked at the fraction $\frac{2}{5}$.

She said this means that there are 5 parts out of 2 total parts.

Joy's answer is incorrect. **ERROR**

Since the denominator is 5, there are 5 total parts. The numerator, 2, tells us that we have 2 parts.

The fraction $\frac{2}{5}$ means that we have 2 parts out of 5 total parts. **CORRECT**

How do we write fractions for whole numbers?

What about whole numbers? How do we write them as fractions? What do they look like as shapes? We can write every whole number with a denominator of 1.

Example 1

Write 2, 5, and 7 as fractions.

$2 = \frac{2}{1}$ $5 = \frac{5}{1}$ $7 = \frac{7}{1}$

When we use a shape to represent 1, we shade the whole thing. We have all the total parts. We add more shapes to show the numbers greater than 1.

Example 2

Use circles to show the whole numbers 2, 5, and 7.

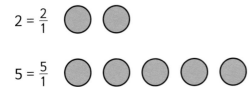

For each of these fractions, the total part is 1. The shaded circles show how many parts we have for each fraction.

 Apply Skills
Turn to *Interactive Text*, page 301.

 mBook Reinforce Understanding
Use the *mBook Study Guide* to review lesson concepts.

▶**Problem Solving: The Median in Data**

What is the median?

The **median** is another important statistic. It is the middle number in a set of data. To find the median, list the numbers in the data from lowest to highest, then count down halfway.

Let's see how this works with this list of numbers.

7   9   10   10   11   12   14   15   20

Notice that these numbers are already listed in order from smallest to largest. That is usually your first step. In this list, there are nine numbers. The 11 is the middle number in the list, so it is the median.

One technique for finding the median is to cross out numbers. Start by crossing out the smallest and biggest number. Then move to the next smallest and next biggest. Keep going until there's one number left in the middle. That middle number is the median.

7̶ 9̶ 1̶0̶ 1̶0̶ (11) 1̶2̶ 1̶4̶ 1̶5̶ 2̶0̶
↑
median

Mean = 12

Median = 11

How do we compute the median when we have an even number of data in the data set?

The cross-out method works well when we have an odd amount of numbers in our data. But what happens if we have an even amount of numbers? There will be two numbers left in the middle. When we have an even amount of numbers, the median is in between the two middle numbers.

Let's add 22 to the data set we used in the last example. Now we have 10 numbers in our list. The two middle numbers are 11 and 12. The median is the number that comes between them. What is between 11 and 12? We know that $11\frac{1}{2}$ is the number in the middle.

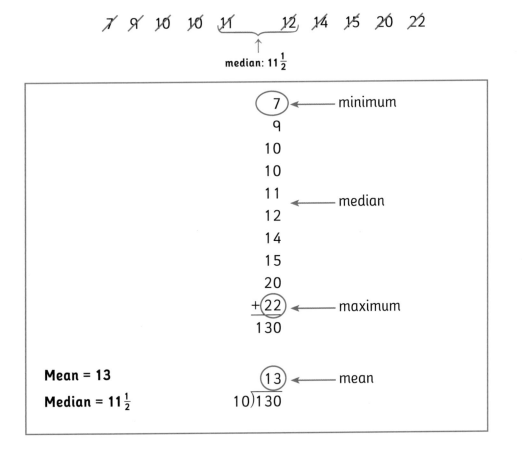

7 9 10 10 11 12 14 15 20 22

↑
median: $11\frac{1}{2}$

7 ← minimum
9
10
10
11 ← median
12
14
15
20
+22 ← maximum
130

Mean = 13

Median = $11\frac{1}{2}$

13 ← mean
10)130

Problem-Solving Activity
Turn to *Interactive Text*,
page 302.

 mBook Reinforce Understanding
Use the *mBook Study Guide*
to review lesson concepts.

Homework

Activity 1

Draw these shapes on your paper. Divide the circle into fourths, the square into thirds, and the hexagon into sixths.

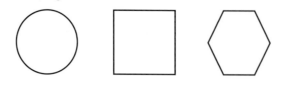

Activity 2

Fill in the missing fractions and decimal numbers on the number lines.

1. Fourths

0   1

2. Thirds

0   1

3. Halves

0   1

Activity 3

For each set of data, write the maximum, the minimum, and the range. You may need to put the numbers in order from smallest to largest to find this information.

1. 8 14 10 11 9 8 14 12 11 10

2. 17 16 18 19 12 14 19 15 13 14

3. 1 5 10 11 12 13 14 15 12 19

4. 12 1 30 25 5 19 9 16 12 25

Activity 4 • Distributed Practice

Solve.

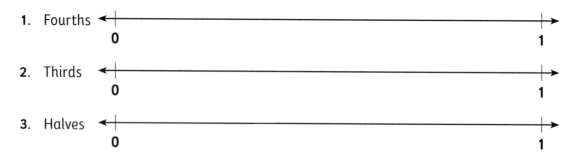

1. 15,876
   + 9,934

2. 1,500
   − 900

3. 27
   × 86

4. 150
   × 4

5. 90)‾360

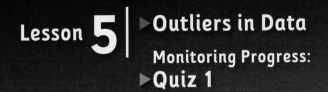

Lesson 5 | ▶Outliers in Data
Monitoring Progress:
▶**Quiz 1**

▶**Problem Solving: Outliers in Data**

Vocabulary
outlier

What is an outlier?

Sometimes in a set of data, we have a number that is a lot bigger or a lot smaller than the other numbers. We call that number an **outlier**. Outliers have a bigger impact on the mean than on the median.

Let's look at an example.

Let's add 310 to the list of numbers we used in the last lesson. Remember that the total from our example before was 130, and the mean was 13. Let's see how adding 310 affects this list of numbers.

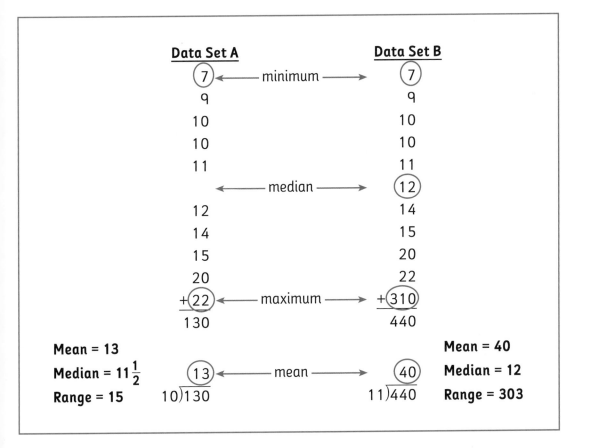

Data Set A

| 7 | ← minimum → | 7 |

7 (minimum)
9
10
10
11
← median → 12 (median)
12   14
14   15
15   20
20   22
+22 (maximum) ← maximum → +310 (maximum)
130   440

Mean = 13
Median = 11½
Range = 15

13 ← mean → 40
10)130   11)440

Data Set B

Mean = 40
Median = 12
Range = 303

When we added the large number, or outlier, the mean changed a lot. It went from 13 to 40. The range also changed a lot. In the data set without the outlier, the range was 15. In the data set with the outlier, the range was 303.

But the median changed only a little when we added the outlier. It went from $11\frac{1}{2}$ to 12. The median 12 is a much better representation of the middle of the data set than the mean of 40.

The median is an important statistic because it does not change much when our data set has an outlier. This makes it a much better indicator of the numbers in the list when we have an outlier.

Other statistics, like mean and range, can change a lot with an outlier.

POWER CONCEPT

The median is a better indicator of the numbers in a list when there is an outlier.

 Problem-Solving Activity
Turn to *Interactive Text*, page 304.

 Monitoring Progress
Quiz 1

 mBook Reinforce Understanding
Use the *mBook Study Guide* to review lesson concepts.

Activity 1

Draw each of the shapes on your paper. Divide two of the shapes into halves and the other two into thirds.

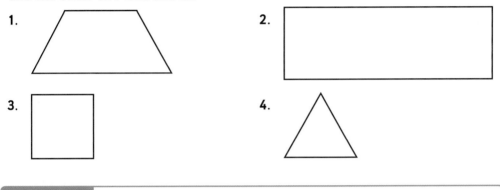

1.

2.

3.

4.

Activity 2

Find the maximum, minimum, range, median, and mean for the set of data.

52   10   13   14   11   21   19

Activity 3

Solve.

A high school basketball team scored the following points in their first six games of the season: 54, 44, 48, 52, 54, and 36. What was the average number of points scored?

Activity 4 • Distributed Practice

Solve.

1. $\begin{array}{r} 5,876 \\ -1,097 \end{array}$ 2. $\begin{array}{r} 4,800 \\ +9,000 \end{array}$ 3. $\begin{array}{r} 60 \\ \times 40 \end{array}$ 4. $\begin{array}{r} 791 \\ \times \quad 9 \end{array}$ 5. $8\overline{)79}$

▶**Fractions Equal to, Less Than, and Greater Than 1**

What are fractions that equal one whole?

In earlier lessons, we learned about fair shares. The term "fair shares" means that fractional parts need to be the same size. We also learned about counting fractions. Let's review with the fraction $\frac{2}{3}$.

There are 3 total parts in the rectangle, so the fractional part is thirds.

Each part is one third, which is written $\frac{1}{3}$.

We count the fractional parts that are shaded like this: one-third, two-thirds.

The shaded parts represent two-thirds, or $\frac{2}{3}$. We have two parts out of three total parts.

Let's think about other kinds of fractions—fractions that equal one whole.

In this example, we still have three total parts, so we are still talking about thirds. We shade 3 parts.

$\frac{1}{3}$	$\frac{1}{3}$	$\frac{1}{3}$

How many parts do we have? We have three out of three parts.

When we shade three-thirds, we shade the whole rectangle.

Now we can count the fractional parts: one-third, two-thirds, three-thirds (or one whole).

How does a number line help us see fractions that are less than, equal to, and greater than one whole?

Fractions can be less than, equal to, or greater than one whole. It is easy to see this on a number line. Let's look at different fractions involving fifths.

Example 1

Using fifths and number lines, show: a fraction less than 1, a fraction equal to 1, and a fraction greater than 1.

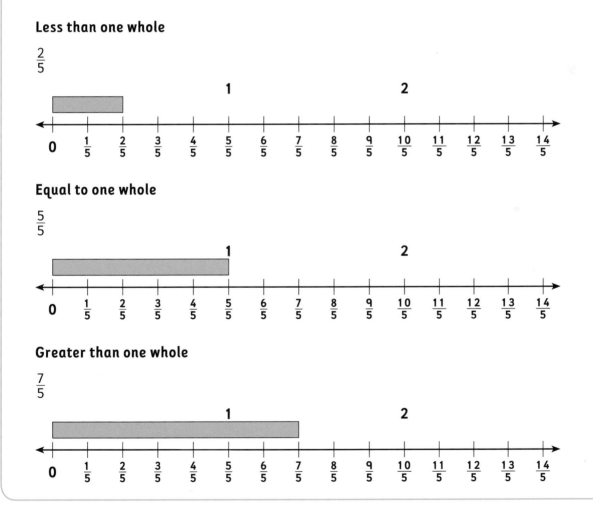

Less than one whole

$\frac{2}{5}$

Equal to one whole

$\frac{5}{5}$

Greater than one whole

$\frac{7}{5}$

How do we use different shapes to count fractions equal to and greater than 1?

Let's look at the fraction $1\frac{1}{2}$. That is one whole rectangle and one half of another rectangle. To count the fractional parts, we first count the whole rectangle: one-half, two-halves. That makes one whole. Then we count the remaining fractional part: three-halves.

We see in the drawing that we have a fraction that is greater than 1.

One Whole   One Half

We can also see this with other shapes. Let's look at an example.

Example 1

Use triangles and circles to show a fraction greater than 1: $1\frac{1}{2}$.

One Whole   One Half

We can also see this with circles.

One Whole   One Half

 Apply Skills
Turn to *Interactive Text*, page 306.

 mBook Reinforce Understanding
Use the *mBook Study Guide* to review lesson concepts.

▶**Problem Solving: Comparing Tables of Data**

What are the effects of extremes in tables of data?

We learned that an outlier has a big effect on the mean but not on the median.

A good example is salaries in professional sports. Players on sports teams make a wide range of salaries. If we just looked at the mean salary, we could get the wrong idea about how much all of the players make. Two or three very high salaries on a baseball team would make the mean salary look very large. Look at the following list.

Example 1

Find the outliers in this table of data.

Salaries for the Starting Nine Players	
Right field	$75,000
Center field	$85,000
Left field	$110,000
Second base	$140,000
First base	$150,000
Third base	$160,000
Catcher	$190,000
Pitcher	$1,500,000
Shortstop	$2,000,000

← median (at First base row)

Here are the statistics for the team:

Mean Salary = $490,000   Median Salary = $150,000   Range = $1,925,000

The mean salary for the team is $490,000. Two players—the pitcher and the shortstop—make much more money than the mean. The pitcher makes about three times as much money as the mean. The shortstop makes about four times more money than the mean.

The outliers of this data are the pitcher, who makes $1,500,000, and the shortstop, who makes $2,000,000.

Example 2

What happens if we take out the salaries for the two top-paid players? How do our statistics change?

Salaries Without the Pitcher and Shortstop	
Right field	$75,000
Center field	$85,000
Left field	$110,000
Second base	$140,000
First base	$150,000
Third base	$160,000
Catcher	$190,000

← median

Now we have new statistics:

Mean Salary = $130,000   Median Salary = $140,000   Range = $115,000

The mean and median are much closer together because we do not have the two outliers.

Getting rid of the outliers gives us a much better picture of the salaries on the baseball team, especially if we want to know what the "average player" on the team makes.

 Problem-Solving Activity
Turn to *Interactive Text*,
page 307.

 mBook Reinforce Understanding
Use the *mBook Study Guide*
to review lesson concepts.

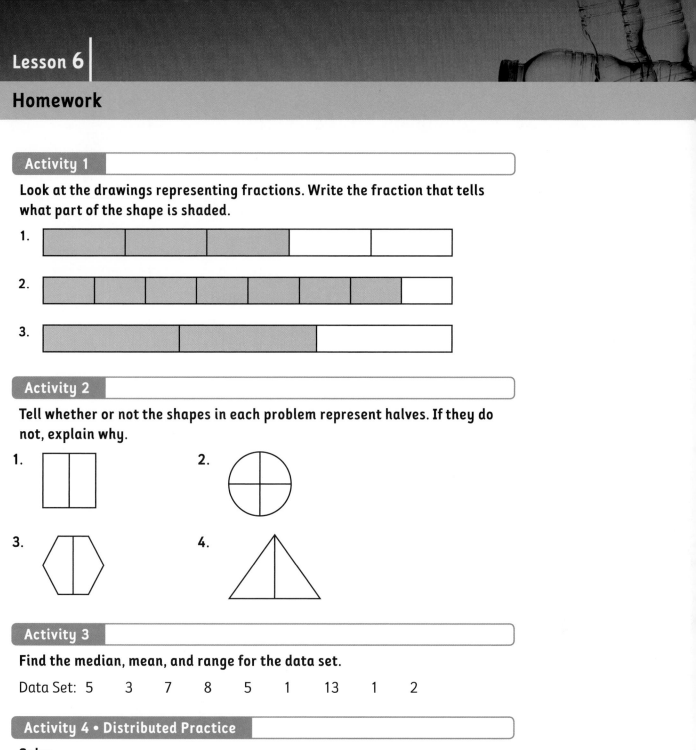

Activity 1

Look at the drawings representing fractions. Write the fraction that tells what part of the shape is shaded.

1.

2.

3.

Activity 2

Tell whether or not the shapes in each problem represent halves. If they do not, explain why.

1.

2.

3.

4.

Activity 3

Find the median, mean, and range for the data set.

Data Set: 5   3   7   8   5   1   13   1   2

Activity 4 • Distributed Practice

Solve.

1.   800   2.   1,700   3.   12   4.   347   5. 6)367
    + 800   − 900   × 22   ×   8

▶Estimating Fractional Parts

Vocabulary

benchmark

How do we estimate fractions and decimal numbers?

Different shapes can be used to show the same fraction. Here's a circle, a triangle, and a rectangle. They all show $\frac{1}{2}$.

We know they show $\frac{1}{2}$ because each shape is divided into two parts. The two parts look like they are the same size. So they are fair shares.

When we estimate fractional parts, we use **benchmarks** . These are common fractions or decimal numbers from our everyday lives.

We estimate the size of a fraction or decimal number by thinking about fair shares. Here's an example using benchmarks on a number line.

Example 1

Estimate fractions or decimal numbers using benchmarks on a number line.

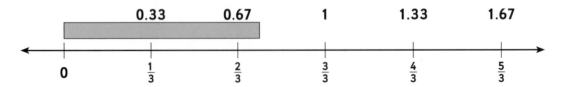

The bar is about $\frac{2}{3}$, or 0.67. Now look at the number line without fair shares marked. We can see that the bar is about $\frac{2}{3}$ or 0.67.

Here's another example. This bar is about $\frac{1}{2}$ or 0.5.

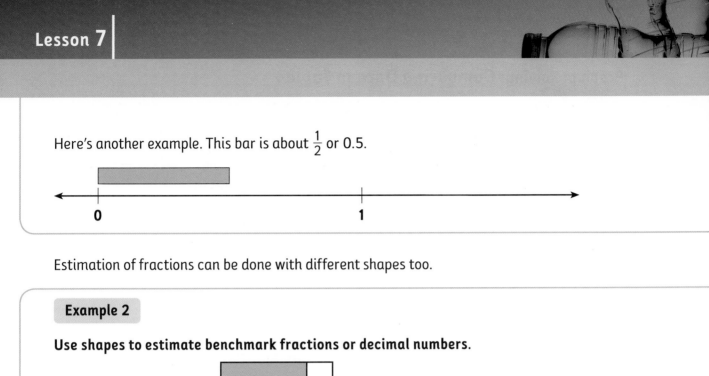

0   1

Estimation of fractions can be done with different shapes too.

Example 2

Use shapes to estimate benchmark fractions or decimal numbers.

This is about $\frac{3}{4}$, or 0.75.

The circle also shows a fractional part of about $\frac{3}{4}$, or 0.75.

Estimation is a very important skill. We use it with whole numbers and the basic math operations, and now we can use it with fractions and decimal numbers too.

 Apply Skills
Turn to *Interactive Text*,
page 309.

 mBook **Reinforce Understanding**
Use the *mBook Study Guide*
to review lesson concepts.

▶Problem Solving: **Comparing Data in Tables**

How do tables help us interpret data?

We learned to find mean, median, range, and outliers. They allow us to interpret and understand data. In the example, we will interpret the data by finding the mean, median, range, and outliers.

Example 1

Use the data charts to interpret the data.

Bauer High School recently had a track meet with two other high schools—Parkside and Landers. Seven students from each school competed in the long jump. The tables show how far each student jumped. All distances are in inches.

The table also shows the mean, median, range, and any outliers for the distances jumped for each school.

BHS	PHS	LHS
18	42	30
25	44	30
68	47	35
72	49	36
72	50	37
74	52	73
77	52	74

BHS		PHS		LHS	
Mean	58	Mean	48	Mean	45
Median	72	Median	49	Median	36
Range	59	Range	10	Range	44
Outliers	18, 25	Outliers	none	Outliers	73, 74

> Remember, outliers are extreme scores. They stand out from the rest of the data when we order the data from lowest to highest.

Here are some observations about the data:

- On average, BHS jumped the farthest.
- On average, LHS jumped the least far.
- BHS had the biggest difference between its longest and shortest jump.
- PHS had the most accurate mean because it is closest to the median. The range tells us it had the smallest difference from its longest and shortest jumps.

Problem-Solving Activity
Turn to *Interactive Text*, page 310.

mBook Reinforce Understanding
Use the *mBook Study Guide* to review lesson concepts.

Homework

Activity 1

Write the mixed numbers represented by the rectangles.

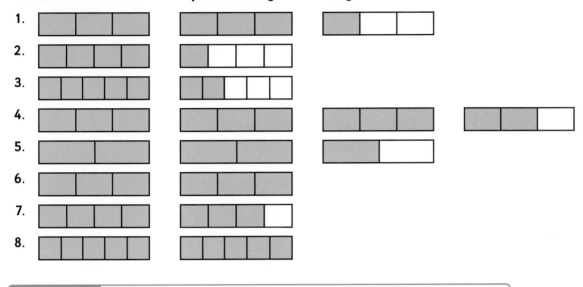

1.
2.
3.
4.
5.
6.
7.
8.

Activity 2

Look at the shapes. Estimate the fractional part of the shape that's shown by the shading. Give the nearest fraction or decimal number benchmark.

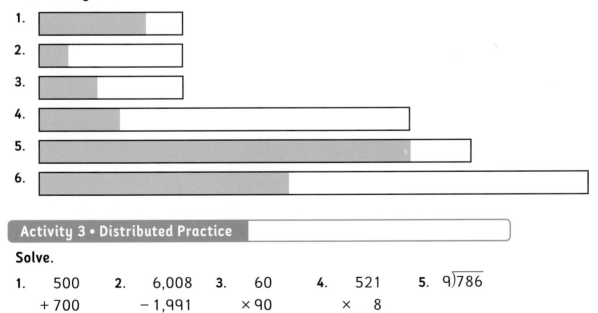

1.
2.
3.
4.
5.
6.

Activity 3 • Distributed Practice

Solve.

1. 500
    + 700

2. 6,008
    − 1,991

3. 60
    × 90

4. 521
    ×   8

5. 9)786

▶**Surveying Students—Fractions and Statistics**

How do we use fractions every day?

We talk about fractions all the time in our daily lives. Here are some examples:

> *"About half of the people invited came to the party."*
>
> *"There's about $\frac{3}{4}$ of a pizza left."*
>
> *"We're about $\frac{1}{3}$ of the way there."*

We form fractions in the same way we discussed earlier in this unit. We find the total parts, or the denominator, and then we look at the parts we have, or the numerator.

People form fractions from survey results all the time. Suppose advertisers want to know what kinds of sports are popular on TV for people between the ages of 18 and 24. They might survey 50 people in that age range, asking them, "What is your favorite sport on TV?" Here are sample results.

Sport	Number of People
Football	10
Basketball	15
Baseball	5
Auto Racing	13
Extreme Sports	7

To form fractions from these results, we need to look at the total parts, and the parts we have. If 50 people were asked about their favorite sport, 50 is the total parts.

Total Parts = 50

Now we can make fractions for each of the sports.

Sport	Number of People
Football	$\frac{10}{50}$
Basketball	$\frac{15}{50}$
Baseball	$\frac{5}{50}$
Auto Racing	$\frac{13}{50}$
Extreme Sports	$\frac{7}{50}$

Each response represents a fraction of the total. We might say that 10 out of 50 people liked football best. That's the same thing as the fraction $\frac{10}{50}$.

 %÷ Apply Skills
Turn to *Interactive Text*,
page 312.

 mBook Reinforce Understanding
Use the *mBook Study Guide*
to review lesson concepts.

▶**Problem Solving: Stem-and-Leaf Plots**

What are stem-and-leaf plots?

We have been working with data arranged in columns, but that's only one way to organize numbers. We've also seen that it sometimes helps to rewrite the numbers in order from smallest to largest so that we can find the median.

Another way to organize numbers is to use a **stem-and-leaf plot** , like the one here. We'll start with a column of numbers listed in order from smallest to largest.

Column of Data	Stem-and-Leaf Plot	
	Stem, or Tens	Leaves, or Ones
21	2	1 1 3 4 5 6 7
21		
23		
24		
25		
26		
27		
31	3	1 3 3 5
33		
33		
35		
40	4	0 2 2 5 7
42		
42		
45		
47		
51	5	1 2 3 8
52		
53		
58		

To make a stem-and-leaf plot, all we have to do is think of place value. We take the numbers in the list and break them apart. Let's see how this is done.

What are the steps for putting numbers in a stem-and-leaf plot?

We will see in later lessons in this unit that stem-and-leaf plots make it easy to find the median and the range. Note that it's not necessary to start with a list of numbers arranged from smallest to largest to make a stem-and-leaf plot. When the numbers are not arranged in order, just follow these three steps:

Steps for Creating a Stem-and-Leaf Plot

STEP 1
Identify the **stem**, or the way the numbers can be grouped. In this case, we are looking for the different 10s numbers (10, 20, 30, 40, etc.).

STEP 2
Fill in the "stem" column with the 10s numbers.

	Stem	Leaf
21 →	**2**	

STEP 3
List the remaining part of each number, or the **leaf**, in the "leaf" column. In this case, the remaining parts are the ones.

	Stem	**Leaf**
21 →	2	**1**

We can already make some observations about the data from the stem-and-leaf plot on the previous page. We can see that the numbers start at 21 and end at 58. There are more numbers in the 20s than in the other 10s places.

The stem-and-leaf plot is a simple way to organize and show the data so that it's easier to interpret. We can make stem-and-leaf plots with numbers of any size.

 Problem-Solving Activity
Turn to *Interactive Text*, page 313.

 mBook Reinforce Understanding
Use the *mBook Study Guide* to review lesson concepts.

Activity 1

Choose a shape to represent each of the fractions. Be sure to divide the shapes into equal parts, or fair shares. Use rectangles, circles, or other shapes that you have seen in previous lessons.

1. $\frac{1}{3}$

2. $\frac{1}{4}$

3. $\frac{3}{4}$

4. $1\frac{1}{2}$

Activity 2

Look at the survey results. Ten students were asked what their favorite food is. Tell the fraction for each choice.

Food Choice	Number of Students Choosing This Food	Fraction
Pizza	4	(a)
Hamburgers	3	(b)
French Fries	3	(c)

Activity 3

Make a stem-and-leaf plot for the set of data. Remember that the first column is the tens place and the second column is the ones place.

35   36   42   42   43   45   52   53   53   55   60   61

Activity 4 • Distributed Practice

Solve.

1. $\begin{array}{r} 7,898 \\ + 8,978 \\ \hline \end{array}$

2. $\begin{array}{r} 8,018 \\ - 1,081 \\ \hline \end{array}$

3. $\begin{array}{r} 88 \\ \times 77 \\ \hline \end{array}$

4. $\begin{array}{r} 900 \\ \times \quad 6 \\ \hline \end{array}$

5. $9\overline{)360}$

Problem Solving:
▶Creating Stem-and-Leaf Plots

▶**Estimating Fractional Parts on a Number Line**

How do we estimate fractional parts on a number line?

We learned in Lesson 7 that we can use common locations on a number line to estimate a fractional part. We call these locations benchmarks.

The most common benchmark is $\frac{1}{2}$ or 0.5. We can see that the dot on the line is near $\frac{1}{2}$ or 0.5. That's easy to see when we have the tick mark for $\frac{1}{2}$ or 0.5 on the number line.

> Remember that benchmarks are common fractions or decimal numbers from our everyday lives.

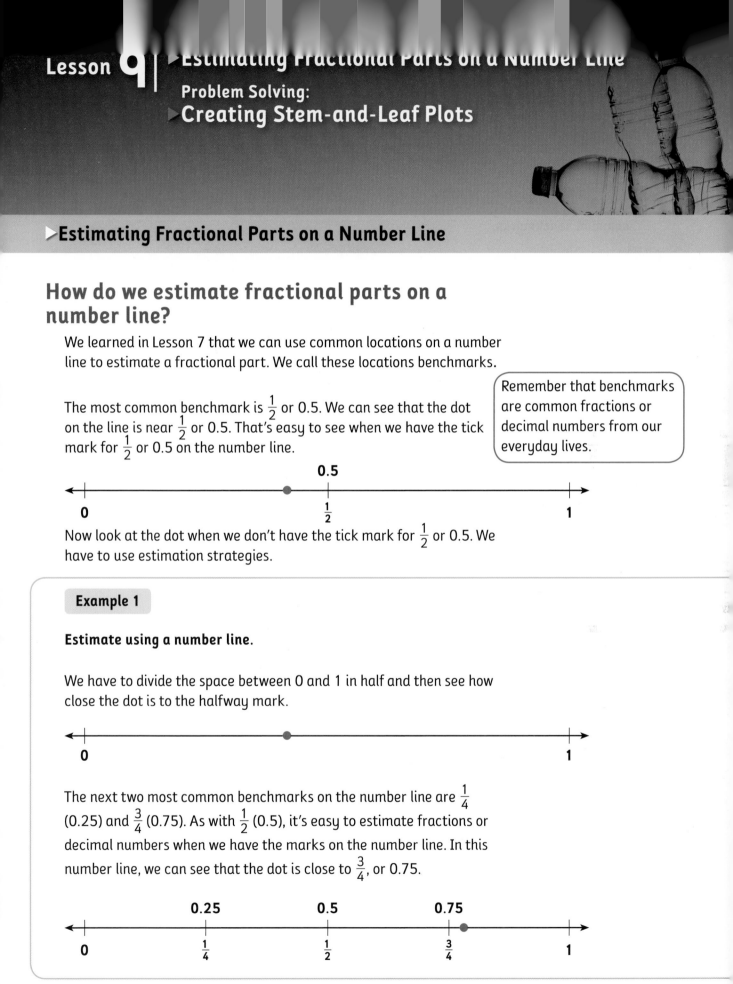

Now look at the dot when we don't have the tick mark for $\frac{1}{2}$ or 0.5. We have to use estimation strategies.

Example 1

Estimate using a number line.

We have to divide the space between 0 and 1 in half and then see how close the dot is to the halfway mark.

The next two most common benchmarks on the number line are $\frac{1}{4}$ (0.25) and $\frac{3}{4}$ (0.75). As with $\frac{1}{2}$ (0.5), it's easy to estimate fractions or decimal numbers when we have the marks on the number line. In this number line, we can see that the dot is close to $\frac{3}{4}$, or 0.75.

Example 2

Estimate $\frac{3}{4}$ (or 0.75) on a number line by first estimating other common benchmarks.

0   1

This is a little more difficult. The dot is near $\frac{3}{4}$, or 0.75. We have to imagine $\frac{1}{2}$ or (0.5) and then go halfway from there to the 1. That makes $\frac{3}{4}$, or 0.75.

With practice, we can become good at estimating where fractions and decimal numbers are on a number line.

Remember, we also need to look at the whole numbers when estimating fractions.

Example 3

Estimate fractions by looking at whole number benchmarks.

Look at the dot on the number line. It is between 5 and 6.

5   6

The dot is at about $5\frac{3}{4}$, or 5.75.

 Apply Skills
Turn to *Interactive Text*, page 315.

 mBook Reinforce Understanding
Use the *mBook Study Guide* to review lesson concepts.

▶Problem Solving: **Creating Stem-and-Leaf Plots**

How do we make a stem-and-leaf plot?

In the last lesson, we learned about stem-and-leaf plots. Now we will learn how they are used. The tables show the final standings for all of the baseball teams at the end of a season. We are interested in seeing the differences between the teams in terms of the number of games they won. For example, how many teams won about 80 games? How many won about 90 games? A good way to show that is with a stem-and-leaf plot.

Team 1 and Team 2 Final Standings

Teams in League 1

East	Wins	Losses	Percentage	Central	Wins	Losses	Percentage
New York	103	58	.640	Minnesota	94	67	.584
Boston	93	69	.574	Chicago	81	81	.500
Toronto	78	84	.481	Cleveland	74	88	.457
Baltimore	67	95	.414	Kansas City	62	100	.383
Tampa Bay	55	106	.342	Detroit	55	106	.342

Teams in League 2

East	Wins	Losses	Percentage	Central	Wins	Losses	Percentage
Atlanta	104	59	.631	St. Louis	97	65	.599
Montreal	83	79	.512	Houston	84	78	.519
Philadelphia	80	81	.497	Cincinnati	78	84	.481
Florida	79	83	.488	Pittsburgh	72	89	.447
New York	75	86	.466	Chicago	67	95	.414

We can analyze the data more easily when we put it in a stem-and-leaf plot. Today we want to compare the wins, so we will only plot the data for the wins.

Example 1

Make a stem-and-leaf plot using the data about the number of wins for each baseball team.

STEP 1
List the data for the wins in numerical order.

STEP 2

Write the stems, or numbers in the tens place, in the stems column:

5   6   7   8   9   10

STEP 3

For each stem, write the ones digits in the leaf column.

55
55
62
67
67
72
74
75
78
78
79
80
81
83
84
93
94
97
103
104

Stem, or Tens	Leaves, or Ones
5	5 5
6	2 7 7
7	2 4 5 8 8 9
8	0 1 3 4
9	3 4 7
10	3 4

Problem-Solving Activity
Turn to *Interactive Text*,
page 316.

mBook Reinforce Understanding
Use the *mBook Study Guide*
to review lesson concepts.

Activity 1

Draw a number line with a dot at the fraction's location.

Model $\frac{3}{4}$

0 ●————— 1

1. $\frac{2}{3}$ 2. 0.25   3. $\frac{1}{2}$ 4. 0.33   5. $\frac{3}{4}$

Activity 2

Make a stem-and-leaf plot for the set of data.

46 47 49 50 52 52 58 67 68 70 73 73 87 88 90
91 110 114 127 129

Activity 3 • Distributed Practice

Solve.

1. 1,500
   − 700

2. 867
   + 981

3. 47
   × 74

4. 600
   × 6

5. 9)982

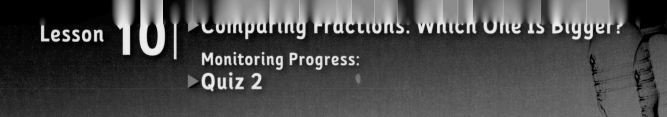

▸**Comparing Fractions: Which One Is Bigger?**

What strategies can we use for comparing fractions?

So far in this unit we have learned how to write fractions and how to estimate fractions. Here's a quick review. Look at the fraction shown by the circle.

How many parts do we have? 3

How many total parts? 4

We write the fraction this way: $\frac{3}{4}$

We have also learned how to estimate fractions. Look at the fractional part in the circle.

We cannot tell exactly what the fraction is because we cannot see the fair share parts. But we can estimate the fraction. Look at these two representations of fractions side by side. They are about the same. So the fractional part is about $\frac{3}{4}$.

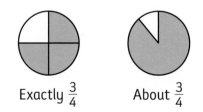

Exactly $\frac{3}{4}$ About $\frac{3}{4}$

We can use the same kind of thinking to compare fractions of different sizes in our heads.

Let's think about the fractions $\frac{3}{4}$ and $\frac{1}{3}$. Which one is bigger? We can answer this if we think about a circle for each fraction. Then we break the circles into their total parts, think about the parts we have, and compare the fractions.

Example 1

Compare the fractions $\frac{3}{4}$ and $\frac{1}{3}$ using shapes.

Think of circles first.

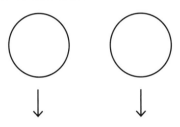

Then think about total parts.

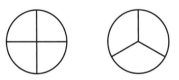

4 Total Parts   **3 Total Parts**

Then think about parts we have.

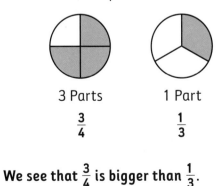

3 Parts   1 Part

$\frac{3}{4}$ $\frac{1}{3}$

We see that $\frac{3}{4}$ is bigger than $\frac{1}{3}$.

Apply Skills
Turn to *Interactive Text*, page 319.

Monitoring Progress
Quiz 2

mBook Reinforce Understanding
Use the *mBook Study Guide* to review lesson concepts.

Lesson 10

Homework

Activity 1

Tell the fraction or decimal benchmark for each of the shaded areas.

1.

2.

3.

4.

5.

Activity 2

Look at the fractions in each problem. Tell which fraction is bigger using the estimation strategy you learned in this lesson.

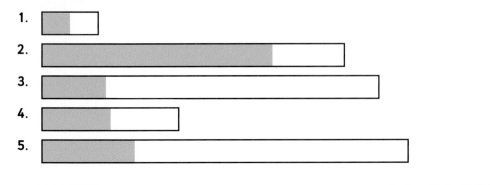

Model   Which is bigger: $\frac{2}{3}$ or $\frac{3}{4}$?

$\frac{2}{3}$ $\frac{3}{4}$

Answer: Comparing the shaded regions, we see that $\frac{3}{4}$ is bigger than $\frac{2}{3}$.

1. Which is bigger: $\frac{1}{3}$ or $\frac{2}{5}$?

2. Which is bigger: $\frac{3}{4}$ or $\frac{4}{7}$?

Activity 3

Find the mean number of hits.

Inning	Number of Hits
1	4
2	0
3	5
4	9
5	10
6	8
7	6

Activity 4 • Distributed Practice

Solve.

1. $17,000 - 8,000$

2. $6,782 + 4,328$

3. 80×74

4. 123×8

5. $9\overline{)778}$

Lesson 11 ▸Fraction Bars

Problem Solving:
▸**Finding the Median on a Stem-and-Leaf Plot**

▸**Fraction Bars**

Vocabulary
fraction bars

What are fraction bars?

We have been representing fractions using a lot of different shapes. Here are some examples of $\frac{1}{3}$.

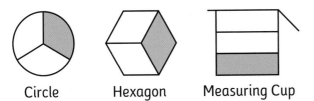

Circle   Hexagon   Measuring Cup

One shape that we've used to show fractions is the rectangle. The rectangles used to show fractions are called **fraction bars**. We'll be using fraction bars for the rest of this unit. Note that the length of every fraction bar is the same. Equal lengths let us compare fractions. Here are some examples of different fraction bars.

Example 1

Represent the fractions $\frac{1}{2}$ and $\frac{1}{4}$ using fraction bars.

The fraction bar for $\frac{1}{2}$ looks like this:

The fraction bar for $\frac{1}{4}$ looks like this:

We see right away that $\frac{1}{2}$ is bigger than $\frac{1}{4}$.

Fraction bars are very helpful because they allow us to compare two fractions to see which one is bigger.

Here are two more fractions. If we look at them as numbers, we can't tell very easily which one is bigger.

Example 2

Use fraction bars to compare the fractions $\frac{3}{8}$ and $\frac{3}{10}$.

Which is bigger, $\frac{3}{8}$ or $\frac{3}{10}$?

We can easily tell which one is bigger if we use fraction bars:

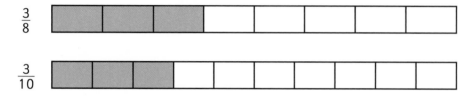

We see right away that $\frac{3}{8}$ is bigger than $\frac{3}{10}$.

All we have to do is line up the fraction bars, and we can see right away which fraction is bigger or smaller.

Fraction bars are helpful tools for looking at fractions. We can see how fractions compare in size, including when they are the same size. This will be something we look at a lot in future lessons.

 **Apply Skills**
Turn to *Interactive Text*,
page 321.

mBook Reinforce Understanding
Use the *mBook Study Guide*
to review lesson concepts.

How do we find the median on stem-and-leaf plots?

With lists of numbers, we found the median by finding the number in the middle of the list.

- With an odd set of numbers, the median is the number in the middle.

- With an even set of numbers, it is the number halfway between the two numbers in the middle.

Odd Set of Numbers (11 Numbers)	Even Set of Numbers (10 Numbers)
12	30
12	32
13	35
14	38
16	40 ← median
median → 21	50
22	55
23	56
26	60
29	63
35	

In the "even set of numbers" example, the median is halfway between 40 and 50, or 45.

Here are the stem-and-leaf plots for these two sets of numbers. Again, like we did in an earlier lesson, we can use the technique of placing one finger on the smallest value and the other finger on the largest value, and then move to the next smallest/biggest value, and the next, and the next, and so on.

With the set of 11 numbers, the median is the number that's left in the middle, or 21.

Odd Set of Numbers (11 Numbers)				
1	2 2 3 4 6			
2	1 2 3 6 9			
3	5			

median: 21 →

When finding the median in a stem-and-leaf plot, remember to cross out the smallest value and the largest value first. Then cross out the next smallest value and next largest value, and so on.

With the set of 10 numbers, it's the number between the two numbers left in the middle, or 45.

Even Set of Numbers (10 Numbers)			
3	0 2 5 8		
4	0		
5	0 5 6		
6	0 3		

median: 45 →

 Problem-Solving Activity
Turn to *Interactive Text*, page 322.

 mBook Reinforce Understanding
Use the *mBook Study Guide* to review lesson concepts.

Homework

Activity 1

For each of the fractions given, draw a number line labeled with 0 and 1 and estimate where the fraction falls on the number line. Use a dot to show the approximate location.

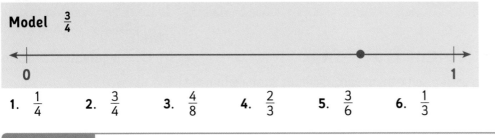

Model $\frac{3}{4}$

0   1

1. $\frac{1}{4}$ 2. $\frac{3}{4}$ 3. $\frac{4}{8}$ 4. $\frac{2}{3}$ 5. $\frac{3}{6}$ 6. $\frac{1}{3}$

Activity 2

Write the fraction and decimal benchmarks for each of the shapes.

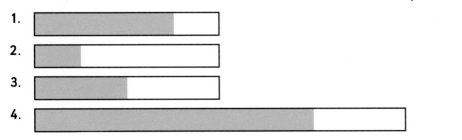

1.

2.

3.

4.

Activity 3

Look at the fraction bars and tell the fraction for each.

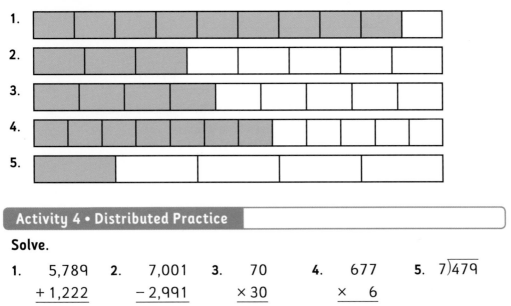

1.

2.

3.

4.

5.

Activity 4 • Distributed Practice

Solve.

1. $\begin{array}{r} 5,789 \\ + 1,222 \\ \hline \end{array}$
2. $\begin{array}{r} 7,001 \\ - 2,991 \\ \hline \end{array}$
3. $\begin{array}{r} 70 \\ \times 30 \\ \hline \end{array}$
4. $\begin{array}{r} 677 \\ \times \ \ 6 \\ \hline \end{array}$
5. $7\overline{)479}$

Problem Solving:
▶**Line Plots**

▶**Equivalent Fractions**

Vocabulary
equivalent fractions

What are equivalent fractions?

Fraction bars help us see something very difficult to see when we look at fractions. They help us see when two fractions are equal. Equal fractions represent the same amount.

$$\frac{1}{4} \qquad \frac{3}{12}$$

If we don't work with fractions a lot, it can be hard to see when fractions are equal. But if we use fraction bars, it's easy to see when they are equal. Here are the fraction bars for $\frac{1}{4}$ and $\frac{3}{12}$, one beneath the other.

Example 1

Use fraction bars to help us see fractions that are equal.

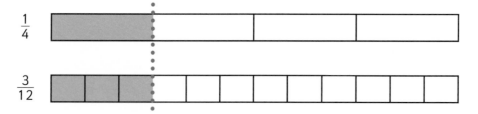

We can see that the fractions are equal because the same area in each fraction bar is shaded.

Fractions that have different numerators and denominators but represent the same fractional part are called **equivalent fractions** . We will be using fraction bars to learn more about equivalent fractions.

Let's look at another example of equivalent fractions. This time we can see how three fractions are equivalent.

Example 2

Show that $\frac{1}{2}$, $\frac{3}{6}$, and $\frac{5}{10}$ are equal by comparing fraction bars.

Compare $\frac{1}{2}$, $\frac{3}{6}$, and $\frac{5}{10}$.

We can use fraction bars.

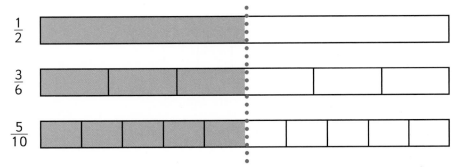

It's easy to see that $\frac{1}{2}$ of the area of each fraction bar is shaded. Let's think about this carefully. If we look at these three fractions, we can see that 1 is half of 2, 3 is half of 6, and 5 is half of 10. All of these fractions represent half. We can make this statement about the three fractions:

$$\frac{1}{2} = \frac{3}{6} = \frac{5}{10}$$

Equivalent fractions have different numerators and denominators, but they are all equal to the same fractional part. In this example, they are all equal to half. We can call the fractional part half using many different fraction names. They are all equivalent.

Equivalent fractions are equal to the same fractional part.

Here is one more example of equivalent fractions.

Example 3

Show that $\frac{2}{3}$, $\frac{4}{6}$, and $\frac{8}{12}$ are equivalent by comparing fraction bars.

Compare $\frac{2}{3}$, $\frac{4}{6}$, and $\frac{8}{12}$.

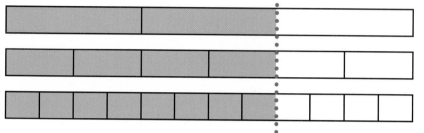

- The first fraction bar shows $\frac{2}{3}$, so 2 out of 3 parts are shaded.

- The second fraction bar shows $\frac{4}{6}$, so 4 out of 6 parts are shaded.

- The third fraction bar shows $\frac{8}{12}$, so 8 out of 12 parts are shaded.

> When comparing fractions using fraction bars, if the shaded area is the same, the fractions are equivalent fractions.

We can see how the lengths of the three fraction bars are the same, and that the same portion of each bar is shaded. The only difference is that they are divided into a different number of total parts.

- The fraction bar that shows $\frac{2}{3}$ is divided into 3 total parts.

- The fraction bar that shows $\frac{4}{6}$ is divided into 6 total parts.

- The fraction bar that shows $\frac{8}{12}$ is divided into 12 total parts.

Even though the number of total parts is different, the area that is shaded is the same in each fraction bar. That is what makes these three fractions equivalent.

$$\frac{2}{3} = \frac{4}{6} = \frac{8}{12}$$

 Apply Skills
Turn to *Interactive Text*, page 325.

 mBook **Reinforce Understanding**
Use the *mBook Study Guide* to review lesson concepts.

▶**Problem Solving: Line Plots**

What are line plots?

We have learned a lot about representing data in this unit. Here is one last way we are going to show data on a graph. A line plot looks a lot like a vertical bar graph, except that we use Xs instead of bars. Look at the following data on goals scored by the Women's Soccer Team. Then look at the line plot created from the data.

Number of Goals the Women's Soccer Team Scored in 12 Games	
Game	Goals
1	3
2	2
3	3
4	5
5	9
6	1
7	2
8	1
9	5
10	2
11	2
12	1

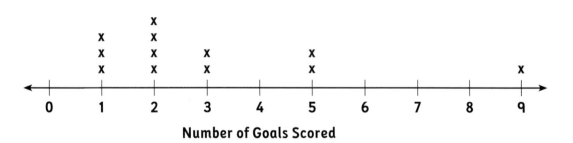

Number of Goals Scored

This line plot is helpful because it lets us see very quickly how many times the team scored each number of goals. Most of the time, they scored between 1 and 3 goals. They scored 9 goals in one game, but that was unusual. Remember, we call that score an *outlier*. It lies far outside the other scores.

 Problem-Solving Activity
Turn to *Interactive Text*, page 326.

 Reinforce Understanding
Use the *mBook Study Guide* to review lesson concepts.

Homework

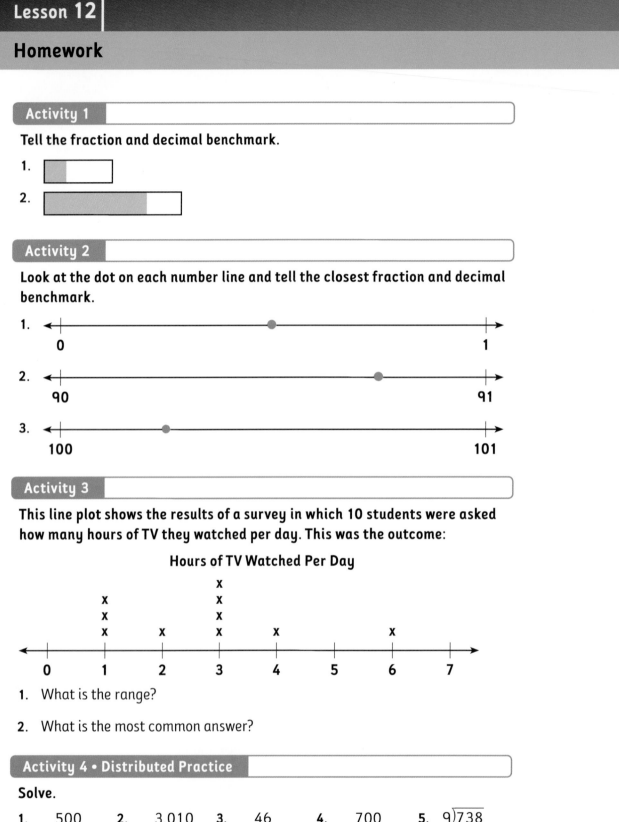

Activity 1

Tell the fraction and decimal benchmark.

1.

2.

Activity 2

Look at the dot on each number line and tell the closest fraction and decimal benchmark.

1.
0   1

2.
90   91

3.
100   101

Activity 3

This line plot shows the results of a survey in which 10 students were asked how many hours of TV they watched per day. This was the outcome:

Hours of TV Watched Per Day

1. What is the range?

2. What is the most common answer?

Activity 4 • Distributed Practice

Solve.

1. 500
   + 800

2. 3,010
   − 1,909

3. 46
   × 88

4. 700
   ×   8

5. 9)738

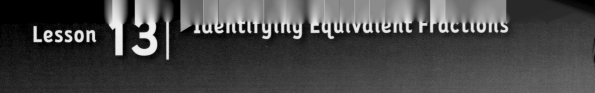

▶**Identifying Equivalent Fractions**

How are fraction bars and number lines related?

In this lesson we will use what we know about fraction bars to identify equivalent fractions. Here are two fraction bars. Let's use them to identify equivalent fractions.

First we look to see if any of the parts of the fraction bars "line up." What does that mean?

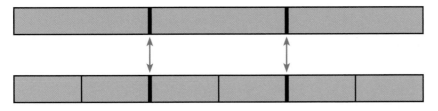

We can see that they line up in two places. At each place they line up, we find equivalent fractions.

Next, we need to identify the fractions at these points.

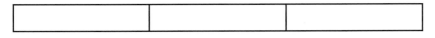

$\overline{3}$ ← total parts

$\overline{6}$ ← total parts

We start by writing the total parts that we have for each fraction bar. Remember, we call the total parts the denominator, or the number down below the line.

Now we look at the parts we have. This is the number that goes on top, or the numerator. For the equivalent fractions in this example, we have the following:

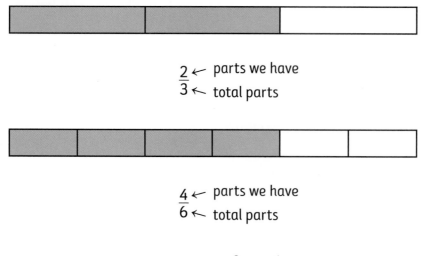

$$\frac{2}{3} \quad \begin{array}{l}\leftarrow \text{ parts we have}\\ \leftarrow \text{ total parts}\end{array}$$

$$\frac{4}{6} \quad \begin{array}{l}\leftarrow \text{ parts we have}\\ \leftarrow \text{ total parts}\end{array}$$

So, one set of equivalent fractions is $\frac{2}{3}$ and $\frac{4}{6}$.

$$\frac{2}{3} = \frac{4}{6}$$

Notice that the fraction bars also line up at $\frac{1}{3}$ and $\frac{2}{6}$, so they are also equivalent fractions. If we extended these fraction bars, we would see they line up in other places as well. For instance, they line up at $\frac{3}{3}$ and $\frac{6}{6}$, $\frac{4}{3}$ and $\frac{8}{6}$, and so on. These are all examples of equivalent fractions.

What are other ways to identify equivalent fractions?

We can also use grid paper to identify equivalent fractions.

Example 1

Show equivalent fractions using grid paper.

We will find a fraction that is equivalent to $\frac{1}{3}$. We start by drawing a rectangle on the grid paper, and dividing it into thirds.

Then we shade one of the thirds to show $\frac{1}{3}$.

We can find an equivalent fraction by simply drawing horizontal lines in our rectangles. The horizontal lines make smaller rectangles in each third that are the same size. Remember fair shares. Each part has to be the same size.

We see how the rectangles now also represent $\frac{3}{9}$, and that $\frac{1}{3}$ is the same as $\frac{3}{9}$.

We can do the same thing with even larger rectangles.

Example 2

Show how we can use grid paper to prove that $\frac{1}{3} = \frac{4}{12}$.

Here's how we can show that the fraction $\frac{1}{3}$ is equal to $\frac{4}{12}$.

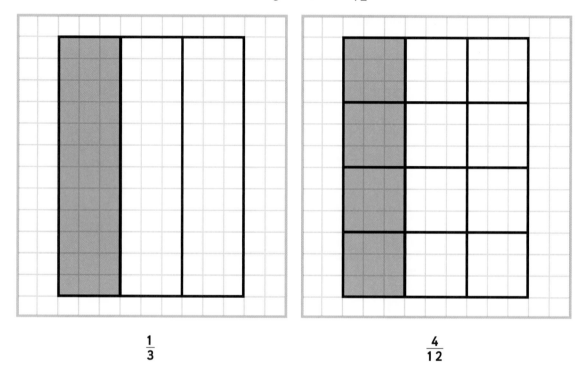

$$\frac{1}{3} \qquad\qquad\qquad \frac{4}{12}$$

All we did was break up $\frac{1}{3}$ into smaller rectangles that had the same number of rows. We drew heavy lines every 3 rows. Remember fair shares. Each part has to be the same size.

We can see how we now have 12 total parts with 4 parts shaded. The 4 parts are the parts we have.

We now have these equivalent fractions: $\frac{1}{3} = \frac{4}{12}$.

 Apply Skills
Turn to *Interactive Text*,
page 328.

 mBook Reinforce Understanding
Use the *mBook Study Guide*
to review lesson concepts.

Activity 1

Tell an equivalent fraction for each of the problems.

1. Write $\frac{2}{3}$ as an equivalent fraction using ninths.

2. Write $\frac{4}{6}$ as an equivalent fraction using twelfths.

3. Write $\frac{1}{2}$ as an equivalent fraction using sixths.

4. Write $\frac{3}{4}$ as an equivalent fraction using eighths.

5. Write $\frac{2}{5}$ as an equivalent fraction using tenths.

6. Write $\frac{1}{4}$ as an equivalent fraction using twelfths.

Activity 2

Estimate the fraction and decimal benchmarks.

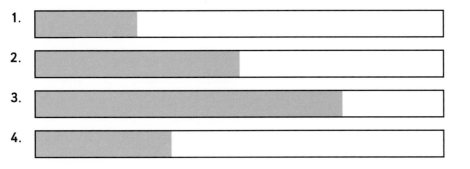

1.
2.
3.
4.

Activity 3

Find the mean, median, and range of the data.

12 13 11 19 13 15 15

Activity 4 • Distributed Practice

Solve.

1. $\begin{array}{r} 5{,}873 \\ + 1{,}237 \\ \hline \end{array}$

2. $\begin{array}{r} 1{,}200 \\ - 900 \\ \hline \end{array}$

3. $\begin{array}{r} 50 \\ \times 60 \\ \hline \end{array}$

4. $\begin{array}{r} 872 \\ \times 4 \\ \hline \end{array}$

5. $8\overline{)579}$

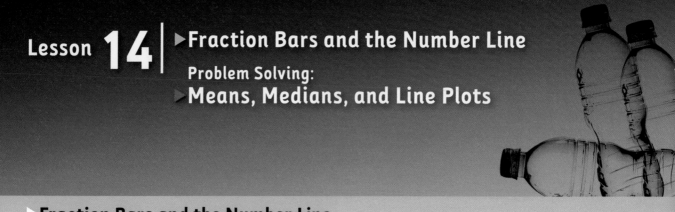

▶ **Fraction Bars and the Number Line**

How do fraction bars connect with number lines?

In this lesson, we will learn how number lines and fraction bars are related. Let's look at a number line for one whole number and its corresponding fraction bar.

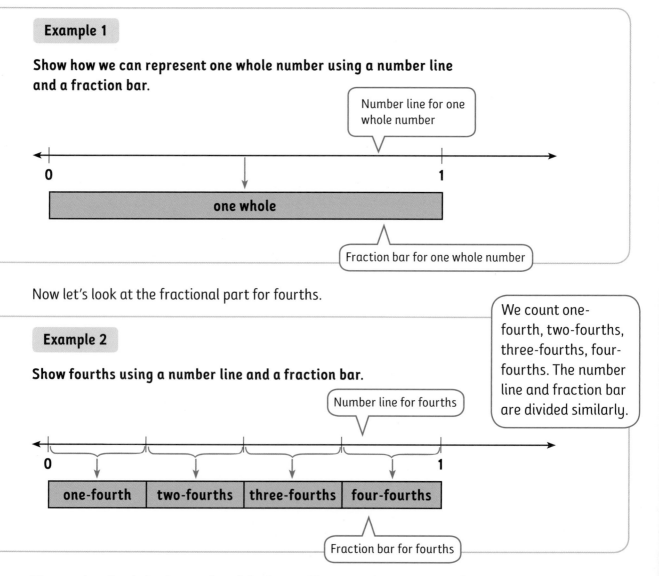

Example 1

Show how we can represent one whole number using a number line and a fraction bar.

Number line for one whole number

one whole

Fraction bar for one whole number

Now let's look at the fractional part for fourths.

Example 2

Show fourths using a number line and a fraction bar.

Number line for fourths

We count one-fourth, two-fourths, three-fourths, four-fourths. The number line and fraction bar are divided similarly.

one-fourth | two-fourths | three-fourths | four-fourths

Fraction bar for fourths

The number line is broken up into fair shares. The space between 0 and 1 has 4 equal shares.

Example 3

Let's look at twelfths. Show twelfths using a fraction bar and a number line.

Number line for twelfths

0   1

Fraction bar for twelfths

We can identify equivalent fractions when we look at twelfths and fourths on the number line and on the fraction bars.

Example 4

Show equivalent fractions for twelfths and fourths using number lines and fraction bars.

12ths

0      $\frac{3}{12}$ $\frac{6}{12}$ $\frac{9}{12}$ $\frac{12}{12}$

4ths

0      $\frac{1}{4}$ $\frac{2}{4}$ $\frac{3}{4}$ $\frac{4}{4}$

We can also identify equivalent fractions using fraction bars for twelfths and fourths.

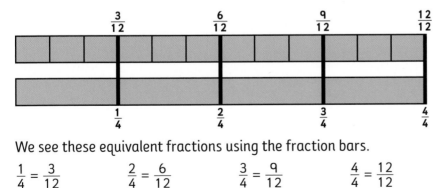

$\frac{3}{12}$ $\frac{6}{12}$ $\frac{9}{12}$ $\frac{12}{12}$

$\frac{1}{4}$ $\frac{2}{4}$ $\frac{3}{4}$ $\frac{4}{4}$

We see these equivalent fractions using the fraction bars.

$\frac{1}{4} = \frac{3}{12}$ $\frac{2}{4} = \frac{6}{12}$ $\frac{3}{4} = \frac{9}{12}$ $\frac{4}{4} = \frac{12}{12}$

 Apply Skills
Turn to *Interactive Text*, page 330.

mBook Reinforce Understanding
Use the *mBook Study Guide* to review lesson concepts.

▶Problem Solving: Means, Medians, and Line Plots

How do we use line plots to solve problems?

When we have a lot of information in a table, it is hard to get a clear idea about the statistics. When we transfer the data to a line plot, we can more easily understand the data. The line plot helps us find the mean and median of the data. Let's look at an example.

Example 1

Use a line plot to find the mean and median of the data.

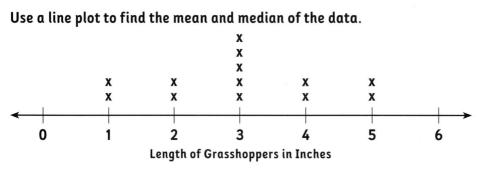

To find the median, we work from each end toward the middle. The median is 3.

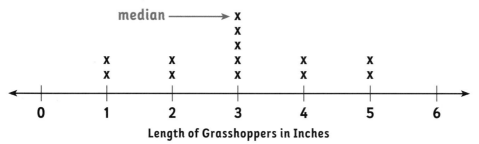

The median length is 3 inches.

We use a different process to find the mean. Each X on the line plot represents the length of a grasshopper. We need to add up the lengths of all the grasshoppers and divide by the total number of grasshoppers.

1 + 1 + 2 + 2 + 3 + 3 + 3 + 3 + 3 + 4 + 4 + 5 + 5 = 39

39 ÷ 13 = 3

The mean length is 3 inches.

Using line plots to find the mean and median helps us solve problems involving data.

 Problem-Solving Activity
Turn to *Interactive Text*, page 331.

 mBook Reinforce Understanding
Use the *mBook Study Guide* to review lesson concepts.

Activity 1

Tell the equivalent fraction.

1. Write $\frac{1}{2}$ as an equivalent fraction using eighths.

2. Write $\frac{1}{3}$ as an equivalent fraction using twelfths.

3. Write $\frac{3}{4}$ as an equivalent fraction using eighths.

4. Write $\frac{2}{8}$ as an equivalent fraction using fourths.

Activity 2

Estimate the fraction and decimal benchmarks.

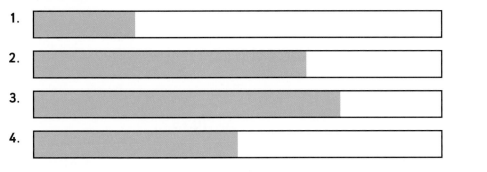

1.

2.

3.

4.

Activity 3

Find the mean, the median, and the range of the data.

21 28 27 29 24 22 25 26 23

Activity 4 • Distributed Practice

Solve.

1. $500 + 900$

2. $7{,}118 - 1{,}779$

3. 63×97

4. 872×4

5. $9\overline{)976}$

Problem Solving:
▶**Introduction to Statistics**

▶**Concept of Fractions**

What are fractions?

Fractions can be found between every whole number on a number line. The same is true of decimal numbers, which are another way of describing fractional numbers.

> **Review 1**
>
> **How do we find fractions and decimal numbers on the number line?**
>
> Dividing the space into fourths:
>
> | 10 | 10.25 | 10.5 | 10.75 | 11 |
> |---|---|---|---|---|
> | 10 | $10\frac{1}{4}$ | $10\frac{1}{2}$ | $10\frac{3}{4}$ | 11 |
>
> Dividing the space into thirds:
>
> | 10 | 10.33 | 10.67 | 11 |
> |---|---|---|---|
> | 10 | $10\frac{1}{3}$ | $10\frac{2}{3}$ | 11 |
>
> Dividing the space into halves:
>
> | 10 | 10.5 | 11 |
> |---|---|---|
> | 10 | $10\frac{1}{2}$ | 11 |

We can use different shapes to show fractions. The example shows how the fractions $\frac{1}{2}$, $\frac{2}{3}$, and $\frac{3}{4}$ can be represented with circles, squares, and hexagons.

Review 2

How do we use shapes to represent common fractions?

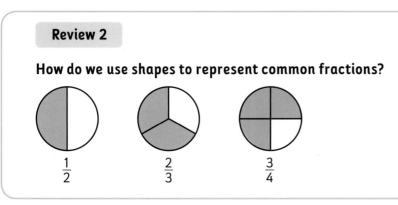

$\frac{1}{2}$ $\frac{2}{3}$ $\frac{3}{4}$

Each fraction has a numerator and denominator. The denominator in the fraction $\frac{2}{3}$ tells that there are 3 total parts, and the numerator tells us that we have 2 parts.

One of the most convenient ways for working with fractions involves fraction bars. They help us see that fractions aren't just "less than one." They can be equal to or greater than one, as shown in the example.

Review 3

How do we use fraction bars to show a fraction less than one, equal to one, and greater than one?

A fraction less than one

$\frac{7}{8}$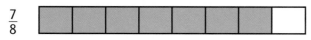

A fraction equal to one

$\frac{8}{8}$

A fraction greater than one

$\frac{12}{8}$

Review 4

What are equivalent fractions?

$\frac{2}{5} = \frac{4}{10}$

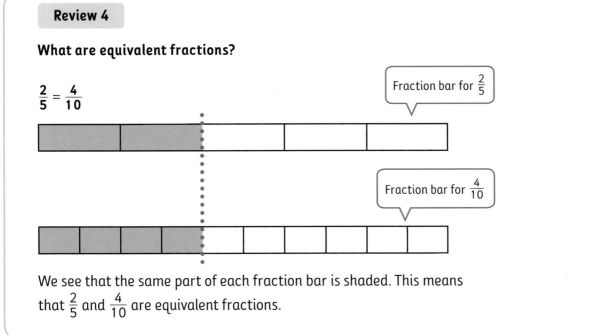

Fraction bar for $\frac{2}{5}$

Fraction bar for $\frac{4}{10}$

We see that the same part of each fraction bar is shaded. This means that $\frac{2}{5}$ and $\frac{4}{10}$ are equivalent fractions.

Review 5

What are some commonly used fractions and decimal numbers?

Location on a number line

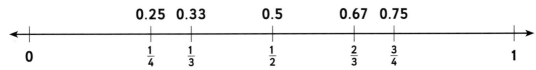

The shaded area in the shape is about $\frac{1}{4}$ or 0.25.

 **Apply Skills**
Turn to *Interactive Text*,
page 333.

 mBook Reinforce Understanding
Use the *mBook Study Guide*
to review lesson concepts.

How do we analyze data from tables using basic statistics?

We are surrounded by data in the world today. Tables are a particularly good source of data. However, we need to be able to read and interpret data in an intelligent way. We can use basic statistics.

Let's review some basic terms by looking at a column of data from a table.

The example shows the number of burgers sold per hour at Jack's Burger Palace from 10 in the morning until 9 at night on Monday. The column on the right is difficult to interpret because the numbers go up and down.

Review 1

How do we use a table to show data?

Monday's Burger Sales	
10–11 AM	19
11 AM–12 PM	28
12–1 PM	47
1–2 PM	35
2–3 PM	21
3–4 PM	20
4–5 PM	27
5–6 PM	41
6–7 PM	31
7–8 PM	26
8–9 PM	24

Time	Tues.	Wed.	Thurs.	Fri.	Sat.	Sun.
10–11 AM	21	26	20	17	25	16
11 AM–12 PM	30	29	33	27	34	31
12–1 PM	48	45	44	49	54	51
1–2 PM	34	31	33	36	39	35
2–3 PM	20	19	23	18	26	22
3–4 PM	19	21	22	18	24	17
4–5 PM	28	31	26	24	32	25
5–6 PM	44	41	45	43	49	42
6–7 PM	33	32	34	30	35	28
7–8 PM	24	27	25	24	30	23
8–9 PM	21	23	22	25	27	20

The column of data in the previous section is difficult to read because the numbers go up and down. Let's say we don't care about the time the burgers were sold. Now we have rearranged the data by listing the numbers in order so that we can look at our key information for data analysis.

Review 2

How do we organize the data in a table?

Total burgers sold: 319

$319 \div 11 = 29$

We are able to understand the data by organizing the column of data and doing a basic calculation to find the mean. The number of burgers sold varied from 19 (the minimum) to 47 (the maximum). This range tells us something about the extremes, or "the distance," from

19	minimum
20	
21	
24	
26	
27	median
28	
31	
35	
41	
47	maximum

the mean of 29. The range makes sense because we know that we are going to sell a lot more burgers at lunch or dinner time than early in the morning.

The mean of 29 and median of 27 are close together. Remember, the mean is a good predictor. We could use that as the basis for predicting the average number of burgers per hour we would sell on Tuesday. The median is important because it helps guard against extremes in the data. It is halfway between the minimum and the maximum.

Suppose that three traveling sports teams stop by Jack's at 7 PM and order another 132 burgers. This would be an extreme and unusual example, and would exaggerate the mean. That's why the median is so important. It doesn't change very much, even if we have something like three sports teams stopping by the restaurant without any notice.

Review 3

How do we use a stem-and-leaf plot to show data?

The data from Monday's burger sales:

19 20 21 24 26 27 28 31 35 41 47

1	9
2	0 1 4 6 7 8
3	1 5
4	1 7

Range = 28

Median = 27

What is a line plot?

Finally, a line plot is a good way of showing data if we have a lot of numbers that are repeated. The example shows the number of milkshakes sold at Jack's Burger Palace on Monday.

Review 1

How do we use line plots to show data?

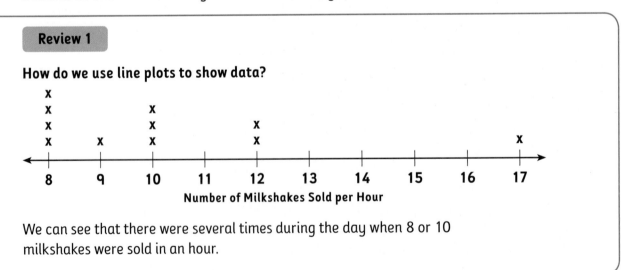

Number of Milkshakes Sold per Hour

We can see that there were several times during the day when 8 or 10 milkshakes were sold in an hour.

 Problem-Solving Activity
Turn to *Interactive Text*,
page 334.

 mBook **Reinforce Understanding**
Use the *mBook Study Guide*
to review lesson concepts.

CALVIN AND HOBBES (c) 1986 Watterson. Dist. By UNIVERSAL PRESS SYNDICATE.
Reprinted with permission. All rights reserved.

THE WORLD'S BIGGEST PANCAKE

was cooked in Rochdale, England, in 1994. It was nearly **50 feet** (15 meters) in diameter, weighed over three tons and contained about 2,000,000 calories.

What? You mean that pancake was almost as long as my truck?

TASTY SYRUP

Basic Pancake Recipe

Ingredients: 2 cups all-purpose flour
2½ teaspoons baking powder
½ teaspoon salt
1 egg, slightly beaten
1½ cups milk
2 tablespoons melted butter

Mix together flour, baking
and salt. In a separate bow
opping. Serves 4 adults,
y hungry teen.

uttermilk Pancake

,450 Pounds Buttermilk
800 Pounds Eggs
350 Pounds Butter
450 Gallons Water

Mix all ingredients. For
results use 39 grills. Top
4,700 pounds of butter and
gallons of maple syrup.

OBJECTIVES

Building Number Concepts

- Add and subtract fractions with like and unlike denominators

- Find the least common multiple of two or more whole numbers

- Use least common multiples to find common denominators

Problem Solving

- Understand common units of measurement

- Convert units using a conversion table

- Measure objects to the nearest quarter inch

Lesson 1 | ▶Same Denominator

Problem Solving:
▶Everyday Measurements

▶Same Denominator

Vocabulary
fractional parts

What do the numerator and denominator tell us about a fraction?

We learned in the last unit that the denominator of a fraction tells us how many total parts there are and the numerator tells the parts we have. The numerator tells how many **fractional parts** to count out of the total parts.

Let's review.

Example 1

Use a fraction bar to show a numerator and denominator.

Let's think about the fraction $\frac{3}{4}$.

First, we look at a fraction bar for fourths.

Then we count the fractional parts to find the parts we have. Here, we want to count three-fourths. We count one-fourth, two-fourths, three-fourths.

1	2	3	

Then we shade the parts we have.

Now we have a fraction bar that represents $\frac{3}{4}$.

How do we add fractions with the same denominator?

We count fractional parts when we add fractions that have the same denominator. We just count more of the same fractional part—thirds, fourths, fifths, tenths, or any other type of fraction.

Example 1

Add $\frac{1}{4} + \frac{2}{4}$.

$$\frac{1}{4} + \frac{2}{4} = ?$$

First, we decide if both fractions are using the same fractional parts, or fair shares. We look at the denominator to find total fractional parts. Both fractions are fourths, so we are counting the same fractional part in both fractions.

We start with $\frac{1}{4}$ and we add $\frac{2}{4}$ to it.

Let's look at this using fraction bars.

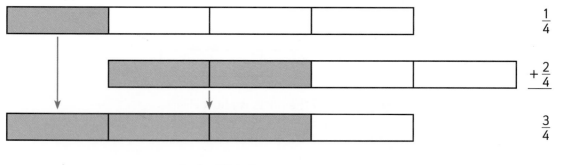

$$\frac{1}{4} + \frac{2}{4} = \frac{3}{4}$$

We add the numerators of these fractions because the denominators are the same.

We don't have to use fraction bars to see how this works. We can use circles, measuring cups, or other shapes. If the denominators in two fractions are the same, we add the numerators. When the denominators are the same, the fair shares are the same.

Example 2

Show $\frac{1}{4} + \frac{2}{4}$ using circles.

$$\frac{1}{4} + \frac{2}{4} = \frac{3}{4}$$

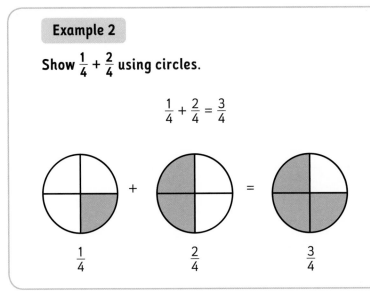

Example 3

Show $\frac{1}{4} + \frac{2}{4}$ using measuring cups.

$$\frac{1}{4} + \frac{2}{4} = \frac{3}{4}$$

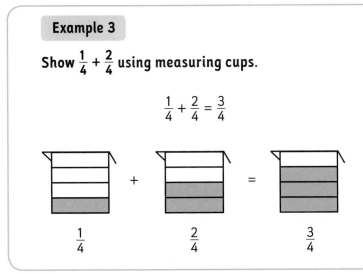

How do we subtract fractions with the same denominators?

We take away fractional parts when we subtract fractions that have the same denominator.

Example 1

Show $\frac{4}{5} - \frac{1}{5}$ using fraction bars.

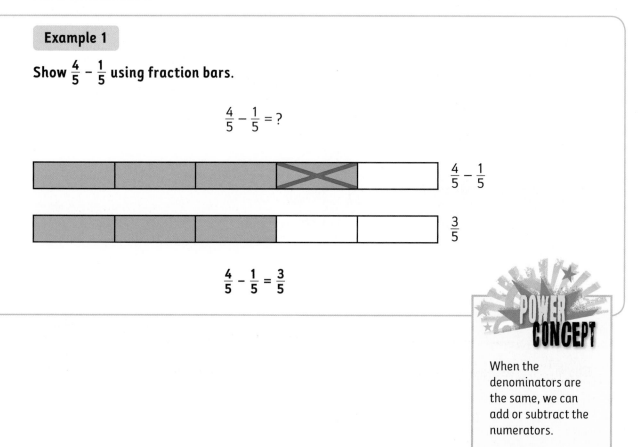

$$\frac{4}{5} - \frac{1}{5} = \,?$$

$$\frac{4}{5} - \frac{1}{5} = \frac{3}{5}$$

POWER CONCEPT

When the denominators are the same, we can add or subtract the numerators.

 Apply Skills
Turn to *Interactive Text*, page 337.

 mBook Reinforce Understanding
Use the *mBook Study Guide* to review lesson concepts.

▶**Problem Solving: Everyday Measurements**

Vocabulary
converting

What are some common measurements used in the import and export industry?

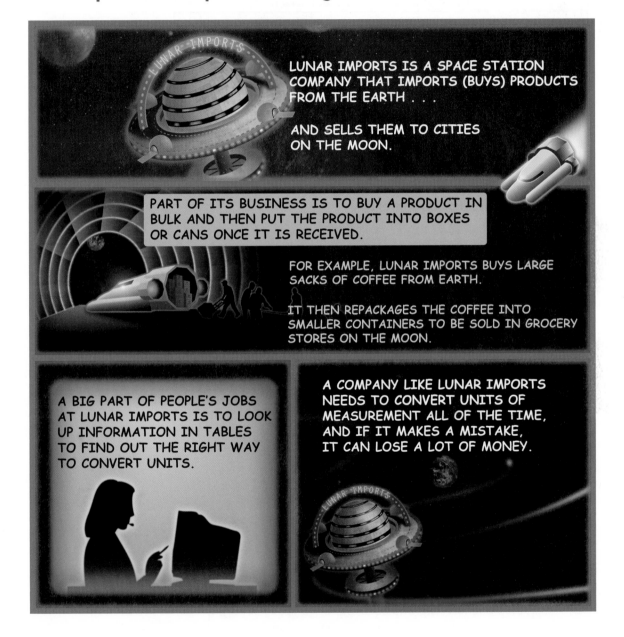

LUNAR IMPORTS IS A SPACE STATION COMPANY THAT IMPORTS (BUYS) PRODUCTS FROM THE EARTH . . .

AND SELLS THEM TO CITIES ON THE MOON.

PART OF ITS BUSINESS IS TO BUY A PRODUCT IN BULK AND THEN PUT THE PRODUCT INTO BOXES OR CANS ONCE IT IS RECEIVED.

FOR EXAMPLE, LUNAR IMPORTS BUYS LARGE SACKS OF COFFEE FROM EARTH.

IT THEN REPACKAGES THE COFFEE INTO SMALLER CONTAINERS TO BE SOLD IN GROCERY STORES ON THE MOON.

A BIG PART OF PEOPLE'S JOBS AT LUNAR IMPORTS IS TO LOOK UP INFORMATION IN TABLES TO FIND OUT THE RIGHT WAY TO CONVERT UNITS.

A COMPANY LIKE LUNAR IMPORTS NEEDS TO CONVERT UNITS OF MEASUREMENT ALL OF THE TIME, AND IF IT MAKES A MISTAKE, IT CAN LOSE A LOT OF MONEY.

We will look at different ways of measuring things. We will practice changing, or **converting** , units of measurement. For example, we might convert ounces to pints, quarts, or gallons. We might convert pounds to tons.

This table shows conversions of liquid measurements.

Table of Liquid Measurement		
16 ounces	1 pint	
32 ounces	2 pints	1 quart
128 ounces	4 quarts	1 gallon
4,032 ounces	$31\frac{1}{2}$ gallons	1 barrel

Example 1

Solve the word problem by converting.

Problem:

Lunar Imports receives a large shipment of cooking oil. The oil comes in large drums. Each drum holds 768 ounces of oil. Julian at Lunar Imports needs to put the oil in gallon containers. He uses the table of liquid measurement to find out how many gallons of oil he should get from each drum. Julian uses a calculator to go through the steps.

To convert ounces to gallons, we divide:

total ounces ÷ ounces in a gallon = total number of gallons

$$768 \quad ÷ \quad 128 \quad = \quad 6$$

$$\begin{array}{r} 6 \\ 128\overline{)768} \end{array}$$

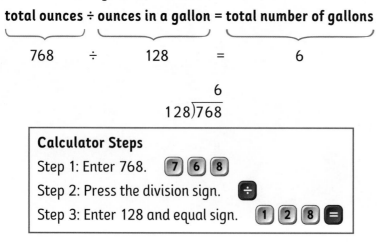

Calculator Steps

Step 1: Enter 768. [7] [6] [8]

Step 2: Press the division sign. [÷]

Step 3: Enter 128 and equal sign. [1] [2] [8] [=]

Julian finds that he can get six gallons of oil from every big drum.

 Problem-Solving Activity
Turn to *Interactive Text*,
page 338.

 mBook Reinforce Understanding
Use the *mBook Study Guide*
to review lesson concepts.

Homework

Activity 1

Draw fraction bars to show each fraction.

1. $\frac{3}{5}$
2. $\frac{4}{9}$
3. $\frac{7}{10}$
4. $\frac{3}{4}$
5. $\frac{6}{12}$

Activity 2

Solve the problems that have the same fair shares and can be solved without finding a common denominator.

1. $\frac{3}{5} - \frac{1}{5}$
2. $\frac{2}{9} + \frac{4}{10}$
3. $\frac{11}{12} - \frac{7}{12}$
4. $\frac{4}{8} + \frac{3}{8}$
5. $\frac{6}{7} - \frac{4}{7}$
6. $\frac{1}{11} + \frac{1}{10}$
7. $\frac{6}{10} - \frac{2}{5}$
8. $\frac{3}{6} + \frac{2}{6}$
9. $\frac{1}{4} + \frac{1}{4}$

Activity 3

Add and subtract. Use fraction bars to help you.

1. $\frac{11}{12} - \frac{6}{12}$
2. $\frac{1}{9} + \frac{7}{9}$
3. $\frac{1}{5} + \frac{2}{5}$
4. $\frac{8}{11} - \frac{4}{11}$

Activity 4

Use this conversion table to help answer the questions.

Table of Liquid Measurement		
1 pint		16 ounces
1 quart	2 pints	32 ounces
1 gallon	4 quarts	128 ounces
1 barrel	$31\frac{1}{2}$ gallons	4,032 ounces

1. How many pints are in a quart?

2. How many quarts are in a gallon?

3. If you have two barrels of cooking oil, how many gallons is that?

Activity 5 • Distributed Practice

Solve.

1. $376 + 295$

2. $8{,}001 - 4{,}723$

3. 658×2

4. $8\overline{)344}$

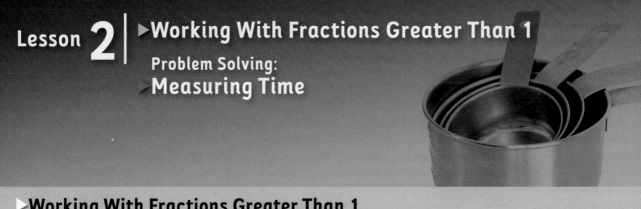

Lesson 2 ▸ Working With Fractions Greater Than 1

Problem Solving: ▸ Measuring Time

▸**Working With Fractions Greater Than 1**

How do we show addition of fractions?

When we think of fractions, we usually think of something smaller than 1. But fractions can be found everywhere on the number line.

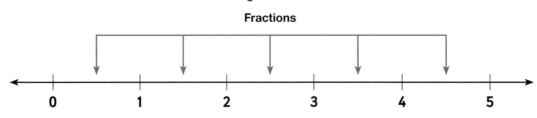

Fractions

When we add and subtract fractions, we often get numbers that are bigger than 1. Here are two examples. We will use a number line and fraction bars to show addition. Remember, we need to have the same denominators when we add fractions.

Example 1

Show $\frac{4}{6} + \frac{5}{6}$ on the number line.

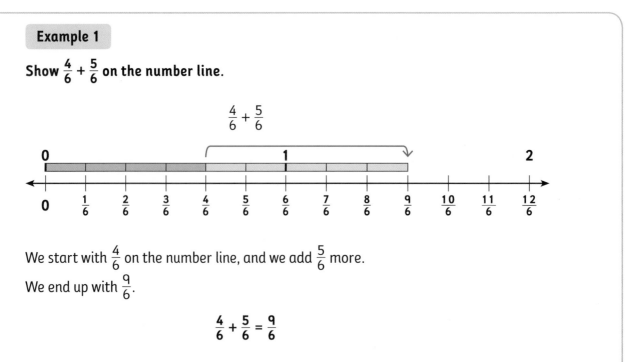

We start with $\frac{4}{6}$ on the number line, and we add $\frac{5}{6}$ more.

We end up with $\frac{9}{6}$.

$$\frac{4}{6} + \frac{5}{6} = \frac{9}{6}$$

On the number line, we see that we have a fraction greater than 1.

We see the same thing when we use fraction bars. Let's look at $\frac{4}{6} + \frac{5}{6}$ using fraction bars.

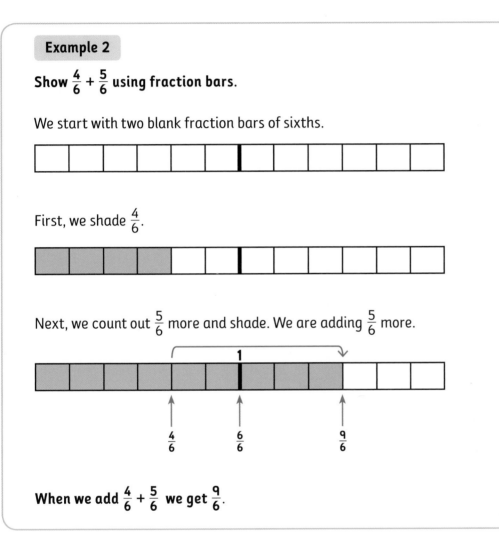

Example 2

Show $\frac{4}{6} + \frac{5}{6}$ using fraction bars.

We start with two blank fraction bars of sixths.

First, we shade $\frac{4}{6}$.

Next, we count out $\frac{5}{6}$ more and shade. We are adding $\frac{5}{6}$ more.

When we add $\frac{4}{6} + \frac{5}{6}$ we get $\frac{9}{6}$.

How do we show subtraction of fractions?

We also use the number line to show subtraction. We start with the larger fraction and cross out the fractional parts we are subtracting. We will use Xs to show that we are crossing out parts.

Example 1

Show $\frac{7}{4} - \frac{5}{4}$ on a number line.

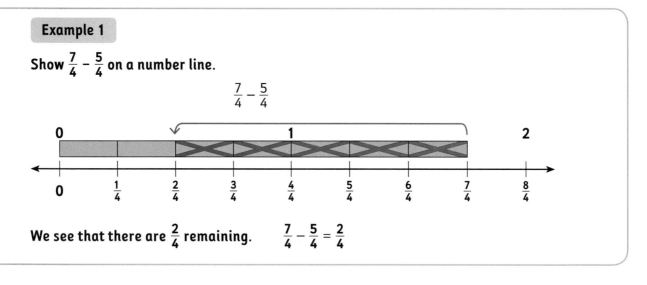

We see that there are $\frac{2}{4}$ remaining. $\frac{7}{4} - \frac{5}{4} = \frac{2}{4}$

Example 2

Show $\frac{7}{4} - \frac{5}{4}$ using fraction bars.

We see the same thing when we use fraction bars. We start by showing $\frac{7}{4}$ with fraction bars. Notice that it takes two fraction bars to make $\frac{7}{4}$.

Then we count down $\frac{5}{4}$. We go past $\frac{4}{4}$, or 1 whole, so we know our answer will be less than 1. It is $\frac{2}{4}$.

Apply Skills
Turn to *Interactive Text*, page 340.

mBook Reinforce Understanding
Use the *mBook Study Guide* to review lesson concepts.

▶**Problem Solving: Measuring Time**

What are common conversions involving time?

IN A BUSINESS LIKE LUNAR IMPORTS, EVERY SECOND COUNTS. IT IS IMPORTANT TO MOVE GOODS AS FAST AS POSSIBLE.

Here is a table of time units. Lunar Imports uses a table like this to figure out how long it will take for something to be shipped from one place to the next.

Table of Time Units	
60 seconds	1 minute
60 minutes	1 hour
24 hours	1 day
7 days	1 week
30 days*	1 month
12 months	1 year
365 days	1 year
100 years	1 century

*Note: Some months have 31 or 28 days, but we will use the number 30 to represent one month.

Let's use the table to convert 72 hours into days.

Example 1

Convert 72 hours into days.

To convert hours into days, we divide:

total number of hours ÷ hours in a day = total number of days

$$72 \div 24 = 3$$

72 hours = 3 days

 **Problem-Solving Activity**
Turn to *Interactive Text*, page 341.

 mBook Reinforce Understanding
Use the *mBook Study Guide* to review lesson concepts.

Homework

Draw fraction bars to show the fractions.

1. $\frac{1}{4}$ 2. $\frac{2}{8}$ 3. $\frac{1}{3}$ 4. $\frac{2}{6}$

Activity 2

Add and subtract. Circle the fractions that are greater than or equal to 1. Use fraction bars to help.

1. $\frac{5}{4} + \frac{2}{4}$

2. $\frac{9}{6} - \frac{3}{6}$

3. $\frac{9}{9} + \frac{5}{9}$

4. $\frac{3}{2} - \frac{2}{2}$

Activity 3

Use this conversion chart to find the missing numbers in the problems. Write the answers on your paper.

Table of Time Units			
60 seconds	1 minute	30 days	1 month
60 minutes	1 hour	12 months	1 year
24 hours	1 day	365 days	1 year
7 days	1 week	100 years	1 century

1. 60 seconds = _____ minute

2. _____ hours = 1 day

3. 12 months = _____ year(s)

4. _____ days = 1 year

5. 100 years = _____ century

6. 120 seconds = _____ minute(s)

7. 48 hours = _____ day(s)

8. _____ months = 2 years

Activity 4 • Distributed Practice

Solve.

1. $\begin{array}{r} 37 \\ \times\ 48 \\ \hline \end{array}$

2. $80\overline{)720}$

3. $\begin{array}{r} 487 \\ -\ 199 \\ \hline \end{array}$

4. $\begin{array}{r} 52{,}701 \\ +\ 87{,}199 \\ \hline \end{array}$

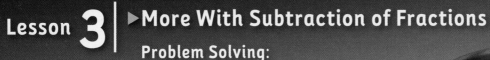

Lesson 3 | ▶More With Subtraction of Fractions

Problem Solving:
▶More With Converting Units

▶More With Subtraction of Fractions

What are some common errors when subtracting fractions?

When we subtract fractions, it is easy to make mistakes. Let's look at some common errors that can happen when we subtract fractions using fraction bars.

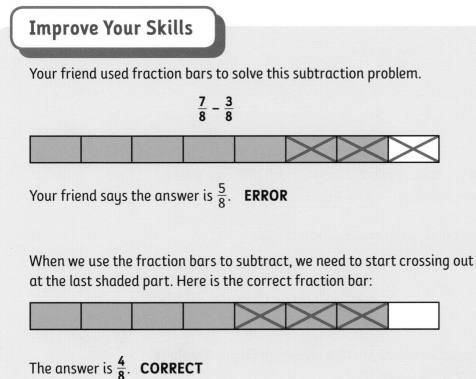

Improve Your Skills

Your friend used fraction bars to solve this subtraction problem.

$$\frac{7}{8} - \frac{3}{8}$$

Your friend says the answer is $\frac{5}{8}$. **ERROR**

When we use the fraction bars to subtract, we need to start crossing out at the last shaded part. Here is the correct fraction bar:

The answer is $\frac{4}{8}$. **CORRECT**

%÷
=
<× **Apply Skills**
Turn to *Interactive Text*,
page 343.

mBook **Reinforce Understanding**
Use the *mBook Study Guide*
to review lesson concepts.

▶**Problem Solving: More With Converting Units**

What do we do with remainders in conversion?

We practiced converting units. For each problem, the answer was a whole number. That doesn't happen very often in real life. Usually, there is a remainder, or parts of a unit left over. For example, suppose we wanted to figure out how many weeks are in 17 days.

To convert days to weeks, we divide:

total number of days ÷ days in a week = total number of weeks

---

Example 1

Convert 17 days into weeks using long division.

$$
\begin{array}{r}
\overset{\text{2 weeks}}{}\quad\overset{\text{3 days}}{} \\
2\ \text{R3} \\
7\overline{)17} \\
-14 \\
\hline
3
\end{array}
$$

When we divide 7 days into 17 days, we get 2 weeks and 3 days. Let's think about what we are doing. We are taking the unit of 7 (one week) and dividing the total number of days by that unit.

We have 2 weeks (or 2 units of 7) and 3 days left over.

It is important to see that when we convert days into weeks, we get two different types of units—weeks and days.

We have two strategies that we use to solve division problems like these. We use long division or a calculator.

Long division works relatively well when the numbers are small. But it can lead to mistakes with much larger numbers. Using a calculator is one way we work with bigger numbers.

Example 2

Convert days into years using the calculator (divide, multiply, then subtract).

There are 365 days in a year. How many years is 1,000 days?

STEP 1

In this example, we divide 1,000 by 365 to find the number of years.

- Enter the total number of days.   [1] [0] [0] [0]
- Press [÷].
- Enter the number of days in a year.   [3] [6] [5]
- Press [=].

The whole number in the answer is the number of whole years in 1,000 days.

Now we need to understand what the remainder is. The remainder is the digits after the decimal point.

STEP 2

Multiply the whole number in the answer (2) by 365 to convert it to days.

We multiply 2 · 365. Now we know that two years is equal to 730 days.

STEP 3

Subtract the number of days in two years from the total number of days to get the number of days left over.

Subtract 1,000 − 730 = 270.

The answer is 2 years and 270 days. We get 2 years (or 2 units of 365) and 270 days left over.

When we convert units, we need to think about what our units are. This is especially true if we are using a calculator. The answer to a division problem with a remainder involves two different units. In the last example, the whole number 2 stood for years, and the number 270 stood for days. That means there are two different kinds of units—years and days.

Improve Your Skills

The students were asked to convert 123 hours to days. Here are four answers. Only one of them is correct.

$$\begin{array}{r} 53 \\ 24\overline{)123} \\ -120 \\ \hline 3 \end{array}$$

123 hours = 53 days

ERROR: The remainder was not separated from the whole number of days.

$$\begin{array}{r} 5\ R3 \\ 24\overline{)123} \\ -120 \\ \hline 3 \end{array}$$

123 hours = 8 days

ERROR: The quotient and the remainder were added together.

$$\begin{array}{r} 5\ R3 \\ 24\overline{)123} \\ -120 \\ \hline 3 \end{array}$$

123 hours = 3 days, 5 hours

ERROR: The days and hours were switched.

$$\begin{array}{r} 5\ R3 \\ 24\overline{)123} \\ -120 \\ \hline 3 \end{array}$$

123 hours = 5 days, 3 hours

CORRECT: This student was correct.

 Problem-Solving Activity
Turn to *Interactive Text*, page 344.

 mBook Reinforce Understanding
Use the *mBook Study Guide* to review lesson concepts.

Activity 1

Draw fraction bars to show the fractions.

1. $\frac{1}{4}$
2. $\frac{9}{7}$
3. $\frac{3}{6}$
4. $\frac{3}{3}$

Activity 2

Add and subtract the fractions.

1. $\frac{5}{4} + \frac{8}{4}$
2. $\frac{4}{6} - \frac{3}{6}$
3. $\frac{10}{12} + \frac{5}{12}$
4. $\frac{6}{2} - \frac{4}{2}$
5. $\frac{10}{5} + \frac{5}{5}$
6. $\frac{14}{7} - \frac{7}{7}$

Activity 3

Use the table to answer the questions.

Table of Time Units	
60 seconds	1 minute
60 minutes	1 hour
24 hours	1 day
7 days	1 week
30 days*	1 month
12 months	1 year
365 days	1 year
100 years	1 century

*Note: Some months have a total of 31 or 28 days, but we will use the number 30 to represent one month.

1. If you are going on a vacation for 23 days, how many weeks will you be gone on your vacation?

2. If you will graduate from high school in 17 months, how many years is that?

3. There are 790 more days until your car is paid off. How many years is that?

4. A tortoise at the zoo is 138 years old. How many centuries is that?

5. It took Timmy 95 seconds to print his report. How many minutes is that?

Activity 4 • Distributed Practice

Solve.

1. $\begin{array}{r} 14{,}000 \\ -\ 8{,}000 \\ \hline \end{array}$

2. $\begin{array}{r} 965 \\ +237 \\ \hline \end{array}$

3. $\begin{array}{r} 437 \\ \times\ \ 8 \\ \hline \end{array}$

4. $9\overline{)857}$

Lesson 4 | ▶Common Denominators

Problem Solving:
Measuring Dry Weight

▶**Common Denominators**

Vocabulary
common denominator

What are common denominators?

So far, we have been adding and subtracting fractions with denominators that are the same. What happens when the denominators are not the same? Remember the rule:

> **Rule:**
> When we add or subtract fractions, the denominators have to be the same.

If the denominators are not the same, we need to make them the same by finding equivalent fractions. We know from earlier lessons how to find equivalent fractions using fraction bars.

How does that work when we have a problem like $\frac{1}{2} - \frac{1}{3}$?

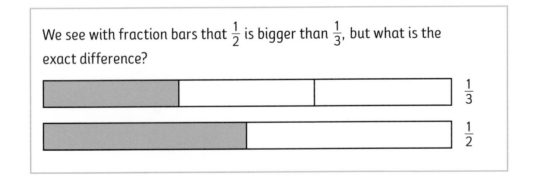

We see with fraction bars that $\frac{1}{2}$ is bigger than $\frac{1}{3}$, but what is the exact difference?

$\frac{1}{3}$

$\frac{1}{2}$

The units, or fair shares, of the two fractions are not the same, so we can't just subtract. Before we subtract, we need to find a **common denominator** .

Here's a story that will help us remember that we have to use common denominators when adding and subtracting fractions.

After the story we will learn how to solve $\frac{1}{2} - \frac{1}{3}$.

The Fable of the Peasants and the King

Hundreds of years ago, people didn't always use money. They would trade work for food or a place to live. One day, a king was giving out bread to the peasants who had done some work for him. Two peasants came to get their bread.

Peasant George got $\frac{1}{3}$ of a loaf of bread, and Peasant Tom got $\frac{1}{2}$ of a loaf of bread. George was upset that his loaf of bread was smaller than Tom's loaf of bread. George asked the king, "Why did I get less bread?" The king asked, "Did you get less bread? If you have less, how much less? If you can tell me exactly how much less, I will give you the same amount as your friend." This was a big problem for George, because he had to figure out exactly the difference between $\frac{1}{2}$ and $\frac{1}{3}$.

Exactly how much less is George's loaf than Tom's?

To solve a problem like this, we need to make the denominators the same. Let's use fraction bars to see how to do that.

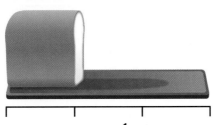

Peasant George's $\frac{1}{3}$ loaf of bread

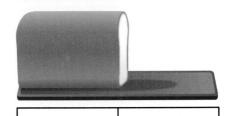

Peasant Tom's $\frac{1}{2}$ loaf of bread

Example 1

Find the difference between $\frac{1}{3}$ and $\frac{1}{2}$.

We need to find a fraction bar with fractions that line up with both $\frac{1}{3}$ and $\frac{1}{2}$.

$\frac{1}{2}$

Let's try sixths.

The fraction bar for sixths

$\frac{1}{3}$

We use sixths because they line up with both thirds and halves. That means that we can find equivalent fractions for both $\frac{1}{2}$ and $\frac{1}{3}$ on the fraction bar for sixths. Let's look at how this works.

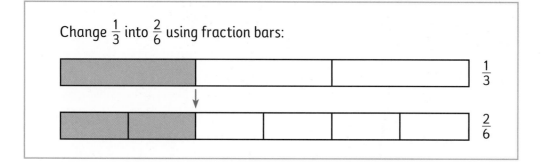

Now we can subtract because we have the same fair shares, or the same denominators.

What is $\frac{1}{2} - \frac{1}{3}$?

We use fraction bars to find equivalent fractions. We

see that $\frac{1}{2} = \frac{3}{6}$ and $\frac{1}{3} = \frac{2}{6}$.

Now we can rewrite the problem $\frac{3}{6} - \frac{2}{6} = \frac{1}{6}$.

What does Peasant George tell the king? "The difference is $\frac{1}{6}$."

Try to remember the story about the peasants and the king when adding or subtracting fractions. It will help us remember that we must have denominators that are the same.

 Apply Skills
Turn to *Interactive Text*,
page 346.

 mBook **Reinforce Understanding**
Use the *mBook Study Guide*
to review lesson concepts.

▶**Problem Solving: Measuring Dry Weight**

How do we make conversions with dry weights?

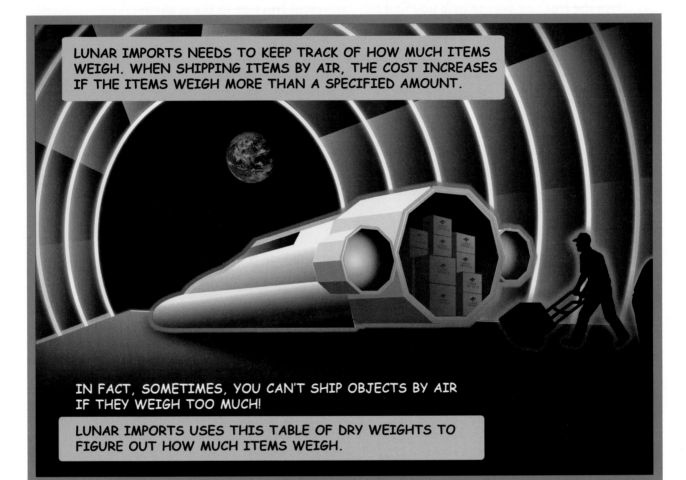

LUNAR IMPORTS NEEDS TO KEEP TRACK OF HOW MUCH ITEMS WEIGH. WHEN SHIPPING ITEMS BY AIR, THE COST INCREASES IF THE ITEMS WEIGH MORE THAN A SPECIFIED AMOUNT.

IN FACT, SOMETIMES, YOU CAN'T SHIP OBJECTS BY AIR IF THEY WEIGH TOO MUCH!

LUNAR IMPORTS USES THIS TABLE OF DRY WEIGHTS TO FIGURE OUT HOW MUCH ITEMS WEIGH.

Table of Dry Weight Units	
16 drams	1 ounce
16 ounces	1 pound
100 pounds	1 hundredweight
2,000 pounds	1 ton

 Problem-Solving Activity
Turn to *Interactive Text*, page 347.

 mBook Reinforce Understanding
Use the *mBook Study Guide* to review lesson concepts.

Homework

Activity 1

Use the fraction bars to help you find the equivalent fraction in the problems.

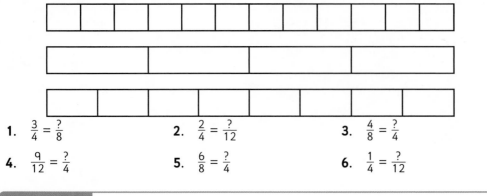

1. $\frac{3}{4} = \frac{?}{8}$

2. $\frac{2}{4} = \frac{?}{12}$

3. $\frac{4}{8} = \frac{?}{4}$

4. $\frac{9}{12} = \frac{?}{4}$

5. $\frac{6}{8} = \frac{?}{4}$

6. $\frac{1}{4} = \frac{?}{12}$

Activity 2

Add and subtract the fractions. Use fraction bars to help find equivalent fractions with the same denominators.

1. $\frac{3}{4} + \frac{2}{12}$

2. $\frac{4}{8} + \frac{2}{4}$

3. $\frac{6}{12} + \frac{1}{4}$

4. $\frac{1}{4} + \frac{2}{8}$

Activity 3

Use the table to answer the questions.

Table of Dry Weight Units	
16 drams	1 ounce
16 ounces	1 pound
100 pounds	1 hundredweight
2,000 pounds	1 ton

1. How many drams are in 1 ounce?

2. How many ounces are in 1 pound?

3. How many pounds are in 1 hundredweight?

4. Two thousand pounds is the same as how many tons?

Activity 4 • Distributed Practice

Solve.

1.
$$\begin{array}{r} 36 \\ \times 46 \\ \hline \end{array}$$

2. $90\overline{)810}$

3.
$$\begin{array}{r} 565 \\ - 299 \\ \hline \end{array}$$

4.
$$\begin{array}{r} 48,002 \\ + 97,909 \\ \hline \end{array}$$

▶ **Problem Solving: Using More Than One Table of Information**

When do we need more than one table?

Sometimes we need to use more than one table of information to solve a problem or answer a question. It helps to use paper, pencil, and a calculator to keep track of what we are doing.

Let's look at a type of problem that the employees at Lunar Imports have to solve every day. It involves shipping costs, which are based on weight.

Problem:

How much does it cost Lunar Imports to ship a box that weighs 48 ounces?

To determine shipping costs, Lunar Imports employees first have to figure out how much something weighs. Then they have to use a table of shipping costs to figure out the cost of shipping the item. That means the employees have to use two tables, like these:

Table of Dry Weight Units	
16 drams	1 ounce
16 ounces	1 pound
100 pounds	1 hundredweight
2,000 pounds	1 ton

Table of Shipping Costs	
Weight	Cost
Less than 1 pound	$5
1 pound or more	$2 per pound
1 ton or more	$950 per ton

Let's look at the steps we go through to solve a problem using one or more tables.

Steps for Using More Than One Table to Solve a Problem

STEP 1

Read the problem. Determine what you need to know to solve the problem.

Problem:

> How much does it cost Lunar Imports to ship a box that weighs 48 ounces?

We need to know how much something weighs. Then we need to know the cost of shipping the item.

STEP 2

Use the Table of Dry Weight Units to convert the weight to pounds. We can use long division or a calculator to do this. We are dividing 48 by 16.

$$16\overline{)48}^{3}$$

The weight is 3 pounds.

STEP 3

Use the Table of Shipping Costs to find the shipping cost. We see from the table that for anything weighing between 1 pound and 1 ton, we need to multiply $2 times the number of pounds. Here we multiply 3 pounds by $2 per pound.

$$3 \text{ pounds} \cdot \$2 \text{ per pound} = \$6$$

It costs $6 to ship a 48-ounce box.

 Problem-Solving Activity
Turn to *Interactive Text*, page 349.

 Monitoring Progress
Quiz 1

 Reinforce Understanding
Use the *mBook Study Guide* to review lesson concepts.

Activity 1

Draw fraction bars on your paper to show these fractions.

1. $\frac{6}{12}$

2. $\frac{5}{10}$

3. $\frac{3}{4}$

4. $\frac{6}{8}$

Activity 2

Add and subtract the fractions. Use fraction bars to help find equivalent fractions with the same denominators.

1. $\frac{2}{6} + \frac{1}{3}$ 2. $\frac{2}{3} - \frac{3}{9}$

3. $\frac{1}{3} + \frac{4}{6}$ 4. $\frac{3}{4} - \frac{1}{12}$

Activity 3

Solve the word problems involving fractions that have the same fair shares. Use fraction bars, if necessary. Show the equation as well as the answer.

1. Shondra and Liza bought a long piece of candy at the store. Shondra ate $\frac{3}{5}$ of the candy. Liza ate $\frac{1}{5}$ of the candy. How much candy did the two girls eat?

2. Humberto has a piece of wood that is $\frac{10}{12}$ of a foot long. He needs a piece of wood for his model airplane that is $\frac{5}{12}$ of a foot long. How much does he need to cut off the piece of wood that he has?

3. Evan has a job painting a neighbor's house. On Tuesday, he painted $\frac{2}{6}$ of the house before lunch and then painted $\frac{3}{6}$ of the house after lunch. How much of the house did he paint on Tuesday?

Activity 4

Use the two tables to answer the questions.

Table of Dry Weight Units	
16 drams	1 ounce
16 ounces	1 pound
100 pounds	1 hundredweight
2,000 pounds	1 ton

Table of Shipping Costs	
Weight	Cost
Less than 1 pound	$5
1 pound or more	$2 per pound
1 ton or more	$950 per ton

1. How much does it cost to ship something that weighs 12 ounces?

2. How much does it cost to ship something that weighs 10 pounds?

3. How much does it cost to ship something that weighs 1 ton?

4. How much does it cost to ship something that weighs 2,000 pounds?

Activity 5 • Distributed Practice

Solve.

1.   14,000
   − 8,000

2.   37
   × 82

3.   1,589
   + 6,927

4. 8)756

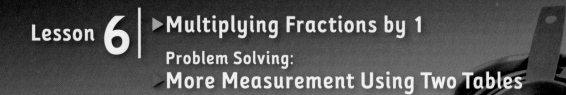

►**Multiplying Fractions by 1**

What is important about fractions equal to 1?

We have been using fraction bars to find equivalent fractions. Fraction bars work for small fractions. Using fraction bars for large fractions like 100ths would be difficult. The fraction bars would be far too big and would take too much time to create. Fortunately, there's a faster way to make denominators the same. Let's start with a simple fraction bar example, then show a faster way of changing the fraction.

Example 1

Change $\frac{2}{3}$ into sixths using fraction bars.

If we line up the two fraction bars, we can see right away that $\frac{2}{3} = \frac{4}{6}$.

$\frac{2}{3}$

$\frac{4}{6}$

But there is another way to find this answer. We do it by multiplying $\frac{2}{3}$ by a fraction equal to 1.

We know that any number multiplied by 1 is the same number.

$$23 \cdot 1 = 23 \qquad 4{,}399 \cdot 1 = 4{,}399 \qquad 2 \cdot 1 = 2$$

The same thing is true for fractions.

$$\frac{2}{3} \cdot 1 = \frac{2}{3} \qquad \frac{4}{5} \cdot 1 = \frac{4}{5} \qquad \frac{7}{8} \cdot 1 = \frac{7}{8}$$

Now let's look at fractions equal to 1.

$$\frac{4}{4} = 1 \qquad\qquad \frac{230}{230} = 1 \qquad\qquad \frac{89}{89} = 1$$

All of these fractions are equal to 1. Let's look at an example.

Example 2

Show fractions equal to 1 with fraction bars.

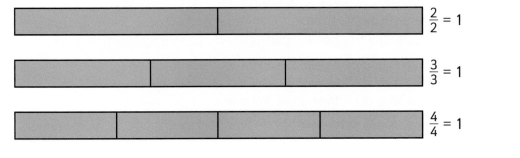

$\frac{2}{2} = 1$

$\frac{3}{3} = 1$

$\frac{4}{4} = 1$

Any number over itself is equal to 1. We see that with these fraction bars.

Speaking of Math

Here's how we explain our thinking when using fraction bars to find a fraction equal to 1:

- *First, I look at how many total parts there are. This tells me the denominator.*
- *Then, I shade in all of the parts of the fraction bar. This is the numerator.*
- *Finally, I write the fraction using the numerator and denominator.*

Knowing how to explain the process for writing a fraction equal to 1 is important as we continue to study math.

We can use this thinking to find equivalent fractions.

How do fractions equal to 1 help us find equivalent fractions?

We find equivalent fractions by multiplying by a fraction equal to 1. Changing the fraction to an equivalent fraction helps us add and subtract fractions easily.

Let's see how this works when we change $\frac{2}{3}$ into sixths.

Steps for Changing Fractions to Equivalent Fractions

STEP 1

We start with the denominator and think about multiplication. What number can we multiply the denominator by to get the new fraction? In this case, what number can we multiply times 3 to get 6?

$$\frac{2}{3} \cdot \frac{}{} = \frac{}{6}$$

We multiply 3 · 2 to get 6.

$$\frac{2}{3} \cdot \frac{}{2} = \frac{}{6}$$

STEP 2

Now we make the fraction in the middle equal to 1.

$$\frac{2}{3} \cdot \frac{2}{2} = \frac{}{6}$$

STEP 3

Then we make the new fraction by multiplying the numerators.

$$\frac{2}{3} \cdot \frac{2}{2} = \frac{4}{6}$$

This is the same answer we got at the beginning of the lesson using the fraction bars.

There is a big advantage to changing fractions by multiplying by a fraction equal to 1. We can use this method to change large fractions, which would be difficult with fraction bars.

Let's see how this works with larger fractions.

Example 1

Change $\frac{4}{10}$ into 30ths.

$$\frac{4}{10} \cdot \frac{}{} = \frac{}{30}$$

If we think about our multiplication facts, we know that $10 \cdot 3 = 30$. So,

$$\frac{4}{10} \cdot \frac{3}{3} = \frac{12}{30}$$

$$\frac{4}{10} = \frac{12}{30}$$

We could show that $\frac{4}{10}$ and $\frac{12}{30}$ were the same if we used a fraction bar for 30ths. But the multiplication method is faster and easier.

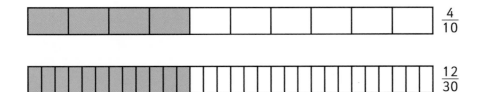

$\frac{4}{10}$

$\frac{12}{30}$

POWER CONCEPT

Any number over itself is equal to 1.

 Apply Skills
Turn to *Interactive Text*, page 351.

 mBook Reinforce Understanding
Use the *mBook Study Guide* to review lesson concepts.

570　Unit 9 • Lesson 6

▶Problem Solving: **More Measurement Using Two Tables**

What measurement conversions are necessary for building a new warehouse?

LUNAR IMPORTS NEEDED TO EXPAND ITS SPACE BECAUSE BUSINESS INCREASED.

THE NEW LUNAR IMPORTS CENTER WILL HAVE LARGE WAREHOUSES AND PLACES TO LAND CARGO SHIPS.

In developing plans for its plant, Lunar Imports used two tables to figure out how long different parts of the plant would be, and how big the overall space would be.

Table of Linear Measurement	
12 inches	1 foot
36 inches	1 yard
3 feet	1 yard
5,280 feet	1 mile
1,760 yards	1 mile

Table of Surface Measurement	
144 square inches	1 square foot
9 square feet	1 square yard
4,840 square yards	1 acre
640 acres	1 square mile

- The table of linear measurement gives different lengths. It was used to tell how long or wide a structure would be.

- The table of surface measurement gives different areas. It was used to tell how much space a structure would occupy.

The architect used both of these types of measurement to design the warehouse.

 Problem-Solving Activity
Turn to *Interactive Text*, page 352.

 Reinforce Understanding
Use the *mBook Study Guide* to review lesson concepts.

Homework

Activity 1

On your paper, write the numbers that go in the blanks in the problems. Make sure the fractions you are multiplying by are equal to 1.

Model $\frac{2}{5} \cdot \frac{2}{2} = \frac{4}{10}$

1. $\frac{2}{3} \cdot \underline{} = \frac{4}{6}$

2. $\frac{3}{4} \cdot \underline{} = \frac{12}{16}$

3. $\frac{6}{10} \cdot \underline{} = \frac{18}{30}$

Activity 2

Solve.

1. $\frac{2}{3} + \frac{4}{9}$

2. $\frac{5}{6} + \frac{6}{12}$

3. $\frac{7}{9} - \frac{1}{3}$

Activity 3

Answer the questions about measurement. Decide which table you need to use to answer each question. You may use a calculator.

Table of Linear Measurement	
12 inches	1 foot
36 inches	1 yard
3 feet	1 yard
5,280 feet	1 mile
1,760 yards	1 mile

Table of Surface Measurement	
144 square inches	1 square foot
9 square feet	1 square yard
4,840 square yards	1 acre
640 acres	1 square mile

1. If a road is 2,700 yards long, how many miles is that? Give your answer in miles and yards.

2. If your house is $2\frac{1}{2}$ yards from the street, how many inches is that?

3. If the area of a football field is 57,600 square feet, how many square yards is that?

Activity 4 • Distributed Practice

Solve.

1. $\begin{array}{r} 700 \\ + 900 \\ \hline \end{array}$

2. $\begin{array}{r} 1,407 \\ - 892 \\ \hline \end{array}$

3. $\begin{array}{r} 400 \\ \times \quad 3 \\ \hline \end{array}$

4. $80\overline{)640}$

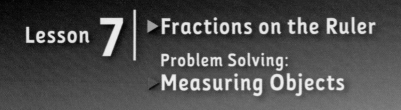

▶**Fractions on the Ruler**

How can fractions make measurement more accurate?

We are going to use a ruler in this lesson. The picture shows some of the markings on the ruler. As we can see, the markings work just like a number line. The fractions get bigger as we move toward the whole number 1.

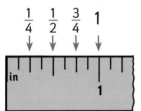

We will measure objects to the closest $\frac{1}{4}$, $\frac{1}{2}$, $\frac{3}{4}$, or whole inch. Don't worry about trying to measure the objects exactly. Just round the number to the nearest $\frac{1}{4}$, $\frac{1}{2}$, $\frac{3}{4}$, or whole inch.

Example 1

Measure this line segment to the nearest $\frac{1}{4}$ inch.

When we look at the ruler, we see that the line is somewhere between $2\frac{1}{4}$ and $2\frac{1}{2}$. The length is closer to $2\frac{1}{4}$. Rounding to the nearest fourth, the line is about $2\frac{1}{4}$ inches long.

In this case, rounding to the nearest $\frac{1}{4}$ inch resulted in a fractional part of $\frac{1}{4}$. This is not always the case.

Let's look at another example.

Example 2

Measure this line segment to the nearest $\frac{1}{4}$ inch.

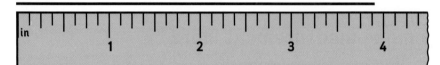

When we look at the ruler, we see that the line is somewhere between $3\frac{3}{4}$ and 4. Its length is closer to 4. Rounding to the nearest $\frac{1}{4}$ inch, the line is about 4 inches long.

POWER CONCEPT

Rounding to the nearest fourth does not always mean we will have $\frac{1}{4}$ in our answer.

Sometimes when we round to the nearest fourth, our answer is a mixed number and sometimes it's a whole number.

Let's look at one more example.

Example 3

Measure this line segment to the nearest $\frac{1}{4}$ inch.

When we look on our ruler, we see that the line is somewhere between $1\frac{1}{4}$ and $1\frac{1}{2}$. It's closer to $1\frac{1}{2}$ inches long. Rounding to the nearest $\frac{1}{4}$, the line is about $1\frac{1}{2}$ inches long.

This is another example of the kind of fractional part we can get if we round to the nearest fourth. We can get an answer that includes the fraction $\frac{1}{2}$.

 Apply Skills
Turn to *Interactive Text*, page 354.

 mBook Reinforce Understanding
Use the *mBook Study Guide* to review lesson concepts.

▶**Problem Solving: Measuring Objects**

How do we measure objects with a ruler?

Buyers for stores often need to know the size of items they are interested in buying. The buyer for a hobby shop, for example, might ask, "How big is that model car?" The buyer wants to know because he or she has to plan where to put the model cars in the store. Which shelf? Is there enough room?

To measure an object, we need to choose a unit of measurement. We will use inches for this model car. We start with the length. We line up one edge with the zero and measure length from the longest parts.

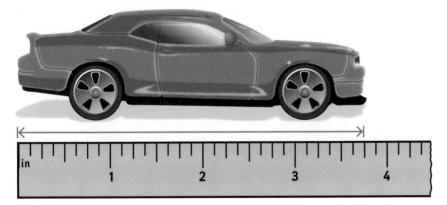

This model car's length is about $3\frac{3}{4}$ inches.

Next, we measure the height. We measure the height the same way we measured the length, by measuring from the lowest to the highest parts of the car.

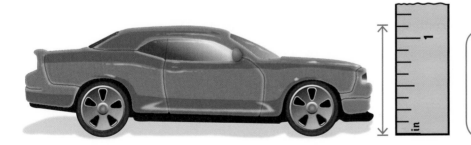

> When measuring length and height of an object, remember to measure from the outermost points.

The height of this car is about $1\frac{1}{4}$ inches.

 Problem-Solving Activity
Turn to *Interactive Text*, page 355.

 mBook Reinforce Understanding
Use the *mBook Study Guide* to review lesson concepts.

Activity 1

On your paper, write the numbers that go in the blanks in the problems.
Make sure the fractions you are multiplying by are equal to 1.

1. $\frac{2}{4} \cdot \underline{} = \frac{4}{8}$
2. $\frac{3}{5} \cdot \underline{} = \frac{9}{15}$
3. $\frac{1}{6} \cdot \underline{} = \frac{4}{24}$
4. $\frac{1}{2} \cdot \underline{} = \frac{5}{10}$

Activity 2

The word problems involve fractions with unlike denominators. Use fraction
bars to help find equivalent fractions with the same denominators. Then
add or subtract. Be sure to write the equation as well as the answer
for each problem.

Model $\frac{1}{4} + \frac{1}{2}$

$\frac{1}{4} + \frac{2}{4} = \frac{3}{4}$

1. Hector's class voted on its favorite foods. Of the students in the class,
   $\frac{2}{6}$ chose pizza and $\frac{1}{3}$ chose hamburgers. The rest of the class had many
   different answers. What fraction of the students liked pizza or hamburgers?

2. Hillary needs a piece of material that's $\frac{3}{4}$ of a yard long to make a scarf.
   The piece of material she bought is $\frac{7}{8}$ of a yard long. How much does she
   need to cut off the material to get the size she needs?

3. At a talent show, $\frac{2}{3}$ of the contestants were singers and $\frac{1}{6}$ were dancers.
   What fraction of the contestants in the talent show were either singers
   or dancers?

Activity 3

Use a ruler to measure the line in each problem to the closest $\frac{1}{4}$, $\frac{1}{2}$, $\frac{3}{4}$, or whole inch. Write the length of each line on your paper.

1. ——————

2. —

3. ———————

4. ————

5. —————

6. ————————————

Activity 4

Answer the questions using this table of linear measurement. Be sure to give your answer in the correct units.

Table of Linear Measurement	
12 inches	1 foot
36 inches	1 yard
3 feet	1 yard

1. If the box holding a toy car is 4 inches long, how many of these boxes can you fit on a shelf that is $1\frac{1}{2}$ feet long?

2. You have 6 feet of shelf space available. You have two types of toy cars to put out. One type has a 3-inch box. The other has a 4-inch box. How many more of the 3-inch boxes could you put on this shelf space?

3. If you have 14 feet of shelf space to fill, how many yards is that? Give your answer in yards and feet.

Activity 5 • Distributed Practice

Solve.

1. 3,000
   + 1,999

2. 5,061
   + 9,809

3. 45
   × 98

4. $4\overline{)337}$

Lesson 8 | ▶Finding Common Denominators for Two Fractions

Problem Solving:
▶Measuring With Fractions in the Real World

▶**Finding Common Denominators for Two Fractions**

How do we find common denominators for two fractions?

We learned two ways to find the common denominators for fractions so that we could add them. One way was to use fraction bars. The other way was to multiply one of the fractions by a fraction equal to 1.

Suppose we wanted to add $\frac{1}{3}$ and $\frac{5}{6}$. Using fraction bars, it's easy to see that $\frac{1}{3} = \frac{2}{6}$. We just line up thirds and sixths.

Example 1

Find a common denominator for $\frac{1}{3}$ and $\frac{5}{6}$ using fraction bars.

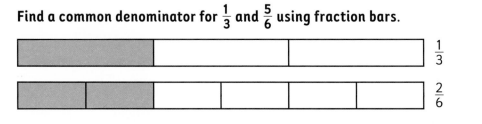

Now we can replace $\frac{1}{3}$ with $\frac{2}{6}$ and add: $\frac{2}{6} + \frac{5}{6} = \frac{7}{6}$.

The common denominator is 6.

We also learned to find the common denominator by multiplying one of the fractions by a fraction equal to 1. Again, let's look at $\frac{1}{3} + \frac{5}{6}$.

Example 2

Find a common denominator for $\frac{1}{3}$ and $\frac{5}{6}$ by multiplying by a fraction equal to 1.

We could multiply $\frac{1}{3} \cdot \frac{2}{2}$ to get $\frac{2}{6}$.

Then we could add $\frac{2}{6}$ to $\frac{5}{6}$ to get $\frac{7}{6}$.

The common denominator is 6.

How do we add using common multiples?

Let's look at another addition problem involving fractions: $\frac{2}{3} + \frac{1}{4}$. The fraction bars for thirds and fourths don't line up anywhere. Also, there isn't an easy way to multiply one of the fractions by a fraction equal to 1, but we need to find a common denominator. So what should we do?

There is a fast and easy solution, and it's a method we can use to find a common denominator for any two fractions:

- Find the least common multiple for the denominators 3 and 4.
- Change each fraction to a fraction that has the least common multiple as its denominator.

Steps for Adding Fractions Using Common Multiples

STEP 1
Find the least common multiple.

We can use a number line or count by multiples of the numbers.

Using a Number Line
If we think about number lines, we can easily find the least common multiple of 3 and 4.

Multiples of 3

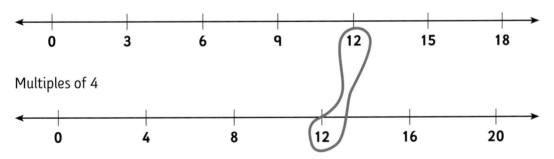

Multiples of 4

We see that 12 is the least common multiple of 3 and 4.

Counting by Multiples of the Number
Another way to do this is to count by each number in our heads.

3s: 3–6–9–12–15

4s: 4–8–12–16

They both have 12 as a multiple, so the least common multiple of 3 and 4 is 12.

We can use common multiples to find common denominators.

STEP 2

Multiply each fraction by a fraction equal to 1 that will give the common multiple.

In this case, the common multiple is 12.

$$\frac{2}{3} \cdot \frac{4}{4} = \frac{8}{12}$$

$$\frac{1}{4} \cdot \frac{3}{3} = \frac{3}{12}$$

STEP 3

Add the two fractions together.

$$\frac{8}{12} + \frac{3}{12} = \frac{11}{12}$$

STEP 4

Check the answer.

In this case, we will check the answer with fraction bars.

We change $\frac{2}{3}$ into 12ths.

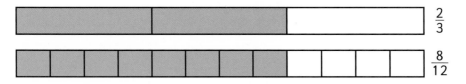

$\frac{2}{3}$

$\frac{8}{12}$

Then we change $\frac{1}{4}$ into 12ths.

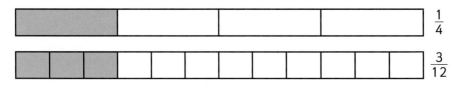

$\frac{1}{4}$

$\frac{3}{12}$

When we add $\frac{8}{12} + \frac{3}{12}$ we get $\frac{11}{12}$.

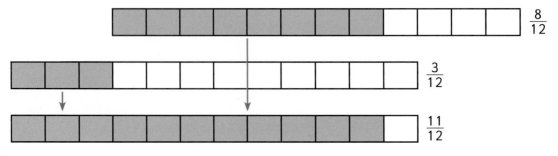

$\frac{8}{12}$

$\frac{3}{12}$

$\frac{11}{12}$

 Apply Skills
Turn to *Interactive Text*, page 357.

 mBook Reinforce Understanding
Use the *mBook Study Guide* to review lesson concepts.

▶**Problem Solving: Measuring With Fractions in the Real World**

How are fractions used in real-world situations?

As we saw in the last lesson, fractions are used in measurement. Measuring to the nearest fraction allows us to get an accurate measurement. We use fractions in many different areas of everyday life. Let's look at fractions used in sports.

Fractions are used in sports to measure lengths and distances accurately. Often, these fractions have to be added or subtracted.

Example 1

Answer the problem by finding common denominators.

Problem:

Teala runs on the cross-country team. How many miles does she run in a week?

Day	Sun.	Mon.	Tues.	Wed.	Thurs.	Fri.	Sat.
Miles	Rest	$4\frac{1}{4}$	$4\frac{1}{4}$	$3\frac{1}{2}$	3	$4\frac{3}{4}$	3

First, add the fractions by finding the common denominator.

$\frac{1}{4} + \frac{1}{4} + \frac{1}{2} + \frac{3}{4}$ is the same as

$\frac{1}{4} + \frac{1}{4} + \frac{2}{4} + \frac{3}{4} = 1\frac{3}{4}$

Then add the whole numbers, including the sum of the fractions, $1\frac{3}{4}$.

$4 + 4 + 3 + 3 + 4 + 3 + 1\frac{3}{4} = 22\frac{3}{4}$

Teala runs $22\frac{3}{4}$ miles in one week.

 Problem-Solving Activity
Turn to *Interactive Text*,
page 358.

 mBook Reinforce Understanding
Use the *mBook Study Guide*
to review lesson concepts.

Activity 1

On your paper, write the numbers that go in the blanks. Make sure the fractions you are multiplying by are equal to 1.

1. $\frac{3}{4} \cdot \text{---} = \frac{9}{12}$　　2. $\frac{4}{5} \cdot \text{---} = \frac{16}{20}$　　3. $\frac{3}{6} \cdot \text{---} = \frac{6}{12}$　　4. $\frac{2}{3} \cdot \text{---} = \frac{10}{15}$

Activity 2

Find multiples for the numbers in each problem. Then write the least common multiple for each pair of numbers.

Model	2 and 5
	2:　2　4　6　8　10
	5:　5　10
	LCM = 10

1. 3 and 4　　　2. 4 and 6　　　3. 2 and 8　　　4. 3 and 5

Activity 3

Use the least common multiple to find common denominators for the fractions. Write the new equation with the common denominators. Then add or subtract.

1. $\frac{3}{4} + \frac{2}{3}$　　　2. $\frac{1}{4} - \frac{1}{6}$　　　3. $\frac{1}{2} + \frac{1}{8}$　　　4. $\frac{1}{3} - \frac{1}{5}$

Activity 4 • Distributed Practice

Solve.

1.　　3,497
　　$-\ 1,089$

2.　　6,000
　　$+\ 8,000$

3. $7\overline{)498}$

4.　　438
　　$\times\ \ \ 5$

How do we write a word problem using common conversions?

We looked at different ways to measure objects. We looked at how things are measured if they are liquid or dry. We measured time, and we measured length. The tables show some of the key units that are used for these types of measurement.

Units of Liquid Measurement
Ounce
Pint
Quart
Gallon
Barrel

Units of Dry Measurement
Dram
Ounce
Pound
Ton

Units of Time Measurement
Second
Minute
Hour
Day
Month
Year

Units of Linear Measurement
Inch
Foot
Yard
Mile

We're going to make up some word problems that involve both fractions and units of measurement. We'll include answers to the problems.

Example 1

Write a word problem using fractions and common units of measurement.

- It takes $\frac{1}{4}$ of a day to unload a train car filled with boxes.
- It takes another 7 hours to put the boxes in the right place in a warehouse.
- How much of a day does this work take altogether?

We need to convert 7 hours into days. We know there are 24 hours in one day. We can write a fraction to show this relationship.

$$7 \text{ hours} = \frac{7}{24} \text{ of a day}$$

Now we can add our fractions.

$$\frac{1}{4} + \frac{7}{24} =$$

$$\frac{1}{4} \cdot \frac{6}{6} = \frac{6}{24}$$

$$\frac{6}{24} + \frac{7}{24} = \frac{13}{24}$$

It takes $\frac{13}{24}$ of a day.

 Problem-Solving Activity
Turn to *Interactive Text*, page 360.

 Reinforce Understanding
Use the *mBook Study Guide* to review lesson concepts.

Homework

Activity 1

Solve. Be sure to find a common denominator if you need one.

1. $\frac{1}{4} + \frac{1}{8}$

2. $\frac{3}{7} + \frac{2}{3}$

3. $\frac{4}{5} + \frac{1}{5}$

4. $\frac{8}{9} - \frac{2}{3}$

5. $\frac{7}{9} - \frac{1}{6}$

6. $\frac{3}{4} - \frac{1}{4}$

Activity 2

Fill in the blanks. Write the answers on your paper. You may look back at the tables in your book if you need help.

1. _____ inches = 1 foot

2. _____ feet = 1 yard

3. 1 hour = _____ minutes

4. _____ days = 1 week

5. _____ ounces = 1 pound

6. 1 ton = _____ pounds

Activity 3

Solve the word problems.

1. Joe spent $\frac{1}{3}$ of the day mowing the yard and $\frac{1}{4}$ of the day weeding the garden. How much of the day did he spend on these two activities?

2. Patty made a recipe for her famous oatmeal cookies. She had to mix $\frac{2}{3}$ cup butter into the cookies and $\frac{1}{4}$ cup of butter into the icing. How much butter did she need?

3. Stuart was building a little fence around his little house. He made the length of the fence out of scrap pieces of wood he had in the garage. He had a piece of wood that was $\frac{1}{8}$ foot long and a piece of wood that was $\frac{1}{6}$ foot long. How long was the total length of the fence?

Activity 4 • Distributed Practice

Solve.

1.
$$\begin{array}{r} 1,700 \\ -\ \ 900 \\ \hline \end{array}$$

2.
$$\begin{array}{r} 6,892 \\ +\ 4,327 \\ \hline \end{array}$$

3.
$$\begin{array}{r} 50 \\ \times\ 40 \\ \hline \end{array}$$

4. $8\overline{)672}$

Unit Review

▶ **Adding and Subtracting Fractions**

Problem Solving:
▶ **Converting Units of Measurement**

▶ **Adding and Subtracting Fractions**

Why do we change denominators when we add or subtract fractions?

This unit focused on one of the most important rules in working with fractions—when we add or subtract fractions, we have to make sure the denominators are the same. The fractions must have the same fair shares. If we try to add or subtract fractions with different denominators, the answer will be wrong. Think about the story of the peasants and the king when adding or subtracting fractions, and make sure the denominators are the same.

In a problem like $\frac{1}{3} - \frac{1}{4}$, the denominators are not the same. We have to find a common denominator. The first review shows how we use fraction bars to find the answer.

Review 1

How do we find common denominators using fraction bars?

We need to find a fraction bar with fractions that line up with both $\frac{1}{3}$ and $\frac{1}{4}$.

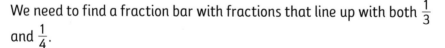

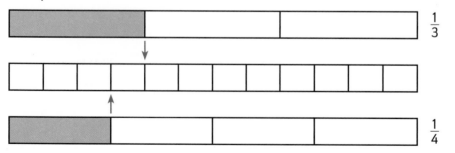

We use twelfths because they line up with both thirds and fourths. We can find equivalent fractions for $\frac{1}{3}$ and $\frac{1}{4}$ on the fraction bar for twelfths.

$$\frac{4}{12} - \frac{3}{12} = \frac{1}{12}$$

The next two examples present different strategies for finding common multiples of 3 and 4.

Review 2

How do we find the least common multiple of 3 and 4?

Using Tables of Multiples

Use tables of multiples for each number.

3	3	6	9	12	15
4	4	8	12	16	

The least common multiple is 12.

Using Fact Families

The numbers 3 and 4 are part of the multiplication and division fact family of 3, 4, and 12.

$$3 \cdot 4 = 12 \text{ and } 4 \cdot 3 = 12$$

That means 12 must be a common multiple for 3 and 4.

Using Number Lines

Multiples of 3

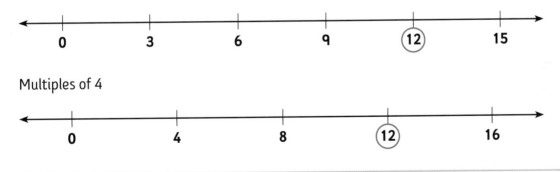

Multiples of 4

Once we find the least common multiple, we change the denominators so that they are the same. Review 3 shows how we multiply by a fraction equal to 1 to get common denominators. It also shows how we solve the rest of the problem.

Review 3

How do we find common denominators for the fractions $\frac{1}{3}$ and $\frac{1}{4}$?

We begin by finding fractions that are equal to 1 that will give us a common denominator. We use the fractions $\frac{4}{4}$ and $\frac{3}{3}$.

$$\frac{1}{3} \cdot \frac{4}{4} = \frac{4}{12}$$

$$\frac{1}{4} \cdot \frac{3}{3} = \frac{3}{12}$$

We can now add or subtract because we have the same denominators or the same fair shares.

$$\frac{4}{12} + \frac{3}{12} = \frac{7}{12}$$

$$\frac{4}{12} - \frac{3}{12} = \frac{1}{12}$$

Adding or subtracting fractions with denominators that are not the same takes a number of steps. But the more problems we work, the faster we will get. If we get stuck, we can remember our strategies of finding multiples: counting by a number to find its multiples, and using number lines to find multiples. We can also use fraction bars as a way to check our answers.

 Apply Skills
Turn to *Interactive Text*,
page 362.

 mBook **Reinforce Understanding**
Use the *mBook Study Guide*
to review lesson concepts.

Lesson 10

▶**Problem Solving: Converting Units of Measurement**

How do we use information from tables to solve problems?

This unit presented a number of problems where we had to use tables to make calculations and convert units of measurement. We converted units like ounces into pounds, seconds into minutes, and quarts into gallons. We need to think carefully when we change one unit to another. Sometimes, changing from one unit to another works out evenly. If we have 12 inches, we can change that into 1 foot. If we have 24 inches, we can change that into 2 feet.

However, changing from one unit to another does not always work out evenly. When we come across this situation, we have two strategies we can use:

- Change the unit using long division.
- Change the unit using a calculator—divide, multiply, and subtract.

Let's say we want to change 55 inches into feet and inches. The example shows two strategies for converting these units.

Review 1

What are two strategies for converting units in a table?

Using Long Division
We know there are 12 inches in a foot. How many feet are in 55 inches? Divide 55 by 12.

$$
\begin{array}{r}
4 \text{ R7} \\
12\overline{)55} \\
-48 \\
\hline
7
\end{array}
$$

We get 4 feet and a remainder of 7 inches.

The remainder is a different unit from the whole number. The whole number is feet, and the remainder is inches.

Steps for Using a Calculator

STEP 1
Divide using a calculator.
In this example, we divide 55 by 12. The whole number in the answer is the number of feet in 55 inches.

STEP 2
Multiply the whole number in the answer (4) by 12 to change feet into inches: $4 \cdot 12 = 48$.

STEP 3
Subtract that number of inches from the total number of inches to get the number of inches left over.
In this example, we subtract $55 - 48$.

The answer is 4 feet, 7 inches.

The most important thing to remember is that when we are changing a measurement from one unit to the other, the remainder is a different unit than the whole number. In Review 1, the whole number was feet and the remainder was inches.

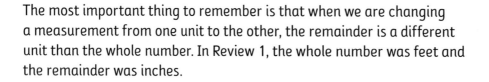
Problem-Solving Activity
Turn to *Interactive Text*, page 363.

mBook **Reinforce Understanding**
Use the *mBook Study Guide* to review lesson concepts.

Glossary

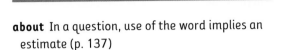

about In a question, use of the word implies an estimate (p. 137)

algorithm A set of steps for solving a problem (p. 35)

area The total number of square units inside a shape (p. 210)

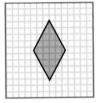

Approximate Number of Square Units: 26

array A picture of the factors and products of a multiplication problem (p. 269)

average The middle value (p. 463)

bar graph A graph where the length of a bar represents a certain amount (p. 20)

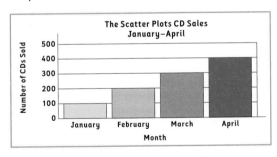

base The bottom, or horizontal, part of a shape (p. 201); when working with prime factorization, it is the number that is being multiplied repeatedly (p. 411)

basic addition facts One-digit math facts that we either memorize or compute quickly in our heads (p. 9)

benchmark Common fractions or decimal numbers from our everyday lives (p. 496)

budget An estimate of income and expenses (p. 120)

C

common denominator Denominators that are the same (p. 558)

common factor A factor that two or more numbers share (p. 347)

common multiples Multiples that are the same for two numbers (p. 425)

commutative property The property that lets us change the order of the numbers without changing the sum (p. 57)

commutative property of multiplication The property that lets us change the order of multiplication facts without changing the answer (p. 135)

composite numbers A number with more than two factors (p. 289)

congruent Two shapes that are exactly the same (p. 369)

consecutive Numbers placed in order (p. 387)

contract Objects starting at the outermost point move in (p. 383)

converting The changing of units of measurement (p. 545)

D

decimal number The quotient when we divide on a calculator and we have a remainder (p. 218)

denominator The number below the line in a fraction (p. 480)

difference The answer to a subtraction problem (p. 78)

digits Any numeral from 0 to 9 (p. 3)

dividend A number to be divided by another number (p. 203)

divisibility rules Rules for the numbers 2, 5, 10, 3, and 6 used to divide larger numbers (p. 319)

division The act of breaking up a larger number into smaller, equal groups

divisor The number dividing the dividend into parts (p. 203)

E

equivalent fractions Fractions that have different numerators and denominators but represent the same fractional part (p. 518)

estimate An approximate answer or a guess (p. 46)

expand Objects expand when moving from the center of the design out (p. 383)

expanded addition Numbers that are added in expanded form (p. 19)

expanded division Numbers that are divided in expanded form (p. 233)

expanded form Numbers written in a way that shows place value (p. 10)

expanded multiplication Numbers that are multiplied in expanded form (p. 147)

expanded subtraction Numbers that are subtracted in expanded form (p. 77)

expenses Money spent (p. 115)

exponent The number of times we multiply the base (p. 411)

extended addition facts Basic facts multiplied by a power of 10 (p. 9)

F

fact family A set of facts with the same three numbers (p. 73)

Fact Family for 2, 8, and 10	
8 + 2 = 10	10 − 2 = 8
2 + 8 = 10	10 − 8 = 2

factor list A list of all the factors (p. 279)

factor rainbow All the factors of a number displayed as a rainbow to show their relation (p. 284)

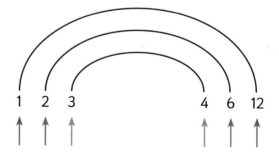

factors The numbers being multiplied (p. 139)

fair share Equal fractional parts (p. 472)

Fourths

flip Flipping an object from front to back or top to bottom (p. 418)

formula A rule shown with symbols, for example, Area = base × height (p. 275)

fractional parts Divide a whole into smaller parts (p. 460)

fraction bars Rectangles used to show fractions (p. 513)

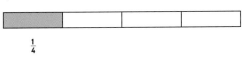

$\frac{1}{4}$

G

greatest common factor (GCF) The largest of all the common factors (p. 360)

H

height The vertical part of a shape (p. 201)

horizontal axis The line across the bottom of a graph (p. 20)

horizontal expanded addition The process of writing the problem across the addition page on one line (p. 56)

I

icons Another word for pictures, such as used in a pictograph (p. 63)

Things in My Room	
Items	**Number**
CDs	◎ ◎
T-shirts	👕 👕
Books	📖 📖 📖

income Money earned (p. 115)

infinite Endless (p. 294)

infinite fractional parts Endless amount of whole numbers that go in the gaps between whole numbers on a number line (p. 460)

interval How the scale in a graph changes, for example, by hundreds (p. 20)

K

key A table that shows the amount of data (p. 63)

key
◎ = 10 CDs
👕 = 10 T-shirts
📖 = 10 books

L

least common multiple (LCM) The smallest multiple that two or more numbers have in common (p. 428)

line of symmetry A line that divides an object in half so that the two halves are mirror images of each other (p. 422)

M

maximum The greatest number in the data set (p. 476)

mean Average (p. 475)

median The middle number in a set of data (p. 484)

meter The basic unit of measurement in the metric system (p. 152)

metric system System of measurement based on the meter (p. 152)

minimum The smallest number in the data set (p. 476)

multiples All the products of a number and another whole number (p. 425)

N

near extended fact Extended facts that are close to the larger division problems (p. 246)

near fact Facts that are close to a basic fact (p. 226)

number line A line where numbers are placed in order, like on a ruler (p. 45)

numerator The number on top of the line in a fraction (p. 480)

$$\frac{1}{2} \qquad \frac{1}{3} \qquad \frac{1}{4} \qquad \frac{1}{6} \qquad \frac{3}{4} \begin{array}{l} \leftarrow \text{numerator} \\ \leftarrow \text{denominator} \end{array}$$

O

order of operations The rules we use to simplify expressions correctly

outlier In a set of data, a number that is a lot bigger or smaller than the other numbers (p. 487)

P

perimeter The distance around a shape (p. 296)

pictograph A way of showing data that uses pictures (p. 63)

place value The value of a digit as defined by its place in a number (p. 3)

place-value chart Chart that determines the value of each digit in a number (p. 3)

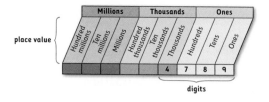

power The base and exponent together (p. 411)

power of 10 A number that can be written as a product of tens (p. 9)

prime factors The most basic factors of a number (p. 300)

prime factorization The process of finding the prime factors of a number (p. 300)

prime factor tree Method of finding the branches, or factors, of a large number (p. 300)

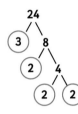

prime numbers A natural number that has exactly two distinct natural number divisors: 1 and itself (p. 290)

product The answer to a multiplication problem (p. 139)

profit The amount of money remaining after all the expenses are paid (p. 115)

properties The elements of a shape, such as straight edges, curves, number of sides, etc. (p. 422)

Q

quarter rounding The process of rounding to the nearest quarter (p. 102)

quotient The answer to a division problem (p. 203)

R

range The difference between the biggest number and the smallest number in a data set (p. 476)

referent Common objects that represent units of measurement (p. 157)

reflection symmetry A property of shapes in which two halves are exactly the same (p. 422)

regroup The changing of numbers, for example from hundreds to tens, from tens to ones (p. 29)

remainder The number that is left after dividing (p. 217)

rotational symmetry Objects that still look the same when turning (p. 440)

rounding The process of changing the value of a number to its closest surrounding number (p. 47)

S

scale The numbers along the vertical axis in a graph (p. 20); scaling an object is to make it bigger or smaller by a certain amount (p. 383)

scale drawing A drawing that shows objects in a size relative to their actual size (p. 187)

slide The process of moving an object in one direction (p. 418)

specifications The exact measurements of a design (p. 182)

square number An integer that can be written as the square of some other integer, that is, it is the product of some integer with itself (p. 386)

square unit Unit of measurement that allows us to measure in two dimensions (p. 201)

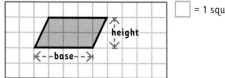

= 1 square unit

standard form The way you usually write a number: 328, 487, 24 (p. 10)

standard unit of measurement Established measurements used by everyone, such as feet, yards, inches, or metric units (p. 149)

stem-and-leaf plot A way to organize numbers and show data so that it is easier to interpret (p. 502)

survey A study of people's opinions (p. 61)

T

table A set of data organized in rows and columns (p. 32)

Hipster Records CD Sales January–April	
Band	**CD Sales**
The Hammerheads	$30,000
One Later	$24,000
4 Floors Up	$19,000
The Scatter Plots	$12,000
Three Ears	$6,000

tangram A puzzle made from a square that is divided into seven shapes (p. 408)

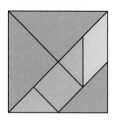

tessellation A design repeatedly using the same shape (p. 363)

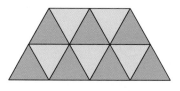

title The name of something, such as a graph or a table, that tells us what this something is about (p. 20)

traditional addition An addition algorithm that is faster and more efficient than expanded addition (p. 35)

traditional long division A division algorithm that is faster and more efficient than expanded division (p. 241)

traditional multiplication A multiplication algorithm that is faster and more efficient than expanded multiplication (p. 165)

traditional subtraction A subtraction algorithm that is faster and more efficient than expanded subtraction (p. 90)

transformation A type of change (p. 418)

transpose The process of switching the numbers around (p. 109)

trend A pattern in data over time (p. 27)

triangular numbers A number that has an array that looks like a triangle (p. 405)

turn The process of rotating an object so that it rests at a new angle (p. 418)

U

unit Smaller, equal groups in division (p. 208)

unit of measurement The object we use to measure other objects (p. 137)

U.S. customary units A standard measurement, such as an inch (p. 149)

V

vertical axis The line along the left side of a graph (p. 20)

W

whole The larger number in division (p. 208)

Index

expanding objects, 383–384, 388–389, 394, 402

expenses, 115

exponents, defined, 411, 446. *See also* powers (of 10)

extended addition facts, 9–10, 74

extended division facts
  basic facts and, 205–207
  described, 205–207
  near extended facts and, 246–247, 250–251
  on number lines, 214–216

extended multiplication facts, 136, 193, 376

extremes in data, 493–494

F

fact families
  addition, 73
  defined, 73
  division, 201–202
  for extended facts, 74
  multiplication, 201–202
  subtraction, 73–74

factor lists
  for determining prime/composite numbers, 292
  for finding GFC, 366
  using arrays to write, 279–280
  what they are, 279

factor rainbows
  finding all multiplication facts for, 286
  what they are, 284–285

factors. *See also* common factors; greatest common factor (GCF)
  arrays of. *See* arrays
  defined, 139, 445
  factoring out 10, 139–140
  factoring out powers of 10, 143–144, 194
  prime. *See* prime factor trees; prime factorization; prime factors

fair shares
  of circles, squares, hexagons, 473
  defined, 472
  fractional parts and, 473–474, 490
  of triangles, 472

flip, defined, 418

floor plans
  area of, 277
  designing, 253

formula, defined, 275

fraction bars
  adding fractions on, 549
  common denominators on, 558–560, 586
  defined, 513
  equivalent fractions on, 518–520
  number lines and, 523–524, 528–529
  showing fractions equal to 1, 568
  subtracting fractions on, 550
  using, 513–514

fractional parts (fractions). *See also* common denominators
  between 0 and 1, 467–468
  adding. *See* adding fractions
  changing, for adding/subtracting, 569–570
  comparing, 468, 510–511, 513–514
  decimals and, 459
  defined, 459, 460
  denominator defined, 480, 541
  equal to one, 490, 491, 492, 568, 569–570
  equivalent, 518–520, 523–526, 529, 535, 569–570
  estimating, 496–497, 505–506
  everyday uses of, 500–501
  examples of, 460–462
  fair shares and, 473–474
  fourths, 460, 462, 467, 468, 473
  greater than one whole, 491, 492
  halves, 461, 467, 468, 473, 474
  Improve Your Skills, 482
  less than one whole, 491
  measuring with, 573–574, 575, 581
  missing on number line, explaining, 462
  multiplying by 1, 567–570
  of number lines, 459–462, 491, 505–506, 532, 535
  numerator defined, 480, 541
  real-world uses for, 500–501, 581
  review, 532–535
  of shapes, 473, 533
  subtracting. *See* subtracting fractions
  thirds, 460, 461, 462, 467, 468, 473, 474
  using shapes to count, 492

first steps in solving, 7, 69
geometry of square numbers, 388–389
good number sense and, 122–123
irregularly shaped objects, 272, 288
line plots for, 521, 530, 538
looking for patterns, 337
making a ruler, 149
measurement problems. *See* measurements; units of measurement
median in data. *See* median
metric system and. *See* metric system
perimeter of shapes. *See* perimeter
rounding for. *See* rounding
shapes and. *See* irregular shapes; shapes; specific shapes
stem-and-leaf plots, 502–503, 507–508, 515–516
tables and. *See* tables
tessellations, 363–364
understanding budgets, 120
understanding income, expenses, profit, 115
using division in everyday life, 231
product, defined, 139. *See also* expanded multiplication; multiplication
profit, 115
properties. *See specific property names*
properties, defined, 422
properties of numbers summarized, 444–446

Q

quarter rounding, 102–103
quarts, 545, 546
quotient, defined, 205. *See also* division

R

range
computing, 476
defined, 476
stem-and-leaf plots for finding, 502–503, 507–508, 538
rectangles. *See* squares and rectangles
referents, 157, 196
reflection symmetry, 440
regrouping

in division, 238–239
in expanded addition, 29–31, 36, 40
to hundreds place, 39–41
in subtraction, 82–83, 86–87, 91
in traditional addition, 35–36, 41
remainders, 219–221
in converting units, 554–556
defined, 219
rounding, 223–225
in word problems, 236
rotational symmetry, 440–442, 447–448, 456
rounding
in bar graphs, 54
defined, 47–48
differences, 95
in division, 223–225, 228–230
estimating and, 46–47, 51–52, 95, 131
Improve Your Skills, 49
near facts and, 228–230, 246–247
on number lines, 47–48, 49, 95, 102–103
quarter, 102–103
real-world uses for, 53
rules for, 49
ruler
fractions on, 573–574
making, 149
measuring objects with, 575
metric, 152

S

scale
of bar graphs, 20, 21, 23
of objects, 383
scale drawings, 187
shapes. *See also* irregular shapes; *specific shapes*
areas of. *See* area
base of, 275
changing, 418
classifying, 350–351, 357–358, 400
common properties of, 400
comparing sizes of, 208, 212
complex designs from simple, 408–409, 414
congruent, 369, 377, 401
contracting. *See* contracting objects

Photo and Illustration Credits

PHOTO CREDITS

Unit 1 Biscuit ©istockphoto.com/Bridgette Braley. Handed biscuit ©istockphoto.com/Ivan Solis. Pawprint ©istockphoto.com/Jane Tyson. Adding machine ©istockphoto.com/bluestocking. Scratches ©istockphoto.com/Ernest King. Dave the Math Dog courtesy of Frank and Debbie Ferris. Maggie the Wonder Dog courtesy of Jesse Treff. Dog begging ©istockphoto.com/Leigh Schindler.

Unit 2 Postcard ©istockphoto.com/Valerie Loiseleux.

Unit 3 Fish (dad) ©istockphoto.com/Dan Thornberg. Fish (son) ©istockphoto.com/Dan Thornberg. Fish (mom) ©istockphoto.com/George Peters. Guitar (small) ©istockphoto.com/Steffen Skopp. Guitar ©istockphoto.com/pixhook.

Unit 4 Girl ©Jupiter Images. Lockers ©istockphoto.com/P. Wei. Tape measure ©istockphoto.com/Shawn Gearhart. Ruler ©istockphoto.com/dny59.

Unit 5 Mirrored ball ©istockphoto.com/Mustafa Deliormanli.

Unit 6 Louvre pyramid at night ©ICONOTEC. Burj Dubai ©Mohamed El Zeiny. Image from BigStockPhoto.com. Dubai cityscape ©istockphoto.com/Matt Kunz. Pyramid (daytime) ©Michael Mattox. Image from BigStockPhoto.com.

Unit 7 Mountain bike jump ©istockphoto.com/Peter Brutsch. Alexander Calder holding 21 Feuilles Blanches in Paris, 1954 ©2008 Calder Foundation, New York/Artists Rights Society (ARS), New York. Cuckoo clock ©istockphoto.com/Brendon DeSuza.

Unit 8 Green monster ©istockphoto.com/Stephen Strathdee. Buildings ©istockphoto.com/Nikada. Garbage bag ©istockphoto.com/Ever. Cardboard ©istockphoto.com/Rose DeGrie. Soda can ©istockphoto.com/J. R. Trice. Taxis ©istockphoto.com/Nikada. Television ©istockphoto.com/bluestocking. Light bulb ©istockphoto.com/Skip O'Donnell. Water bottle ©istockphoto.com/Skip O'Donnell.

Unit 9 Waffle ©istockphoto.com/stocksnapper. Pancake ©istockphoto.com/Bella Logachova. Waitress ©istockphoto.com/Sharon Dominick. Measuring cups ©istockphoto.com/Norman Pogson. Measuring spoons ©istockphoto.com/A. E. Knost.

ILLUSTRATION CREDITS

Unit 1 Boy ©istockphoto.com/Aldo Murillo. Dog ©istockphoto.com/Li Kim Go.

Unit 2 Cartoon CALVIN AND HOBBES ©1992 Watterson. Dist. by UNIVERSAL PRESS SYNDICATE. Reprinted with permission. All rights reserved.

Unit 4 Tree ©Jupiter Images.

Unit 7 Mountain biker ©istockphoto.com/4x6. Background bikers ©istockphoto.com/Brandon Laufenberg.

Unit 9 Cartoon CALVIN AND HOBBES ©1986 Watterson. Dist. by UNIVERSAL PRESS SYNDICATE. Reprinted with permission. All rights reserved.